The Heart's Narrative

· ·

For Jeanie and Verna —
the harbour of love

The Heart's Narrative

*Therapy and
Navigating Life's Contradictions*

Johnella Bird

Published by Edge Press
PO Box 80089
Green Bay, Auckland
New Zealand

www.heartsnarrative.cc
email: edgepress@ix.net.nz

Johnella Bird © 2000 Edge Press
First Published 2000
Second Edition 2002

ISBN 0-473-06558-4

Cover and text designed by Mary Egan
Typeset by Egan-Reid Ltd, Auckland, New Zealand
Cover photograph by Kathryn Bartlett
Glass sculpture by John Abramczyk
Printed by Publishing Press Ltd, Auckland

Contents

. . . . . .

	Acknowledgements	vi
	Introduction	vii
Chapter One	Just Talk	1
Chapter Two	Therapeutic Narratives in Action	48
Chapter Three	The Therapeutic Relationship	88
Chapter Four	Building the Therapeutic Relationship	140
Chapter Five	Working with Contradictions	167
Chapter Six	Working with Time	209
Chapter Seven	Where There is a Relationship, There is Gender	246
Chapter Eight	Trust and Fear	284
Chapter Nine	Disconnection and Desperation	314
Chapter Ten	Endings	344
	Notes	352
	Bibliography	356

Acknowledgements

The ongoing support and encouragement I received from my community of friends and family provided me with the impetus to cloister myself within the writing enterprise. I appreciate their generosity and contribution to this book. I particularly want to acknowledge the following people. Leela Anderson who gifted her passion for therapeutic ideas, justice and connection, to the reading and re-reading of the manuscript. Isobel Rose who gifted precious time, her passion for the written word and her passion for this book in particular. Ruth Jackson and Carol Lynch who gifted practical advice and enthusiasm. Jill Kelly who gifted patience and dedication as she typed and retyped the manuscript. Pat Rosier who brought a fresh persective to the writing when I had become weary of it.

When I think of acknowledgements I find myself moving into the past. Writing and working from the heart has been and is, supported by my relationship with my grandparents, Jeanie and Alwyn Nelson and my parents, Verna and Tom Bird. Jeanie and Verna spun a protective cloak of light, love and laughter around me. Alwyn and Tom knew and expected that I could do anything.

Introduction

The title of this book represents an exploration that I have been engaged in for 20 years. Over this time, I have been drawn to the mysteries and vagaries of language, the creation and maintenance of change within the unique context provided by the therapeutic relationship and the enactment of justice and compassion within the therapeutic relationship.

Each one of these passions has its roots firmly planted in the whisperings of generations past and the louder memories and stories of childhood. The community I lived in as a child was geographically isolated by horizon-defining folds of mountain ranges that plateaued briefly before the sea. It was here that fortunes were often hard won and loosely lost. People moved easily within the knowledge of fortunes lost and found, thus inhibiting the building of status walls. This was however no utopian place; Irish bitterness continued to play itself out among immigrants, and those who belonged to the land, the indigenous Maori people, disappeared from Pakeha consciousness.[1] Differences were often subsumed and invisiblized, however, under the title 'coaster' which covered all locals and was produced proudly for any outsider. I mention my childhood because the resources and values that have enabled my pursuit of therapeutic ideas and practices developed within my extended family living in this unique environment; a place of laughter, appreciation of language, conversations on justice and compassion, demonstrations of the importance of love and connection, and a steady relationship with the possibility of injury or death.

I have often been asked, 'Why do you feel so strongly about things?' to which I reply, 'Why do you feel so lukewarm for this?' To feel strongly, passionately, in a field that has saturated itself with detached explanations and representations of people's lives is tantamount to declaring oneself pathologically inclined.

My first experience of such pathological sense making was the correspondence between an assessor and myself, following my proposal that a presentation I gave the year before at the annual Child Psychotherapist Association should suffice as assessable for membership. The assessor's response was to declare that I obviously had a problem with authority and that I should investigate my relationship with my father in my personal supervision. The certainty of this declaration interested me as it turned a procedural point into a psychological deficit. I didn't accept this analysis, mostly because the tone of the letter betrayed irritation with my enquiry. The texts I was absorbing at this time were psychodynamically orientated. Within these texts I also experienced intellectual rationalisations that were not representative of either my clinical experiences or life experiences.[2]

In 1981, after reading Lyn Hoffman's *The Foundation of Family Therapy* (14) I attempted to find common ground between the ideas of Family Therapy and the psychodynamic ideas with which I was familiar. When my head threatened to explode with the effort of finding a resting ground within these conceptual differences I made a decision and committed myself to immersion in the ideas and practices of Systemic Family Therapy. I was drawn towards Family Therapy because it represented an active engagement with the ideas and practices that supported people (clients) to change.[3] During this time I was surrounded by the excitement generated within Family Therapy by a climate of discovery where new ideas were being considered, challenged and used. To a certain extent my colleagues and I felt like pioneers and discoverers championing the cause of change-focused therapy. I still feel like a pioneer and discoverer, and I hope that this stays with me throughout my working life.

Throughout the book I have attempted to accurately represent my engagement with clinical work. The representation of any clinical work however is just that, a representation; it isn't the clinical work itself. Inevitably all psychological/counselling texts remain incomplete. This book represents my thinking and practice up until the moment I put down my pen and say, 'That's enough for now.'

WHAT IS THE MODEL?

I have been frequently asked to define my therapeutic work and ideas using a model. I am loath to do this because I believe the development of therapeutic models is very dangerous. The danger lies in our desire for certainty. Within the professional classes certainty provides comfort, privilege, belonging and access to a commodity. The Narrative way of working has provided a challenge to those therapeutic models that adhere to fixed psychological truths. However, the very construction of the term 'narrative model' creates an environment of inclusion and exclusion. Instead of engaging with ideas and practices that are described as Narrative, there is a temptation to replicate certain templates of the ideas and practices, and this replication encourages imitation, together with definitiveness about what is and what is not an accurate representation of the model. The idea that 'the Narrative model' actually exists overshadows the existence of differences as practitioners attempt to engage reflexively with ideas and practices. It is ironic that our attempt to engage with the idea of 'the model' contradicts many of the presuppositions that underpin our engagement with the ideas and practices of what is called Narrative.

I have struggled with defining the ideas that I use and the work that I do, under 'the model' umbrella. I feel a sense of colleagueship with people who call themselves Narrative Therapists because we share a passionate engagement with issues of justice and ethics. The development of the technical skills that I use in the work has its foundations in the Milan group's questioning process (26) and in Michael White's early definition and application of externalisation and relative influence questioning (33, 34). The ideas that I engage with are eclectic and wide-ranging. Over recent years my focus has been on feminist theory in relationship to post-structuralism, together with literature — fiction and non-fiction. The colleagueship, technical skills and theoretical ideas I hold come together within a rare environment of discovery. This environment relies on a compassionate connection with, and acknowledgement of, the people (clients) we work with in the therapeutic relationship. The theoretical ideas and practices which underpin the therapeutic models are discovered and rediscovered, supported and challenged, confirmed and changed within this environment.

In order to consider inventing and reinventing theoretical ideas within clinical practice, I engage with a particular language strategy. I have called this language strategy the relational externalising conversational process. When we use the relational externalising conversational process, we move into a relational paradigm. This relational paradigm acts to construct a 'relational I'. The 'relational I' is a direct challenge to the Western cultural construction of self, which presupposes an autonomous self-regulated self. The relational externalising enquiry challenges psychological ideas which are linguistically constructed and maintained by the conventional rules of correct English usage. When we engage with the relational externalising enquiry, we are in a position to consider the coherence of the theoretical representations of the therapeutic work. The relational externalising enquiry supports the establishment of a climate for discovery. We can thus continually engage with the relationship between theoretical ideas, clinical practice and ethics. This protects us from a process of conversion by the self-referential logic of one set of ideas that challenge the self-referential logic of another set of ideas. This climate of discovery refutes the idea that it is possible to ever engage with a formed and complete model. Instead, we engage in an ongoing evolution of theoretical ideas in relationship to clinical practice.[4]

The title of the book *The Heart's Narrative* reflects my particular engagement with technical skills and intellectual ideas that support my relationship with therapeutic practice. The complexity and challenge of the therapeutic work I represent is centered in our persistent living engagement with ethics. A living engagement with ethics moves us outside of compliance with the traditional professional position which engages us with linguistic strategies that internalise lived experiences. Internalisation captures the individual as solely responsible and culpable for the psychological development of concerns; the individual is thus available for scrutiny, evaluation, diagnosis and intervention by the detached psychological expert. The conventions of the English language thus generate the traditional professional position which captures these people as 'other'. The 'other' is outside of normal, often medicated in an attempt to find normal, and counselled back to normal.

In moving outside of the traditional professional position, I am challenged to move beyond a two-dimensional relationship with the significant ideas that I hold, i.e. respect, honouring and collaboration. The ongoing negotiation of these ideas in the practice of the therapeutic relationship requires me to continually engage with the practice of ethics.

The Heart's Narrative is my attempt to provide technical and intellectual tools to support both or all participants in the therapeutic relationship to engage as a subject with a subject. Within this therapeutic environment I am able to bring to the therapeutic work the total resources of my mind, heart and spirit.

INTRODUCING THE CHAPTERS

I began to write *The Heart's Narrative* guided in particular by the clinical and teaching discoveries of the last ten years. When I put down my pen I had more than one book. In this one I focus primarily on clinical work with people (clients) who have been psychologically, emotionally and sexually abused. Chapter One 'Just Talk!' represents the technical and theoretical foundation stones on which my clinical work rests. In this chapter I attempt to demystify the complexities of a relational externalising conversational process.

I propose in Chapter Two 'Therapeutic Narratives in Action' that a special kind of talk is the tool that will facilitate a change/healing focused environment. The structure of conventional therapeutic talk can inadvertently act to engage people (clients) in experiences of retraumatisation and hopelessness. I describe a relational externalising conversational process that positions us for discovery. These discoveries are located within the environment that shapes the meanings attributed to experiences. By orienting our listening, re-search and language usage we support people (clients) to engage with their relationship with abilities, strengths and competence.

In order to do this we would ask people to reflect on instances where the concerns were partially present or absent in their lives. We would also shift our language use to reflect an enquiry that emphasises a non-pathologising discourse. This shift of language is reflected in the subsequent enquiry. Inevitably this process brings forward knowledge of those experiences that stand outside of the pathologising discourse.

In Chapter Three 'The Therapeutic Relationship' I re-view the understandings and engagement with the therapeutic relationship. The therapeutic relationship has the potential to provide an important site for discovery. These discoveries draw our attention towards unique relational experiences that can occur in the present moment. In order to utilize the relationship potential of the therapeutic relationship, I propose a particular engagement with the therapeutic relationship understanding. This engagement requires an ongoing self and other reflective process.

The complexity of this process is determined by our willingness to engage with an ongoing relationship that reflects 'living respect'. Living respect exists within the bounds of the therapeutic relationship understanding. It is within this environment of living respect that we can direct our hearts and minds towards an engagement with the complexities of people's (clients') lived experience. The ideas and practices presented in this chapter provide an alternative to the transference and counter-transference paradigm.

In Chapter Four 'Building the Therapeutic Relationship' I reflect on the balance between detachment and connection within the therapeutic relationship. The common professional understanding of the acceptable detachment position for therapists is in my opinion an over-detached position. The elevation of over-detachment as the normal and preferred professional practice subjects people (clients) to therapeutic environments that support professional truth claims. These truth claims subsequently define normality and pathology. Finding the balance between connectedness and detachment within the bounds of the therapeutic relationship understanding engages us in a dynamic process. In this chapter I reflect on the strategies that we can use to maintain this balance. This includes identifying the implications for the therapist's sense of self of engaging in the therapeutic relationship.

In Chapter Five 'Working with Contradictions' I consider the complexities of people's (clients') lived experiences, complexities which can often take us beyond our experience. In these moments people (clients) are immensely vulnerable to our seeking refuge in psychiatric and psychological classification. With courage and skill we can identify and re-search these contradictory moments. The enquiry has profound implications for the discovery of a liberating way of making sense of people's (clients') lives, contradictions which have subjected people (clients) to silence and torment are exposed and stripped of a central place in determining their life direction. This conversation can require us to willingly engage with the profundities of life.

I passionately believe that those of us who work with people (clients) who have been abused (emotionally, sexually, physically) have a responsibility to move past the simplistic classification processes that establish right and wrong, good and bad, normal and not normal. In this movement we seek to understand people's (clients') experiences of living with contradictions. At the same time we seek to find a new place for people (clients) to be in the self. In order to achieve this, we work with people (clients) to find liberating ways of thinking and being, in order to diminish the influence of sometimes unendurable emotional pain.

In Chapter Six 'Working with Time' I consider working across time from within the present moment. The relational externalising enquiry supports an exploration of the past while holding people (clients) within the present. The experience of being in the present resources people (clients) to reflect on the 'child's sense of events and feelings' from the adults or young person's perspective. The advent of strong feelings is thus connected to reflections on the past. Reflecting on the past is experientially different from feeling 'lost in the past'. When people (clients) feel 'lost in the past' they experience the experiences of the past in the present. Instead I am committed to processes that support people (clients) to relate to the past.

The enquiry over time (past, present and future) creates an experience of movement which challenges people (clients) to view/know their lives as evolving rather than static. The movement over time exposes both the conditions which support and strengthen people's (clients') ideas of self and the conditions which weaken and undermine people's (clients') ideas of self. In this enquiry process the exposure of moments of movement, change and self determination challenges ideas of the formed, damaged, bad and mad self. The influence of societal and others' ideas and practices on what is remembered and what is forgotten is also made apparent in this enquiry process. The enquiry over time is essential to the search for people's (clients') engagement with unique experiences and ideas.

Chapter Seven 'Where There is a Relationship There is Gender' focuses on the discovery of gendered practices and ideas from within the therapeutic relationship. These ideas and practices have implications for both the therapeutic relationship and the therapy. We (therapists) are ideally positioned to either contribute to ongoing gender blindness or expose gender relations for exploration and negotiation of meaning. I believe we have an ethical responsibility to unmask the operation of gender relations in people's (clients') lives. Once unmasked by naming, we conduct an enquiry to discover how gender relations are negotiated and maintained. In this chapter I discuss how we can participate in this enquiry by making apparent to our selves and others our gender relations blindness and gender relations shorthand.

Chapter Eight 'Trust and Fear' and Chapter Nine 'Disconnection and Desperation' focus on the work with fear and trust, connection and disconnection and desperation. I have highlighted these areas because our inability to work effectively with people (clients) in the grip of fear, terror, distrust, disconnection and desperation has resulted in incalculable injury. We are often challenged in this work to go beyond our lived experience. We utilise our imaginations in order to explore with people (clients) their intricate relationship with fear, trust, disconnection and desperation. This exploration requires a negotiation of safety conditions. These safety conditions are necessary in order for people (clients) to experiment with claiming and holding the self free from the influence of the past.

In this work we are challenged to use language strategies which move us beyond binaries such as trust/mistrust. The movement away from binaries provides conditions for a rich and multidimensional exploration. This exploration focuses on working with people (clients) to expose the influences that are shaping their relationship with the self and with life.

Chapter Ten 'Endings' is included because the process of ongoingly negotiating the therapeutic relationship with people (clients) inevitably includes negotiating the end of the therapeutic relationship. People (clients) often expect therapists to determine the ending and therapists often expect this of themselves. Negotiating the ending supports a therapy of collaboration. This chapter provides ideas and questions for the negotiation of session endings, therapy endings and the end of the book.

THE LIMITATIONS OF TEXT
When I read the reference section of most therapy orientated books and articles, I am reminded of a piece of writing by Owen Marshall (18) titled, *The Lenny Fudge Bibliography* (pp. 58–63). Lenny Fudge's writings are listed over six pages. The titles include 'Lenny Fudge to the Rescue', 'Come Back Lenny Fudge', 'Twenty Quick Feminist Hotpots', 'Lenny Fudge', 'Fudge Speaks Out — Again', 'The Family Fudge: A Celtic Genealogy' and 'A Life Among the Ngai Tahu: Lenny Waka Fudge'. The Lenny Fudge bibliography represents a desperation to commit ideas to writing, thus staking an ownership claim. Once ownership of ideas is

determined through text, future texts then validate this process through a process of referencing.

I have previously been reluctant to write, for many reasons. In exploring this reluctance, several common explanations come forward — a lack of time, financial constraints and the belief that ideas that originate rather than replicate established clinical practices have a long germination process. Two recent events however galvanized me into action, demanding that I take up the textual challenge. In two situations where I had considerable prominence and visibility my contribution and literal existence was disappeared by the authors of texts. Authorship is a dominant western cultural strategy for the securing of ownership of ideas and practices. Its dominance can relegate conversation to the status of free floating ideas and practices. These events confirmed a realization that twenty years of participation in clinical work and twelve years of teaching was likely to disappear under its conversation status.

The disappearing goes beyond its personal effect; it reflects the disappearing of many women's experiences and ideas. I decided that I would not disappear. The decision brought into sharp relief the idea that no one was going to give me the time, space and financial support to write. I needed to take time and space and make the financial sacrifices. I was startled that this idea had not occurred to me until that moment. Taking the space and time to write requires enormous access to privilege, including financial privilege. Those who write determine ownership of ideas and practices. This continuously excludes people who live outside of privilege, people who warrant and deserve acknowledgement. Authors who talk about justice are not necessarily doing justice. The doing of justice means providing people outside of privileged circumstances with the opportunity to claim their place and ways of representing their knowings.

Outside of academic circles (which provide structure, funding and an explanation for self-preoccupation) a limited number of clinicians find the emotional, physical and financial space needed to write. Ethnic, gender and class perspectives on clinical work remain unavailable as academics (both men and women) retain the positions of authority as teachers and writers. In order to challenge this status quo, it is necessary to find new ways of securing physical, emotional and intellectual space.

I have 'taken' the time to write with the hope that my personal account of the therapeutic work will stimulate further discovery and exploration within a climate that recognises our daily engagement with ethics.

WHO OWNS IDEAS?

A friend was telling me a story about a woman who was a book editor. She saw a gap in the book market for a Greek cookery book. She approached a number of people about the possibility of writing such a book but to no avail. Finally she decided to write the book her self. She was not a particularly impressive cook of any cuisine, however she was able to relate well to people and she was passionate about the project. She travelled to Greece and over a six month period sat in women's kitchens, watching, asking questions and writing recipes that had been orally handed down through the generations. The book was written and was very successful.

Is the collector of the recipes the author of the recipes? Is the transcriber of oral knowing the author of that knowing? In this instance the writer didn't create or originate any of the recipes, therefore is she morally the author?

Margery B Franklin (8) in the chapter, 'Interviewing and Narrative Representation' describes the interviewee as 'author' and the interviewer as 'interpreter'. This distinction is interesting as it raises the issue of ownership of the ideas that are generated in therapeutic conversations.

Throughout a recent year-long consultation/teaching process the participants and I found numerous opportunities for discovery. These discoveries occurred within a climate of collaboration that defied the conventions of ownership and authorship. Answers to the questions 'What is mine?' and 'What is yours?' became blurred. It was often impossible to entirely attribute a new idea to any one individual member of the consultation group. Consequently we considered this question — 'What is an adequate and appropriate acknowledgement of other people's contribution to any one idea?'

It is clear to me that new metaphors of acknowledgement need to be experimented with. For example, the production of a play or a film requires a multiplicity of contributors who perform quite specific functions. Each is acknowledged and appreciated for their specific expertise, i.e. producers, director, screenwriter, writer, actors, sound, lighting, costumes, musicians, conductors, etc., etc.

The discoveries that emerge from the consultation group sit more comfortably within these metaphors of acknowledgement. The discoveries are produced in and by a particular environment that includes particular relationships. The position of the author needs, in my view, to be moved alongside others rather than retaining its central position as the principle generator of therapeutic ideas and practices.

Conventional practice dictates that authorship of psychology texts lies with the writer. The ownership of ideas is thus retained within the community of privilege. For all our egalitarian rhetoric, the status quo is safely maintained and supported.

Lauris Edmond, a New Zealand poet, commented firmly in a recent article, 'If you put art before life you will kill them both.' I really believe that. Life itself must be primary, and art, whatever it is, must serve it. And if you start to reverse that you're in great danger of isolating your self from experience, inflating your own idea of what you are or do.

'The only place for the writer to be is on the bottom rung of the ladder — not because I'm an especially modest person, but that's the only place to be. If you catch your self even once saying, "I'll do that so I can write a poem about it" — that's the worst thing.'[5]

Lauris Edmond's comments reflect my beliefs about therapy/counselling and teaching. To see this more clearly read her comments again interposing therapy/counselling/or teaching in relationship to life. It is challenging for those of us who write and teach to continuously and purposefully defy conventional career hierarchies to place our selves at the bottom of the ladder. The actions involved in placing the self at 'the bottom' are unstated and unheralded. In other words it is reflected in our engagements with life and the work. It is beyond the public performance of the modest or self effacing positioning of the self. I hold the belief that acting to defy conventional career hierarchies is one of the principle supports for the maintenance of integrity and creativity of the work.

LIVING COMPLEXITY

The commitment to text of the ideas and practices that I have found useful posits a dilemma. John Shotter (27) has reflected on 'the centrality of texts and the processes of their production in the conduct of psychology as a professional enterprise'.

While expressing this concern, 'For we all know texts are nothing if not the medium par excellence of fiction of story telling,' (p. 157) I have attempted to challenge the production of psychology/counselling as a movement from text to text by writing subjectively. I have drawn attention to the 'living complexity' of our (therapist and client) engagement within the therapeutic relationship. This 'living complexity' is expressed in our (therapist and client) willingness to engage with reflecting on the languaging of experiences and emotions within a therapeutic relationship bound by time restrictions. These reflections often require us to travel to the edge of known morality and ethics. Standing on this edge challenges us to find the courage to both look into the face of death and into that of life. In this place we re-search the relationships that support destruction and those that support resilience. We consider the existence of evil while marvelling at the human capacity to love.

In challenging my reluctance to write, will I succeed in drawing your attention towards the complexity of engaging within the therapeutic conversation? Will I lift your gaze away from the psychological certainty inherently represented in the psychological/counselling texts, a certainty that provides definitive explanations for people's behaviour and lives? Will I challenge you to construct a 'relational I' through a radical engagement with language? Will you join me in an ongoing exploration of the Talk That Sings? That is my hope.

Throughout the book I present numerous examples of therapeutic dialogue. Unless I indicate to the contrary, all the examples are constructions of my imagination. I have used these examples in order to provide a context for a theoretical idea or a practice. I use my imagination because all verbatims represented in psychological/counselling texts are transformed from dialogue to written text, a transformation that makes the interview more intelligible to the reader. The changes, however, move us away from the actual dialogue to a representation of the dialogue — a fiction constructed by the author. My fiction, or the telling of the clinical stories, is constructed from the accumulation of twenty years of clinical work and forty years of living.

A GUIDE TO THE TEXT

A central tenet of my work is that our effectiveness is enhanced when we position our selves in such a way as to be open to the reinvention of the theoretical ideas we stand beside and the technical abilities we use. The process of reinvention acknowledges the source of the idea or practice while affording us the opportunity to move a particular idea and practice beyond rote learning and imitation to something that is reflective of our selves.

In the process of reinvention we position our selves both within and in relationship to an idea or practice so that we can be in it while re-viewing it. This allows us to achieve an ethical practice by experiencing and noting the nuances and subtleties of the theoretical ideas in relation to the practice. We do this while also re-viewing the success or failure of the technical practices to achieve change within ethical parameters. In this re-view process, we stand back from the theoretical ideas and the description of the technical abilities to ask, Does this description adequately represent what I have experienced within the therapeutic relationship?

If it does not adequately reflect experience, we can position our selves to experiment with the naming and re-searching of our experiences, and ask,

How much does this description rely on our automatic concurrence with the ideas that we are immersed within?

The positioning of our selves for discovery and re-view protects the therapeutic relationship from the imposition of dogma. Dogma is the inevitable consequence of our desire to join a therapy that is bound by a beginning, a middle and an end, and results in a 'How to do it' or 'How to think about it' manual of set techniques that provide us with certainty.

I have attempted to protect this book from becoming a 'How to do it' or 'How to think about it' manual by using a variety of processes to engage you (the reader) in and with the text. The book is written as a personal reflection on the experiences I hold of the therapeutic work together with the ideas and practices that support me in this work. I have highlighted my engagement with ethics in order to expose the ethics that have and do reflect in my work. At the end of each chapter I have included a section called 'Working with the Text'. This is an attempt to protect the reader from objectifying people (clients) as the other. I have often included questions at the end of each section. These questions are directed at people who identify as either clients or therapists. However both sections are relevant to the reader and I encourage readers to engage with both sections.

There is a glaring absence of the knowledges and practices of Maori (the indigenous people of New Zealand) in this book. Although I consider issues of justice and equality throughout the text while highlighting the centrality of ethnicity, sexuality, gender and class in the making of meaning, this consideration has severe limitations. The very construction of the text and the language used is culturally bound and therefore limited.

ETHICS

A number of years ago I was sitting in a lecture hall listening to a clinical presentation reflecting on the consequences of therapists' lack of awareness of gender relations, for women (clients).[6] Well known and revered Family Therapists appeared on screen demonstrating a cringe-making ignorance of gender relations. This ignorance clearly subjected women to explanations and interventions that confined them within oppressive stereotypes. I left this lecture chastened. I wondered how the practices and ideas that I engage with would be understood in the next ten or twenty years. I considered how my relationship within privilege was acting to exclude the knowledges and practices that more adequately reflected people's lived experience. I explored ideas about the context that would support an ongoing engagement with ethics, and I pondered the role of therapists, counsellors, psychiatrists, psychologists and social workers in maintaining the status quo for the ongoing comfort of the dominant group.

These wonderings were to the forefront in the writing of this text.

During the writing process I spent some time preparing to write a theoretical chapter. I turned towards post-structuralist texts whilst holding a desire to not simply replicate there ideas. I was also aware that although many of the post-structuralist ideas provided me with an explanation for many of the ideas and practices I've struggled with, these ideas are not the fulcrum on which my clinical discoveries rest.

At some point in my textual re-search I decided to engage with reflecting on the ethical underpinnings of each chapter. This engagement with ethics is an attempt to remind us to consider that therapy is always an ethical endeavour that is situated historically and culturally.

PEOPLE WHO ARE READING THIS TEXT FROM THE POSITION OF CLIENTS

This text is slanted towards people who are described as therapists/or counsellors. The therapeutic relationship understanding (see Chapter Three) attributes responsibilities to the participants in the therapeutic conversation. This understanding draws the distinction between people who are therapists and people who are clients.

The understandings represented in this text have developed over time as a result of the therapeutic conversations between myself and the people (clients) I've worked with. The text is therefore also relevant to people (clients) who have in the past been in a therapeutic relationship and those who are presently engaged in a therapeutic relationship or may consider engaging in a therapeutic relationship in the future. In other words, during our lifetime we could all engage on all sides of the therapeutic relationship.

When you read this book reflect on the text and ask your self the following:

▼ Does this in some way represent my understandings of past, present, future experience?

▼ What did I notice that was similar to the experience I hold?

▼ What were the differences?

▼ How do I make sense of the similarities and the differences?

▼ What would I want the author to know in order that she would appreciate the differences and similarities between the text and the knowledge I hold?

These questions are an attempt to protect readers from a relationship with texts as a true representation of all people's lived experiences. Inevitably texts will always be a partial representation of people's lived experience. At the end of each chapter I have developed questions to support you to engage with the text. These questions are not finite, you may discover that you have other questions that you would prefer to ask your self.

When you read and think about the questions directed towards people who are identifying as therapists, this may raise questions for you about a past or present therapeutic relationship. I encourage you to explore this further.

PEOPLE WHO ARE READING THIS TEXT FROM THE POSITION OF THERAPISTS

A strong belief that supports my work is that our effectiveness is strengthened when we continuously re-search the relevance of the theoretical ideas from within the practice. This principle attempts to move us away from reproducing others' ideas in the therapy or becoming mimics of teachers or writers. The relational externalising enquiry is the cornerstone linguistic support for therapeutic conversations that expose the operation of power relations between competing sets of ideas. This power relations is inherent in any institutional requirement for classification, assessment and diagnosis.

In reading this book, you are engaging with my relationship to the ideas and practices. I would like to encourage you to also use this book in order to make your discoveries in the therapeutic practice. In order to do this, at the end of each chapter I have often extracted from the text questions that can be explored in study groups of two to four people focusing on how you relate to these ideas within and outside of the clinical practice. Once you have engaged with these exercises, I would suggest that you re-read the text. In the re-reading you may formulate questions or wonderings about the relationship between the discoveries represented in the text and the discoveries you've made in reflecting on your relationship with the clinical work. When you read and think about the questions directed towards people who are identifying as clients, this may raise questions for you about how you would support people's (clients') initiatives or challenges. I encourage you to explore this further.

CONCLUSION

This text is a personal account of therapeutic work. I hope that the text resonates in some way for you and supports you to actively engage with the ideas and practices that shape the therapeutic work you are involved with.

CHAPTER ONE

· · · · · · · · · ·

Just Talk

WHAT SORT OF TALK IS JUST TALK ?
In this chapter I attempt to describe the foundational ideas that underpin *The Heart's Narrative*. My therapeutic practice has been the primary venue where I have re-searched[1] the ideas and practices reflected in this book. Reading what others had written often came later. I was guided within this climate of discovery by a relationship with ethics and a particular engagement with externalising conversations.

The story that follows is fictional because therapeutic transcripts are often read as accurate reflections of lived experience. The smooth movement between question and response in such transcripts belies the complexity of the conversation by sheltering the reader from the emotional exchange between people (therapist and client). Transcripts protect us from the contradictory moments where a choice of therapeutic direction can send people (clients) tumbling into despair. We are safe-guarded from profoundly confronting those taken-for-granted values that support the pathologising of people on the margins. We are encouraged by our insider position to consider that we know what it means to relationships and a sense of self to live within certain conditions. We are deluded by the thought that the hours spent in therapy can accurately represent people's (clients') actual lived experience.

The story introduces Sophie, Jacob, Sam and Rebecca. Different members of this family might approach a therapist for many different reasons. I present some possibilities.

The family could be referred by Sam's school. Sam has been masturbating both inside and outside of the classroom, which has resulted in his being ostracised and teased by other children. Sophie and Jacob (Sam's parents) have noticed the same behaviour at home and have responded to it by suggesting that masturbation is a private activity that Sam should conduct in his room. The school principal suggested to them that Sam may have been sexually abused. Sophie and Jacob are both very concerned about Sam, however he appears detached from the conversation.

or,

Sophie is referred by the hospital social worker after her discharge from a psychiatric ward as, due to economic restructuring, counselling is not available in her community. She begins the interview by describing her self according to her current psychiatric diagnosis. She appears resigned to her life and has little or no expectations of the therapy. She is here because she has been sent.

or,

Sophie and Jacob seek out a therapist together. Jacob explains that Sophie has a psychiatric illness that is contained with medication. He is concerned that they have not had a sexual relationship since the birth of their daughter, Rebecca. He indicates that the relationship is very important to him. Sophie is also concerned about their sexual relationship, however she adds that she just doesn't ever feel like being sexual. She wonders if she has been sexually abused as a child.

A FICTIONAL STORY

Sophie

The walls are greyish/white. Greyed with age and shock. I sit naked, cold, concrete cell cold. I stare into myself and see my mother and grandmother talking while sharing a well-earned cup of tea. I was seated at the table seemingly doing something. The something that children do while listening for information about the adult world.

'She had a beautiful head of hair, shiny, thick black hair. Hair you'd die for. They were such a close family you wouldn't see one without another being nearby. Then that dreadful accident. It was on Macky

St. A drunk went through the stop sign. There was nothing anyone could do, it was a head on. She was the only one to survive. They say it took them four hours to get her out of the car. The next day she was completely grey, completely, not a black hair left on her head. Amazing to go grey just like that.'

I am grey like these walls. Together we have greyed with groans and screams, bodies thrashing and silences that have a death aura. I study the grey, reading the cracks and chips and in turn make my mark with fists, head and feet until dragged back, bloodied, battered, held and sedated, I see my blood seep into these cracks to join the others. They can't wash me away. I've marked the place, greyed it as it has marked me.

It truly was and is us and them. 'They' know as much about what goes on here as zoo-keepers know what's in the minds and hearts of their charges. Secrets create the fabric of this small society. New residents learn the protocol after a couple of sessions in solitary. I seemed to take longer than most, but then I preferred this solitary place where I could scream and tear at the air. For this is not a place to expose pain and rage. It is not a place to wonder if disappearing into death is preferable to this life that I endure. No, for this is a place of timetabled order, no messiness is allowed here. At least no messiness that can be seen, for the truth is, messiness abounds.

Me — oh what messiness do we have here? Jesus Christ why did they make me do it? I told them what would happen, I screamed, I won't be able to cope. I begged, let me carry the child to term and then adopt. I knew abortion wasn't possible. I didn't want an abortion, I wanted them to just listen, listen I can't have this child, I can't, I can't.

They said I didn't know what I was saying. They said I wasn't myself, that I'd feel different when the baby arrived. They said it was all hormonal. They said I'd never forgive myself. They said I was being selfish denying Jacob the child that he'd wanted for years. They said Sam needed a little brother or sister, otherwise he'd be lonely or spoilt. They said I wasn't natural. On and on it went with no one join- ing me on my solitary side. It was them, Jacob and his parents, against me. The medical profession stood on neutral ground. I thought of killing myself but I just couldn't. I was held in life by the relentless voice of past indoctrination and a genetic predisposition to belief in mortal sin. I wondered about engineering an accident and went through each scenario with precision and more than a modicum of pleasure. When it came to it, I couldn't cross the line, it was still suicide. My stomach grew as my hatred grew for this body that had betrayed me. The only way it could redeem itself was to give up this package it was delicately holding and nurturing. It didn't achieve redemption so I punished it, depriving it of food and drink, giving it pain with small burns and scratches, denying it by never once looking at it. I smashed every mirror in the house. I brought on a bout of madness, easy to enter, not so easy to leave behind. But this time, carrying madness and a precious cargo like a prize cow coming to term, I was whisked off to the colour coordinated rooms with a view, service with a smile and a menu that the Regent would be proud of. No expense spared. For this little bundle couldn't begin its life in the desolate outreaches of the psychiatric wards.

They tell me it was an easy birth. She was born on 16 August at 7.30 a.m. She slipped into the world, eyes open, and was greeted by a rapturous Jacob. He swept her into his arms and although I carried her, she, Rebecca, was his. I wasn't there to see this life miracle. I had disappeared into the recesses of my mind, refusing stubbornly to reappear. I even resisted the consciousness-dragging chemicals they pumped into me. This stopped a week before the event because 'it became difficult to judge the effects that the drugs would be having on the baby'. So relatively free of chemical aids I found myself at one point looking down on the joyful gathering, post-theatre. There I was, looking like death itself while life was celebrated. Jacob was holding Rebecca, a nurse stood to his left gazing lovingly at this scene. She then looked over at Jacob's Mum and Dad with a smile that said, 'Isn't he a special man.' I was mentioned in the self-congratulatory conversations that followed. The nurse (I don't remember her name, they all look alike to me) threw me a pitying look that could be taken for compassion and said, 'It will make a world of difference when she sees this beautiful little girl.' The others nodded and smiled politely while catching each other's eyes nervously. That's right, I thought, it's not that easy. I have nothing to give this little girl. I am barren, a wasteland where nothing can feed.

So here I am, I have come home to the desolate outreaches. Not to rest, for this place is full of restless motion. Not to heal, for the injuries remain mostly hidden to all who are injury free. Not to hope, for hope is drowned in the deafening mutterings of death's numerous possibilities. I have come home to a sense of belonging. A belonging that is founded on an acceptance of all that the others, the outsiders, the normals, deem outrageous and unacceptable. Knowledge of past acts and deeds is not a precursor to acceptance. Acceptance just is. It sits between us as we move from banal activity to banal activity — basketmaking, exercise classes, lunch, rest time, card playing, TV watching. Exposure of that which is still unthinkable and therefore unknowable is not a requirement in this world. We know that exposure has the potential to liberate but it also carries the potential to destroy. I am caught within the dreams of others. This asylum is my only place of shelter.

Jacob

I never once lift my gaze from the triangle that has at its apex flesh that surges and retreats around a seemingly vacuous cavern. Quivering and stretching, the cave voraciously consumes my vision, threatening to leap beyond the legs. Finally it is filled with the head of my child. The head is grasped and turned gently enabling one shoulder to slip out and then the other.

'It's a girl. She's just perfect.' Her eyes are open. They fix on me and I fix on her. 'You're so beautiful,' I say and ask to hold her as soon as the midwife has checked and wrapped her. While holding her, I glance over at Sophie. She is so motionless she could be dead. Momentarily I hope that while we've all been preoccupied with the birth she has slipped away. But no, the beeps of the machine affirm a life force.

Rebecca you have given me the opportunity to eradicate the intruder that invaded my soul eight years ago when Sam was born. I have waited to slide you into my consciousness. In the waiting, I protected myself by not listening, seeing and remembering those things that brought forth the intruder. I fought off loneliness by praying, praying for you, Rebecca. Now you're here I can dedicate all my listening, seeing and memory towards you.

Rebecca don't ask me to tell you what happened eight years ago. I won't go back there. Know this, while witnessing Sam's birth I gazed upon my death. A sight that literally froze me. I couldn't move a muscle, even my eyes froze in their sockets. My mind however moved with the frenzy of those that are trapped. This is where I

stayed until shocked back by a rude psychiatric invention, ECT. That's
all I will tell.

Sam

Rocking, hand on my willie,
Rocking, turn up the sound,
Sway and rock,
Sway and rock,
Rippling pleasure
As I grasp this stick hard, until
exhausted and wet I lie
looking at the ceiling, the ride complete.
I exist again, beyond the body edges
filled in with warmth.
Knowing that at other moments eyes stare through a void that is me.
Pinching confirms an existence
but this works best.

DISCUSSION

In this chapter I discuss the ways we position our selves in order to
facilitate discovery. I am interested in the conditions that support our
willingness to engage with the complexities of people's (clients') lives,
and in exploring the style of enquiry that brings forward what is known,
but often unspoken. Throughout this chapter I will be referring to this
story to illustrate and translate a theoretical idea into the activity of the
therapeutic conversation.

The discussion that follows is my response to these questions:

▼ What style of conversation will help us explore with people
   (clients) the complexity of their lived experience?

▼ What style of conversation promotes a connected exploration that
   is emotionally coherent?

▼ What style of conversation challenges detached diagnostic
   categorisation that turns tragic circumstances into personal
   deficit?

▼ What style of conversation respects the identified concerns
   while exploring the context of meaning that surrounds these
   concerns?

EXTERNALISING — A RADICAL WAY OF RELATING

I was introduced to externalisation in a workshop facilitated by Michael White in 1986. At that time the emphasis was on externalising the problem and externalising the unique outcome. When I began working predominately with individual adults in 1988, I became engaged in conversations that reflected the complexities of adults' lives. It was clear that people's (clients') life stories were often torn with contradictions. People (clients) were persecuted by descriptions of self, drawn from interpretations of experiences riddled with common sense and taken-for-granted truths. The concept of 'problem' thus disappeared under a plethora of concerns. During this time I discovered that I was using a different externalising process in order to construct a linguistic relationship. This linguistic relationship allowed me to negotiate meaning differently. I subsequently named this conversational process relational externalising.

The conventions of English language usage locate experiences within people (clients), e.g. 'I'm sad'. In this example the languaging practice ('I'm sad') acts to encourage the speaker and the listener to consider that sadness exists within the body of 'I'. Its static representation of experience has severe consequences for those people (clients) who are struggling with life experiences and circumstance. Conventional English language strategies create the conditions where the I is seen/experienced/known as autonomous, self directed, singular and independent. Whenever we use the English language conventionally in clinical work, we unwittingly support conversational processes that persistently subject people (clients) to 'self' and 'other' evaluation, categorisation and diagnosis.

A relational externalising conversation shifts linguistically what has been/or is subjectified (i.e. attributes, ideas, feelings, experiences that are conceptualised as belonging to the person) to the status of an object in relationship to the person (client). This way of languaging acts to shift the focus, from that of an individual self to a self always in relationship.

This literal explanation of the relational externalising conversation reduces its complexity. In engaging in this style of conversation we are living out or practising a philosophical belief, which is that the 'I' is never singular. The 'I' is known and experienced always in relationship.

Engagement with *the self in relationship to* whatever has been named as significant or meaningful to people (clients) creates linguistic space. This linguistic space provides people (clients) with a perspective of distance which illuminates the relational paradigm. For example, we can explore people's (clients') relationship to the following:

▼ The ideas and practices of fear
▼ The ideas and practices of shame
▼ The ideas and practices of terror
▼ The ideas and practices of guilt
▼ The light at the end of the tunnel.

We can reflect on, re-search, get to know the feelings and activities of each externalisation e.g. the ideas and practices of shame, in relationship to people (clients') lives, in relationship to the past, present, future, in relationship to others, and in relationship to prevailing cultural ideas.

The relational externalising conversational style is experienced or felt rather than heard. Although we are speaking relationally and thus unconventionally, we are utilising the language of everyday experience. People (clients) engage with the languaging of everyday experience while experiencing the linguistic space which is generative of a relational construct that inevitably builds a sense of hope and possibility. When we use relational externalising talk we imply through our use of the language that people (clients) are not totally the identified concern, feeling, life event, or diagnosis. This style of talk enables us to research the institutional and other supporters of the development of this concern, feeling, life event, or diagnosis. The relational externalising conversation thereby challenges the idea that the self is the sole regulator of life events and the meanings attributed to these life events.

In this work, we focus on the languaging of lived experience in order to challenge the practices of psychological detachment. Exploration of people's (clients') lived experience by using the language of lived experience supports us to move beyond the shorthand of diagnosis and categorisation. This shorthand subjects people (clients) to institutional categorisations of normal/not normal. Inevitably this acts to support dominant institutional values and regimes of meaning. When we use a relational externalising conversation we engage with an enquiry process that connects us (therapist and client) in an exploration of the intricacies and complexities of human experience. In this exploration we expose the power relations inherent in the support of one meaning paradigm over another.

When the static languaging of life experiences is replaced by a relational externalising conversational process, the everyday becomes spectacular, fascinating, engaging and life changing.

It is noticeable in the following example that I have moved what has been/or is subjectified to the status of an object in relationship to a person (client) by using a noun, i.e. the attribute, the feeling, the word, the it, the high horse, the hitting out, etc. Once this externalisation is recognised by people (clients) as relevant or meaningful I will often change the noun by introducing this, that or these attributes, feelings, ideas and so on. The movement to create the demonstrative adjective and/or pronoun draws our attention towards what has already been named, while emphasising an increasing linguistic distance between 'it' and the self. This distance is not a separation. It allows for a perception of or emphasis on the relational.

Carl is a 45 year old, Pakeha[2] man. He has made an appointment for counselling as a result of his partner threatening to leave him.

Johnella: What brings you to counselling?

Carl: I feel a bit embarrassed about that. I don't think there's much of a problem. Pauline won't take my word for it, so I've come here so she can see I'm making an effort.

Johnella: What's involved in *the word* that you've given her?

Carl: Well, I said that it won't happen again and it won't. I know that, I'm a hundred per cent certain.

Johnella: What is *the 'it'* that won't happen?

Carl: It is a bit of a long story. I don't know how relevant it is really.

Johnella: I'd like to hear what *the it* is because otherwise I won't know what we are talking about. Is there anything that I can do or say that would help you to tell me what *the it* is?

Carl: Well, I hope you're not one of those feminist types that get on their high horse about things.

Johnella: What could I do or say that might indicate *getting on a high horse?*

Carl: I don't know, I just wouldn't feel comfortable.

Johnella: Would you be willing to tell me if you felt you were listening to me engaging with *'high horse' statements or questions?*

Carl: Yes I suppose?

Johnella: What are the first signs, feeling or thinking signs, that these *'high horse' statements or questions* are around?

Carl: Irritation first, then anger.

Johnella: Could you tell me, as soon as you notice *this irritation?*

Carl: Yeah, that would be okay.

Johnella: Okay, I'd like to hear what *the it* is.

Carl: I'd had a few beers after work, I don't do this often. I was feeling stressed out, we had just got a big order out. I'd been working 12 hour days for four weeks so I was really buggered. I was celebrating with the guys. Time got away from me and so I arrived home tiddly I suppose, not drunk. Anyway, I came in the door and went to greet Pauline and she's all snitchy with me. She tells me that I smell like a brewery and that I can sleep it off on the couch. It was then that I saw red, here I am working my guts out and I come home to this. Well one thing led to another and next thing I know I've hit her. She's holding her face and her nose is bleeding. That stops me in my tracks, I couldn't believe I had done this. I went over and said I'm sorry and tried to hold her. She pushed me away, calling me a bastard and screaming at me to leave her alone. I was shattered, I didn't sleep a wink and we talked a bit in the morning. She said she'd had enough and I needed to sort myself out. So here I am.

Johnella: Has this *hitting out* happened at any other times?

Carl: Only once, about 12 years ago. We had just bought our first house and I thought I'd do a few things to surprise her. When she saw what I'd done she was furious, said

that I hadn't consulted her and this was not the sort
of relationship she wanted. I just lost it. I was so
disappointed.

Johnella: Twelve years ago did you express the same promise that
it — the hitting out wouldn't happen again?

Carl: Yeah, I did and I meant it. It didn't happen again for
nearly fifteen years.

Johnella: Would you be willing for *it* to happen again in the next
fifteen years?

Carl: No, I don't want it to happen again.

Johnella: Does your engaging in *this hitting out*, go against your
hopes or wishes for your-self in this relationship?

Carl: Yes it does, this isn't the person I see myself as being.

In this example I am neither avoiding Carl's hitting out behaviour nor
am I launching into an anger management programme. I am primarily
attempting to understand the context within which the hitting out
occurred.

Relational externalising presents a challenge to conventional
language use and provides us with a vehicle to consider *the self in
relationship*. Engaging with the *self in relationship* creates conceptual
space within which alternative explanations for life concerns can be
explored and considered. Utilising a practice that engages with *the self
in relationship* is in itself challenging to a Western cultural preoccupation with autonomous self direction.

For example, let's return to the previous story of Jacob, Sophie, Sam
and Rebecca.

Jacob: I feel so delighted with Rebecca. She is everything I
imagined she would be. It's strange though, even while
I feel happy there is this gnawing like sadness that just
sits in me.

Therapist: If we think about *the sadness* for a moment, what first
alerts you to its presence?

What do you do when you notice *the sadness* enter your
life ?

If you were to welcome *the sadness* into your life rather
than push it down and away, what do you think would
happen?

In this example we can consider the history of the sadness, the appearance and reappearance of the sadness, the effects of the sadness, the
effects of pushing away or welcoming sadness. This provokes a complex
engagement with the experience and meanings of sadness.

Using the relational externalising conversation positions us as
explorers of people's lived experience rather than expert knowers of
people's lives. This is an example of the beginning of a relational externalising conversation with Sam.

Johnella:	Sam, do you mind if we talk about this masturbation? Do you call it masturbation or do you call it something else?
Sam:	Wanking. I call it wanking.
Johnella:	Sam, other people have told me that they think this wanking is a problem. Do you think it's a problem?
Sam:	I suppose.
Johnella:	Are you not too sure — are there times that wanking feels good?
Sam:	What do you think?
Johnella:	I'd like to know what you think?
Sam:	(Shrugs)
Johnella:	Before *the wanking* happens do you think to your-self, I feel like wanking now?
Sam:	No, of course not.
Johnella:	What happens?
Sam:	I just do it.
Johnella:	Are there any times during the day when *doing it* happens more or times when *doing it* happens less?
Jacob:	I notice it happening in front of TV.
Sam:	(Shrugs)

Johnella:	What about at school Sam? Does *doing it* happen more there, or only sometimes, or *does it* happen less at school?
Sam:	I don't know.
Johnella:	As soon as you get to school in the morning *does it* happen?
Sam:	No, of course not.
Johnella:	Hey, why not? What stops *it* happening then?
Sam:	I've got other things on my mind, I'm thinking about the day.
Johnella:	Thinking about the day, how does this thinking stop it, *the wanking*?

Engaging in a relational externalising conversation requires us to locate within conversations the attributes, concerns, feelings, ideas and experiences that seem central to people's (clients') meaning-making processes.

Whenever I engage with an relational externalising enquiry I comprehensively re-search the following:

▼ The context.[3]

▼ The movement between the polarity positions, e.g. success/failure, stealing/honesty. This includes developing language for in-between positions, e.g. partial forgiveness, hope with protection.

▼ The positions outside of polarity positions (e.g. if we were to put to one side all consideration of forgiveness or not, what are the other considerations that stand out to you?).

▼ The exploration of one position, and then others — without a requirement to commit to one position over another. This exploration inevitably brings forward ideas and practices that don't comply to a rigid adherence to either position.

A relational externalising enquiry frees us from the static internalising representation of experience, which is embedded in everyday usage of language. Words that have previously imprisoned, tormented, limited and pathologised people are reshaped and reformed in order to act as a medium for transformation and healing.

WHAT DO I EXTERNALISE ?

What we are listening for is critical in determining what is available to be re-searched within the therapeutic conversation. Students frequently ask me how I know what to externalise? The answer to that question is shaped by what I am listening for.

▼ I am drawn towards those parts of the conversation that seem to emotionally resonate for people (clients).

▼ I am drawn towards significant life themes.

▼ I am drawn towards key descriptive words or phrases that encapsulate or reflect lived experience.

▼ I am drawn towards parts of the conversation that reflects people's (clients') relationship with resilience, abilities, strength.

▼ I am drawn towards an exploration of the contextual environment of concerns and the contextual environment of those relationships, experiences, beliefs and practices that contradict the truth regimes that support the concerns.

▼ I am drawn towards words and/or metaphors that imply movement. A movement towards or a movement away. The existence of movement inevitably implies change, thereby challenging belief in the static nature of all that constitutes pathology and normality.

When I am drawn towards an idea, theme, word, experience, I hold it as a tentative support for the enquiry. I attempt to put to one side any psychological theories or complete hypotheses in order to construct a question that promotes exploration. Even though I sometimes have a sense of people's (clients') response to this question, I make myself available to the possibility of a different response. The relational externalising enquiry requires us to engage with presence listening. Presence listening is a turning of all of our facilities towards the other/ s. In the present moment we are totally available to engage with the therapeutic conversational process. This depth of listening involves our emotional, intellectual and physical selves. It is listening beyond the everyday. It is listening that defies Western cultural strategies of detachment. It is listening that positions us on the line between knowing and not knowing. In this listening place we make our selves available to have our life knowledges overturned, added to and/or confirmed.

Relational externalising constructs a relational 'I'. When I am engaging with the relational externalising process I am drawn towards a multiplicity of possibilities. These possibilities include people's (clients') relationship with problems and concerns as well as people's (client's) relationship with resilience.

EXTERNALISING— A FEELING FOR WORDS

I am attempting in this section to describe or define the activity of externalising relationally. Relational externalising is a central part of my practice.

My attempts to describe relational externalising as a practice seem paltry when I consider the implications this practice has for psychiatry, psychology and counselling. There are numerous counselling or therapy tactics for creating distance between people (clients) and their concerns. The creation of distance attempts to provide people (clients) with an observer's view/experience of life events. From this view/ experience it is hoped that people will make discoveries that will act to shift people's (clients') relationship with their life concerns.

The relational externalising conversation is not a counselling/therapy tactic. It is the way I talk and engage with the world. It is an ethic and it supports my relationship to and with ethics. The linguistic shift that occurs when we are externalising relationally profoundly shifts our engagement with the self. This shift occurs through a linguistic practice. In contrast, everyday usage of the English language creates the logio- centric voice that delivers comprehensive arguments. This linguistic practice supports certainty and forms a static and fixed engagement with language. For example, within poststructuralist texts, discussion of subjectivity, diversity and the multiplicity of truth claims are embedded within an engagement with language that is static and fixed. This adherence to the conventions of English usage inevitably results in one textual truth claim being replaced by another. This way of using language continues to support the Western language strategy that confirms the self as the autonomous purveyor of cultural meaning. The linguistic practice that is relational externalising profoundly shifts our engagement with words and meanings through the implication that the self and all that constitutes the self exists relationally. I describe the ethics of the relational externalising style of talking on pages 34–43. I engage with the practice of relational externalising throughout the book. In this section I will describe the relational externalising style of talking.

Finding the descriptive language to adequately respond to the question 'What is relational externalising?' is tormenting. How do I describe a process without succumbing to the language strategies that contradict the process? How do I describe being in the air that I breathe without reproducing chemical formulas and describing the physiology of breath? How do I describe an engagement with others that uses language that includes a technical knowledge of a languaging style *with a feeling for words*?

In the struggle for description, I think of Peter Høeg's novel *Miss Smilla's Feeling for Snow*. (13) I think of a knowledge relationship of snow that moves beyond the binary of snow or not snow, towards descriptions that incorporate the qualities, consistencies, colour ranges, smell and shapes that support a 'feeling for snow'. If this knowledge relationship of snow is put into language, the subtleties of our relationship to and with snow are extended until we too may have a feeling for snow. With this feeling for snow, we may become resourced to read the weather and we may engage differently with the rhythm of seasons.

A relational externalising practice extends my thinking beyond binaries. Once freed from the binary, static nature of conventional English language use, I move into a different relationship with the everyday. Development of *a feeling for words* was multifaceted, and stretched beyond my cognitive awareness of the relational externalising process. The following influences shaped my engagement with a feeling for words.

▼ A *feeling for words* develops in a family where playful engagement with language is the everyday.

▼ A *feeling for words* is shaped through an ongoing appreciation of literature.

▼ A *feeling for words* is strengthened through experiencing directly and indirectly the capacity of words carried and delivered by a detached authoritarian source (text or person) to injure, silence, pathologise and torment people's spirit-filled selves.

▼ A *feeling for words* is strengthened through years of listening, watching and reflecting on therapeutic relationships where words are used to negotiate and renegotiate meaning.

▼ A *feeling for words* is shaped through experiencing directly and indirectly the capacity for words to liberate, strengthen and heal people's spirit-filled selves.

When words are the medium I use to facilitate change, my focus of study is my ongoing engagement with words. Within this dedication to expose and study my engagement with words and meanings I continually discover *a feeling for words*.

In order to develop *a feeling for words* it is helpful to see, feel and hear the words that you use. In the following practice you will have an opportunity to:

▼ Identify language habits.

▼ Practice a contextual enquiry.

▼ Reflect on the structure of the language used within a relational externalising conversation.

▼ Challenge and extend the meanings ascribed to the words used to describe significant thoughts, feelings and events.

PRACTICE EXERCISE

Think of and write down every word or collection of words that describes the essence of you.

Once you have completed the list re-view it, reflecting on how many attributes appear on this list. Spend a moment reflecting on the attributes. (I ask you to do this because struggles or deficits, rather than successes or desirable traits, seem to move into prominence whenever people are asked to describe the self.)

Next, list the significant people in your life (past and present). Ask your-self — 'How would this person describe what they consider represents the essence of me?'

Using descriptive words from both lists, develop a list of questions that explores each quality in a range of contexts.

For example, here are some questions that begin an enquiry of the quality of loyalty:

▼ What ideas support your engagement with the loyalty ability?

▼ What relationship qualities bring forward this loyalty ability?

▼ Is loyalty expressed in relationship to others and the self?

▼ How would the loyalty ability be expressed in relationships?

▼ Is this loyalty ability also found in relationship to ideas?

▼ Have other people appreciated your engagement with this loyalty ability?

▼ Is this an ability that has been supported or acknowledged in your family?

▼ What sort of loyalty occurs when the person carrying authority in a hierarchical relationship demands loyalty from the other person in the relationship?

This list is not in any way definitive. For ideas on how to create questions refer to the contextual enquiry (Chapter Two). The practice of developing questions will assist you to strengthen a feeling for words. It is important to remember that the questions you develop here are a response to an exercise; these questions are not 'the therapy'.

RELATING TO FEELINGS

An enquiry that emphasises a relational externalising process is extremely evocative of emotions. I don't, however, doggedly set out to provoke emotions, rather the expression of emotions is a natural consequence of an enquiry process that explores the fullness of human existence. When we listen to people's (clients') experiences we are listening for opportunities to participate in an experimental and experiential enquiry that explores the multiplicity of meanings that can be made of life events. This listening includes listening to the body and listening to and for the emotions. The relational paradigm assumes a relationship between ideas, feelings and body sensations. The enquiry brings forward ideas, feelings and body sensations as a potential knowledge resource for the therapy. The meanings attributed to this knowledge resource are an ongoing negotiation between us (therapist and client). Dominant discourses reside most comfortably within ideas, thus saturating people's (clients') thinking. When we negotiate the meanings attributed to significant life events by utilising the resources of ideas, feelings and the body, we access a richer tapestry of potential meanings. In these moments we can find our selves engaging with issues of morality, life and death. This engagement will often occur in the present moment within the therapeutic relationship. Together we face and name what has previously been unknowable and unimaginable. We reach this unknowable and unimaginable place when there is a meeting of words that touch the heart. These words cross the experiential divide and generate a spirit-filled environment. In this spirit-filled environment we sit together, stripped bare of pretence, facing our humanity in all its fragility and magnificence.

As you read Sarah's story consider the question: 'How do we prepare to meet the challenge of spirit-filled conversations using a relational externalising conversation?'

SARAH'S STORY

I am white light that is surrounded by an electronic low hum. This knowing accompanies me to consciousness. My auto-focus works without a cue as the shadows move into the light. They take form and so do I, finding and defining myself by the pressure points forming against the bed. I remember the searing, unrelenting pain, the scream that detached itself into the air and fear on the face of my lover. There was movement, which surrounded me, lifted me away from the body that was being pushed, pulled, held, cut, rudely entered. In this frenzy there was nothing of me. I gladly departed.

But only it seems for a blink of the eye. Returning, I felt the ache that spread unsympathetically across the lower part of my body.

God, so much for natural childbirth, give me pain relief and more of it any day. This self-muttering was responded to with much activity. Looming faces of strangers in white followed by the familiar loved one. These eyes calm me, hold me, force the panic down and away. 'The baby'. Exclamation mark together with a question mark equals the baby is dead. A gentle, tear-swelling response that cuts me again, enters me, carving a deep hole into my chest, and next, darkness. A pain and darkness.

My lover raged, stormed accused, demanded, sobbed through the days that I was lost to the darkness and now some small but vital parts of me remain, held, cushioned, captured by that darkness place. I am left with soul-aching missing which throws itself over every-thing.

I can speak this now but I can't feel it. When I tell the story, it's a story of patronage and tragedy. A small tragedy, its scale measured by a small paragraph in the newspaper.

Obstetrician censured by the Medical Council for not adequately informing his patient of the result of an ultrasound which showed severe abnormalities in the foetus. Mr Beckett's defence was that he believed that the information would have severely affected the mental state of his patient. This same belief guided his decision to deny the

patient access to the baby's body. At this time he cited hospital policy
rather than informing his patient of the accurate state of the body thus
denying her of the options to view the body. Mr Beckett was fined
$500.00 and ordered to pay all costs.

Is this all there is to say about this small tragedy? No. I placed a
small advertisement. Black edged, bold print on page 3. I've taken the
personal into the public realm and address all who know and have
experienced the enormity of this personal tragedy. The heading was
'Jamie conceived by love on 10 Feb 1989, died Oct 26 1989'. The
body is and was Jamie, a little miracle that I held for nine months and
now he and I are lost together.

A betrayal of faith can damage the spirit to the extent that there appears
only one choice available and that is to disengage from life. It is
challenging for us to know that this is a life possibility and to understand the emotional depth of the betrayal. We can only be invited into
this knowing by the person who has experienced it. We can only indicate
readiness for the invitation. Readiness is determined by our ability to
both use the language of lived experience and re-search the words,
emotions and body sensations in order to negotiate an accurate representation of lived experiences. The act of inviting can result in a
momentous decision to trust. This is a sacred moment between people
where we must tread with great care and respect. Our hearts and minds
are reflected in the words we choose and in this we need to be very
thoughtful. When we speak with emotional coherence we inevitably use
the language of feelings. In these moments feelings naturally move to
expression. The expression and exploration of feeling is the inevitable
consequence of engaging fully with the complexity of people's (clients')
lives.

As I have previously emphasised, the textual explanations of
relational externalising conversations belies its complexity in practice.
In engaging in this style of conversation we are living out or practising
a philosophical belief, which is that the 'I' is never singular, the 'I' is
known and experienced always in relationship.

WORDS THAT REPRESENT AN ACTIVITY
Conventional use of English supports the strong adherence to polarities
such as success/failure, belongs/abandoned, forgiveness/resentment.

These polarities function to categorise, measure and assess. Engaging with these polarities subjects us to self definitions that are finite and internalised, for example, 'I never belonged', 'I can't forgive.' The 'I' is thus engaged as the arbiter of meaning and is understood as the self-determining, autonomous agent.

When people (clients) adhere to the dominant use of language which represents experiences as static, they become trapped in these oppositions. People (clients) respond to the experience of being trapped in a variety of ways, such as depression, anger/rage, or compulsive behaviour. When we are able to use a process that moves past the polarities, we can experiment with ways of using language that suggest movement, activity and context.

Here is an example where people are fixed in oppositions:

Jessie: Are you committed or not?

Tom: I don't know.

Jessie: Its easy, just decide, yes or no?

Here are some questions that begin to move the conversation away from oppositions:

▼ Do you think the commitment to talk together today is the beginning of building an understanding of commitment?

▼ How did you come to the commitment to talk together today?

▼ Do you think building an understanding of commitment will help you both decide if you're willing to engage in the practice of commitment?

In the work with Jessie and Tom I would engage in an enquiry that:

▼ Locates the history of commitment ideas and practices between men and women.

▼ Examines the building of an understanding of the nature of these commitment ideas and practices.

▼ Negotiates the movement from an understanding of commitment to developing the practice of commitment.

▼ Reflects on the commitment practices that Jessie and Tom have already engaged with.

▼ Reflects on a hierarchy of relationship commitment understandings and practices in the community.

When we talk about experience in these ways we move away from the conventional language rules that locate commitment as a personal quality. We imply that commitment is constructed of ideas and practices that may have different meanings according to the following:

▼ Gender relations.

▼ A history of commitment ideas and practices.

▼ Family, community, cultural and institutional preferences.

We may also discover that several commitment ideas and practices are being practised or partially practised within the relationship.

By languaging experience in ways that imbue words with movement, we offer hope and the possibility of new discoveries. This way of expressing and exploring experience requires a rejection of certainty. Rather, we come to each conversation holding what we know while ready to have this knowledge challenged, overturned or added to by the process of the therapeutic conversation.

Relational externalising is the tool I use in the therapeutic relationship to work with people (clients) to expose past meanings and possible future meanings that have been made of physical and psychological injuries, betrayals and experiences.

For example, Jacob said in couple counselling, 'We have an equal relationship.' I explored this further in order to understand *equality* as a practice by asking these questions:

▼ How is this equality reflected in the practice of the relationship?

▼ How do the two of you determine what is equal?

▼ If you had a difference of opinion about the practice of equality in one area of the relationship, what would you both do?

▼ Has equality always been a feature of this relationship?

▼ Do you think equality will be represented differently over time?

In this example the exploration of equality as an activity interrupts an argument for belief in equality as a theoretical, valued idea. Thus, the relational externalising enquiry has the potential to move the conversation beyond one person's lived experiences. In the consideration of others' lived experience, people (clients) are given the opportunity to consider/see beyond dominant, and thus taken-for granted and not consciously known, values and ideas.

In the following example the questions are **not** a representation of the therapeutic work. The exercise is considering *the activity of* forgiving, *the activity of* not forgiving and the relationship between forgiveness, partial forgiveness and no forgiveness. In moving away from polarities (forgiveness or not) we create opportunities to generate *language for the in-between. The language of the in-between* generates an experience of movement. This is illustrated in these questions regarding forgiveness:

▼ What creates a climate of forgiveness/partial forgiveness?

▼ What creates a climate without forgiveness?

▼ What and whom would support a climate of forgiveness/partial forgiveness?

▼ What and whom would support a climate without forgiveness?

▼ How is forgiveness or not, understood in the wider community?

▼ How does this understanding impact on your relationship with forgiveness?

▼ What is the relationship between forgiveness and forgetting?

▼ What is the relationship between not forgiving and forgetting?

▼ If you were to forgive/partially forgive what would you be forgiving?

▼ What action steps would you take if you were to move towards forgiving?

▼ What form will remembering take in a climate of forgiveness/partial forgiveness?

▼ What form will remembering take in a climate of not forgiving?

▼ How will forgiveness/partial forgiveness act to liberate you?

▼ How will not forgiving act to liberate you?

▼ What do you imagine will change in and for you with this liberation?

▼ Does forgiveness/partial forgiveness carry any burden for the person who acts to forgive?

▼ Does not forgiving carry any burden for the person who doesn't act to forgive?

▼ If so, what is this burden?

▼ What are your expectations of the person who has injured you in this climate of forgiveness?

▼ What are your expectations of the person who has injured you in this climate of not forgiving?

▼ If you were to consider your relationship to this injury outside of the notion of forgiveness or not, what comes to mind or to heart?

The creation of the *language for the in-between*, such as partial forgiveness or good enough belonging, prepares people to consider their experiences beyond the definitive and fixed. Engaging with words as signifiers of an activity helps us to move outside of polarities. Once our language reflects activity, we generate an environment that implies movement, movement to a place of, for example, good enough belonging and movement to a more or less desirable place. Re-searching movement to or from highlights people's (clients') active engagement with their lives. Highlighting people's active engagement with their lives generates hope and evokes a belief in the possibility of change.

To continue with the example of belonging, people often situate themselves by saying 'I belonged' or 'I didn't belong'. When we consider *the activity* of belonging we open up arenas for expression and exploration that offer people (clients) new relational explanations and experiences. To this end I could explore:

▼ What constitutes good enough belonging?

▼ What is the evidence for the presence of good enough belonging?

▼ How can the belonging be supported if there is fragile early belonging?

▼ What would partial belonging mean to relationships?

▼ If I wanted to strengthen belonging how would I go about it?

▼ What were the life circumstances, ideas or practices that supported a past experience of belonging?

▼ What contributes to the sense of belonging outside of the nuclear family context?

▼ How is belonging constituted when it exists through a connection with ideas, through a connection with the emotions/heart or through a connection of the spirit?

In this example we have constructed concepts of good enough belonging, fragile early belonging, partial belonging, belonging outside of the nuclear family. Each belonging construction is available for exploration when and if it resonates with people's (clients') experience. Constructing language beyond polarities offers us (therapist and client) new areas of re-search that extend our awareness of and engagement with our potential for creativity.

The generation of language beyond polarities provides depth to any relational externalising enquiry. Without the words for the in-between positions there is no possibility of an enquiry that extends beyond the bounds of polarities.

WORDS THAT CONNECT

When we are sensitive to the words people (clients) use to describe experiences, this sensitivity protects people (clients) from an imposition of our ideas and meanings. So, when we consider the issue of forgiveness in relationship to Sarah's story, some therapists may consider that Sarah 'needs' to forgive Mr Beckett in order to reclaim or move on in life. To introduce forgiveness in this context would be an intrusion and an imposition that could either immobilise Sarah, such as 'I think I should forgive but I can't forgive' or provoke an angry response, such as 'How dare you suggest I forgive him, I'll never forgive him' or encourage forgetting in order to consider forgiveness, such as 'I should just forget the past and get on with my life'. Here is an example of a relational externalising conversation with Sarah:

Johnella: Sarah, did the response by Mr Beckett and the medical authorities reflect the impact Jamie's death had on you?

Sarah: It isn't even in the same league. It's like being in two realities. Their reality and then there's mine. When I remember the way they talked about what happened, I am surprised I didn't go mad!

Johnella: When you remember that time, what supported you to hold on to the reality of your experience?

Sarah: It was really tough. I sat through the inquiry with my partner squeezing my hand. It helped me to feel I existed. It stopped me from just screaming at them sometimes. After the process Tim's hand was marked from my fingernails. I just held on.

Johnella: In *the holding on*, what were you holding on to?

Sarah: What it means for Tim and me, the loss of Jamie. It felt like my soul was aching.

Johnella: When you were being subjected to *this inquiry style of talking*, if you hadn't been able to hold on what do you think would have happened?

Sarah: I don't know, its hard to say. I could have begun to think the way they thought, that Jamie's death was for the best, that I should get over it, put it behind me.

Johnella: What gave you the idea that that was their thinking?

Sarah: The smallness of the fine, the way they talked. It all added up to the same thing.

Johnella: Is *the holding on against* their view of what you should do, is that holding on still present?

Sarah: Yes it is. I suppose I don't want them to win. I don't want to prove them right.

Johnella: So in *the grief,* is there any room for your relationship with grief to change over time or does any change signal that *the holding on against their views* is weakening?

Sarah: It signals that the holding on against their views is weakening.

Johnella: Is there a way for your relationship with grief to change without the change weakening *the holding on against*?

When we engage with the static representation of experience we attribute fixed characteristics and fixed knowledge to human behaviour. Consequently any evidence that contradicts these fixed characteristics or knowledges can be either heard as irrelevant or used as indicators of pathology. People (clients) can censor themselves according to these knowledges or can be censored or cured by members of the professional classes. In this climate hopelessness and helplessness is pervasive. In contrast, we can engage dynamically with language by breaking the conventional rules of language use and playing with language possibilities. This prepares us for therapeutic work that connects with peoples' (clients') lived experience.

This exploration can occur once we position psychological constructs, i.e. forgiveness, as one possibility among many possibilities.
Holding these constructs, i.e. forgiveness, as one possibility among
many, orientates our listening towards people's (clients') actual
representation of experience. The emotionally significant words they
use is the primary focus for the relational externalising enquiry. This
enquiry process breathes life into the words. Feelings and thoughts, i.e.
'the stand taken' which previously just 'felt right' is through the enquiry
process given substance. This substance provides people (clients) with
a place to stand. A place to stand which may contradict available
psychological ideas or institutional wisdom. Breathing life into the
words is something we (therapist and client) do together. People (clients)
will often describe this as 'being seen'. Being seen by the self and by
another. Listening for and exploring the words that connect with
people's (clients') lived experience, takes me beyond the certainty of
psychological theories and sometimes beyond my lived experience.

IN SEARCH OF THE WORDS

One of the complexities inherent in facilitating a relational externalising
conversation is that we are positioning our selves outside of the
dominant discursive practice that confirms the individual as autonomous, self determining and central to the production of meaning. The
only way I know to withstand this dominant discursive practice is to
purposefully and consistently practice the relational externalising style
of thinking and conversation.

I take the opportunity to practice this style of thinking and
conversation both inside and outside of my work. Consequently I
attempt to engage with thinking and practices that constitute my
relationship with life in a relational externalising way. This ongoing
practice supports me to remain in relationship to dominant discursive
practices rather than being unknowingly constituted by or immersed in
the dominant discursive practice.

When we work with people (clients) we extract what emotionally
resonates or identify key descriptive words or phrases from a plethora
of words. This is not an easy task. An externalisation is formed once I
decide what might be significant for people (clients). I then check the
externalisations' relevance to them by using an enquiry process.

The enquiry process consists of our (therapist) formulation of a
question (which includes a relational externalisation) and people's

(clients') response to this question. The question format reduces the risk of therapists imposing their meanings on people (clients). Questions that are constructed in a relational externalising way are assembled from the fabric of people's (clients') talk. The nature of such questions implies that we (therapists) are wondering and exploring possibilities. This allows for an acknowledgment of the power relation within the therapeutic relationship, while privileging collaboration rather than imposition and expert knowing. Within this atmosphere of collaboration we invite a range of responses from people (clients), including responses that challenge our presuppositions. This challenge can include a challenge to the language we have selected as meaningful. For example, if I (therapist) asked the question: 'How often in a day do you find your-self engaging with this worry?' and Mary (client) responds to my question by saying, 'It's more like a nagging concern rather than a worry,' this can alter the direction of the enquiry in a way that I had not anticipated. In these moments we can uncover the assumptions that are directing the enquiry and begin a process of discovery that takes us beyond our lived and professional knowledge. In these moments the enquiry process can change and challenge us. For example, an exploration of people's (clients') relationship with fear moves into a different dimension of meaning when terror becomes the principle focus for exploration.

The relational externalising practice is in contrast to those therapeutic practices where therapists focus only on identifying problems. In the latter instance the search for an externalisation is shaped by the following: 'What is the problem and where is the unique outcome?' This practice is problematic when working with the complexity of many people's (clients') experience. The practice encourages us (therapists) to pursue an enquiry direction that doesn't account for people's (clients') responses to our questions. We can find our selves engaging with binary thinking, such as, 'If I can find a unique outcome for this problem, then I'll have a solution.' This binary thinking inevitably directs us towards imposing our meanings on people (clients).

I believe it is important that we listen intently for dominant discursive practices that hide the complexity, colour and tone of lived experiences. On 11 August, 1994, the *New Zealand Herald* published an interview with the New Zealand pianist, Michael Houstoun. He describes the various abilities of an outstanding musician as physical mastering of the notes, intellectual memory and spiritual understanding. The spiritual understanding he interpreted as getting to grips with what lies underneath the notes. For many people (including children), words are and have been meagre representatives of their experience. In order for people's (clients') experiences to become available for reflection and review, we listen to all that reverberates in the room. We listen for and to the messages conveyed by the body, by feelings, expressions, thoughts, visions, dreams, the imagination, smells and we listen to what is said, partially said and not said. In that listening and from this place of partial knowing we call on all that we know about human existence while not assuming to intimately know the other's (client's) experience. Instead we bring into the conversation our wonderings.

I referred earlier to the fact that the language we use in the therapeutic conversation is at times intensely provocative of emotions. The tragedy and glory of human existence and experience is represented by metaphors that approximate people's lived experience. We are concerned with tragedy, despair, cruelty, death, life, love and hope. This cannot be sanitised or compartmentalised. The metaphors we use to expose the complexity, colour, tone of lived experience imbue our conversations with life and with emotional meaning. These metaphors will be coherent only if the emotional meaning is known by both therapist and client. To talk of torture, concentration camps, prisons, etc., without a sense of what it would mean to experience torture, or be in a concentration camp or prison, is to use language as a detached representation of experience.

A common description people (clients) use to distinguish between living a disconnected life and living a connected life is that 'it was like moving from a black and white existence, devoid of smell, walled off from touch, to a life that was bursting with colour and sensitive to touch and smell'. The difference between a disconnected life and a connected life reflects the difference between a therapeutic conversation that uses dominant discursive practices and a therapeutic conversation that uses the relational externalising practice. When we engage with the relational externalising practice we are indicating our preparedness to explore with people (clients) their intimate experiences of what it is to feel such despair and powerlessness, to experience such abuse and senseless cruelty, to feel and reclaim opportunities for connection and love.

It is important to note that *knowing* is different from *experiencing*.

We can have a sense of knowing without experiencing. The life we speak of with people (clients) is part of our world. The effectiveness of our words is determined by our courage to know, as closely as it is possible to know, another's experience. Coming to this knowing requires an exploration that involves our holding on to several ways of making sense of experience, including the possibility that we will discover a way of making sense beyond our previous knowing.

In connecting with another person's experience, we act as witnesses. We stand beside and engage with people (clients) as they find ways to understand, describe, and feel the experience while telling and retelling, remembering and re-remembering.

TALK THAT SINGS

When I sing, I am at times surprised by an upsurge of emotion. Occasionally I can identify a lyric or melody that provokes a memory or response to the day's events. At other times it appears that the activity of singing allows me to touch emotions that have been previously censored or dismissed. Singing can move us past the time-honoured and invisible mind constraints that can shape the way we engage with our selves and with our environment.

In a similar way, conversation that uses a relational externalising process can become talk that sings. This style of talking provides people (clients) with the experience of engaging actively with identified concerns and abilities, relationships, ideas, practices and time. *Engaging with* is experientially different from being *acted upon* by another (the knowledgeable professional) or being submerged in problems that take on the form of an additional limb or organ as though that problem existed within the person.

Engaging with talk that sings brings us closer to the experience of poetry than to the experience of objective sciences. The words we (therapist and client) use are sometimes extremely provocative of emotions as what is spoken moves past the conventional censorship structures of thinking. We do this within a relationship where one human spirit meets with another's human spirit. Talk that sings exists within this relationship. It is not located in the therapist's self or in the questions.

Censorship structures of thinking are mechanisms that allow us to watch graphic television reports of people starving, being tortured, murdered, in grief and in despair while we eat dinner. Censorship structures of thinking disallow, screen-out, reduce and invisibilize thoughts and experiences that stand outside the regimes of meaning that dominate or prevail. For example, people (clients) who have been abused have often been induced by threats, fear, silence and explanations into colluding with the ideas of victim complicity.

Talk that sings also moves us away from reliance on individual, internal, self-referential thought processes while moving us towards an engagement with the relational. In engaging with the relational enquiry we challenge the concept of static knowledge, replacing it with developing or evolving knowledges that tolerate an ongoing relationship to, and exploration of, what is known and what is not known.

Censorship structures of thinking are then exposed as the primary support of a particular regime of truth, where the meanings made of experiences are biased towards maintaining existing power relations. This power relations can leave abusers free from censure while tormenting and trapping others in the loud silences created by ideas of guilt, shame, fear and doubt. Censorship structures of thinking are exposed when we utilise a relational externalising conversation that assists us to investigate the following:

▼ The supports, including the institutional supports, that privilege one explanation of events over another.

▼ The benefits and disadvantages to people of holding particular ideas.

▼ The effect that regimes of truth have on individuals' sense of wellbeing and belonging.

In the exposure and exploration of one particular regime of truth, we inevitably engage with other regimes of truth. In these moments I choose to stand somewhere with people (clients), which requires that I know I am choosing this set of ideas and practices over others. The ethic that supports me in this involves a commitment to continuously engage in practices that expose the ideas and practices of the power relations which inevitably act to include and exclude.

The knowledge that we are engaging with the inevitable consequence of power relationships, which is to include and exclude, alerts us to the possibility that we may unwittingly act as agents of social control. The

Western cultural relationship with consciousness relies on individuals'
internal self referential thought processes. We have been trained in this
consciousness from birth. Over time we generate a reality that moves
us out of an intimate relationship with the everyday. This form of
consciousness is starkly illustrated in work with couples, where each
person argues for their version of events. The need to argue is strengthened by the belief that 'If my version doesn't win, the other person will
dominate, thus putting me in the wrong'. This belief frequently stops
any listening to the other, apart from listening for errors or inaccuracy.
Gender relations, as manifest in contemporary Western society, can
support men to determinedly argue for a version of events and support
women to comply to the other person's version of events. Both of these
positions act to support the ideas and practices of male dominance.

The internal self referential thought processes are created and
maintained by static language. Static language is a contrast to talk that
sings. In order to illustrate this contrast, I have considered the
languaging of consciousness. In many psychological texts the conscious
and the unconscious are described as fixed structures of the mind with
the unconscious regarded as a repository for repressed childhood
desires. A more open explorative approach is to consider the conscious
and the unconscious as language signifiers that we are in relationship
with.

In order to assist in an exploration of consciousness, I have
constructed a number of questions:

▼ If consciousness is fluid rather than fixed, how is consciousness
   directed?

▼ Is there such a thing as partial consciousness or fleeting
   consciousness? If there is, where does the history of this
   consciousness reside?

▼ What happens to our memory of partial or fleeting consciousness?

▼ If consciousness has been shaped by immersion in ways of
   engaging with the self in the world, including a way of languaging
   experience and knowledge, is it inevitable that experiences and
   knowing that don't fit within this frame would be out of
   consciousness?

▼ Does what is out of consciousness cease to exist?

▼ In the process of consciousness training do we engage in other relationships with consciousness?

▼ If we do, are we active in the discrimination of what is recognisable as consciousness?

▼ In this discrimination do we recognise something that does not fit within our consciousness paradigm?

▼ If we do, then does the recognition give the impetus for existence?

▼ Does our everyday relationship with consciousness require that this knowing is stored, censored and forgotten?

These questions reflect a relational externalising process. This process supports an exploration of consciousness beyond the fixed limitations of Western cultural languaging. In response to these questions I believe it is possible that what is out of everyday consciousness exists if it has been recognisable at some point in our lives, including our early years. We can access what is out of everyday consciousness by:

▼ Engaging in a relational externalising conversation, thus challenging the dominant discursive practice.

▼ Engaging in a relationship with time in contrast to being immersed in time.

▼ Engaging with knowings in contrast to being immersed in the knowing.

▼ Engaging with what is described as intuition.

Engaging with the first three items above is discussed elsewhere in this book. Engaging with what is often described as 'intuitive' provides therapy with another knowledge resource. I believe the intuitive represents the fluidity of consciousness, and intuitive knowledge can be accessed through movement music, writing, voice, art, touch, dreams, language, meditation and presence listening.

Also, talk that sings constitutes a relationship with the intuitive through language and presence listening. Questions bring the intuitive forwards, while the enquiry process establishes the usefulness or not of this intuitive possibility for people (clients). Talk that sings engages us in sensing and experimenting with the putting into language of that which sits between and beyond the words, including what sits between and around us (therapist and clients) in the therapeutic relationship. The enquiry process protects people (clients) from an imposition of metaphor or analogy or wondering that doesn't belong to or resonate with their own experiences. If a metaphor, analogy or wondering is recognised, then this serves as a beginning point for further therapeutic enquiry. Unlike its role in interpretive therapies, recognition is the beginning point rather than the end point. The enquiry that explores and expands on the initial recognition often takes a form and direction that is beyond our (therapists') lived experience. While we engage in this enquiry, we are also critiquing the strategies used to shape consciousness. Talk that sings supports an enquiry process that can extend our (clients' and therapists') understanding of everyday consciousness. It is talk that exists in a climate of synergy, talk that can propel us outside of our lives of comfort. It is talk that can change us.

THE ETHICS OF TALK

In celebration of subjectivity and diversity

Counselling and therapy is always political. It is political because the therapeutic conversation can be constrained within the narrow parameters of one's (the therapist's) regime of truth thereby subjecting people's (clients') experience to a definitive explanation. It is also political when the conversation exists within multiple truth regimes. Within multiplicity it is nonetheless impossible to represent all the possible truth regimes or explore the mechanisms and processes that elevate one regime of truth over another. Within multiplicity there are also preferences, demonstrated and perpetuated, in the emphasis on certain questions and responses. This emphasis has the inevitable consequence of relegating parts of people's (clients') explanations of their experience to the background.

Weedon (32) argues that no discursive practice is outside of power/ knowledge relations.

> Meaning is always political. It is located in the social networks of power/ knowledge relations which give society its current form. Not all areas of discourse are equally significant in the hierarchy of power/knowledge relations but no discursive practice is outside them. (p. 138).

Whenever I consider these ideas in relation to therapeutic practices and ideas, I use the following questions to assist me in an ongoing reflective practice:

▼ What assumptions underpinned my decision to highlight, using an enquiry process, some themes over others?

▼ When I consider these assumptions, is there a taken-for-granted truth statement embedded in the languaging of the assumption?

▼ When I reflect on this taken-for-granted truth statement, what are the cultural practices that this statement serves?

▼ Who is advantaged by these cultural practices?

▼ If I was to consider other possibilities for meaning making, how would that have altered the development of the questions?

▼ What is the relationship between the enquiry direction and power/knowledge relations?

▼ How did the enquiry direction invisibilize or visibilize power/knowledge relations?

In therapeutic work and in lives, we need to locate our selves somewhere and establish at least a temporary fixing on meaning. To not do this leaves us with a fluidity of non-position that renders us incapable of taking a stand to support people's (clients') suffering under the influence of oppressive and invisiblising practices and ideas. The non-position inevitably supports that which is prevalent or dominating as it offers no form of resistance.

Weedon (32) comments:

> Post-structuralism most particularly in its deconstructive forms, stresses the non-fixity and constant deferral of meaning. As a text-based theory, deconstruction is not interested in the implications of this for the reading subject beyond the primary assumption that this subject is not full unitary or in control of meaning. However as I have argued throughout this book subjectivity is of key importance in the social processes and practices through which forms of class, race and gender power are exercised. We have to assume subjectivity in order to make sense of society and our selves. The question is what modes of subjectivity are open to us and what they imply in political terms. Modes of subjectivity like theories of society or versions of history are temporary fixings in the ongoing process in which any absolute meaning or truth is constantly deferred. The important point is to recognise the political implications of fixing identity and meaning. From this perspective it is clear that we are far from achieving a society in which gender, race or class are non-issues. (pp. 172–173).

When we consider Weedon's statement that:

the important point is to recognise the political implications of particular ways of fixing identity and meaning (p. 173),

then therapy/counselling with a focus on making sense of lived experience through a process of exposing and negotiating meaning, is inevitably political. Acknowledging the political implications of therapy enables us to both render our selves available to ongoing critique of our certainties, and find strategies to engage enthusiastically with the relationship between knowing and not knowing.

Therapeutic/counselling work which has as its focus a relational externalising enquiry process creates a climate of discovery rather than imposing meanings. When we know that particular discursive regimes can torment, oppress and silence people, and that those discursive regimes are often carried and believed in by the same people (clients) who are oppressed by them, we can feel stuck between two positions. These positions are identified by two questions:

▼ Do I expose these ideas by presenting an alternative version? If I don't, will I be supporting the ongoing oppression of these people (clients)?

▼ If I do expose these ideas, will people (clients) experience me as another agent of control?

For example: In the first session with a young Maori woman, I asked her what had supported her decision to see me, a Pakeha woman. She responded by telling me that she had been raped by a Maori man when she was a young woman. Consequently she said she felt more comfortable and safe with a Pakeha. I gently asked if she could imagine a young Pakeha woman who had been raped by a Pakeha man choosing to see a Maori counsellor in order to feel more comfortable and safe. She responded by saying that she thought this was unlikely. We then began to identify the ideas she carried that directed her decision, at the same time exposing the strategies of power that elevated those ideas over other ideas.

When knowledge is presented to people (clients) in a definitive, comprehensive, logiocentric way, the following circumstances emerge:

▼ Knowledge, including alternative knowledges, are represented as static, unified truths.

▼ There is pressure to comply with one truth over another.

▼ The knowledge is presented as comprehensive and people (clients) may not feel entitled or able to argue against it.

▼ The knowledge carriers, including the alternative knowledge carriers, become the arbiters and gatekeepers of the one truth.

▼ To decline the other person's (therapist's) particular regime of truth is to potentially lose the relationship. This has serious implications for the therapeutic relationship understanding.

▼ To accept the other person's (therapist's) regime of truth is to potentially endanger other close relationships (partner, friend-ships, family members).

▼ The activity of accepting a particular regime of truth offered in this way threatens to capture the person as a convert.

▼ The activity of declining a particular regime of truth offered in this way threatens to alienate people from a member of the professional classes. The professional can then interpret the rejection as evidence of psychopathology and act on the person in accordance with this view point.

However, when ideas and practices that oppress people (clients) remain unexposed then our silence is a compliance with these ideas and practices. Instead of either presenting people (clients) with an alter-native knowledge or remaining silent, we can use a relational external-ising enquiry that orients us (therapist and client) towards discovery. The relational externalising enquiry process I use can provide us with a technical skill that exposes the history, activity and power implications of particular discursive regimes. This exposure provides a climate for an exploration of the implication of other discursive regimes, including those the therapist doesn't have access to. The enquiry creates a climate for discovery and re-search that people (clients) can embark on both inside and outside of therapy. Weedon (32) comments that:

> To speak is to assume a subject position within discourse and to become subjected to the power and regulation of the discourse. (p. 119)

To speak using the relational externalising enquiry process represented in this chapter is to speak relationally. Speaking relationally assumes a subject position in relationship to a discourse. From this position people (clients) can view, experience, explore and re-search the regulatory function of the discourse. Speaking and engaging in relationship to and with discourse using an externalising other or self enquiry creates an environment where all discursive regimes are experienced as potentially temporary and serving a purpose that supports a particular community. This method of engaging protects us from the processes of conversion, where one comprehensive counselling/therapy truth stands against others. When we hold counselling/therapy truths, we can find our selves arguing for superior status by using theoretical constructs that ignore the ethical implications of practices. We can also be tempted to engage with ethics as fixed truth positions. Once we claim a fixed truth position we can relax into privileging our ideas of, for example, justice or equality. Of necessity any fixed truth position exists outside of an engagement with both the practice of inclusion of marginalised voices and the practice of ongoingly reflecting on the practice of ethics.

The practice of relational externalising engages the self in relationship to the idea, concern, ability, etc., thus supporting us to engage in a conversational process that opens up linguistic space. This opening allows us to engage with ideas and practices rather than being subsumed by ideas and practices.

For example, I have developed the following questions in order to re-search the understandings and experiences of 'desire'. In developing answers to these questions you (the reader) are re-searching your own experience. You can also answer these questions imaging someone who is other than the gender you identify with. This will assist you in the development of further questions.

▼ Is there a physiological response that identifies for you the presence of desire?

▼ If so, how would you describe the qualities of this physiological experience?

▼ What parts of the body first recognise the presence of desire?

▼ Does the experience of desire move throughout the body?

▼ Is there a mind response that identifies for you the presence of desire?

▼ If so, how would you describe the qualities of this mind response?

▼ Is there a relationship between the mind and body in the identification and experience of desire?

▼ Is the experience of desire represented in a multiplicity of forms?

▼ If this is so, what are the forms that you most recognise?

▼ What's the distinction between desire and need?

▼ In the absence of the experience of desire, what would you miss?

▼ What shapes the decision to act, or not act, with the experience of desire?

▼ How is the experience of desire shaped by social prescriptions of success in material and social spheres?

▼ How is the experience of desire shaped by moral and ethical considerations?

▼ What is the relationship between the experience of desire and a relationship with another person?

▼ What is the relationship between the experience of desire and a relationship with creativity?

▼ How do social prescriptions effect the relationship with desire?

▼ How do social prescriptions effect the decision to act or not act on the experiences of desire?

▼ Do you take some expressions of desire for granted?

▼ Is the experience of desire strengthened or precipitated by sensory experiences?

▼ Historically, what were the prevailing ideas that were constructed and supported by various powerful institutions (i.e. Church, state) that acted to police the experience and activity of desire within Western cultural groups?

▼ What are the dominant ideas that circulate in your cultural group in relationship to the experience and activity of desire? Consider the implications of these ideas on gender relations, sexuality, disability, age. What institutions validate these ideas?

Under the heading 'In celebration of subjectivity and diversity', I am claiming that all therapeutic work is inherently subjective. I agree with Weedon (32) when she says, 'We have to assume subjectivity in order to make sense of society and our selves' (p. 173). In the assuming of subjectivity we are concerned with 'what modes of subjectivity are open to us and what they imply in political terms' (p. 173). When I re-search the political, social and personal implications for people (clients) of certain modes of subjectivity I am hoping to:

▼ Expose the strategies for implicating people in the practices and ideas that act to torment and oppress them.

▼ Expose the ideas of the autonomous self which suggest individuals are totally responsible for the success/failure, health/illness, poverty/wealth in their life.

▼ Expose the ideas and practices that act to marginalise one group while rewarding and supporting others.

▼ Develop counter-knowledges and practices that can act to support people (clients) to ongoingly resist the prevailing knowledges and practices that oppress them.

▼ Expose and critique the ethics that define what is legitimate and what is not.

What is the relationship between responsibility and a relational externalising conversation?

The question of responsibility arises when we use an externalising practice that separates people (clients) from their relationship to abilities, problems, ideas and beliefs. The following is a definition of a relational externalising conversation:

'A relational externalising conversation shifts linguistically what has been/ or is subjectified. (i.e. attributes, ideas, feelings and experiences that are conceptualised as belonging to the person) to the status of an object in relationship to the person (client).' This definition and the practice that arises from it, allows people (clients) to consider the relationship between words, actions, responsibility and the self.

In the work with people (clients) who have abused others, we attempt to counter the idea that abusive behaviour arises from an internal pathology that exists outside of the contextual environment. This allows us to move our thinking and conversation away from regimes of punishment, persuasion or telling towards re-searching explicitly and unflinchingly the effects of the abusive behaviour and thinking. In this way we can discover and challenge taken-for-granted beliefs while also discovering abilities and attributes that will create a context allowing us (therapist and client) to engage with the idea of lifelong responsibility.

Regimes of punishment (including self punishment), such as that expressed in 'How can I live with the knowledge of this crime?' often create a context of defense and attack. People (clients) who are responsible for abuses often attempt to defend themselves from self and other definitions that may subject them to a lifetime of isolation as monsters. This defense takes the form of a total redefinition of the events, victim blaming and declarations of innocence. Professionals, together with family members, can respond to this defense with a conversational process that supports the defense directly or indirectly, i.e. by ignoring the abusive behaviour. Professionals, together with family members, can also respond by engaging in a conversational process that subjects the abuser to a similar relationship with power/ powerlessness to the one he/she has previously subjected others to. Submitting to an authority more powerful than the self can thus confirm the abuser's relationship with power.

We engage with a relational externalising conversation in order to join with people (clients) without reflecting a regime of punishment. A relational externalising conversational process allows for exploration of the contradictions that inevitably emerge in people's (clients') relationship with their lives. We can hold, re-search and use these contradictions while maintaining a relationship with responsibility. In this way, people (clients) can experience a relationship to an idea or practice. The relational externalising process thus creates the linguistic space that exposes certain modes of subjectivity; once it is exposed we can critique it. This conversational process enables people (clients) to engage with responsibility knowing the conditions and ideas that support abusive thinking and practices. It also allows a commitment to hold and support alternative thinking and practices.

An Example:
Carl is a 45 years Pakeha man. He has made an appointment for counselling as a result of physically abusing his partner, who is now threatening to leave him. I use this example to illustrate three enquiry processes:

Number One — Questions that reflect an investigative assessment and enquiry.
 ▼ When did you begin acting violently towards your partner?
 ▼ Were you angry when you hit her?
 ▼ Did your anger build up or were you suddenly angry?

Number Two — Questions that reflect an externalising process — this linguistic strategy separates the concern from the person.

▼ How often has *the hitting out* happened?

▼ What ideas support *the hitting out*?

▼ Does *the hitting out* come with feelings?

Number Three — Questions that reflect a relational externalising process — this linguistic strategy acts to separate the concern from the person while maintaining a relationship to the person.

▼ How has *the hitting out* impacted on *the relationship* that you have with your-self?

▼ Were you aware of *the appearance of an idea or feeling* before *the action of hitting out*?

▼ Have you ever had *that idea or feeling* and held back from *this hitting out*?

One of the most frequently asked questions in teaching groups is, 'Doesn't externalising remove responsibility from the person?' When we use an externalising conversation outside of the relational context (as illustrated by the second question sequence), we are at risk of encouraging disengagement from responsibility. When we use a relational externalising conversation then we engage with responsibility in a way that says, 'This behaviour is not the total of you,' and asks, 'What are the conditions that support this thinking and behaviour?' and suggests, 'There is a possibility that you are more than this.' In my interviews I utilise an externalising enquiry process where there is evidence of both the second and third enquiry strategies. A combination of the second and third enquiry processes linguistically emphasises the person as a subject whom is in relationship to discursive strategies. This relationship provides an explanation for the behaviours, while exposing the conditions that support the behaviours. When the second enquiry process is solely utilised it presents the linguistic object, i.e. 'hitting out' as independent of the person and therefore threatens to detach the person from the experience and thereby responsibility.

The investigative and assessment enquiry locates the subject or person as the problem. The subject or person is thus individually responsible for the problem and the solution. This enquiry style denies the implications of discursive strategies within the social environment, thus severely limiting an exploration of the context that supports violence. In the previous example this context may include the history of power relations within heterosexual relationships and the dominant socialisation processes available to and for the development of maleness. An investigative and assessment enquiry thus relies on change occurring as a result of either the effects of social sanctions or the expert/therapist lecturing or informing the person (client) of the contexts that support violence. Social sanctions, lecturing or information giving thus become the major precipitator for change. This format provides the person (clients) with the option of conforming to either the professional person's ideas or social sanctions. The act of conforming represents the domination of one group (professionals) over another group (clients) thus perpetuating the conditions of violence.

The conversational process that uses a relational externalising conversation explores the ideas and practices that support violence. This provides people (clients) with a resource to consider their relationship with the ethics of violence. It is then possible for people (clients) to explore the ideas and practices that support relationships of non-violence.

WORKING WITH THE TEXT

Suggestions for readers

What Am I (Client) Looking/Listening for?

A relational externalising conversation won't particularly stand out to you. Many people who have experienced a relational externalising conversation simply report that they feel understood and attended to. This style of conversation gives you enough distance from the ideas, issues, feelings and strengths that impact on you so that you can consider their effects on your life. When a therapeutic conversation is not a relational externalising conversation you may feel immersed and overwhelmed or you may feel the conversation is going over old ground. You can indicate this to the therapist by saying that you're feeling lost in the conversation or overwhelmed by feelings and/or thoughts, or that you feel like there's nothing new in the conversation. This feedback is consistent with the therapeutic relationship understanding which underlines the importance of your participation in the work.

The therapeutic conversation can be very intensely emotional.

Consequently discoveries made in the therapy can become lost. This can be avoided by asking the therapist to help you remember. Here are a few ideas:

▼ Ask the therapist to write a summary at the end of the session which you can take home. At home reflect on this summary and add to it or change it.

▼ The two of you write or put together a joint summary at the end of the session. Throughout the session you can alert the therapist and your-self to ideas, feelings, strategies, etc. that you want to remember.

▼ Ask the therapist to tape (audio or video) the session and provide you with the tape. It's useful to talk with the therapist about ownership of the tape. It's important to decline permission for the use of technology if it doesn't feel comfortable.

▼ The therapist writes you a letter summarising the discoveries in the session. You can use this letter to help you write a letter to your-self about what stood out for you in the session. You can also add to, or change the therapeutic letter. When therapists write or discuss their ideas or a summary of the session, it represents their understandings, including their understanding of your understanding. Sometimes they don't get this right. Therapists who agree with the therapeutic relationship understanding discussed in this book would welcome and encourage your ideas and opinions.

What Am I (Therapist) Focusing on?

If you are interested in pursuing the work described in this book you are beginning a profound relationship with words and the language used to describe experience. I utilise a relational externalising conversation to mediate a process that can act to liberate people (clients) from the past meanings that have been made of physical and psychological injuries, betrayals and experiences. Words are thus a medium for healing.

Meanings that are assumed in everyday conversation are ineffectual in the therapeutic conversation. Words and meanings are negotiated and renegotiated in order to loosely approximate people's (client's) experiences. This negotiation achieves a consensus of meaning between us (therapist and client) thus protecting people (clients) from the possibility that we will impose our meaning on to their experiences. We then contextualise the discoveries within the broader framework of both culturally dominant and culturally marginalised explanations for experience. At the same time we wonder about the strategies used to maintain these dominant and marginalised explanations and the people who benefit or suffer from the maintenance of these explanations.

This exploration may take you beyond your own experiences, exposing both the benefits you hold, i.e. access to financial and educational resources, and the ideas and practices you take for granted.

In order to engage in a conversation where meaning is negotiated, we are required to develop a relational externalising enquiry. This enquiry incorporates a practice in listening and questioning. The listening does not involve listening for evidence, evaluation or confirmation of a psychological theory, it involves listening for what emotionally resonates for the speaker and for the listeners. It is listening for life themes and transitional points, for what is said and for what is partially said. On identifying one, or several, possible themes we ask questions in order to determine meaningfulness with people (clients).

Our listening can be limited by anxiety, fear, psychological theories, and our adherence to certainty about the meaning of experience. In order to reduce the possibility of limited listening, it may be helpful to consider these questions:

▼ How do I stay connected to what I know while making that knowing available for extension or change?

▼ What practices do I engage in to extend the listening abilities I use in the work?

▼ What practices do I engage in to extend the questioning abilities I use in the work?

▼ How do I remind myself that there are knowledges other than the ones that I'm immersed in?

▼ Do I retain a sense of wonder in and curiosity about people's (clients') lived experience?

▼ If I answer yes, what supports me in this?

▼ If I answer no, what has eroded this and what do I need to do to rediscover it?

▼ How do I extend my repertoire of people's lived experience beyond my lived experience?

▼ What psychological theories do I take for granted as truths?

▼ What ideas support these psychological theories and who benefits from adherence to this theory?

▼ If I consider this theory as an incomplete or partial truth, what would I begin to wonder about in order to extend my knowing?

Sophie's, Jacob's and Sam's stories show some of the emotional complexities of these three people's lives. They come to the therapeutic conversation with all of these experiences which are, however, not immediately available in a coherent form to them or to us. While we work with what people (clients) bring to us, we are also available to and listening for the words which carry emotional significance, and we bring forward what has often been unspoken or invisibilised. This forgetting is often supported by the strength of prevailing ideas/beliefs. The appearance of prevailing ideas and beliefs can overwhelm, minimise and eventually obliterate alternative explanations for life events.

The dilemmas raised in all the stories in this chapter are life dilemmas that may take us to places we have never been. In these instances we can sometimes experience pain, fear and hopelessness which is summed up by the words, 'What can I do?' When we experience this, it is not a failure. It indicates that we are working beyond our experience. We may have never considered what it would feel like to lose a child or what it would feel like to be forced to have a child. We may take our physical and emotional safety for granted. We may never have experienced having limited control over our lives. In order to work with Sophie, Jacob, Sam and Sarah we may need to consider intellectually and emotionally experiences that are beyond our own and maybe beyond our imagination. We don't need to engage in this on our own, we can talk with colleagues, a supervisor or a consultant.

If we wish to protect our selves from becoming agents of social control then, from time to time, we need to explore the values, morality and ethics that shape our lives. This is an example of an exploration of a belief:

Belief: Children need their two biological parents in their lives.

Question: When you consider two biological parents being in a child's life, what is meant by *the being in*?

Answer: Living in the same household.

Question: What difference does being in two different households make to a child's sense of *being in* her/his parent's life?

Question: Do you have some ideas about how *this being in* a child's life is enacted by both parents when they live in the same household?

Question: When parents live in a different household, what sort of *being in my life* would a child want from biological parents?

Question: What is the difference between *the in the child's life* provided by a non-biological parent and *the in the child's life* provided by a biological parent?

This is an example of how an enquiry would begin. The answers to the questions would inevitably determine the next questions. Here, I am exploring the distinction between the same and different households and biological and non-biological parents.

List some of the values, ethics and morals you live your life by and explore these with another person using a relational externalising conversation.

The ability to engage in a relational externalising conversation is central to this book. As you read it look for examples of a relational externalising conversation. You will see that I am very concerned with exploring relationships. Relationship to the concern, relationship to an ability or strength, relationship over time, relationship to prevailing cultural ideas and practices, etc. etc. Dedication to the concept of relationship moves understanding beyond the individual as autonomous, separate and self contained towards the 'I' that exists in relationship to.

This shift of thinking is supported by the technical skills required to engage in a relational externalising conversation. 'How do you know that you are engaging in an externalising conversation?' Try these questions after or during every therapeutic conversation: 'What have or am I externalising?' 'What relationship am I exploring?'

CHAPTER TWO

. . . .

Therapeutic Narratives in Action

WHY TALK?

Kim Chermin (2) in her book *In my Mother's House* records Rose (her mother's) recollections of the death of Kim's sister. The story was known to family members but never spoken of. When the telling finally occurred, the connection between mother and daughter is strengthened. Rose says, 'Why I never talked about it before . . . it's not that you didn't know these things. But to tell them again, that is reliving.' (p. 184)

To tell is to relive and to relive is to feel and to feel is to risk the abysses that we fear may overwhelm us: not an easy journey. As therapists it is our responsibility to prepare, negotiate safety and support people (clients) to reflect on the past without getting lost in the past.

Why tell at all? Kim Chermin reflects on the impact of telling. 'It was the first time I wept because of Nina. The first time in 35 years. It was the beginning of mourning in our family because of Nina's death. And for me it was the beginning of memory.' (p. 199) Without mourning people remain in a state of invisible, unacknowledged grief. Without mourning we are depleted of our memories. The telling moves what is internal and fragmented, known but forgotten, into an external public place where it gathers coherence as the memories are related to, negotiated and rediscovered. Talk is one way to move internal knowing to an external experience of knowing. There are many other methods such as music, writing, drawing, dance that can do this, but the method I most often use is conversation where lived experience is reflected in language.

The therapeutic relationship provides time and space for people's (clients') experiences to be heard, felt, seen and known. The telling moves experiences from an internal private place to an external public place. In this movement, people (clients) begin to experience the pain of holding and living with unspoken knowing. These silent knowings confine people (clients) to a solitary existence. This experience of isolation can occur even when people (clients) are surrounded by loved ones. For example, Phillip had been sexually abused as a young boy. He described the change to his experience of his family that occurred after the abuse:

> I remember sitting at the dining room table. All around me there was activity, noise of conversation and laughter. I felt separate, distanced from the people I needed and loved. I reached out my hand and brushed my father's arm as he lent forwards to cut another piece of meat from the Sunday roast. I felt the touch but it did nothing to remove the feeling. It was as though I was surrounded by a transparent plastic bubble that adapted to my every move. No one could enter this bubble even when they wrapped their arms around me. Their muted voices danced around the edges of this, my shelter and my prison. I felt terribly alone.

The decision to talk about past experiences lies entirely with the person (client). It is important for us to understand what supports this decision in order to negotiate a safe conversational process.

For example, when Louise expressed a sense of urgency to talk about the abuses in her past we explored this. We discovered that she was approaching the past like a cancer that could be cut out and therefore eradicated from her life. Telling was seen by Louise as a cure. She would tell her story and then it would be over. I agreed to listen to the telling, however I said some people found that the telling brought forward strong emotions. In the first telling she described a process by which she would hold her breath and spill out her story, pushing through the emotional and physical pain to get it out. In the second telling, Louise stayed connected emotionally and physically. This allowed us to negotiate the requirements for psychological safety, i.e. Louise could signal her need to stop the conversation before being overwhelmed by emotions.

This negotiation allows people (clients) the opportunity to have authority over the telling, i.e. they may decide to stop, have a break, reconsider their decision, change the conversational direction, or inform us of their internal experiences of visions, nausea, fear and so on. For example, Viv came to see me saying that she wanted someone to listen to her experiences without interruption. I agreed and asked if she had any ideas about how often she would want to tell this story. She responded, 'Five times,' and that is what we did.

Telling must not result in retraumatisation. Retraumatisation occurs when people (clients) psychologically engage with their memory to the extent that they experience what happened in the past in the present. If telling is important for people (clients), then it must occur by reflecting on the past rather than by becoming submerged or lost in it. Therapists must be active in this, watching and listening while people (clients) are observing or commenting on a past event for the indicators that they remain detached enough from the memory to separate themselves from the past. People (clients) indicate that they are lost in the memory by their language and behaviour. They may experience terror or physical pain or speak with a voice that indicates they have entered a memory of themselves at a younger age. If this happens, even though we have established parameters for safety, it is our responsibility to stop the process and move the person into the present. This often involves establishing contact with the person using our voice, eye contact and movement.

In order to avoid retraumatisation, safety parameters for telling are negotiated and renegotiated. Safety parameters include negotiating the time allowed for sessions and discussing signs that indicate moving out of the present, as well as strategies for staying in the present and after-session care. After-session care may include sitting in the waiting room with a cup of tea at the conclusion of the session, being driven home by a friend, not working that day or having someone at home that evening.

The desire to tell someone about past traumatic events can be preceded by emotions, experiences and behaviour that are outside of people's (clients') control. The interference of the past into the present is then the stimulus to attend therapy.

Many people (clients) have successfully conducted their lives without telling others about traumatic events in the past. This success can diminish the serious nature of the abuse. We tread carefully between acknowledging the serious nature of the abuse and acknowledging the strengths and capabilities of people (clients) who successfully negotiate their way through life. For example, an institutional prerequisite for a compensation claim for past sexual abuse required me to write a report on the nature of the abuse and its effects on Josie. I asked Josie to write her response to the institution's questions. Josie had had no difficulty talking about the abuse episodes in her life in therapy. She had readily made the changes in her life that had prompted her to begin therapy. Josie described the writing process as very difficult. She repeatedly put it off until one day she decided to begin. We discussed the discoveries she made while writing and found that the writing process concretised the enormous obstacles she had overcome over the years. In her success, she had taken her tenacity, determination and courage for granted. Writing provided her with a new vision and appreciation of her self.

To tell or not to tell in therapy is always a negotiation between therapist and client. Telling is not necessarily a requirement or prerequisite for healthy psychological functioning. If people (clients) indicate a preference to not talk about past events then it is important that we respect that. We can however negotiate an exploration of the impact of carrying this knowledge on people's (clients') lives, together with an imaginative enquiry centred on how life would change if 'telling' happened? This exploration generates information that supports people (clients) in their decision. Here is an example:

Tim: I don't want to talk about what happened. It seems rather pointless to drag up the past. Talking about it won't change what happened. I want the past to stay in the past so I can move on.

Johnella: I'd like to understand your decision. Do you mind if I ask some questions about the decision? In doing this I won't be asking for details about the past — is that okay?

Tim: Yes, I think so.

Johnella: If you think we're moving towards the past in any way, can you alert me so that we can stop?

Tim: I won't have any difficulty with that.

This conversation represents a negotiation around safety. We are negotiating what can be talked about and what in this moment can't be talked about. In this situation the details of the past are out of bounds to the therapeutic conversation. I can however negotiate with Tim the boundaries of that decision. This negotiation is assisted by these questions:

▼ Is it possible to explore both the implications for Tim's life of the decision, and the beliefs and experiences that support that decision?

▼ Can we explore imaginatively the consequences for Tim's life if the past is actively remembered, rather than actively forgotten?

If we can engage in this exploration both Tim and I get to know what supports and maintains his decision to 'not drag up the past'. This knowledge is often unavailable to people (clients) outside of therapy as the strong feelings that surround the 'not dragging up the past' can exist without a comprehensive exploration and explanation.

INTERPRETATION AND RE-INTERPRETATION, VIEW AND RE-VIEW

The movement of experiences from being held within to being talked about provides people (clients) with the opportunity to re-view and reinterpret the experiences from different perspectives. When working with people (clients) who have experienced emotional, sexual and physical abuse in childhood, this movement allows events in the past to be reinterpreted from an adult perspective. The perpetrator's abusive, coercive and threatening behaviour is placed beside children's vulnerability. This vulnerability extends from the child's developmental maturity (physically, emotionally and intellectually) to the complexity of child/adult relationships where betrayal of trust sits uneasily alongside the expectations, declarations and behaviour of loving relationships. The relationships referred to include family, friends of the family and adult caretakers.

I do not interpret or reinterpret people's (clients') experiences. When I use the relational externalising process I create an environment that introduces emotional and cognitive distance from life events. Generating linguistic space offers people (clients) a perspective that results in life events being experienced differently. These differences are uniquely situated for each person (client). Therapists do, however, carry generalised knowledge which assists us to facilitate the discovery of people's (clients') unique knowings and experiences. For example:

Marcus:	I see those programmes on TV about children who have been physically abused, you know really badly, and I just feel murderous. How can people do that? You just have to look at those kids and you know there's no way they've deserved that. Then I think about the things that have happened to me. When other people, like my girl-friend Jenny, have seen the scars they can't believe it. But I don't feel anything. When I think back to myself as a child, I see a grubby little shit.
Johnella:	What stops the sympathy and anger you extend to others' lives being extended to your young life?
Marcus:	I don't know. I just don't have any feeling for him.
Johnella:	How old were you when the beatings were at their worst?
Marcus:	Anywhere between five, I can't remember anything about myself before then, and 14 years.
Johnella:	Do you know any children between five and 14 years of age?
Marcus:	Yes, I have a niece who's seven years old and a nephew who's 11 years old.
Johnella:	Imagine them both taking your place in the memory of the past. There they are after a beating feeling confused and despondent. No one has bothered to feed them or wash them for a few days. They've had to look after themselves. Can you imagine that?
Marcus:	Yes.
Johnella:	What feelings does that provoke?
Marcus:	I want to rescue and protect them. Pick them up. Feed them. Wash and love them. I want to stroke their heads and tell them it will be okay.
Johnella:	Is this upsetting for you?
Marcus:	Yeah, I feel like having a bawl.

Johnella: If your niece and nephew felt they were to blame for
            what happened, what would you do or say to them?

Marcus: This feels too big. I'm feeling so upset just thinking
            about it.

Johnella: Do you mind if we stay with the upset for a moment?
            I'd like you to tell me if this question is also too big? Can
            you find words for the upset/feelings?

Reinterpretation or re-view of past events is often precipitated when
people (clients) explore and develop a sense of knowing of and
compassion for the child from the past. The child held in everyday
memory may have been labelled as bad, inadequate, dirty, pathetic,
sick, wrong. With the labelling comes a wish to dismiss or eradicate her/
him from their lives and memory. When adults (clients) re-view the past
from an adult perspective, they can often tap into and connect with
strong emotions of love and loss — love for the small child's resilience
and vulnerability; loss for the family they thought they had or should
have had; loss for the life they might have had.

In re-connecting with the past, people (clients) discover emotions
that have previously been hidden, for self-survival. For example,
Stephanie was a successful accountant. She came to see me because
she felt an increasing unhappiness that appeared unrelated to her everyday life. She quickly informed me that she had been sexually abused
as a child by an uncle. This, she said, had not effected her life.
The abuse stopped when a cousin witnessed the assault and told
Stephanie's parents. The adults convened a family meeting. The uncle
was confronted and ordered never to have access to Stephanie and
her family. Stephanie was taken to the doctor, examined, and the
family were told to put it behind them. They never spoke of the assault
again.

When Stephanie spoke about these past events she did so in a matter
of fact, detached manner. She had so successfully 'put it behind her' that
it could have happened to someone else. The problem was, it didn't
happen to someone else, it happened to her. The strategy of 'putting it
behind' had been very helpful in the past, however now something was
seeping through and affecting her life in the anonymous way that life
events and emotions without a name do.

In this situation it wasn't appropriate for me to 'diagnose' what was affecting Stephanie's life. We had a number of possibilities to re-search. Together Stephanie and I worked out a strategy to put the past in front of her so that she could re-view it, feel it, act on it in ways that made sense to her. We discovered the effects of the abuse by re-searching the meaning Stephanie had made as a child of the assault and her family's response to it. The family members' decision to 'put it behind them', which in practice meant never talking about the assault again, left a silence, a gap which the child, Stephanie, filled with her own interpretations. These interpretations included believing that her mother blamed her for the loss of a much loved brother, that her father's withdrawal (he had previously been very physically demonstrative) was revulsion and disgust at her, and that she had been bad and must make it up to her family by being very good. 'Being good' included all the successes in her life. These successes couldn't be claimed by Stephanie as they represented the gifts she gave her family to make up for her 'badness'. When 'the bad' self description was challenged by Stephanie she re-viewed her abilities as belonging to her. Once liberated from the necessity to 'be good' for the family, Stephanie could ask, 'What do I want and need, in and for my life?'

In this example the sexual abuse became seen as a traumatic event that created other traumatic events. When family members are unavailable for an ongoing negotiation of the emotional consequences of the abuse to themselves and to their relationships with the abused person/child, there is fertile ground for misunderstandings and assumptions that shape lives.

It is necessary to explore the events and feelings that surround any traumatic event. This means allowing for the possibility that sexually abusive acts may in some situations be experienced as less traumatic than other events, such as on-going emotional abuse from a parent.

HOW DO WE SITUATE OUR SELVES FOR DISCOVERY?

I know that I bring my accumulated knowledge to every conversation. I also know and believe that the unique nature of each conversation may challenge or add to what I know.

Within the therapeutic conversation I facilitate a complex back and forth process of meaning negotiation in an attempt to reduce the possibility that I may impose meaning on people's (clients') experiences. The enquiry process assists us to test our assumptions in respect to the meaning made of key descriptive and emotionally evocative phrases or words, such as feeling worthy. In the work with Sophie described in the previous chapter, I believed that there had been an agreement about the meaning of worthy in the therapeutic conversation only to find that Sophie was unable to claim worth in her life. After exploration, it was discovered that we (therapist and client) had attributed different meanings to this word. Sophie's understandings were heavily influenced by early experiences with Catholicism.

The exploration of key descriptive and emotionally evocative phrases or words is intricate and detailed. These words often represent the building blocks on which people (clients) build a representation of themselves.

In Chapter One, Sophie's, Jacob's and Sam's stories have been made coherent by the author. Sophie, Jacob and Sam have these experiences but lack any opportunity, willingness, safety or ability to either translate them into a comprehensive understanding or actively deconstruct the everyday assumptions that shape the meanings they make of these experiences. Each comes to therapy believing in her/his interpretation of the problem or concern. Each comes to therapy with beliefs and experiences that shape their ideas and relationship to the therapy. Each comes with threads of knowing that make some sense of their experiences. Each comes carrying unchallenged and often gross expert descriptions for their experiences. The enquiry process involves our asking people (clients) to describe, re-search and wonder about their experiences and the meanings they and others have made of them.

In this activity we are bringing forth what people know but don't know they know. We are pulling forward the threads of knowing that have been pushed into the background by language strategies, power relations and institutional meaning paradigms. In our enquiry we hope to support Sophie, Jacob and Sam (clients) to reconstruct these three stories with all their emotional complexity. The reconstruction then allows us to consider the variety of meanings to be made of experiences, and the strategies used to support one meaning paradigm over another. The emotional complexity inherent in lived experience, as represented here in these three stories, challenges us to stand aside from simplistic notions. We are engaging not with a story, or an alternative story, we are engaging with people's extra-ordinary lives. In the present moments within which therapy is situated, we explore and negotiate the past in the present. Together we pull forward the threads of knowing that weave together a sense of hope and possibility of the self, always in relationship.

UNIQUE EXPERIENCES

Michael White (33) introduced the concept of unique outcome. This concept directed our attention towards a practice of listening and inquiring for instances where people's (clients') experiences and ideas contradicted the experiences and description of the problems/concerns. The enquiry that elicited in conversation what was called a unique outcome significantly altered our (therapist's) relationship to people's (clients') concerns. We directed our attention towards both the possibility of discovering one or more unique outcomes throughout the therapeutic conversation, and we developed a contextual understanding of this unique outcome.

Throughout this book I have referred to unique experiences rather than unique outcomes. I have chosen this renaming because the naming of unique outcome doesn't adequately represent my understanding of this practice. The discovery of a thought or practice that defies people's (clients') prevailing knowledge or practices may be unique. However, its discovery is not the outcome. The discovery provides the impetus for contextually re-searching and making sense of this discovery by utilising a contextual enquiry. I have retained the word 'unique' because, in the process of the therapeutic conversation, something that has been dismissed as irrelevant and/or forgotten is rediscovered anew and is often experienced uniquely. For example, reflect on Sophie's story. Sophie made the decision to remove her conscious self from the environment. She had various diagnoses including schizophrenia and manic-depression. When Sophie came to therapy the power of the diagnosis had removed any consideration that she could be an agent in her life. On exploration of the context that surrounded her life, we brought forward an alternative explanation for her life experiences that highlighted her abilities to act on and for her life, given the limited choices available to her. The conversation might look like this.

Johnella: Sophie, there was a point, a time just before you gave birth to Rebecca?

Sophie: (interrupting) I didn't give birth to Rebecca, I wasn't there.

Johnella: Okay. What do you call your part in the birthing process?

Sophie: I was the vehicle. The vehicle for other people's dreams.

Johnella: Was there any time during the pregnancy and birth where you felt you were more than a vehicle for others' dreams?

Sophie: No, I didn't control anything. I would rather have died than have gone through this.

Johnella: What or who stood beside you in your decision to live rather than die?

Sophie: If I could have died I would have. Even though I don't go to church anymore, those beliefs are still strongly there. I was more scared to die than I was to live.

Johnella: When you decided for life, what sort of life were you deciding for?

Sophie: I didn't have a lot of choice in that. I just had to be here, endure it, I suppose.

Johnella: Is there anything that you did that helped with the endurance?

Sophie: That's hard. I sort of flipped out before it happened, you know, before the birth.

Johnella: In the flipping out was there a moment when you knew that this flipping out was happening?

Sophie: Oh I knew all right, it was coming on for weeks.

Johnella: What are the signs that it's coming on?

Sophie: I begin to disappear or switch off. I can be watching TV and not remember a word. I can miss whole days.

Johnella: When you notice this flipping out, is there anything you can do to slow it down or stop it?

Sophie: I usually go and see my GP who is really good. We talk about it and she asks me to pay attention to whether it's getting worse. Then I usually visit her every 2 or 3 days for checks.

Johnella: Has this talking and monitoring worked in the past?

Sophie: Yes, sometimes it stops it getting worse, other times, if she's worried, she gets my medication re-viewed.

Johnella:	When you noticed the flipping out this time, did you put in place the strategies we've talked about today?
Sophie:	No, I didn't, I didn't want to. I didn't want to talk to anyone.
Johnella:	Do you think at that time you were more interested in going with the flipping out than you were in stopping the flipping out?
Sophie:	Yes, I didn't want to be there. I didn't want any part of it.
Johnella:	So you decided to go with the flipping out and disappear your self from this situation?
Sophie:	In a way I did, yes.

Sophie and I began this conversation with her belief that she had no control over her life and her environment. In the exploration that takes place we enquire and listen for moments of self-direction and self-control. When a moment of self-direction or self-control is identified in the conversation, this moment is used to support the tentative building of a self knowledge that increases Sophie's relationship with self direction and self control. It is critical that this moment is seen and understood in the context of Sophie's life. While we do this, at the same time we hold onto the possible importance of this discovery in order to protect the discovery from being overwhelmed by the context of Sophie's life. For example, if Sophie thought that I thought she had more control of her life than she does, she may say the following:

Sophie:	I suppose I should have done something. I could have been there for Rebecca. They say these first hours between mother and baby are really critical.
Johnella:	Sophie, do you think when I said, 'Do you think at that time you were more interested in going with the flipping out, than you were in stopping the flipping out,' that I was blaming you for flipping out?
Sophie:	Well, I wouldn't blame you if you did. What sort of mother does that?
Johnella:	Do you think you made a choice for mothering?

Sophie: Absolutely not.

Johnella: Okay, you went through pregnancy without any choice, was it hard to have absolutely no choice in this matter?

Sophie: It was shocking. I can't explain how it felt.

Johnella: Do you think that in this environment of absolutely no choice, you took a choice, the only choice available to you and that was to disappear your self?

Sophie: Yes, I did. I did that.

Johnella: Do you think anyone can judge someone who, in an environment of no choice, takes the choice to disappear?

Sophie: No, I don't think that would be fair.

This example illustrates the complexity of conversations that consider what and who supports the meanings that are made of people's (clients') behaviour and ideas. Deciding to 'flip out' is a unique experience of self direction or self control, however it remains lost as a resource to Sophie, because it is overlaid with the prevailing cultural ideas of good mothering and psychiatric illness.

A unique experience can quickly turn to evidence of inadequacy or malevolence if we are not alert to people's (clients') response to it. Our alertness is enhanced by the belief that a unique experience provides us with a thread of understanding; it doesn't in itself provide an answer or solution for people's (clients') concerns. When we work with people who have experienced abusive actions and words, these threads of understanding can assist an exploration that stands on a foundation of knowing what it means (as closely as someone out of the experience can know) to be continuously robbed of self-determination.

In order to adequately re-search what it means to be continuously robbed of the evidence of self determination, we explore, within the context of the person's (client's) life, both the supports for the old descriptions and knowledge of the self and supports for the unique experience.

Our listening for and re-searching of unique experiences in a contextual enquiry expands our knowledge of the unique experience/s. This enquiry demonstrates a philosophical position in respect to the development of individuals' psychological concerns. This philosophical position is based on the following beliefs:

▼ That we facilitate a journey of discovery with people (clients). Over this journey we are prepared to have what we think we know challenged. This belief readies us to listen for and enquire about the possibility of unique experiences that defy conventional psychological theory.

▼ That those who are marginalised are tutored in a deficit view of the self.

▼ That the development of and institutional support for the concept of the autonomous self as the sole agent of self regulation, morality and achievement has orientated people towards psychology as a form of regulation of the self. In this environment people's so-called pathology is exposed and assessed by the expert in the psychological workings of the individual, and this pathology is then corrected by this expert.

When we engage with the self as a relational self we are in a position to wonder about:

▼ The development of the pathological view, idea/experience of the self.

▼ The institutional, environmental and family/other supports of this pathological view of the self.

▼ The experiences, ideas or thoughts that have been excluded because of the belief in the pathologising idea/view of the self.

▼ The emotional experience of re-remembering that which has been excluded (experiences, ideas and thoughts outside of the pathologising view/ideas).

▼ Within the emotional experience, a recognition of the 'making sense of' life experiences that contradicts the pathologising view.

For example, Rena thought she was going mad. Whenever she visited her family and the uncle who sexually abused her turned up, Rena felt paralysed with fear. Days after this event she would often find her self feeling suicidal. When she talked with other family members they said that she was being silly. She just needed to put things in the past. They then reassured her that they would make sure that he didn't hurt her.

Through an enquiry Rena became aware that:

▼ The family members who said they'd protect her had been unable to protect her in the past and were not able to protect her in the present environment where the effects of the abuse were unacknowledged.

▼ The uncle had never been censored or challenged about his abusive behaviour.

▼ The family's silence about the past abuse replicated the secrecy around the abuse and therefore perpetuated the abuse environment.

▼ She had a right to determine how she needed or wanted to protect her self.

▼ She had a right to determine what sort of contact she wanted to have with her uncle.

▼ She had a right to strong feelings about what had happened in the past and what could happen in the future.

▼ The family's motto 'don't cause waves' required her to push away her feelings. This left her without the resource of her feelings which made it difficult for her to determine what action she needed to take for safety. The pushing away of feelings had in the past been a strategy of protection. (Rena's uncle had directly threatened her if she exposed the abuse.) However, in the present the pushing away was an act of compliance with the family mores.

An enquiry that focuses on the relational self contextualises experiences, thoughts and ideas in order that people (clients) are freed from the pathologising view of the self. People (clients) can then recognise or remember the unique resistance steps that they took which had been previously dismissed under the weight of the pathologising discourse. In the above example Rena had significantly defied her uncle's threats by telling her sisters about the sexual abuse. When her decision to do this was re-searched, we rediscovered the strength she carried/carries in order to defy the threats and act for her life. This rediscovery was explored and then situated in the context of her life. Its contextual coherence supported her to take the next steps in determining her needs for emotional and physical protection.

A contextual exploration of unique experiences includes exploring the experiences in relationship to culture, time, gender, sexuality and class. This exploration prevents us (therapists) from determining that a unique experience is a form of answer. Answer-thinking subjects people (clients) to our provision of a unique experience as a solution. When we engage with answer-thinking, indirectly and directly, we imply the following:

If you (client) do more of this (the unique experience) you will be free of these concerns (e.g. fear, depression, anxiety, etc.).

Answer-thinking can also encourage the development of large questions. These large questions move us away from developing an intricate and intimate knowledge of how the unique experience operated/s and survived/s in people's (clients') lives. Large questions also move us away from re-searching the strategies that support the holding of one version of memory over another.

For example, when re-searching a unique experience Emily responded, 'I just do it.' The 'doing of it' is Emily's present knowledge point. We need to start our enquiry from this point:

▼ How do you know that you are coming up to or moving towards *the doing of it*?

▼ Is there any thinking that supports the moving towards *the doing of it*?

▼ When *the doing of it* is happening is there any thinking that you're engaging with?

▼ When *the doing of it* is happening, are there any feelings that you're engaging with?

▼ When you reflect on the coming up to *the doing of it* do you notice any steps that move you towards 'the doing of it'?

▼ After *the doing of it* what thoughts and feelings do you hold about your self, supported by the knowledge of *the doing of it*?

▼ After *the doing of it* how do you hold onto the knowledge and feelings of *the doing of it*?

▼ If you could hold onto the thoughts and feelings of *the doing of it* how would that support you to engage with 'the doing of it' in the future?

In contrast, if we reflected on 'I just do it' by using large questions we might ask the following:

▼ When you *just do it* what changes?

▼ If you were to continue *just doing it* how might your life change?

▼ Do you think you would prefer to *just do it* in order to escape the hold of the problem?

The earlier questions provide an example of how I might begin to put a unique experience into context. As the context gets clarified the naming and understanding of the unique experience may change. The enquiry exposes the fluidity of the unique experience thereby challenging any static construction we (therapist and client/s) may hold.

As I listen for and re-search unique experiences, I also reflect on the way language is used. People (clients) frequently talk about their life experiences using the language of deficit or pathology. Whenever I hear the language of deficit or pathology I re-search all that constitutes those words.

For example, instead of re-searching insensitivity, I focus on re-searching all of the elements of sensitivity. This includes the history of sensitivity, the gendering of sensitivity, the movement towards and away from sensitivity, the strengthening, weakening of sensitivity and the cultural determinants of sensitivity ideas and practices. This style of re-search inevitably includes within it a knowledge of the ideas and practices of insensitivity. However the focus of the enquiry moves us (therapist and client) away from a preoccupation with deficit or pathology. Instead, the enquiry elicits evidence of resilience, abilities and strengths. Unique experiences thus become an inevitable consequence of a unique discourse. The existence of this unique discourse thus contradicts 'the truth' of the pathologising discourse. A relational externalising enquiry over time (past, present and future) generates optimum conditions for discovery of unique experiences. An enquiry conducted over time inevitably highlights movement, movement towards or movement away. Whether we are exploring the contextual development of the concern/s or the contextual development of attributes or abilities, an enquiry over time challenges the static nature of events and experiences. The experience of movement provides us (therapist and client) with an opportunity to experience and re-search moments of change. Within change there are many opportunities to rediscover both unique experiences and hope.

THE CONTEXTUAL ENQUIRY

In a contextual enquiry the context which surrounds significant life events is made available for reflection and re-view within the therapeutic conversation. We situate our enquiry beyond the bounds of the individual and family, to the community within which the individual and family is immersed. This community in turn is affected by the circulation of prevalent ideas and beliefs. A contextual enquiry challenges us to move past the idea that the individual is the independent determinant of meaning; although people carry responsibility for their actions, the conditions that support their actions can be exposed and thus negotiated.

A contextual enquiry provides people (clients) with an opportunity to reflect on their self-understandings, descriptions and experiences in relationship to the ideas for meaning-making that are available to them. When we increase the reservoir of available ideas, people (clients) have the opportunity to reflect on both ideas that persecute them and others and ideas that liberate them and others.

Increasing the reservoir of available ideas can occur through the enquiry process. We ask questions that connect ideas contextually and over time. This provides people (clients) with an exploration of the relationship between power relations and ideas and practices. Consequently people (clients) make connections beyond the static pathologising view or experience of the self. For example:

Jenny: I never had the opportunity to be just a normal thirteen year old. I remember my friends laughing and talking about boys. What they did at the pictures, that sort of thing. I couldn't say a word. I knew that if they knew what had happened to me, they would think I was disgusting. So I just sat there pretending to join in. It was just so lonely.

Johnella: How did the difference between you and your girlfriends result in the thought 'I'm disgusting'?

Jenny: Even though everyone was talking about it, they didn't do it. I mean everyone thought that a girl who did it was just a slut. So I know that's what they would have thought about me if they'd known.

Johnella: Do you think you took these ideas about sexually active girls at thirteen and related them to the sexual abuse that had been happening since you were four years old?

Jenny: Yes I did. I still do now, I think.

Johnella: What's the difference between sexual activity between two 13-year-olds or 16-year-olds or 20-year-olds and what happened to you at four years old?

Jenny: I didn't have any choice when I was four years old. I didn't know what to do. I didn't know what was happening.

Johnella: What ideas and/or people encouraged you to consider consenting sexual activity and sexual assault as the same thing?

Jenny: Well, my cousin kept telling me I liked it and that I had been flirting with him so I deserved it.

Johnella: When you hear your self say that, what do you think of these ideas? Imagine a four-year-old being told this.

Jenny: It's rubbish, pure unadulterated rubbish. I was terrified. He just said that to excuse himself.

Johnella: Do you think when you were thirteen years old and older, that you believed the truth of that excuse? Do you think that belief has contributed to ideas of fault and disgust?

Jenny: Yes they have.

Johnella: What was your experience of the attitudes that surrounded 13 year/15 year/18-year-old boy's and girl's sexual experimentation?

Jenny: Oh, it was really different. Boys would do what they liked. It was all a bit of fun. When girls were sexual, they were sluts.

Johnella: What is the basis, do you think, of this difference? I mean, what ideas supports this difference?

In this example, I am demonstrating a beginning conversation that explores a strong prevailing belief that 'I was a whore, a slut' within a wider meaning-making context. This exploration acts to illuminate the influences that support and determine the meaning an individual makes of experiences. In this instance, the past meanings available to Jenny to make sense of the sexual assault enlisted her as her prime persecutor.

Exploration of the contextual environment extends the focus of the therapeutic conversation beyond simplistic notions of problem and solution. We (therapists) are ideally positioned to make discoveries within this conversation, for although we have constructed the question, the answer may defy, contradict, add to or reflect our experience or current psychological knowledge. We can only add to, or extend our initial questions when we have engaged with or heard people's (clients') response to the question.

The contextual enquiry exposes the relationship between individual suffering and institutional ideas and practices. Once this relationship is exposed we support people to recognise, discover and create strategies for resistance. These moments of resistance are also researched within the paradigm of the contextual self.

Resistance is often thought of as a display of will that counters or subverts the actions or intentions of people who are mandated to represent institutional values, judgments and processes. On the contrary, when we recognise moments of resistance, we are provided with a beginning point for enquiry. The subsequent contextual exploration gives people the opportunity to develop an explanation for themselves. This explanation can then act as a resource for them in their lives. Without this exploration points of resistance remain known to people (clients) as quirks of their nature, such as, I'm stubborn, stupid, crazy, rebellious or I'm 'borderline'.

Central to this exploration is experimenting with the naming and renaming of experience. In this process people (clients) often access their determination to be heard and their ability to fight for their lives in sometimes unconventional ways. When we consider the contextual environment, we are considering these relationships.[1]

THE CONTEXTUAL SELF

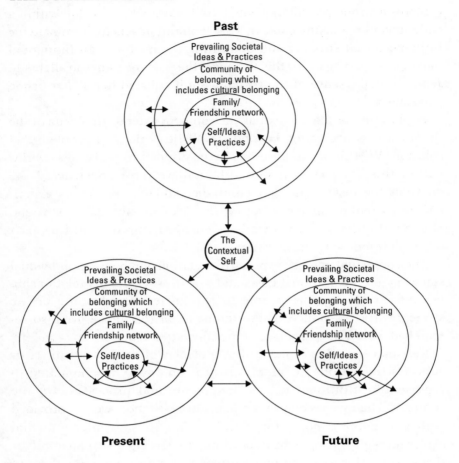

Within the therapeutic relationship the weaving together of words engages us in the present moment. Words that fly us (therapist and client) through time, words that create both a sense of space and a sense of closeness, words that in the experience of detachment from the self bring forward emotional connection with the self; all are spoken in the present moment.

The living narrative is constructed within the therapeutic relationship in the present moment. It is then added to and engaged with outside of the therapeutic relationship. The living narrative is however never complete, whole or finished.

The contextual enquiry that utilizes the relational externalising process provides people with a relational perspective. This relational perspective challenges language strategies that position us and shape us within previously available life narratives. As I outlined in Chapter One, when these narratives are used in compliance with conventional English language usage, experience is reduced to static internalized states. In contrast, when we use relational externalising talk we can feel/experience/know the strategies and privileging of one meaning paradigm over another. To feel/experience/know this is to enter the relational world. In entering this world, we feel/experience/know the relational self which in itself creates an environment that enables change. In this environment of change the static narrative generated by the conventions of English language usage is replaced by a relational engagement with those life narratives available to us.

WHAT ABOUT INFORMATION?

In many interviews I will at times introduce information. This information is couched as a possibility. For example, 'Some parents have told me that they've found . . . useful. These ideas however may not sit comfortably or fit for you. I'm wondering about your thinking in relation to these ideas?'

I believe it is important not to make definitive statements unless we are confronted with a challenge to our ethical position. In order to operate outside definitive statements I select language that defies definitiveness. For example:

▼ 'Some people/parents/women/men/perpetrators, etc. have found that . . . You might be interested in these ideas.'

▼ 'This is one man's ideas of men's friendships, what's your thinking on this?'

▼ 'If you read that a number of other women have had a similar relationship to guilt as the one we've discussed, how would that effect your relationship with this guilt?'

Selecting language that defies definitiveness is an important beginning point in the introduction of ideas to the therapeutic relationship. I carry a resource of thousands of therapeutic conversations and thousands of textual voices. I believe it can be useful to make this resource available for people's consideration. Whenever I do this, I require myself to be available for a variety of responses, including those that are different to mine. I can do this when I use the resource as a support for the enquiry process. I am not interested in obtaining people's (clients') agreement or disagreement to the introduced information. I am interested in people's (clients') emotional and intellectual relationship to it.

However, when people present me with a challenge to my ethical position, I consider it important to disclose this position. Conflicting ethical positions in the therapeutic relationship requires a re-view of the viability of the Therapeutic Relationship. For example, Liz attended counselling in the hope that I would 're-educate' her away from lesbian thoughts and feelings and towards heterosexual thoughts and feelings. The concept of re-education was supported by the community of which she was a member. I told Liz that I was concerned about the idea of re-education. She also needed to know that I carried strong beliefs that endorsed both homosexual and heterosexual relationships, and these beliefs would inevitably shape the therapeutic conversation. It was therefore very likely that any exploration had the potential to challenge the community's doctrine thereby creating the conditions for a loyalty dilemma. Liz agreed that her belonging within the community was paramount. She decided to withdraw from the therapeutic relationship. Two years later Liz recontacted me in order to renegotiate the therapeutic relationship.

THE PRACTICAL DECONSTRUCTION OF EVERYDAY IDEAS AND PRACTICES

I have taken the term 'practical deconstruction' from *Deconstructing Psycholopathology*, written by Ian Parker, Eugenie Georgaca, David Harper, Terence McLaughlin and Mark Stowell-Smith (22). They define 'practical deconstruction' as 'attending to politics and power when you do critical reading and thinking through the effects of your critique on institutions and forms of knowledge'. (p.3) I have used 'practical deconstruction' to reflect a particular engagement with language and meanings which allows us (therapist and client) to attend to politics and power within the therapeutic conversation.

We engage with practical deconstruction of everyday ideas and practices when the meanings given to commonplace roles, attributes, relationships and words are not taken for granted. For example, Jacob stated, 'I am the provider in the family. I expect to come home and see that Sophie has pulled her weight. After all, there isn't a lot to be done.'

In preparing myself for the conversation with Jacob and Sophie, I developed these questions to assist our enquiry.

▼ What is your understanding of the dominant cultural understanding of being a economic and/or emotional 'provider'?

▼ What distinctions do you draw between an economic provider and an emotional provider?

▼ When you look at your family of origin, was the practice of being 'the economic/emotional provider' gendered?

▼ How was the gendering of 'the economic and emotional provider' understood in the family?

▼ What were/are the advantages or disadvantages to the person who occupies these roles?

▼ How has 'the economic and emotional provider' ideas/practices of your family influenced your life?

▼ Have you challenged any of these ideas and practices?

▼ Who and what has supported that?

▼ How do you think Sophie would answer these questions?

▼ If Sophie was to consider being more of an economic provider, what advice would you give her?

▼ If you were considering being more of an emotional provider what advice would you give her?

Attaching 'provider' to both the economic and the emotional moves them into the same arena of consideration. This introduces a consideration of value, skills and status for both the economic and emotional provider. The question, 'What were/are the advantages and disadvantages to the person who occupies these roles?' requires a consideration of institutional power and how it shapes people's lives. For example, the emotional provider doesn't have a sufficient credit rating to apply for a $2000 credit card limit.

In practical deconstruction we are required to consider that the therapeutic conversation is a vehicle for the negotiation of meaning. Within the therapeutic relationship I (therapist) am in a strong position to assume a consensus of meaning which reflects my meaning of the words people use to describe their experience. Acting on an assumption of a consensus of meaning when there isn't one can result in a negotiation with people (clients) around future strategies for their lives based on the therapist's inaccurate assumptions. These inaccuracies can result in the following:

1. People's (clients') inability to think about or act on these negotiated strategies. The following consequences can occur:
    ▼ People's (clients') growing sense of failure followed by hopelessness.
    ▼ Therapists' growing sense of frustration.
    ▼ Therapists' temptation to engage in labelling, e.g. people (clients) as 'resistant'.
2. People (clients) can absorb these strategies and act on them. By acting on the strategies they are further implicated as solely responsible and as sole creators of their concerns and difficulties. This prevents an investigation into the effects of dominant institutional ideas and practices on their sense of wellbeing.

In these circumstances therapy can unintentionally support dominant institutional ideas and practices. This can result in both the ongoing marginalisation of groups of people and the invisibility of ideas and practices that contradict prevalent and available ideas and practices.

In order to prevent myself from assuming meaning I become a negotiator of meaning. I enlist a practical deconstructive process whenever I choose an externalising theme among the myriad of words available in the therapeutic conversation. Reflecting on what draws us to a particular theme is an important part of a self reflection which can protect people (clients) from our impositions. Reflecting on our thoughts and feelings through the therapeutic conversation can alert us to the unspoken. The unspoken can exist whenever there are experiential, class, sexuality, gender, race and age differences in the therapeutic relationship. I believe what is unspoken generally supports the therapist to impose meaning and therefore *act on* rather than *with people (clients)*. A self/other reflective process assists in the naming of the unspoken. Once named it can be re-searched both in the therapist's life and if appropriate, in the therapeutic relationship.

Practical deconstruction of everyday ideas and practices is challenging for us (therapists) as we are also immersed in the 'taken-for-granted'. Engaging with the language that represents and shapes the meanings we make of our lives from the position of wondering or curiosity about this language in practice, prepares us for the therapeutic conversation.

The most challenging questions for us will be those that expose the advantages we retain by adhering to certain ideas and practices. From a position of advantage we are most likely to believe that there are no questions, there is only this particular 'truth'.

PSYCHOLOGICAL LANGUAGE

Psychology, psychotherapy and counselling practitioners construct and present their theories through language. When conventional grammatical rules are used to represent theories these theories are inevitably presented as static, finite and true. When we transfer these theories into our clinical practice, they emerge as truth or knowledge statements.

For example, here are some truth or knowledge statements frequently used by practitioners:

▼ This is the process you need to engage in, in order to grieve in a healthy way.

▼ Commitment is an essential component of successful relationships.

▼ There is no requirement for you to forgive.

▼ Without forgiveness you won't be able to move on.

Even though we may try to protect people (clients) from the directives inherent in the above examples by not making these statements, if we believe these theories we still become stuck in this thinking. When we become stuck, the therapy becomes stuck. What moves the therapy out of stuckness is catching our belief in a particular theory, naming it and then exploring it with people (clients) by using a relational externalising process.

When we use psychological theories as an explanation for people's (clients') lived experience, we engage with a particular power relation. This power relation confirms us as the expert knowers of what constitutes mental illness and mental health or what is normal and what is not. The production of a diagnosis and intervention subsequently maintains the truth of any psychological idea.

People (clients) who don't conform with our diagnosis and intervention by 'getting well' are vulnerable to further labelling. The psychological theories that support diagnosis and intervention are constituted within a detached language strategy. The language of detachment exists in the presence of any grand theory.

In my work I hold psychological theories to one side as one possible explanation for life events. I do this so that I am free to widely explore the meanings available to make sense of people's (clients') life experiences. This experience may be outside of my available psychological theories or it may directly contradict a psychological theory, or it may build onto or extend a psychological theory. It is challenging to direct our listening to people's (clients') actual expression of experience over listening to and for our definitive and detached psychological theories.

People (clients) search for language that accurately describes their experiences. The words that are available to them come from a language reservoir that exists to describe everyday experiences. These words are then used by people (clients) to describe experiences that are outside the everyday. It is an act of defiance whenever we choose to not submit to the universalising nature of psychological theories. Instead, we listen closely to the words people (clients) use to describe their experiences while knowing it is possible that these words require further exploration. We can be alert to these possibilities by:

▼ Listening to the emotions that support the words.

▼ Negotiating the meaning of words rather than taking the meaning of words for granted.

▼ Remaining alert to the contextual environment.

When we engage in a relational externalising enquiry we are supported by the belief that people (clients) have a unique relationship with the words that describe emotionally evocative and significant experiences. In these conversations we sanction the language of lived experience over the detached languaging of psychological theories.

For example, it is very common for people (clients) who have been sexually abused to experience themselves as 'dirty'. People's (clients') strategies for cleansing often involve vigorous scrubbing and washing. This experience of feeling dirty and the cleansing strategy can be distressing. In order to understand the experience of feeling dirty, we need to be able to intensely explore the meaning that surrounds the description 'feeling dirty'. These questions represent a beginning enquiry that extends our (client and therapist's) knowledge of the experience that is represented by 'feeling dirty'.

▼ What does this dirt consist of?

▼ Is it made up of words, thoughts, memories, body feelings?

▼ How would you describe these words, thoughts, memories and/or body feelings?

▼ What are the origins of this dirt?

▼ When you're using the shower to 'get clean', what is it that is being washed away?

These questions do not represent an answer or an extensive enquiry. They form an exercise to illustrate an enquiry process that supports people (clients) to consider, experiment and claim the language that more readily describes their experiences.

When we use an enquiry process in preference to making expert statements we are acknowledging the different experience of vulnerability that a client and a therapist will have in the therapeutic relationship.

In the search for language that accurately describes people's (clients') experiences, we may experiment with metaphors or analogies. Metaphors and analogies are an attempt to closely reflect or mirror people's (clients') experiences. The respectful use of a metaphor or analogy involves closely knowing (as closely as an outsider can) both the meaning people (clients) make of experiences and the potential for reflecting this meaning by using metaphor or analogy. The use of metaphor or analogy does not represent an answer; it is an attempt to flesh out the bones of experience provided by everyday language usage.

WHERE DO THE METAPHORS COME FROM?

I have noticed therapists mimicking phrases commonly used by well known therapists as though they are impregnated with magical qualities. When stock phrases such as 'I was struck by' are used in this way they are flat; the words are disembodied. When we use language in this disembodied way, people (clients) experience a dissonance. This dissonance can then separate people from believing in their own experience.

Our words will either support or challenge the integrity of the therapeutic conversation. In engaging with Sophie's, Jacob's and Sam's lives I'm attempting to illustrate the complexity of working with people's (clients') lives. There is nothing tidy about these lives; there are conflicting experiences and understandings; there are hidden beliefs, tragedies and achievements; there are places of safety and danger; there are strong feelings disguised in politeness.

In many instances, negotiating the naming of experiences generates movement from singular internal knowings to external named reflections. Naming is the first step in establishing a platform for a relational externalising enquiry. This enquiry brings forward new understandings of experiences which allows for a re-connection to and with the self.

In reading Sophie's, Jacob's and Sam's stories, ask yourself what are the themes or descriptions that are imbued with emotional substance. Practising a therapeutic enquiry would involve taking each theme and developing questions that assume a posture of discovery. For example, here are questions towards developing the theme of a place of shelter for Sophie:

Johnella: Sophie, when you think of Kingseat (Psychiatric hospital) as 'a place of shelter', can you tell me about the shelter it provided?

Johnella: Sophie, in looking back over your life, what or who has provided shelter?

Johnella: Sophie, when you have been living in shelter, what do you notice about yourself? What do others notice about you when you are in shelter?

Johnella: Sophie, have you ever been able to take your experiences of shelter with you?

Johnella: Has it ever been possible to have a little bit of shelter outside of the Kingseat shelter?

This is not a definitive list of questions. It is an example of an exercise in developing questions that give depth to a theme that is richly symbolic. Exploration of this theme provides us (therapist and client) with opportunities to experiment with representing the richness of experiential knowings through language. In the therapeutic conversation, Sophie's response to any of these questions may entirely change the direction of the enquiry.[2]

The metaphors we use come from a struggle to listen to what carries emotional or symbolic power for people (clients) while experimenting with matching the feeling, tone, words, with a description or image that is multidimensional. This description or image is suggested as a possibility that people can take up or not. If taken up, it provides the foundation point for an enquiry that may move beyond the original metaphor.

WORKING WITH SECRETS

Any re-view of critical self judgment, blame, shame and guilt, is severely hampered if people's (clients') experiences are held in secret. Secrecy can elevate a sense of shame, blame and fault. The secret often drives an invisible wedge between the carrier of the secret and others, thereby affecting experiences of intimacy and connection. Secrecy situates people (clients) as outsiders, outside of family, friendship groups and community groups. The people (clients) who are the carriers of secrets can feel as though they are leading double lives. The successes they experience in life are often negated, as these successes are considered to be the result of a false representation of the self maintained by the existence of the secret. A 'true' self description is intrinsically linked to the secret which in turn is linked to judgment, criticism, shame and guilt. This 'true' self description remains hidden while taking an enormous emotional toll. The emotional cost can express itself in a number of psychological guises which further support judgment, criticism, shame and guilt. It is only in the exposure of the secret that people (clients) have the opportunity to reclaim their lives from the effects of the past, including the effects of secrecy. The secrets I am referring to extend to any significant life experience that remains as a private knowing.

For example, Maggie had been sexually abused by her father from the age of five years until the age of 10 years. When she came to see me she carried a strong, prevailing belief that she was a whore, a slut. The words, 'whore' and 'slut' were used by her father. She carried these words with the secret of the abuse, she carried these words and found evidence for the truth of these words. Evidence was found in the standing her father held in the community. Evidence was found in the religious teachings of goodness and wrongdoing, in her girlfriend's and boyfriend's judgments of the sexual impropriety of others. Evidence was found in the all-day, every-day messages in the media that indicated what is valued in young women. This evidence was strengthened by a process of self-evaluation that took the community morality position on sexuality and turned this towards the experience of sexual assault.

People (clients) who are forced into secrecy either directly by threats from the abuser or indirectly by societal judgment, can experience enormous isolation and loneliness. This experience of isolation and loneliness is often not softened by a loving family or friends. The exposure of the secret and the strategies that were used to ensure people (clients) continued to carry it, can liberate emotions of joy, anger and sadness. The definition and experience of the self in relationship to:

▼ The past, present and future.

▼ Significant others.

▼ Prevailing societal ideas and practices.

▼ Alternative knowledges.

can be re-viewed anew, once the secret is exposed. This brings to people's (clients') attention what belongs to them and what has been stolen.

RENAMING SURVIVAL STRATEGIES

People (clients) use many methods to protect their emotional, physical, spirit-filled self from the destructive effects of ongoing emotional, physical and sexual abuse. These survival techniques have often been labelled by others as a problem or deficit.

For example, Pat had been severely beaten by her mother for as long as she could remember. The beatings were unpredictable as they appeared unrelated to any event. It seemed to Pat that her mother would look for any excuse to lash out at her. There was little that Pat could do to protect her self. When the beatings began she would offer no resistance. Instead she slid to the floor, covering her head with her arms. After a time she could leave her body and the pain by disappearing to the safe place she had experienced at Aunty Barbara's. When she appeared again in her body, many hours had past. If she was lucky her mother's regret would show in small acts of kindness and comfort. These became treasured relationship memories for Pat who remained ever hopeful that this mother would reappear in her life. Pat became so practised at disappearing into her mind that she found it happened automatically whenever she heard angry or loud voices. Consequently she would disappear in her mind frequently at school, missing large parts of the day. Pat was described by the school authorities as slow. The disappearing had severe consequences for Pat's life. However, without it she may not have survived.

If people (clients) recognise their strategies for survival they can both appreciate the strategies and make a decision to challenge the ongoing presence of the strategies in their lives. Strategies for survival may have outlived their usefulness and become a hindrance. When people (clients) recognise that these strategies have played a part in their life, they can position themselves towards change with compassion. Whenever these strategies reappear in people's (clients') lives this can be seen as an opportunity to reflect on the meaning of this, rather than regarding the reappearance of the strategy as evidence of failure. For example,

Mark: I really enjoyed the evening with Roman. We seemed to have so much in common. It was easy being with him, no tension and no expectations. Then as we were walking to the car he put his arms on my shoulders. I just froze and pulled away. I felt angry with him for no reason. He felt it and looked hurt. I just couldn't talk about it, it seemed so stupid. I feel so stupid. I just don't think I'll be able to have a relationship, I'm just not up to it.

Johnella: When Roman put his arm around you, were you expecting this touch?

Mark: No, it really surprised me, but why should it be such a big thing?

Johnella: Where was Roman standing in relation to you? When this happened, was he standing beside you, in front of you or behind you?

Mark: He was behind me. He had gone to pay the bill and I had started off towards the car. He sort of ran up to me and placed both his hands on my shoulders. He was only being playful.

Johnella: Did this coming from behind touch surprise you? Is this touch similar to other past touches?

Mark: Yes it was. That's what happened all the time walking home from school when these boys used to wait and then ambush me.

Johnella: Do you think your response to Roman's touch is connected to the remembering of that past experience?

Mark: Yeah, it probably is connected but I've got to get over it. If I can't get over it, how can I ever hope to have a relationship?

Johnella: What would happen if whenever strong feelings of freezing or pulling away occur, you thought, This is telling me something about the past. Something I need to listen to and understand.

Mark: That would be okay but how would I talk about it? I mean, what would I say to Roman. I don't want to go on about my past, I've only just met the guy.

Johnella: Well, if you thought that the freezing and pulling away was a sign that the past had moved into the present, then at an appropriate time maybe you could take the experience seriously by re-searching it. This re-search could include questions like:

● Does this belong in the past or is it in the now?

● What's the freezing or pulling away telling me about this situation?

Then maybe you can decide how much you want or need to tell Roman. For example, what would it feel like to say to Roman, 'Hey Roman, I get jumpy when someone comes up behind me suddenly. It would be okay if I could see you'.

People (clients) frequently have an ambivalent relationship with their survival strategies. These strategies protect them but their presence can also brings forwards experiences of shame, alienation and blame. It is important that we (therapists) explore this ambivalent relationship with people (clients). We risk an imposition of meaning if we 'positively connote' the survival strategies without re-searching the possible ambivalent nature of the person's (client's) relationship to them.

PULLING THE CONVERSATIONAL THREADS TOGETHER
Throughout the therapeutic conversation we take opportunities to pull the threads and segments of the conversation together. This:

▼ Creates a sense of conversational integrity.

▼ Provides an opportunity for people (therapist and client) to check if there is mutual understanding.

▼ Provides a platform for further exploration.

▼ Develops a sense of linkage or wholeness that defies the logic or cohesiveness of life-draining explanations.

The process of pulling the conversational threads together needs to include provision of space and time for people (clients) to consider their ideas and responses. Creating a sense of conversational integrity is different from providing an answer. Within the process of exposing the 'taken-for-granted' we disturb people's (clients') relationship with the certainty inherent in the assumed meanings of life events, emotions, experiences and relationships. This disturbance leaves people (clients) to ponder on questions that may lead them in a number of 'making sense' directions. Whenever we pull the conversational threads together, we are drawing on the discoveries from within the therapeutic conversation. People (clients) experience a sense of cohesion in this process. If therapists introduce new ideas during the pulling together process this is an imposition. We can remain alert to any temptation to introduce new ideas during the pulling together time and once alert we can turn the statement into a question or wondering.

ETHICS

How do Foucault's ideas of 'the confessional' relate to this work?

> The confession is a ritual of discourse in which the speaking subject is also the subject of the statement; it is also a ritual that unfolds within a power relationship. (Foucault [7] p. 61)

The other person in this power relationship carries the authority bestowed on her/him as a member of the professional classes. This includes counsellors, therapists, social workers, psychologists and psychiatrists. The work I write about inevitably reflects the authority given to me by my membership of this group. Traditional questioning (i.e. all questioning outside of a relational externalising enquiry) reflects the quasi-scientific notion that there is a set of finite rules that define pathological and normal, good and bad family functioning and appropriate psychological development. This tradition creates a context where the 'neutral' professional questions act to quantify people's (clients') functionality.

This assumes a neutral observer who can assess personal deficit while extolling the benefit to people (clients) of letting go of any thinking or experiences that are outside of 'the norm'. Being outside of 'the norm' is considered by traditional psychological/counselling practices as evidence of pathology or mental illness. People's (clients') reports of unhappiness and dissatisfaction often provide evidence or confirmation of the pathologising explanation. The worker can then assist people (clients) to claim membership of the group that is 'the norm'. The questioning that occurs is often directed by an assessment regime. Responses are evaluated according to the grand psychological theories which are held by the questioner, that allows him/her to intervene in ways that support the psychological theories and ideas of what is 'normal'.

In contrast, the work I describe in this book offers people (clients) an opportunity to explore *the self in relationship to. Being in relationship to* supports people (clients) to see, know and experience the influences that direct and shape their lives. Our questions directs attention to exploring abilities, strengths and experiences outside of or counter to the knowledge of the problems or concerns. *Being in relationship to* encourages us to prepare to challenge known theory by re-searching people's (clients') direct experience. Even though the knowledge we hold of the everyday sits within known and available discourses, resistances to prevailing discourses can be discovered within this everyday exploration. The concept of reverse discourse provides us with an arena for exploration that challenges the constructions of pathology.

> While a discourse will offer a preferred form of subjectivity its very organisation will imply other subject positions and the possibility of reversal — reverse discourse. (Weedon [32] p. 109).

When we hold the idea that other subject positions are implied in the organization of any discourse, we are encouraged to always consider an enquiry and exploration of these other subject positions. This includes movement between subject positions. People (clients) who assess themselves according to prevailing discourses will present substantial evidence of their pathology. An enquiry that attends to this, while also enquiring into the reverse discourse, provides people (clients) with a site for exploration that has previously been negated. Within the exploration of the reverse discourse people (clients) have an opportunity to explore the consequences and processes of the legitimisation of one discourse over another.

> Reverse discourse has important implications for the power of the discourse which it seems to subvert. As a first stage in challenging meaning and power, it enables the production of new resistant discourses. (Weedon [32] p. 110).

Enquiry and exploration of the prevailing discourse exposes its existence. Once exposed, it can be explored in relationship to alternative discourses. For example, in the privileging of couples.

Membership of a couple is considered by psychological developmental theories as evidence of an appropriate movement into adulthood. The rules, obligations and rituals of coupledom disappear from awareness under the guise of 'normal'. With this disappearing comes a lack of analysis of the politics inherent in the wider societal support and privileging of couples. People (clients) who are outside of coupledom often attend counselling holding a pervasive sense of failure. We are in a position to either support this sense of failure or enquire in such a way that exposes the taken-for-granted 'normality' of the couple relationship.[3]

Consider these questions:

▼ What meanings do people attribute to being in a couple/or being identified as a couple?

▼ What are the rules and expectations of coupledom?

▼ What status is attributed to relationships outside of the couple relationship?

▼ What function might be served in the community of elevating the couple relationship over other relationships?

▼ What beliefs underlie the dedication to even numbers at dinner parties?

▼ If the term couple or partnership didn't exist, how would these relationships be described?

The idea of reverse discourse can act as a prompt to move our thinking away from the totalising influence of both the pathologising discourse and the dominant discourse. However, while engaging in an exploration of the *self in relationship* we are interested in exploring the following:

▼ The relationship between power relations and discourses.

▼ The relationship between discourses — dominant and marginalised, accepted and excluded.

▼ Experimenting with languaging strategies that imply movement.
▼ Relating theoretical constructs to practice.

This exploration protects us from engaging with the binaries that simplify life experience, i.e.
discourse — reverse discourse
problem — solution
dominant story — preferred story.

Foucault (7) writes:

Indeed, it is in discourse that power and knowledge are joined together. And for this very reason we must conceive discourse as a series of discontinuous segments whose tactical function is neither uniform nor stable. To be more precise we must not imagine a world of discourse divided between accepted discourse and excluded discourse or between the dominant discourse and the dominated one; but as a multiplicity of discursive elements that can come into play in various strategies. (p. 100.)

It is challenging to stand back from the temptation to simply conform to those discourses that are outside of the dominant discourse. A passion for justice may attract us to the side of currently excluded discourses. This can then move us to argue for this particular version of truth. When we (therapists and counsellors) argue for our version of truth, whether that involves dominant or excluded discourses, we are setting our selves up as arbiters of truth. This position confirms us as dominating meaning-making in the therapeutic relationship. I propose a more complex engagement with the ideas and practices that influence people's lives. This involves re-searching the relationship between discourses, and thus illuminating the complexity inherent in engaging with the discursive elements which influence the available meanings that can be attributed to people's experience.

WORKING WITH THE TEXT

How Does This Chapter Relate to Me (Client)?

In this chapter you will notice an emphasis on a therapeutic convers-ational style that directs our attention towards the impact on you of taken-for-granted commonly held beliefs, theories and ideas. Therapists contravene the therapeutic relationship understanding when they indicate that any one idea or practice is 'the right idea/practice'. We may state the legal ramifications of continuing one practice over another. We may tell you that we had personal beliefs which support one idea or practice over another. We may suggest that certain ideas or practices have been reported by others as useful in and for their lives. However, when we definitely support one idea, theory or practice we begin to engage with certainty. When this occurs the therapy moves away from discovery of your unique engagement with your life and moves towards generalisation. Generalisations support those of us who are comfort-able in the ideas and practices that represent the dominant or prevailing cultural ideas and practices.

The therapy described in this chapter has a focus on making ideas, theories and practices apparent to you. The distance generated by a relational externalising conversation allows you to see, experience, hear and know how a particular theory, idea or practice is being enacted in your life. From this perspective you have the opportunity to determine how you wish to relate to these theories, ideas or practices (including an exploration of your relationship with alternative theories, ideas and practices).

During the therapeutic work we re-search instances in your life where you have acted or thought in ways that contravene the prevailing descriptions of your self in relationship to life themes, significant others, the past, institutional ideas and significant events. We call these moments unique experiences. Outside of therapy, you can do your own re-search for unique experiences. These questions may help your re-search:

▼ Can you remember a time, even the smallest of moments, where you did, said or thought something that contradicted the description you previously held about yourself? This moment may not be recognised by anyone else. In fact people (including family) may have negatively defined this moment by, for example, calling you stubborn, selfish, daydreamer, inconsiderate or a loner. When you reflect on this moment in the context of the knowledge you hold of your life, was this an action of resistance?

▼ Can you remember a time where the problem/concern reduced or disappeared or changed (even temporarily) from your life?

Take these moments and write down:

▼ A description of the moment.

▼ The events that surrounded the moment.

▼ The feelings and thoughts you carried about yourself before, during and after the experience of this moment.

▼ Turn to page 65, The Contextual Enquiry. Develop and answer questions that relate to each category represented in the diagram, for example, 'Did the prevailing societal ideas and practices of the time support or dismiss this moment of difference/resistance?'

▼ Do I know of any theoretical ideas or cultural ideas that support this moment of difference/resistance?

▼ How did my family either support, disappear or contradict this moment?

▼ If there is a collective family memory of this moment, what is it? Does this memory support a pathologising or strength-giving view of myself?

There is no requirement in the therapy for you to talk about something that you don't want to talk about. It's important that if you feel pressure to talk about something, you identify the experience of pressure within the therapy. When you do this a negotiation of your safety require-ments, together with the limitations of the therapeutic relationship, can be discussed.

If you feel yourself becoming submerged in the past, i.e. you feel you're back there in the experience, alert the therapist to this. You may know this before they do. It is possible and preferable to explore and renegotiate the past without re-experiencing it.

How Does This Chapter Relate to Me (Therapist)?

We are challenged throughout this chapter to consider our relationship with certainty: we are asked to listen for the taken-for-granted; we are guided towards the development of an expertise in facilitating conversations of discovery; we are challenged to consider our co-option into believing the truth of ideas and practices that privilege our lives. This includes our 'professional' lives. We can strengthen our selves for the challenge of this work by engaging with a style of listening that alerts us to the gaps in conversation or text. Gaps become apparent when we find our clinical and lived experience/knowings are absent or not reflected in the conversation or literature. Instead of engaging with constructs of right and wrong, we can undertake to name and re-search the gap. These gaps often expose the taken-for-granted. When we become alert to the presence of gaps we are subsequently more able to take part in an enquiry process that deconstructs everyday ideas and practices — the practice of challenging certainty and listening for the gaps is a life strategy rather than a therapeutic strategy. Consequently we may at times find our selves living with marginalisation. This marginalisation may include professional marginalisation as we deconstruct prevailing psychological truths.

Within the therapeutic relationship we engage with people (clients) to construct a living narrative. This living narrative exists in the present moment even when we are reflecting on the past. Our living narratives are never completed, whole or finished. There is no solution. Instead we support people (clients) to engage differently with the self in the present. The self in the present carries both past knowings and future possibilities.

CHAPTER THREE

. . . .

The Therapeutic
Relationship

INTRODUCTION

I became interested in exploring and reflecting on the therapeutic relationship in 1988, when I began working predominantly with people who had been sexually, emotionally and physically abused.[1] For the previous ten years I had worked predominately with children and families. I began working with people who had been abused with these resources:

▼ An attitude of optimism fuelled by a knowledge of people's resilience.

▼ A belief in relating with respect.

▼ A positioning of myself as a discoverer and explorer of people's lived experience.

▼ A confidence that obstacles could be overcome.

▼ A discomfit with conventional therapy wisdom in this area of work.

▼ A feminist critique of the methods and effects of institutional regulation, imposition and privileging of knowledge.

▼ A number of technical skills that had been practised over the previous ten years. This included a dedication to listening for and inquiring around people's strengths and abilities.

When I reflect on the ideas and practices that contributed to how I initially positioned myself with people (clients) in this work, I see before me a multidimensional garment that at first glance appears fragmented and chaotic. It is in perpetual motion, threads loosely tied, seeking new and old connections. There is only a temporary sense of form, shape and direction as this garment exists within movement.

I reiterate that I carried with me into the process of discovery all the therapeutic knowledge I held, but I was particularly assisted by a knowledge of 'externalising the problem' and relative influence questions. (M. White [34]) 'Externalising the problem' enabled me to use a different way of talking, and relative influence questions assisted me to keep listening and enquiring for instances that countered what was then called the 'problem' description.

After a short period of time in this work, I discovered that the idea of 'problem' didn't fit where people's sense of self was under attack and being defined by a range of discursive strategies. These strategies were both supported and maintained by the influential people and institutions that had an impact on people's (clients') lives.

It was while immersed in clinical work that I stopped reading clinical texts. I turned my attention to what had initially attracted me to the Milan group in 1980 — the idea of engaging relationally. Throughout the next ten years I experienced the significance of the therapeutic relationship as a venue for relational experiences and for the negotiation of the meanings made of life events and experiences.

THE THERAPEUTIC RELATIONSHIP
Within Family Therapy the therapeutic relationship has often been either ignored or explained using a psychodynamic explanation. Many family therapists, including narrative therapists, have focused on the therapeutic conversation as a disembodied process of enquiry disconnected from consideration of power relations within the therapeutic relationship. The literature has often elevated intellectual knowledge and technical applications while relegating the therapeutic relationship to obscurity. I have witnessed the consequences of this lack of acknowledgment in my teaching and consultation practice. Many therapists

have been unable to facilitate conversations that enable both therapist and client to negotiate and renegotiate the therapeutic relationship. This inability has often led to serious mis-understandings that have injured the therapeutic relationship. Secondly, therapists have been unable to make use of the moments where there were indicators of change within the therapeutic relationship.

For example, Paul has talked about the lack of trust he holds in anyone in his life. In one session he takes the risk to talk to his therapist about something he's kept secret for years. Although the therapist appreciates this moment he doesn't take the opportunity to explore the steps Paul took to decide to take a risk with trust. Exploration of these steps would contribute to a knowing or unique experience that would then act as a possible resource for Paul's future risk taking with trust in relationships.

I believe we need to reinvent the language, explanations and ethics we use to determine the construction of the therapeutic relationship. This will assist us to respectfully use what happens in the therapeutic relationship as a vehicle for discovery and change. My process of reinvention involved the following:

▼ Re-viewing the language used to describe the therapeutic relationship.

▼ Re-viewing the explanations given for experiences within the therapeutic relationship.

▼ Re-viewing the ethics that shape our intellectual and relational engagement within the therapeutic relationship.

Throughout this re-view I used a relational externalising conversational process. Externalising is both a technical ability to engage with conversation in a particular way and an ethic. It is the fulcrum for my journey of discovery. Before reflecting on my re-view of the therapeutic relationship, imagine for a moment talking with someone, a stranger, about terrifying thoughts, feelings and events that have in the past engulfed you in despair or resulted in physical or emotional attack from others. You begin to talk, tentatively at first, watching for signs of danger and then with growing momentum you dare to speak the unspeakable. As the words form and move from you into the air, it is as though you are hearing them for the first time. The other person listens intently and respectfully. Questions are asked using a tone of voice and pace that reflect compassion. These questions surprise you because you feel a response before you have a response. You feel safe, cared for and seen by another person. Perhaps this is the first time you've felt understood or heard.

Imagine this and then wonder:

▼ What would this relationship mean to you?

▼ Would you want more of this experience in your life?

▼ What feelings might you experience in regard to the other person in the relationship?

Therapies that don't resource people (clients) by providing information about both the therapeutic relationship understanding and the possible experiences within this relationship, risk subjecting people (clients) to powerlessness and dependency. I believe that people (clients) are entitled to an environment in therapy where the meanings of and experiences in the therapeutic relationship are available for ongoing exploration, negotiation and re-view. In order to support this I believe it is important to consider the therapeutic relationship understanding that we use.

Once we have articulated the therapeutic relationship understanding it is then available for ethical scrutiny. I am particularly interested in exposing the pivotal role that the therapeutic relationship under-standing has in determining how we situate our selves in the thera-peutic relationship. The understandings we hold will either position us as the holders and conveyers of knowledge or as the negotiators of the possible meanings that can be made of experiences, feelings and ideas.

Interpretative therapies use people's (clients') experience of strong feelings within the therapeutic relationship as a knowledge resource which reflects early childhood relationships (i.e. parents). This reliance on interpretation inevitably results in therapists imposing meanings rather than exploring the strategies for making sense of life events, experiences and strong feelings.

In moving away from interpretative therapies we situate our selves on the boundary of knowing and not knowing. In this place we bring all of our selves, however we position our selves within the therapeutic relationship, in a unique way. Throughout this chapter I attempt to describe this unique way. I would like, however, to signal a persistent concern, which is that my writing of these ideas will reduce the complexity of a dynamic process. The complexity I am referring to is beyond an intellectual process of describing a set of ideas that determines a practitioner's thinking and positioning of her/himself. It encompasses a range of abilities including the ability to be emotionally and intellectually available to the therapeutic relationship, with enough detachment to make partial sense of self and other information. By partial sense I mean the putting into language of an incomplete explanation, a possibility. This possibility is introduced to the therapeutic conversation as a wondering, a question, in contrast to a certainty or knowledge statement. In exploring this possibility we are more engaged with the present moment. The therapeutic relationship thus becomes a site and resource for discovering experiences and knowledge in respect to the self in relationship to another.

THE THERAPEUTIC RELATIONSHIP UNDERSTANDING
The therapeutic relationship understanding can be simply described. However, it is extremely complex in its enactment. It requires the following:

▼ Commitment to dedicate 100% attention to the therapeutic environment and conversation.

▼ Engagement in a self-reflective process that discriminates between thoughts and feelings that belong to the therapeutic conversation, and thoughts and feelings that belong outside of the therapeutic conversation.

▼ Ongoing monitoring of the balance between connection and detachment within the therapeutic relationship.

▼ Preparation for a style of conversation that negotiates and exposes meaning. This includes exposing the consequences for people's (clients') lives of adhering to one meaning paradigm over another.

Description Of The Therapeutic Relationship Understanding
This is the understanding that I bring to the therapeutic relationship.

The therapeutic relationship is a special relationship in that people (clients) experiment with trusting another person (therapist) with their vulnerability. The vulnerability may range from uncertainty, for example about parenting, to disclosure of intimate thoughts and acts. Therapist and client/s are both participants in the therapeutic conversation, yet each plays a distinctive part. People (client/s) identify, reflect on and re-view emotionally and intellectually the areas of concern and interest. They participate actively in the therapeutic conversation both within and outside of the therapeutic process. The therapist directs her/his energy, skill, knowledge, thoughts, actions and care towards the other/s for a specified time. She/he facilitates an enquiry process that provides people (clients) with an opportunity to negotiate and renegotiate the intellectual and emotional meanings ascribed to events and ideas in relation to the self and others. People (client/s) on agreeing to enter the therapeutic relationship indicate both a willingness to consider trusting the therapist within a process of discovery, and a commitment to dedicate time and energy to self discoveries. The therapist, on agreeing to enter the therapeutic relationship, indicates a willingness to engage with a process of discovery together with a commitment to dedicate time and energy to these discoveries.

The 'therapeutic relationship understanding' provides a broad explanatory frame that allows for a wide range of experiences within the therapeutic relationship. The construction of the frame itself highlights the special nature of this relationship, in that it stands separate from other relationship descriptions. In offering a description of the therapeutic relationship understanding we assist people (clients) to engage in further exploration of the implications of the therapeutic relationship, thus establishing a climate of collaboration and negotiation.

The 'therapeutic relationship understanding' appears to be a very simple understanding; it is however complex in its practice. There are very few instances in life where one person (the therapist) dedicates 100% attention towards the other (the client). Attending requires a multiplicity of skills that are rarely articulated, let alone taught. I believe that engaging in the therapeutic relationship requires us to find a balance between connection and detachment. Connection provides us with an enquiry resource beyond the language used by people to represent experience. Connection assists us to listen for intonation, emotions, body sensations, visions, dreams, the imagination and for what is partially said. Detachment assists us to stand back from the experience and to stand back from the sense made of the experience. If from this standing back position I decide that this knowing belongs to the relationship and not to my life experiences, then I can decide how to use the information so that it enters the conversation as a partial knowing, a possibility. The most effective method for doing this is an enquiry process. For example, 'Just before the words froze, I was listening to you and this thought/wondering came to my mind. It may not be at all relevant to you, what do you think?' Or, 'I noticed a difference today. You seem to be annoyed with the questions, maybe its not annoyed, I don't know. Have you noticed a difference?'

From the standing back position within the session, I may decide that my listening to the other (client) is effected by my lived experiences. When this happens my thinking reflections do **not** enter the therapeutic relationship. Self reflection from within the therapeutic conversation is often difficult to achieve. We may need to hold a thought or feeling and re-search its origins out of the therapeutic conversations using supervision or consultation. If we believe that the thought and/or feeling belongs to the therapeutic relationship, we then explore ways to tentatively introduce a re-searching of this thought and/ or feeling. In the subsequent enquiry we create a context of wondering that can be refuted, added to and/or changed by people (clients). For example:

Kath:	I just felt overwhelmed by the way the family members seemed to talk over every change point that was brought forward. I'd hear something that one of the family members had done differently and then as I re-searched it someone else would jump in with something else.
Johnella:	Let's talk for a minute about feeling overwhelmed and what was happening that supported that feeling. You would catch a moment of difference, where something had changed for family members. As you moved to explore this, what happened?
Kath:	People would just talk about something else.
Johnella:	What sort of talk was it, was it defensive talk, angry talk, taking the attention talk?
Kath:	Um, it was defending talk. Like, look I've done this and this really well.
Johnella:	When people are involved in defending talk, what do you think they're listening for? Imagine you're using defending talk, what would you be listening for in the conversation in order to feel the need to defend?

Kath:	Criticism I suppose, maybe I'd be looking for criticism.
Johnella:	Okay. Do you think it's possible that family members are so on guard against criticism that it's difficult to hear what's happening that's different or positive?
Kath:	That sounds possible.
Johnella:	Okay. Lets experiment with ways you can bring your experience in the family sessions forwards and then re-search with the family what they make of this.

The 100% attending to the other requires us to listen to our thinking, feeling, imagination, theories and body. In this listening we actively determine how and if this knowing relates to the therapeutic relation-ship understanding.

When the therapeutic relationship understanding is made available to people (clients) at the beginning of the therapy, people (clients) are provided with a resource to begin negotiating the limitations and strengths of the therapeutic relationship[2]. The implication that the thera-peutic relationship is a negotiation between therapist and client within the therapeutic relationship bounds, enables people (clients) to continu-ously reflect on thoughts, feelings and expectations that may or may not fit within the therapeutic relationship understanding. For example:

Laura (client):	I know the limitations of the therapeutic relationship, however I'm beginning to feel that I might be depending too much on the relationship.
Johnella:	What tells you that this depending on the relationship is happening?
Laura:	Well, it feels as though this is the only place I feel I can be real. I just so look forward to coming and that feels not very helpful. I know that the therapy is going to end. I just don't want to rely on it too much.
Johnella:	Okay. Can we look at what has happened here that has contributed to the experiences of realness. If we think about these conditions for a bit we could then reflect on places, people and ways to experiment with realness outside of the therapy room.

In this example we (therapist and client) are beginning to explore what 'depending too much' or 'relying too much' means to the person's (client's) life and to the therapy. This exploration is preferable to offering people (clients) reassurance or minimalising their concerns by explanations that normalise these concerns. When we negotiate the meanings that can be made of experiences within the therapeutic relationship we are reflecting the ethic that the therapeutic relationship is a collaboration.

RE-SEARCHING THE THERAPEUTIC RELATIONSHIP
UNDERSTANDING

The therapeutic relationship understanding that I use in my work carries an intention — it is broadly based in order to allow for the variation of needs and experiences within any negotiated therapeutic relationship.

Within this broad base, I continue to engage with naming and re-searching experience within the therapeutic relationship. The position of ongoingly re-searching people's (clients') experience of the therapeutic relationship assists me to ongoingly engage with the evolution of my ideas and practices. Below is part of a conversation between myself and Leslie which occurred after we completed therapy. Leslie and I talked approximately six months after the therapy concluded. It was this conversation that prompted me to continue to provide opportunities throughout therapy to discuss ideas about, and experiences of, the therapeutic relationship.

Leslie's description of the therapeutic relationship

Johnella: I was interested in your thoughts about the therapeutic relationship. We've talked about this earlier and you had some interesting thoughts about that.

Leslie: That became an issue for me when I got to a stage in the therapy where I recognised that I had everything I needed to survive but didn't really need to carry on with the counselling on a routine basis. It was always going to be there, and I wasn't being shut out or anything, but I acted like I was, because I was very mad. I was kind've high at the first instance. I was really high. I've graduated. How wonderful! And the next day I just went 'foonk'. And it felt like this huge void in my life like kind've what's going to fill it?

And I also felt I was angry with you. But it was anger on a funny level because I knew that you hadn't actually done anything wrong. I didn't feel that. I was just angry because I was left with nothing, because you and the whole proof that therapy had been a really huge thing in my life was gone. And I had been one of your clients and part of your work. And those are two very different perceptions. And I kind've felt like we had built up something. Because, for me to trust you, to say the things to you that I've said, then we should be the best of friends that would run into each other when we need someone. That's in my reality. That's how it is.

But because we had kind've like a, sort of, working relationship, from your point view, then you weren't going to be my best friend. So what I questioned was what happened to all that was built up. Okay, I've been through my process and I've come a long way, but what about the relationship we had.

And why . . . if we were friends, I'd be able to ring you up and have a chat and just keep some contact, when I felt like it. If I wanted contact I had to have a crisis to see you again. I'm going to have to have a problem. Why can't I just ring you and say, 'Hi, I've done this and done that?'

And I was really mad about that for a while. And I did think, it was a while ago, but I remember that it was quite intense.

I was quite depressed and feeling very funny about it. And for a wee while I thought ah, maybe I've got a crush on you, and I thought that maybe this is one of those therapist crushes and I thought . . . and then I've thought about it, and I thought, no that's not it. It could actually have been interpreted like that but it wasn't. It was just because it wasn't a friendship, and there wasn't the counselling any more. So what was it? And I think it just felt like this thing had gone.

There was a gap and I talked to someone about it and

they just said it sounds like you need to grieve. And that really clarified it for me actually.

That made me . . . but I wished that I'd been told that sooner, about grieving our relationship. And it was really helpful once what I was going through was put into words. And that allowed me just to grieve and let it go.

I kind've had, by the time I'd talked to someone and they said, ah yeah it sound like you just need to grieve. I had kind've let it go, but still wondered about it. It just felt so painful. I thought, why after all this, do I have to go through this pain now. And it was helpful to eventually get it verbalised.

Johnella: When you wrote that letter . . . what you said was very interesting. You were quite clear about the relationship. I thought the letter was part of trying to explain the relationship to your self and to me. You were saying, 'The reality is that you know all these things about me but I don't know much about your life and if I did I mightn't like you.' I thought that was a very strong statement. You were saying that the relationship had been a certain way and that's been good for you, but in terms of me as a person, in an ongoing relationship, it's possible I'm not the sort of person you'd be friendly with. It's a strong statement. It's a strong knowing that you had about the relationship.

Leslie: Yeah, because I thought, ah I want to be your friend, kind of thing. And then I thought, I don't know you. I don't know you at all. All I know about you is in your role as the counsellor. We just might not have anything in common. And how can I want you as a friend when I don't even know you? You know what I mean? Um, yeah.

Johnella: What do you think would be the best way to describe this special sort of relationship where there is a connection on a very deep level, given some of the things we've talked about in terms of trust? What's the best way to describe it do you think? Let's say somebody came to you and said, I'm thinking of going to a counsellor?

Leslie: I guess it's very special because it's not like a relationship with friends or anything. And it's very intense but it's intense emotionally for the client. But it's not like an emotional intenseness between you and I, and I think that's what makes it unique. Because you've got one person going through this incredibly intense emotional stuff but the other person is kind of facilitating it.

Johnella: What stops it? What do you think stops a person, like a client, from seeing it as their own strong emotional connection or response, as being something between the therapist and the client? What helps distinguish it? What makes the difference? Is it something that I do? Is it something that the therapist does? Or is it something that you do? Or is it something that we both do together?

Leslie: I feel that it's like a boundary that is there, that we probably both set up. That it's just there. What I get from you is that you're very clear about your boundaries. And probably in among it all, when I've felt vulnerable or felt certain things, that's been really good to know your boundaries. And I think that's really important, that counsellors have that really clear. And it's not like you've had to spell it out or something. It's just something that I've got from you really clearly and that. I think that's really important, it's just something that's been there.

Johnella: I think that's really interesting.

This conversation raises numerous questions including these: How do people (clients) make sense of strong emotional responses in therapy? What relationship metaphors are available to the making sense process? What supports the emotional intensity remaining with the person versus between both people? I discuss these questions under the headings:

▼ Where does the boundary lie?
▼ Therapeutic relationships can be different.
▼ Negotiating the relationship.

WHERE DOES THE BOUNDARY LIE ?

The term 'boundary' is common in counselling and psychology texts. It has been used to distinguish the therapeutic relationship from other relationships and to provide safety for both therapist and client. This conventional use of boundary acts to separate therapist and client, and is often experienced as sitting between therapist and client. On one side there's the therapist's professional self and on the other side the client's self. It is understood that neither person can transgress this boundary although it is ultimately the therapist's responsibility to maintain the boundary. I don't like this representation of boundary as it feels like a barrier, something that sits between myself and the other. I prefer to conceptualise the therapeutic relationship as existing within a boundary that surrounds the relationship. The boundary consists of an agreed to, mutual understanding of the therapeutic relationship. The therapeutic relationship is negotiated and renegotiated within the bounds the therapeutic relationship understanding. This boundary surrounds, supports and holds the therapeutic relationship, enabling me to bring to it all of myself. This boundary holds within it an extraordinary relationship to which I believe there are no other relationship parallels in western cultural life.

As discussed earlier, we as therapists are required to engage with self-reflective practices that help us to discriminate between the ideas, theories and feelings that may act as a resource to the therapeutic relationship and those ideas, theories and feelings that don't belong to the therapeutic relationship.

Traditional representation of boundary

Therapist | Client

Alternative representation of boundary

The therapeutic relationship understanding provides the boundary that surrounds the therapeutic relationship, setting it apart from other relationships in life. It remains however a 'real' relationship within which people (clients) can develop relationship knowledge and relationship resources. For example, the therapeutic work with people (clients) who have experienced betrayals of trust by significant others necessitates a focus on the experience of the therapeutic relationship in the present moment. This focus allows us (therapist and client) to negotiate the conditions of safety necessary for people (clients) to take risks in trusting the therapeutic relationship. In taking a risk with trust of the therapeutic relationship, people (clients) are provided with an opportunity to explore a unique experience of safety in relationship.

THERAPEUTIC RELATIONSHIPS CAN BE DIFFERENT

Therapeutic relationships can be as varied as any other relationships. There is a substantial experiential difference between a therapeutic relationship that ends after five sessions and focuses on a young woman's fear of public speaking and a therapeutic relationship that ends after forty sessions and focuses on a young woman's search to escape the effects of terror.

Like all relationships, the therapeutic relationship changes over time. Like all relationships, this change can sometimes show itself in emotions or actions that are surprising. These experiential differences can promote an important conversation that names and explores the strategies people (clients) use to position themselves within the therapeutic relationship, knowing both its limitations and its strengths. When we use a relational externalising conversation, the therapeutic relationship knowledge and experiences can be explored in their context. This style of conversation supports both therapist and client to resist totalising explanations for changes within the therapeutic relationship. Conversations that explore people's (clients') experiences within the therapeutic relationship are based on the premise people (clients) can use the therapeutic relationship as a relationship resource, while also acting to protect themselves from over-estimating the availability of the therapeutic relationship resource. For example:

Raewyn: It is really tempting to rely on this relationship. Coming here feels like an oasis.

Johnella: What happens when this temptation to rely on the relationship is around?

Raewyn: I know it's appealing, but I also know that it doesn't help me. It could keep me dependent on the therapy and I don't want that. I want to have a life outside of therapy, it's just so hard sometimes.

Johnella: What does this relying on the relationship mean? How do you know that relying is happening?

Raewyn: Well, if I'm in a social situation and I start getting scared I say to myself, What would Johnella think about this?

Johnella: Do you answer your self?

Raewyn: Yes, most of the times.

Johnella: How does the answer effect the scared feeling?

Raewyn: Some of the time it reduces it, but I feel I shouldn't be relying on you.

Johnella: How is it that you can guess my thinking so well?

Raewyn: I don't know if it's exactly your thinking. I suppose I remember the things we talk about.

Johnella: Raewyn, it seems you can utilise the memory of our talking to resource you when fear's around. Have you got an idea that using your memory resource is somehow connected with reliance?

Raewyn: I think I have.

THE THERAPEUTIC RELATIONSHIP OVER TIME
In the circumstances where the experience of the therapeutic relationship has changed, the therapeutic relationship understanding takes on new meaning. Over time people's (clients') understanding can move from an intellectual understanding to a living understanding that can be re-searched in practice.

For example, Chrissy (client) was interested in an exploration of what constitutes love in relationships. This interest was provoked by wondering how she would name the feelings she has within the therapeutic relationship.

Opportunities for exploration and discovery occur when we are willing to engage in the ongoing development of a *practice understanding* of the therapeutic relationship understanding. The *practice understanding* of the therapeutic relationship challenges us to engage with the possibility that people could experience strong emotions within it. In order to prepare for a therapeutic conversation that explores these strong emotions, we need to consider both our thoughts and our engagement with strong emotions and where these strong emotions sit within the therapeutic relationship understanding. The exploration is contained within our understanding of the therapeutic relationship.

Engaging with the ongoing development of the *practice understanding* requires us to continually re-view our professional practice guidelines with colleagues, consultants and supervisors. This re-view protects us from mindlessly engaging with ethics as rules and moves us into a living engagement with ethics.

In the following example I demonstrate engaging with therapy rules about time. Instead of cementing our engagement with time into time slots of 1 hour or 1½ hours per session, I'm re-viewing the premises that support this convention:

▼ What are the ideas that promote our adherence to valuing one time frame over another?

▼ What is the history of these ideas?

▼ What are the institutional values that support the adherence to one time frame over another?

▼ How does time given to therapeutic sessions and time between sessions impact on people's (clients') abilities to engage with new ideas?

▼ Is time an issue for negotiation within the therapeutic relationship? What supports the negotiation or lack of negotiation?

▼ If people (clients) engaged with time differently, how would we set about re-searching this?

▼ How do various lengths of therapeutic time effect our ability to contribute to the therapeutic conversation?

Professional practice guidelines are established by members of the professional classes. This group can be captured by a belief that the construction of rules is supported by therapy truths that act to protect both therapist and client. When we follow these rules without enquiry we risk mindless acceptance. Our mindless acceptance of rules has the potential to benefit therapists while limiting the arenas that support people (clients) to engage effectively in their lives.

NEGOTIATING THE THERAPEUTIC RELATIONSHIP UNDERSTANDING IN PRACTICE

I have mentioned negotiating and renegotiating the therapeutic relationship several times. This is only possible if people (clients) have some sense of what the therapeutic relationship understanding is in practice. I have found it useful to provide people with my description of the therapeutic relationship understanding as a beginning point for the conversation. Over time people (clients) are as curious as I am about the relationship in practice. This creates a context of openness for re-searching people's (clients') wonderings, puzzlements and worries about the therapeutic relationship. This supports people (clients) to actively engage in re-searching their experience of the therapeutic relationship.

If the therapeutic relationship understanding is withheld from people (clients) then it is inevitable that people (clients) will search for descriptions and meanings of the extra-ordinary therapeutic relationship. This will often lead them towards comparisons with other important life relationships such as mother, father, lover, partner. When we support this direction for our interpretation purposes we create a therapeutic relationship that encourages dependency and elevates the therapist's expertise or all-knowing status. One person (client) expressed her thoughts on this possibility rather succinctly, 'If I thought you were my good mother, then I would never leave!' Alternatively, if we ignore the therapeutic relationship understanding we risk the development of a strong silence between our selves and the people we work with as people (clients) struggle to cope with strong feelings. When these strong feelings are self-defined, for example as romantic love, a person (client) can vacillate between shame and desperation. We can also experience desperation in this context as we struggle to understand the person's (client's) behaviour, which may reflect the effects of desperation or shame.

Provision of a therapeutic relationship understanding doesn't preclude the experience of strong emotions in the therapeutic relationship. People's (clients') experiences of the central relationships in their lives may result in their bringing their expectations of these relationships into the therapeutic relationship. Whenever I experience behaviour and emotions within the relationship that I don't understand, it provides me with an opportunity to explore the meaning of this. An exploration of meaning is a very different experience from one where we provide people (clients) with an interpretation of meaning.

For example, if a person (client) has experienced her primary relationships throughout life as 'letting her down' then it is possible that she is very sensitive and alert to this. In therapy we can identify the behaviour or thinking indicators of 'being let down' so we can both remain alert to the appearance of 'being let down' within the therapeutic relationship. If these indicators appear we can get to know how they operate in the person's (client's) life and find ways to challenge them in a climate of safety. This provides the person (client) with a unique experience in relationship to another. This experience can then act as a knowledge and experiential platform that supports other relationships including a relationship with the self. We can begin an exploration in a non-judgmental way by wondering about meaning, as follows:

> Johnella: I've noticed that if I don't do what you expect of me there is a lot of disappointment and anger. For example, last week you thought I would read the level of distress well enough to suggest an earlier time. When I didn't you became very angry. I'd like to talk a little about this expectation because I don't think I understand it. Is that okay?

PRIVATE THOUGHTS AND FEELINGS

I believe that the therapeutic relationship understanding requires us to avail our energy, skill, knowledge, thoughts, actions and care to the conversation. In order to respect that commitment, thoughts and feelings that impact on the relationship need to be made explicit to supervisors/consultants. For example, I experienced irritation when working with Paul, a 36-year-old property developer. Throughout our conversations he would introduce information about his latest sexual interest. This information seemed to be introduced randomly and would cut across the topics we were talking about. Paul's body posture, voice tone and facial expressions would change as he recounted his

story. When I reflected on my irritation, I decided that I didn't know
what Paul's intention was in telling these stories. I had some ideas hence
my irritation, however I didn't know. I then developed a number of
questions in order to explore this further. Here are some possible
questions:

▼ Paul, we were talking about the people who supported you in
  your growing up and you began to tell me in detail about a
  woman you are interested in. I'm wondering what we would have
  talked about if we had kept talking about your growing up time?
▼ What feeling did the talk about growing up provoke?
▼ If we had continued the talking, do you think a feeling would
  have come forward?
▼ What feeling would you guess that might have been?
▼ Do you think these stories about who you're sexually interested
  in tells me something about you that you think is important for
  me to know?
▼ What do you want these stories to tell me about your qualities?

These questions are possibilities for beginning an enquiry that allows
me to explore what I don't yet know. Not to listen to my irritation would
leave a silent judgment that would have huge implications for the
therapeutic relationship.

On agreeing to enter the therapeutic relationship, we surrender the
right to private thoughts and feelings in respect of the therapeutic
relationship. The idea that we have a responsibility to surrender our
right to private thoughts and feelings in respect of the therapeutic
relationship is based on the premise that these ideas and feelings have
enormous implications for the therapeutic conversation. The notion of
surrendering our right to private thoughts and feelings, challenges
therapeutic practices that represent the therapist as a detached
pervader of psychological truths. Instead, this conversation relies on a
negotiation of the meanings made of life experiences and therapeutic
experiences. Whenever I use myself as a potential resource within the
therapeutic relationship I attend to all my thoughts and feelings. This
attention precludes censorship of strong thoughts and feelings. The
process of attention involves a self reflective and/or other-initiated
conversation that uses a relational externalising conversation. It is
important that we provide our selves with opportunities outside of

therapy to say out loud, without censorship, what we have been thinking and feeling. A relational externalising process will provide us with an opportunity to re-search and negotiate the meaning of these thoughts and feelings. We can then determine whether these thoughts and feelings belong to the therapeutic conversation. If they do, we can engage with naming the relationship experience in order to practice a tentative enquiry within the therapeutic relationship. This practice contrasts with the practice of interpretative therapies, where the hierarchy of knowing moves from therapist to supervisor. Within the latter paradigm the supervisor will interpret and provide an explanation for strong thoughts and feelings. It also contrasts therapies which privilege technical applications while ignoring the therapeutic relationship where discoveries are made. This lack of acknowledgement of the therapeutic relationship suggests that it is possible for therapists to detach from their experiences. Strong thoughts and feelings within this paradigm are thought to be resolved by the therapist detaching from the self in order to seek 'The Right Question.'

The conversation we engage in with supervisors/consultants is directed towards understanding our thoughts and feelings in a way that enhances the therapeutic relationship. If this is not possible then the therapeutic relationship is unable to be sustained. Instead we accept responsibility for the end of the therapeutic relationship and refer the person (client) elsewhere. This process requires considerable preparation with a supervisor/consultant[3] and may require inclusion of a third party in order to negotiate the ending.

WHAT ABOUT US (THERAPISTS)?

Therapists are ideally positioned to be agents of social control. We work with the disenfranchised, those who have been most hurt by the contradictions within which we are all situated. We are often required to submit to institutional requirements that objectify, categorise and act on these people (clients). We may be intellectually and technically skilled; however, what prepares us to be emotionally, physically and spiritfully on the edge of someone's life experience when their experience is radically different from our own? What prepares us to face the contradictions and find a place to rest within them? What prepares us to make our selves available to another and another and another person? What prepares us to be constantly watchful for the inevitable capturing of radical ideas by conservative institutions? What prepares us to remain connected with our selves while stepping back to wonder about our thinking and experiences? What prepares us to be supported by what is known while being available to discover new knowings in the exploration of people's lived experience?

Rarely are we prepared by institutions of learning to meet these questions and thus we struggle. Many of us succumb to the safety of certainty and prescription, easing our selves into a professional role that categorises and diagnoses those who have apparently failed the societal success criteria.

Most people begin the work as therapists and counsellors because the ideas and practices are exciting and interesting. Perhaps there is a desire to be of service to others. We all choose the work because it satisfies us in some way. The assumption of satisfaction allows us to name and re-search this satisfaction. The re-search may bring to our attention a loss of satisfaction or a search for satisfaction that is limiting our therapeutic ability. When I reflect on my career the criteria for satisfaction has changed substantially over the years. The knowledge that my relationship with this work will change over time, resources me to plan for development and change.

These questions may help to name and re-search satisfaction:

▼ What interests and excites you about the work?

▼ How have you maintained this interest and excitement?

▼ What or who supports you to continue in the work?

▼ How do you benefit from your ongoing participation in the work?

▼ What abilities have you developed and strengthened over the years?

▼ When you look at your self in one year, five years, 10 years, how would you like to answer the above questions?

If we use the therapeutic relationship in order to fulfill needs such as being liked or loved or needed, we will create dependency. If we seek to be liked, loved or needed within the therapeutic relationship we will indirectly or directly inform people (clients) of those needs. People (clients) will attempt to comply in order to be 'good' clients. This may be enjoyed until some limit/line is crossed, for example, being tele-phoned at home or an increase in demands for time. If the response to crossing a limit/line is to react strongly by setting limits on these behaviours then this suggests that people (clients) have the problem. People (clients) are then provided with further evidence of their inadequacy. Interpretative explanations for these behaviours, which can include making psychological connections with people's (clients') behaviour and past parental relationships, once again positions people (clients) as having the problem.

When we have introduced our needs into the therapeutic relationship, the power differential can assist us to direct attention away from our selves while directing attention towards others (clients). This attention is never beneficial for people (clients). Acknowledgement of the power differential accords us the responsibility to continually re-view our participation within the therapeutic relationship. One part of this re-view process is to consider these questions:

▼ How it is that we have chosen and continue to choose this work over other work?

▼ What is the satisfaction we find in engaging with this work?

The re-view process involves reflecting on our participation in the making of meaning within the therapeutic conversation. We can do this through practicing self and other reflection that is assisted by strategies to reflect in the work as well as on the work. Reflecting in the work occurs when we make our actual practice apparent.

IDEAS ON SELF AND OTHER REFLECTIONS

The therapeutic relationship understanding requires a willingness to be transparent to our selves, and to others such as supervisors, consultants and colleagues. Transparency occurs when we make available thoughts, feelings, values, judgments and intuitions for self and other reflection. Therapists are members of a community that gives status to certain ideas, values and attributes. We may benefit from this status and thus find our selves complying with ideas and practices that invisibilize and oppress others.

Ideas about transference and countertransference are based on an assumption that experiences within the therapeutic relationship are made sense of by drawing on early childhood experiences. The 'truth' of these early childhood experiences is determined by psychological theories. Whenever we hold these grand psychological theories we risk imposing them, as the true explanation, on people's (clients') thoughts, feelings and experiences. The theories are delivered as comprehensive truths and consequently they disallow further exploration. When we are strongly influenced by grand psychological theories, our thinking and enquiry of people's (clients') experience becomes limited and sometimes stuck.

For example, Mary was consulting with me about Stefan (a client). She reported that he was feeling hopeless about his life. Mary said she was also feeling a little hopeless about the therapy because he'd had such a horrific life. When I interviewed Mary around the hopelessness, we discovered the presence of grand psychological theories. These theories included an all-encompassing theory of psychological damage that predicted limitations and restraints. I asked Mary to put these to one side for a moment and then interviewed Mary as Stefan. In this process Mary demonstrated her knowing of Stefan, which included emotional knowing. In the interview we discovered that Stefan, with great courage and determination, had given up alcohol four years ago. The interview focused on re-searching Stefan's abilities and the subsequent consequences for his life without alcohol.

Before this interview Mary had been tempted to join Stefan in hopelessness and provide him with an explanation for his psychological state using grand psychological theories. If she had acted on this she would have missed an opportunity to discover, with Stefan, his amazing resilience.

This example illustrates the dangers inherent in any interpretative approach that uses psychological theory as truth rather than as one possibility among many. In order to hold numerous explanations, including the possibility that there are explanations beyond our knowing, the enquiry process needs to be one which uncovers with people (clients) what they know, but often don't know they know.

The above example of my consultation process involved an interview that required the consultee and consultant to engage with an exploration of lived experience. This exploration brought to prominence an account of Stefan's life that challenged the consultee's psychological theory. The psychological theory had been so predominant that the consultee was unable to move past it. *Moving past it means holding the psychological theory as one possibility among many.* This thinking positions us as discoverers rather than interpreters or knowers of people's (clients') lives. Positioning our selves as discoverers requires a self and other reflective practice[4] that emphasises a practical deconstructive process. We are listening for those themes that are central to meaning making. We do this with the knowledge that these themes exist within the protective environment created by the privileging of one discursive regime over others. Once these themes are exposed and high-lighted, the meanings that are made of the language used to represent this central experience is available for re-view.

Central to my work is the presupposition that psychological theory and practice is always situated within an historical and cultural context which determines the frame of reference for making sense of individuals, family and group behaviour. If the frame of reference is unacknowledged then its invisibility prevents critique. Those in the helping professions risk imposing meanings that protect political interests rather than people's (clients') interests. By political interests I am referring to ideas and practices that serve the dominant group within any community.[5]

People (clients) who attend counselling have judged themselves according to invisible, taken-for-granted values and ideas. We can make visible/apparent the privileging of certain ideas, values and attributes, and enquire how these relate to people's (clients') lives. However, we can only do this if we continually engage in exposing the ideas, values and attributes that shape the meaning we make of our lives. This process is lifelong. While we are forever immersed in discursive regimes we nevertheless continue to alter our intellectual and experiential understandings over time. This knowing prepares us to engage with processes of self and other reflection.[6]

This reflective process can help us to remain alert to the institutional privileging of ideas, values and attributes. Consider these questions:

▼ What ideas/values and attributes are privileged within the community? (Particularly focus on culture, sexuality, gender and socio-economic status.)

▼ When and how did you first learn that certain ideas, values and attributes were given higher status than others?

▼ How have you benefited from the privileging of these ideas, values and attributes?

▼ Have the benefits altered over time?

▼ In what ways have you suffered from the privileging of these ideas, values and attributes? For example,

● What are the implications for relationships when people are preoccupied with certainty thinking?

- What are the implications for psychological theory of an elevation of language that represents logical thought over languaging emotional engagement?

- What are the implications for the health of indigenous people when Western medicine is elevated over indigenous healing knowledges?

▼ Has the suffering changed over time?

▼ In your suffering, what helped you to challenge the truth of the privileged ideas, values and attributes?

▼ How have the benefits stopped or aided you in challenging certain ideas, values and attributes?

▼ How do you remain alert to the experience of others when it may be outside your experience?

▼ What knowledge resources strengthen you in your life?

▼ What relationship resources strengthen you in your life?

▼ What or who will support you to be available for the critiquing of all psychological theory and practice?

In the therapeutic enquiry we assume a multiplicity of possible conversational directions, therefore we also assume a privileging of one conversational direction over another. We reduce the risk of imposing meaning by asking questions that support people (clients) to respond in such a way as to challenge, add to or change our thinking or belief. Questions that expose the institutional privileging of some ideas, values and attributes direct the enquiry towards an exploration of the relationship between personal experience and the political context. By moving between the personal and the political, we reduce the likelihood that we will act to support the oppression of others.

SELF AND OTHER REFLECTIONS WITH A FOCUS ON FAMILY AND RELATIONSHIP

I am referring here to our (therapists') families, rather than those families who come to our counselling rooms. Being interested in the ways people negotiate and conduct their lives is an important attribute to have in this work. This interest involves the minutiae of daily life as well as the cultural determinants that impact on families. This interest can and, in fact, at times needs to be, turned homeward towards our selves. Families provide the environment for intimate relationship training from which a sense of self in relationship emerges. The intimate nature of this training acts to invisibilize it until a situation provokes a response or a way of thinking that surprises us or others. We can make sense of our life experiences in ways that are limiting but comfortable; when confronted with someone else's similar experience we may find our selves avoiding the topic or responding inappropriately. For example, a male therapist who experienced his mother as being overly involved in his life to the degree that he perceived she had limited his life experiences became critical of a single parent he was interviewing. The single parent was a woman who was concerned about the behaviour of her adolescent son. The therapist primarily focused his attention on the parent. His tone of voice and the direction and emphasis of his questioning indicated his disapproval. The client responded with irritation and anger which in turn confirmed the therapist's original hypothesis.

This and similar situations are inevitable without an environment that enables transparency in the work together with a self and other reflective practice. I use the following ideas for a self and other reflective practice:

1. We take time to articulate our understanding of our relationship with family members both past and present. When I refer to family I am referring to those people that you consider family. This may include non-biological and biological connections. Once articulated this understanding can be explored using an enquiry process with a skilled, experienced and trusted interviewer. This will provide an opportunity to experience self discovery utilising an enquiry. During the enquiry process the ideas available to make sense of experiences will be considered. For example:

    Bess: My father never told me he loved me. Often as a child I would consider that he didn't love me at all. When I reflect on the past now, I remember that he would often make things for my sister and me. If I think, would dad have considered his making of things reflective of his love for me, I'd say yes, yes he would.

    In this conversation what was considered to reflect love was re-viewed.

2. At times in our career we take the opportunity to re-view our understanding of our self in relationship to significant others.

3. We hold an expectation that understandings about life experiences alter over time according to access to alternative theoretical knowledges (e.g. feminism) and access to experiential knowledge (e.g. parenting).

4. We search out alternative knowing through theoretical texts, literature, film, art, conversation, play, experience, language, etc.

5. We find ways to explore and experiment with the translation of ideas and beliefs into a practice that reflects those ideas and beliefs.

WHERE AM I IN THIS RELATIONSHIP?

Narrative and Systemic Family Therapies commonly leave the therapist out of descriptions of the therapeutic relationship. A proliferation of articles on the technical application of ideas together with success stories has unwittingly created a context where trainees and experienced therapists ignore their own experiences in search of the 'right' question? For example, June (therapist) felt increasingly uncomfortable about the demands that Ann (client) was making for extra clinical times. These demands escalated, culminating in Ann spontaneously turning up several times a day hoping to talk with June between sessions. Ann expressed suicidal feelings and was clearly feeling very desperate. June ignored her own feelings of discomfort about Ann's demands for the relationship. She set limits on meeting times and during sessions focused on an enquiry process that would free Ann from depression.

The putting aside of feelings of discomfort deprived both June and Ann of the opportunity to negotiate the therapeutic relationship. Consequently the therapy became stuck with both June and Ann feeling very desperate. Negotiating the therapeutic relationship would involve discussing expectations, limitations, experiences and the meaning made of the relationship. When we use a relational externalising conversation to negotiate the therapeutic relationship we sustain an environment of exploration. An environment of exploration directs our (therapist's and client's) attention towards the therapeutic relationship as a vehicle for discovery.

In order to use our selves as a resource in the negotiation of the therapeutic relationship understanding we need to allow our selves to express our thoughts, feeling and experiences without censorship. Lack of censorship allows us to speak fully while knowing that an enquiry process will assist us to make sense of our thoughts, feelings and experiences. In speaking out loud I frequently find a theme that provides me with language that supports a relational externalising enquiry. It was by using this process that I discovered a way to engage with different and often gendered conversational styles. (Refer Chapter Seven: Working with Gender).

In the uncensored speaking to our selves, colleagues and consultants/supervisors we acknowledge our thoughts, feelings and experiences while hoping that we can use this knowing as a therapeutic resource. Engaging with this self and other reflective practice requires us to be very connected and present to our selves.

A self and other reflective process may provide a knowledge resource about the self (therapist) or about the therapeutic relationship. We can gauge the therapeutic merit of this discovery by reflecting on the therapeutic relationship understanding. Whenever the discovery enters the therapeutic conversation, it provides us with an enquiry resource which is unencumbered by the therapist's emotions, preferences and/or life experience.

I have found that four simple questions provide me with a quick self-check before, during and after sessions. The questions are:

▼ What do I think about this person (client)?
▼ What do I feel about this person (client)?
▼ Do I like the person I'm working with?
▼ What are my thoughts and feelings about the concerns?

These questions help me to articulate and thereby explore thoughts and feelings while reflecting on how these thoughts and feelings will impact on the therapeutic process. If we believe that these thoughts and feelings will interfere with the therapeutic relationship understanding then we need to participate in a self, and other, reflective process that explores and contextualises these ideas and feelings.

For example, a heterosexual couple were attending counselling sessions as a result of escalating conflict. The couple were both in their forties with three children, all of whom had recently left home. Over the last year, Mrs Rowlings had been attending night classes and had re-entered the paid work force. She had, as a result of night classes and her job, made a number of friends with whom she socialised. Mr Rowlings has become increasingly distressed whenever his wife attended night classes. He didn't like her new friends and made it clear that he would prefer it if She would stop socialising with her friends. Discussions escalated to arguments with Mr Rowlings demanding that Mrs Rowlings give up her night classes. She refused and at the point of attending counselling the couple were considering separation.

Throughout the interview Mr Rowlings displayed the same behaviour Mrs Rowlings complained about at home. That is, he continuously repeated that she was the problem and that if she only would stop night classes their relationship would go back to normal.

Mrs Rowlings reiterated that she didn't want the relationship to go back to normal as she had been unhappy prior to obtaining paid employment and going to night school.

The therapist found her self becoming increasingly irritated with Mr Rowlings irretractable opinions. This irritation was an important signal that a new direction of enquiry was essential if counselling was to be successful.

The irritation she experienced was a result of her belief that Mr Rowlings was being unreasonable. Mr and Mrs Rowlings both persisted in the belief that the other was the problem throughout the interview. The therapist found her self siding with the idea that it was reasonable for Mrs Rowlings to go to night classes. Any attempt to explore this with Mr Rowlings resulted in a restatement of his position.

The therapist's irritation was a signal that she was taking sides. She had quickly and easily understood Mrs Rowlings' experience. She had not, however, developed a context in this session for understanding Mr Rowlings' experience. In order to develop a context of understanding she needed to find a way to inquire about Mr Rowlings, experience rather than assume that she knew it.

In the next session the therapist directed her attention towards Mr Rowlings and asked him a number of questions:

▼ When you were first married what ideas did you have about your role as a man and a husband? What were your ideas of a woman's/wife's role?

▼ Where did these ideas come from?

▼ What did you think your father expected of you as a man? What did he expect of himself as a man and as a husband?

▼ If you weren't the only provider in the household, would that diminish your idea of your self as a man?

▼ What do you think are Mrs Rowlings' ideas about her self as a woman and a wife?

▼ If her ideas have changed over the years, how would you know?

▼ What do you think she expected of you as a man and as a husband when you were first married and now?

▼ If you were to make changes in your expectations of each other, how would you negotiate that?

▼ Do you know of other couples who have successfully made changes?

At the end of the questioning process it became clear to Mr and Mrs Rowlings that Mrs Rowlings' actions, in reclaiming another direction after twenty years of being employed as a primary parent, challenged the covert understanding of the marriage. Mr Rowlings felt confused and desperate. The old understanding had disappeared and there was nothing to replace it. His actions, which were previously understood as controlling, were seen as a desperate bid to hold on to the old relationship understanding. Mrs Rowlings had been unable to renegotiate the original understanding because it was covert. However she could act to re-establish the sense of self that had been put to one side over the last twenty years.

The couple left counselling with the intention to renegotiate a new relationship understanding. This would require Mr Rowlings to discover and appreciate Mrs Rowlings' new self-direction. Mr Rowlings was also committed to think about the ideas he carried and whether these ideas both limited and/or extended him and limited and/or extended the relationship.

In this situation the therapist used her self and the therapeutic relationship as an important information source in the therapeutic process.

A self and other reflective practice includes re-viewing any apprehension that occurs before meeting with people (clients). Again apprehension can mean many things — exhaustion, feelings of stuckness, fear related to a lack of knowing, fear generated by meeting

a challenging situation, over-rehearsal of the conversation, or predictions of being directly challenged and so on. Whenever apprehension
occurs we begin by acknowledging it and then seek out a way of making
sense of the apprehension.

When you (therapist) reflect on the question, 'Do I like the person I
am working with?', and the answer is, 'No,' this signals that the
therapeutic relationship is in difficulties. The idea of 'liking' is a simple
concept that in no way describes the complexity of the therapeutic
connection. Its simplicity, however, makes it readily accessible. In the
above situation we are bound by the therapeutic relationship understanding to speak about this experience in supervision/consultation in
order to explore what it means. If it is impossible to find a new way to
engage in the relationship with the person (client) after supervision,
peer and self re-view, then the contract of the therapeutic work needs
to end (refer Chapter Ten: Endings).

The other questions, 'What do I think about this person (client)?',
'What do I feel about this person?', 'What do I think about her/his
concerns?', prepare us to articulate our thinking and feeling beyond
psychological theorising. In doing this we are assuming that our
subjective thinking and feeling will have an influence on both the
therapeutic relationship and the direction taken in the therapeutic
enquiry. Whenever we reflect with another (supervisor, consultant,
colleague) on our response to these questions, the conversation will
mirror the therapeutic conversation by its emphasis on a relational
externalising enquiry. The relational externalising enquiry protects the
therapeutic relationship and the supervisory/consultative relationship
from imposed meanings supported by grand psychological theories.

SELF REFLECTION IN RESPECT TO SEXUAL THOUGHTS AND FEELINGS AND STRONG FEELINGS

There are clear ethical guidelines for counsellors and therapists
prohibiting sexual relations between therapists and clients. Therapists
who agree with this ethical position are sometimes shocked to experience sexual thoughts and feelings in relation to a person (client). Given
that people (therapists) are meeting with people (clients) it is possible
that sometime in our career we could experience sexual thoughts and
feelings, or strong feelings, about a person (client) with whom we are
working. It is important not to ignore our response but to engage in a
self/other reflective process that honours our commitment to the

therapeutic relationship understanding. To disclose sexual thoughts and feelings within the therapeutic relationship directs the therapeutic process away from the other (client) and towards our selves. This is a betrayal of the therapeutic relationship understanding. The therapeutic relationship is bound by the therapeutic relationship understanding, which in turn governs behaviour within the relationship. Acting outside of this understanding creates an abusive therapeutic climate.

The self/other reflective process I'm referring to requires that sexual thoughts and feelings, and strong feelings in relation to a person (client), must never be thought of as private. When experiencing sexual thoughts and strong feelings in relation to a person (client) we are obliged by the therapeutic relationship understanding to disclose these thoughts and feelings to a supervisor/consultant. Once they are disclosed, we attempt to make sense of them in a way that diminishes the sexual and/or strong feeling response to the person (client). If the sexual or strong thoughts and feelings remain after a process of supervision/consultation, then it is important that the therapeutic relationship is ended. Once the therapeutic relationship has ended, under no circumstances is it appropriate for an ongoing relationship to exist between therapist and client.

Sexual thoughts and feelings are often easier to identify than strong feelings. Fear can accompany sexual thoughts and feelings, encouraging denial of sexual thoughts and feelings, leaving in their place strong feelings. Strong feelings can precede sexual feelings or they can be a distraction from facing sexual feelings. We are all affected by a Western cultural bias to sexualise strong feelings when in fact strong feelings can also occur without sexual feelings.

Ethical guidelines in relationship to sexual relations between therapists and clients can create a rule culture that limits disclosure and enquiry. Within a rule culture we can become mainly concerned with whether we adhere to the rule. I am interested in developing a culture of sensitivity to strong thoughts and feelings, and sexual thoughts and feelings. Once identified, these thoughts and feelings are made available for a relational externalising enquiry dedicated to upholding the therapeutic relationship understanding. An enquiry process that researches our engagement with strong feelings in our lives provides us with an environment to wonder about the multiplicity of meanings that we can attach to strong feelings.

For example, if a man has been socialised to make sense of strong feelings of connection with others as sexual, what are the implications for the therapeutic relationship where there is an environment of connection?

Whenever we identify that we have strong feelings for a person (client), this must be disclosed to a supervisor/consultant. We can identify strong feelings by asking our selves the following questions:

▼ How often do I find myself thinking about this person (client)?

▼ Have I made this person (client) special in some way?

▼ Do I go out of my way for this person (client), for example, by agreeing to appointments that are not convenient or usual for me?

▼ Do I look forward to sessions with this person (client) in a way that is different?

▼ Is there any difference in my physical proximity to this person than with others?

▼ How much do I disclose about myself to this person (client)?

▼ Do I go out of my way to encourage or meet this person (client) outside of the therapeutic context?

I am interested in finding constructive ways to acknowledge that sexual thoughts and feelings, and strong thoughts and feelings, can and do occur within the therapeutic relationship. A relational externalising conversation within a self/other reflective process allows these thoughts and feelings to be identified and re-searched in a non-totalising way thereby liberating us from the effects of shame.

It isn't shameful to experience sexual thoughts, feelings and strong feelings towards a person (client). There is, however, considerable shame in maintaining these sexual thoughts, feelings and strong feelings in secret. If we do so, we abuse the therapeutic relationship understanding, abuse the trust of people (clients) and put people (clients) emotionally and physically at risk.

SPECIALNESS

The creation of a special relationship can occur so gradually that the participants remain unaware of its special status. The relationship doesn't begin with a decision for specialness, it may begin simply with a sense of ease. We need to be alert to the creation of a climate of specialness as its insidiousness development can have dire consequences for both therapist and client. This includes the possibility that specialness can provide the climate within which strong feelings and sexual thoughts and feelings develop.

The creation of a special relationship can leave people (clients) feeling disloyal or ungrateful if they express a lack of ease with some part of the relationship. Special relationships can support people (clients) to comply with requests, ideas or practices out of respect for our good natures. When agreements are obtained primarily as a result of a sense of our 'goodness' then this precludes the development of a conversation that focuses on people's (clients') best interest.

The following questions will help you to reflect on any special relationships:

▼ Have you ever discovered that you had participated in creating a special relationship with a person (client)?

▼ When/how did you recognise specialness? (This includes special-ness that you had participated with and specialness that you noticed from the other person's (client's) thoughts and actions)?

▼ How did specialness impact on the therapeutic relationship? Was there any benefit for the therapeutic relationship? If it was detrimental, in what way was it detrimental?

▼ What would stop/help you talk with a supervisor/consultant about noticing specialness in the relationship?

▼ When you reflect on what would stop you talking about noticing specialness, what do you need to negotiate with your supervisor/ consultant in order to make such a conversation possible?

▼ Have you used therapeutic conversations for teaching, re-search or articles? What impact do you think these requests have had on experiences of specialness?[7]

Whenever the experience of specialness is a consideration in the therapeutic relationship, I suggest that it is named and explored. Any negotiation of the relationship must occur however within the bounds of the therapeutic relationship understanding. The experience of specialness that can occur with the use of audio and video taped material and transcripts will become a concern if the meaning made of specialness isn't clarified. We can prevent the specialness from becoming an issue by providing people (clients) with a comprehensive permission process. Specialness can be indicated whenever people (clients) give us gifts. Receiving cards and gifts from people (clients) however can mean many things. The way I position myself in respect to this is to enquire with people (clients) about what is meant by the gifts or cards. Receiving gifts or cards doesn't necessarily mean that people (clients) are over-connected to us. They can simply be tokens of respect and appreciation. We can respond in numerous ways. For example: 'I'd like to ask you what the thinking or feeling was behind your decision to give this to me?' or, 'I've noticed this is the fourth card you've sent me this month, what do these cards represent to you?'

These questions provide openings to renegotiate the therapeutic relationship understanding if that proves necessary. It is important to situate any gift-giving within the person's (client's) cultural and familial understandings.

AN ENVIRONMENT OF RESPECT

The therapeutic relationship understanding only exists within an environment of respect. Within this environment, respect is experienced as a dynamic practice rather than a static state. Anything that disrupts a respectful practice needs to be identified, named and negotiated. If the disruption belongs to our thoughts and feelings, then consultation/supervision is used to attempt to enable the maintaining of an environment of respect. If this isn't possible then the person will need to be referred elsewhere. (Refer Chapter Ten: Endings.)

If the disruption to an environment of respect belongs to people (clients) then it is our responsibility to name and explore this in a respectful way. If people (clients) are unwilling or unable to engage with us in an environment of respect, then the therapeutic relationship is untenable. For example, Jack is 23 years old and is involved in counselling as a result of being caught intruding on people's property while looking through windows at women. After 15 minutes of conversation, Jack's eyes have not left my chest.

Johnella:	Jack, I've noticed that since we've been talking together your gaze hasn't shifted from my chest. I'm wondering if you have any other ways of gazing at women or at men?
Jack:	You've got to be joking, I don't look at blokes like that.
Johnella:	What sort of look would you be using if I was a bloke?

Jack:	(Shifts in his chair looking down and to the side, runs his hand through his hair) I dunno.
Johnella:	I noticed when I talked about your talking with a bloke, you looked down and to the side. Is that the look you use with blokes, do you think?
Jack:	I dunno, it could be.
Johnella:	There are possibly two looks we've discovered. One for women and one for men. I'm wondering if you know any others ways of looking.
Jack:	I dunno.
Johnella:	If the look you use is down and to the side, how does that effect listening?
Jack:	What do you mean?
Johnella:	Okay. if you are using the look you find your self using with women — I don't want you to use that look right now. Just think about it — If you used that look, how would that effect listening?
Jack:	I dunno.
Johnella:	Would you find your self listening to my words or would you be listening to the words in your mind?
Jack:	Like what words?
Johnella:	I don't know. As you're imagining the look used on women, do you find your self thinking things?
Jack:	Yeah, I do.
Johnella:	What do you find your self thinking?
Jack:	I don't want to say.

This is a *beginning* conversation that represents Jack and I negotiating as to whether an environment of respect is possible.

When the disruption to an environment of respect belongs to the people (clients) we are working with, then the first indicator of a lack of respect may be our emotional response. The possibility of a respectful conversation is limited whenever we experience strong feelings.

In protecting the therapeutic relationship from the effects of our strong feelings we miss an opportunity to use the therapeutic relationship as a vehicle for change. Within the context of the therapeutic conversation we may be unable to move in the moment past strong feelings in order to name and explore the behaviour/s. In this instance, we can reflect out of session and come back to the experiences in order to negotiate an environment of respect. This negotiation is particularly relevant when the behaviour represents a socially sanctioned attitude or value. We may find our selves in this position whenever there is a cultural, gender or social difference between us and the people (clients) we work with.

For example, a woman therapist reported that after a couple session the man waited until his partner had left the room and then told the therapist how much he had enjoyed the session. He then patted her on the head and left. The therapist reported that she felt furious about this behaviour, but didn't know how to address it therapeutically.

The ideas we discussed included the following:

▼ Stan, I'm not sure what you meant when you patted me on the head at the end of the last session. Is this something you do with everyone, men and women?

▼ Do other people engage in this patting behaviour with you?

▼ What would you make of it if they did?

▼ Are you interested in my experience of this patting behaviour?

In order to use the experience of the therapeutic relationship as a vehicle for change we provide our selves with the opportunity to express thoughts and feelings without censorship. When we move outside of censorship we can listen to the strength, colour, emotional substance of our experience. Uncensored expression is followed by a self/peer/consultant conversational process where we find a way to name the interaction, thought and feeling so that it can be re-searched. The starting point for the re-search is with the therapist's experience. If we decide that the experience belongs to the therapeutic relationship we determine an appropriate way to bring the interaction forwards as a wondering. This wondering is constructed by using a relational externalising process. This construction protects the therapeutic conversation from the effects of totalising language and provides for the possibility of an ongoing negotiation of naming and meaning. When we use this practice we are challenging the idea that respect is an attribute that belongs to our character. Instead we are representing respect as a negotiated practice.

Engaging with respect requires us to expose our disrespectful thinking with the intention that a relational externalising exploration will take us to a new level of knowing. When we consider that our relationship with respect is shaped by gender, class and cultural presuppositions it is inevitable that limitations of our experience can initially propel us into disrespectful thinking. For example, 'Sam's just too comfortable to change,' or, 'I'd want to leave the relationship too if I had to put up with those insistent accusations.'

Pretend respect occurs when we censor our thoughts and feelings and continue smiling. Whenever pretend respect appears within the therapeutic relationship it signals a therapy that is moving towards stuckness. Engaging with respect is an ongoing challenge that has the potential to support us (therapist and client) to go beyond conventional knowledge. Engaging with respect ensures that we are experienced by people (clients) as 'real'; discoverers rather than knowers.

TRANSPARENCY WITH RESPONSIBILITY

Transparency in the therapy means disclosing intention to people (clients). This may require us to articulate the thinking behind the therapeutic direction, the enquiry process, the exercise or activity. If the intention of an enquiry is an attempt to make sense of someone's experience, then that is its intention. Transparency allows people (clients) to engage with us rather than be passive respondents to our interventions, whether they are conversational intervention or activities. For example:

Johnella: Peter, you may have noticed that I have spent some time today asking you about your memory of the relationship between you and your mother as a young boy. What took me in that direction was a comment you made about the effects of a belief that you hold. You said that given your Dad left the family and you when you were two years old, you were therefore damaged as a man. In asking those questions I was wondering about the contribution the relationship between you and your mother had on the qualities you appreciate in your self? I'm wondering how easy it is to hold onto an appreciation of those qualities we discovered given the belief in

damage? I'm also wondering how your appreciation
of those qualities would have changed if the relationship
between you and your dad had contributed to the
development of those qualities?

In this example, I could have made the conversational direction
transparent at the beginning of my exploration of Peter's early relationship with his mother. However, in this example I had changed the
direction of the enquiry before I was clear about which idea was
supporting the change of direction. Disclosing intention serves to
illuminate that the therapeutic conversational direction is subject to the
knowledges we have access to. In the above example, I am wondering
if, the recent strengthening of the already prevalent Western cultural
belief that men's psychological well-being is determined predominantly
by their relationship with their father, had subjected Peter to
experiences of hopelessness. The questions ask Peter to consider the
relationship with his mother as a focus for the development of
worthwhile qualities. In exposing these qualities we can then wonder
what would support or hinder the valuing of these qualities.

Transparency in the therapeutic process does not equate with therapist self disclosure.

Selfdisclosure is only appropriate if we are clear that it fits within the
therapeutic relationship understanding. Legitimate self disclosure is
determined by its benefit to people (clients). Even when we decide that
self disclosure is beneficial we continue to protect the therapeutic
relationship understanding by re-viewing that decision in supervision/
consultation.

THE PROFESSIONAL SELF IS NOT A DETACHED SELF
When I interview people (clients) about what in the therapy has
contributed to the changes they've made in their lives, people regularly
say it was significant for them that I was 'real'. This realness constitutes
a meeting between people, where terror, shame, rage, grief and pain are
expressed and we do not avert our eyes or close down our hearts. We
offer to meet these experiences/feelings while agreeing to retain hope
for life within the bounds of the therapeutic relationship understanding.

'Realness' is supported by intellectual and technical knowledge
that allows us to engage in the therapeutic conversation as a 'subject

with a subject'. Each subject engages with the therapeutic conversation differently. However, both are aware of the subjectivity of the conversation.

The adoption of a subject position within the therapeutic relationship understanding creates an interesting relationship between knowing and not knowing. Although I know something, that knowing is available for reflection and re-view both within and outside of the therapeutic conversation. When what I think I know is presented to the conversation as a question, the response may shift or add to what it is that I know.

When what I think I know is presented in the therapeutic conversation as a possibility, as in for example, 'Some people have found that . . .,' the context is set for discovery rather than certainty such as the certainty expressed in the sentence, 'This will help you with temper tantrums.'

In order to position our selves for discovery we position our selves to hear the responses to questions and experimental practices even though the response may contradict the ideas we hold. Hearing involves holding this new possibility as a possibility rather than arguing against it or dismissing it if it doesn't fit our meaning paradigm. This challenge to the idea of objective knowledge positions us as re-searchers of people's (clients') experiences.

The power relations that operates within the therapeutic relationship determines that we have a substantial influence over the conversational direction such as what draws us to one conversational theme over another. Our economic and social privileging may dull us to the experience of others. We may find our selves so much on the inside of privilege that we are unable to see the other sides. If this happens we risk becoming agents of social control. When we recognise our subjectivity then ethically we are challenged to expose our work and our selves to ongoing critique by:

▼ Actively searching for what is said and what is partially said and not said.

▼ Establishing conditions of safety where our work is critiqued for the subjectivity produced by privilege in relationship to socio-economic status, gender, sexuality, ethnicity, etc.

▼ Seeking out and listening to marginalised voices.

In engaging with the above critique process, we may find our selves conducting our professional lives on the border between those groups of people who dominate and those who are marginalised.

ETHICS AND THE THERAPEUTIC RELATIONSHIP UNDERSTANDING

How is power represented in the therapeutic relationship understanding?

Therapists, counsellors, psychologists and psychiatrists play a considerable role in maintaining normalising and pathologising discourses that hold the individual responsible for both their problems and/or concerns and the solution to these problems. When people (clients) cross the line between what is considered normal and what is not, not only do they feel alienated, they are also often socially and economically disadvantaged. In using the descriptions 'normal/not normal', I am including any experience that is not supported by the prevailing descriptions of normality. For example, 'I am a successful accountant, I am financially secure, married with two children, yet I don't feel happy. What's wrong with me?'

In this example the person is affected by the following beliefs:

▼ Happiness is important and possible.

▼ Happiness can be expected if people engage with life in a particular way.

▼ A lack of happiness is the individual's responsibility, 'Something is wrong with me.'

Normality for this person would involve being happy. Relational externalising allows us to move happiness away from a static internalised states towards re-searching happiness in relationship to. We can then consider the following:

▼ The conditions that promote the experience of happiness.

▼ Happiness ideas that foster an expectation of happiness.

▼ The knowledge of happiness as a state.

▼ The effect on relationships of happiness-advertising which promotes happiness by product.

The movement towards a self in relationship allows for the historicising, culturising and genderising of problems, concerns and abilities in relationship to the self and others. The therapeutic relationship understanding draws our attention to the power relation within the therapeutic relationship. People (clients) are talking about and exposing thoughts, feelings and actions to another person who is deemed a member of the professional classes, i.e. therapist, counsellor, psychologist, psychiatrist. The traditional role of members of the professional class (doctors, lawyers, teachers, therapists, social workers, accountants) is to classify, assess and interpret according to over-riding principles of success/failure, right/wrong, normal/ abnormal, well/sick. The social sanction that enables us to engage in assessment and classification places us in a powerful position within the therapeutic relationship. This position of power exists beyond our politics, personal attributes, social and class membership and gender. It exists beyond our theories, intentions and technical abilities. It exists because we cannot stand outside of power relations. With this knowledge of power relations within the therapeutic relationship, we can however undertake conversations about how we ethically engage with power difference. These conversations can be held both in and outside of the therapeutic relationship.

The power difference in the therapeutic relationship belongs to our categorisation as therapists/counsellors in Western society rather than to our theoretical orientation. This idea enables us to scrutinise therapeutic practice and ideas. We can no longer hide behind the acquisition of ever-increasing qualifications, or teaching status, or years of experience, or complex theory, or revolutionary new theory that exposes the old theory. Complacency and intolerance of difference are the forerunners of a therapy or counselling practice that alienates and subjugates others. Understanding the power relation inherent within the therapeutic relationship obliges us to remain forever ethically available to the challenge of what we don't yet know by listening to and for the voices of difference. The listening for and to difference, together with exploring the context within which difference exists, engages us with the ethics of the everyday. Knowledge of the power relations that exist in the therapeutic relationship supports us to consider and negotiate the meaning made of gestures of support, the lack or presence of physical contact, the personal stories told or not told, the implications of acknowledgement and the understanding of the therapeutic relationship itself. This knowledge of the power relation also enables us to consider the questions people (clients) don't ask us because of assumptions that we carry fixed and absolute knowledge and that our intentions are beyond questioning.

When people's (clients') experience of difference is constructed as individual pathology (which then translates to individual responsibility), people (clients and others) inevitably turn to counselling and therapy. When we listen to these pathologising discourses while searching for a theoretical explanation located in universaling and essentialising theories, we inevitably prop up the western construct of the individualised and autonomous self.

The therapeutic work represented in this book draws on a way of talking that moves the self from its isolated position as represented in everyday talk and in most texts, to a self in relationship. For example,

Johnella: How did the search for happiness impact on your life decisions, for example, your choice of career?

Ted: I'm not sure what you mean by search for happiness. I thought from an early age that there were things I needed to do to be happy.

Johnella: What were those thoughts?

Ted: I knew that I needed financial security. When I was young I dreamed of having my own boat and car, and these things don't fall off trees.

Johnella: How did having these things, a car and a boat, relate to happiness, do you think?

Ted: A lot. I thought they'd make me happy but they don't.

Johnella: When you were deciding on the financial security direction for happiness, did you turn away from other directions?

Ted: Yes, I did. I remember it clearly. I was in my fifth form year and I had to decide on my sixth form subjects. I loved art and drama, but they clashed with maths and accounting. I didn't know what to do.

Johnella: How did you decide?

Ted: I talked with my Dad and he said I had to think of my future, there was no future in art and drama. Everyone knows there's no money in those jobs.

Johnella:	Do you think at that point you moved away from those subjects or knowledges that you loved, towards the idea of a future that had a job and money in it?
Ted:	Yes, I did, but that's realistic.
Johnella:	In the movement towards a realistic future, did you think you were also moving towards happiness?
Ted:	Yes, I did.
Johnella:	In this movement, did you ever take the opportunity to pick up on engaging with the things you loved?
Ted:	No, I left those things behind.

The pathologising self-gaze that interprets difference as problematic is so common place that counsellors/therapists when asked to reflect on their work, readily identify what they are struggling with as a skill, idea or personal deficit, while straining to identify what it is that they are doing well. It is interesting to note that on my teaching courses, women who are therapists report their deficits with ease while often struggling to present their abilities. Men who are therapists are more at ease presenting abilities. From this we could hypothesise that the pathologising self-gaze is strengthened when people experience themselves as outside of the ruling discourses.

How do I know that I'm acting as an agent of social control?

This question requires us to confront the contradictory nature and the limitations of our work. As in the previous example with Ted we work primarily with people who locate problems/concerns within themselves. If we consider engaging with the idea of a relational self rather than an autonomous individual self, then problems/concerns move from belonging intrinsically to the person to being in relationship to the person. This shift in thinking is sustained by a relational externalising conversational process that creates the linguistic space to investigate the impact of ideas on wellbeing. For example,

John:	I'm unemployed, I guess I'm a bit of a no-hoper.
Johnella:	How has not being able to find work made you into a no-hoper?

John:	I don't know. I've looked for work, applied for heaps of jobs. I sometimes get my hopes up when I get an interview but no luck so far.
Johnella:	What is it about you that keeps you applying and looking for work, despite all that disappointment?
John:	I just really want to work. Sometimes I feel like giving up but I pull myself up and start again.
Johnella:	When you hear your self say that you just really want to work, when you hear your self say that even under the weight of disappointment you start again, how does that relate to this no-hoper idea?
John:	I don't know, it's just the way I feel.
Johnella:	What do you think supports the sense of being a no-hoper? When you think about the newspapers or the TV or other people, how do these relate to the no-hoper idea?
John:	Oh yeah, that advertisement on TV really makes me mad. I mean I don't want to be on the dole, yet they make it look like it's a bloody holiday.
Johnella:	The TV makes it look different than what it is?
John:	Yeah, they sure do.
Johnella:	How do you think TV and other media, effect the no-hoper idea?
John:	Well, that's what people think if you're not working.
Johnella:	Do you think that when the getting mad at the TV wears off you're left with the TV idea — the no-hoper idea?

This conversation could go on to explore what would be different if 'the no-hoper idea' was replaced with a sense of 'I'm doing everything I can to get a job'. It would also explore who and what benefits from 'the no-hoper idea'. In this example I have used language to move 'the no-hoper idea' away from an internal state to a construction supported by an ideology. The success of any ideology is marked by the ease with which it is incorporated into the person, as an internal feeling state or idea.

We act as agents of social control whenever we fail to explore the strategies used to move a collective responsibility on to the individual as the sole agent of responsibility. We act as agents of social control whenever we fail to identify the groups that are advantaged and disadvantaged by adherence to certain ideas and practices.

The nature of our work positions us as either regulators and maintainers of power relations in everyday life or as deconstructors of the power relations in the everyday. When we engage as deconstructors of the power relations within the everyday, we need to go beyond an exploration of ideas and practices that produce personal discomfort. When we sit with ease within a particular ideology, we remain ignorant of the implications for our selves and others. In order to continue to reflect on the question 'How do I know that I'm acting as an agent of social control?' we must actively position our selves to deconstruct the ideas and practices that contribute to our sense of comfort.

How do we engage with the contradictory nature of therapy?

The relational externalising therapeutic conversation may challenge the concept of the autonomous, individualised, self directed self. However, this challenge as I am describing it, occurs within the context of therapy. Therapy is contradictory in its very structure as it exists because individuals believe their psychological pain is a problem of the self, and that the self can be changed in therapy. Therapies that expose the effects of adherence to particular ideologies for people's (clients') sense of wellbeing, do this within the contradiction created by the structure of therapy itself.

I believe we can involve our selves in conversations that expose and explore this contradiction both inside of and outside of the therapeutic relationship. This may mean establishing discussion groups, action groups, newsletters, etc. In these ways the individual's experience of their experience is explored in a community. Collective experience challenges the pathologising of individuals, while drawing attention to the group who benefits from the beliefs in the prevailing discourses. These conversations are supported by the raising of questions rather than the presentation of a counter-discourse. In raising questions and reflecting on these questions, we create room for multiple discoveries and explanations. Here is an example from the conversation with John.

Johnella: When you think of work, what is work made up of? For example, if you spend your time in the garden, is that work?

John: No, that's not work, work is a real job,being paid.

Johnella: If you were working as a gardener, getting paid, would that constitute work, a real job?

John: Yeah, it would.

Johnella: Does payment then legitimise work?

John: Yeah.

Johnella: How is it decided that one form of work is legitimate and thus paid, and another form of work isn't legitimate and isn't paid?

John: It's a matter of producing. Producing something to sell, I suppose, or selling a skill.

Johnella: Okay, so I know that you've been doing a lot of child care lately.

John: Yeah, I've pretty much taken over that job.

Johnella: Do you think the job you've taken over requires skills?

John: Heaps of patience for a start and I've had to get really organised around the house to do everything.

Johnella: So you've developed organisational and patience skills. Have these skills been recognised with payment?

John: No way.

Johnella: Some skills and work are legitimatised with payment and some are not.

This example represents a partial enquiry where the taken-for-granted meaning of work is explored. It is our responsibility to develop questions that expose the taken-for-granted, thus rendering the taken-for-granted available for re-view. In this re-view a multiplicity of meaning, possibilities are seen to exist within the ruling discourses. The power structures that support and strengthen certain regimes of meaning while diminishing and undermining other meaning possibilities are then uncovered. The language used to signify all that is meaningful in our lives is no longer regarded as natural or taken for granted.

WORKING WITH THE TEXT

What do I (Client) need to consider on entering a therapeutic relationship?
On entering a therapeutic relationship, you need the definition of the therapeutic relationship understanding to be made available to you. Once you know what it is, you have the opportunity to negotiate what it means in therapy. Through the experience of therapy you may discover expectations, thoughts and feelings about the therapy that were previously unavailable to you. If this occurs, it is useful to ask your self, 'What do I need to know in order to feel safe enough to discuss this?' Answering this question can provide you with a beginning point for negotiation of safety with the therapist.

When the therapist provides you with an understanding of the therapeutic relationship, remember the understanding is not set in concrete. Throughout your experience with the therapeutic relationship you have the opportunity, in conversation with the therapist, to develop this understanding within the ethical boundaries, (In order to prepare for this you can ask for the therapist's professional associations's guidelines and refer to pages 92 and 93).

If you don't feel listened to, comfortable, respected or safe in this relationship, take this experience seriously. In order to consider an environment of respect it may be useful to reflect on these questions:

▼ When I've raised issues of concern to me in therapy, have I felt listened to and respected?

▼ If I have felt listened to and respected will this knowledge support me to raise present or future concerns?

▼ If I haven't felt listened to and respected in the past, what needs to change so that I can feel listened to and respected?

▼ How can I safely ask the therapist to consider these concerns?

▼ Would it assist me to have someone else present when I do this?

If it's not possible to discuss, or raise, these issues with the therapist, then this is an unsafe environment for you.

The therapeutic relationship is a negotiated relationship within certain bounds. If it's not working, then the expectations and limitations of the therapeutic relationship need to be considered. When the therapeutic relationship is not working for you, attempt to stand aside from self-accusation and self-blame and reflect on the therapeutic relationship understanding by asking your self, 'How have I been enacting this understanding?'

The therapeutic relationship has limitations of availability. The therapeutic relationship may fail to meet your expectation of availability and that may leave you feeling vulnerable and disappointed. If this happens, negotiate availability with the therapist and ask for information about other resources.

If you believe that you are experiencing strong feelings within the therapeutic relationship, then it's useful to acknowledge and identify these feelings. Strong feelings can precede strong expectations of the therapeutic relationship. Once strong feelings are named, consider raising the issue of strong feelings with the therapist. When you raise this issue the conversation should be directed towards undermining the effects of fear, silence and shame, and negotiating ways to protect you and the therapeutic relationship from strong feelings.

If the therapist talks about her/his own strong feelings towards you, or discusses her/his personal issues, then this contravenes the therapeutic relationship understanding. For example (therapist), 'You make me feel comfortable, happy, listened to, cared about, etc.' You are not safe in this context. Either leave or immediately introduce a third party of your choice to act as a witness and a facilitator. The facilitator's role may include negotiating the ending of the therapeutic relationship. Refer to Chapter Ten: Endings for further comment on this.

What do I (Therapist) need to consider on entering a therapeutic relationship?

In order to provide people (clients) with a therapeutic relationship understanding you need to establish what this understanding is. Reflect on the therapeutic relationship understanding discussed in this book and ask your self the following:

▼ What is the therapeutic relationship understanding that I bring to the work?

▼ What are the theoretical presuppositions that support my engagement with this therapeutic relationship understanding?

▼ Are the understandings that I hold similar to or different from the one represented in the book?

▼ When I reflect on my clinical practice, what questions are unanswered in the book?

▼ How do I make myself available to new discoveries about the therapeutic relationship understanding from within my clinical practice?

▼ How do I inform people (clients) of the therapeutic relationship understanding that I work with?

The ability to listen to your thoughts, feelings and experiences within the therapeutic relationship is highlighted in this chapter. Noticing your thoughts, feelings and experiences provides you with an opportunity for exploration in order to determine the effects of these thoughts and feelings on the therapeutic relationship. These thoughts and feelings can be both a resource and a hindrance in the therapeutic relationship.

Refer back to the questions asked throughout this chapter. Then reflect on the following questions:

▼ What emotions do I have easy access too?

▼ How do those emotions find expression?

▼ What emotions do I rarely notice experiencing?

▼ What sense do I make of that?

▼ Do other people notice the presence of emotions that remain invisible to me?

▼ Does my body alert me to the presence of emotions? If so, how?

▼ What are the thoughts/practices/life habits that are supportive of emotional expression?

▼ What are the thoughts/practices/life habits that reduce or suppress emotional expression?

▼ Are certain relationships more/less supportive of my engagement with emotional expression?

▼ When I hold on to an emotional response that I experience in a therapy session, that takes me outside of the therapeutic relationship understanding. What strategies do I have to reconnect with this emotional response in safety outside of the therapeutic relationship in order to make sense of it?

In a similar way you can re-search your thoughts and experiences. For example,

▼ When I thought, 'I hope the Jackson family don't turn up today,' what is that thought telling me?

▼ Is it telling me I'm tired and want a break from the work?

▼ Is it telling me something about the last session?

▼ Is it telling me something about the therapeutic relationship?

Taking thoughts, feeling and experiences seriously

It's important to take thoughts, feelings and experiences within the therapeutic relationship seriously as this provides us with information.

The following questions provide a focus for taking your experiences seriously. This can protect people (clients) from your responses, which they may experience as overwhelming, confusing and punishing.

Think of a time when you felt a lack of respect from people (clients) in the therapeutic relationship. Reflect on the following questions:

▼ How would you describe the lack of respect experience?

▼ How do you think the other person (client) would describe it?

▼ What past or present experience in your life, the therapy's life, the person's (client's) life may have contributed to this lack of respect experience?

▼ Did differences contribute to the lack of respect experiences, i.e. gender, ethnicity, class, sexuality?

▼ How would you describe this experience so that it can become part of a relational externalising enquiry?

▼ Develop questions that would support a relational externalising enquiry.

Together with listening to your thoughts, feelings and experiences, consider the environment that will support you to listen to people's (clients) thoughts, feelings and experiences when these may be different from your own. It is within these moments that people (clients) are most vulnerable to labelling, expert interpretation, and indirect or direct blame.

When people (clients) indicate directly and indirectly that there is a difference in understanding, consider the following:

▼ When people raise concerns about the therapeutic conversation or the therapeutic relationship, how do I ensure I can respond with openness and enquiry rather than defensiveness or silence?

▼ How do I or can I make myself available to learning something new, without this reducing my sense of competence?

▼ If I feel uncertain or overwhelmed in a conversation, what can I say in order to stop the conversation direction, while indicating that the therapeutic relationship needs outside assistance? Can I do this and still hold on to my sense of competence?

Self reflection in respect to sexual thoughts, feelings and strong feelings protects the therapeutic relationship. You can regularly use the questions on pages 120 and 121 while you reflect on the people (clients) you are engaged with. Remember disclosure of strong feelings is appropriate with a supervisor/consultant. It is not appropriate to disclose strong feelings directly to people (clients).

Moving outside of comfort

We inevitably live with ideas and practices that provide us with a sense of comfort. Given the power relations operating in the therapeutic relationship, we are ongoingly obliged to scrutinise these ideas and practices in relationship to benefit. This doesn't mean that we must surrender those benefits we enjoy. We are however re-viewing the implications of ideas and practices that benefit one group while disadvantaging others.

CHAPTER FOUR

. . . .

Building the Therapeutic Relationship

NEGOTIATING THE EXPECTATION OF MEANINGFULNESS
When I began to reflect on my engagement in the therapeutic relationship I was drawn towards what I now describe as the practice of 'negotiating the expectation of meaningfulness'. I was most interested in the situations where I ended the therapeutic session feeling I had worked very hard to achieve a connection with people (clients). I was often left with the thought that people (clients) were subsequently attending therapy as a result of my enthusiasm or eagerness for them to do so.

I consider that the counselling/therapy protocol of 'joining' encourages us (therapists) to create an environment of connection, safety and care towards others (clients). The 'joining' can encourage us to 'win over' people (clients) to the possibility that counselling/therapy will be beneficial.

When we use a relational externalising conversational process we are equipped to consider and explore people's (clients') ideas about the usefulness of meeting within the bounds of the therapeutic relationship understanding. This negotiation process sets the scene for the practice of collaboration.

In order to engage in and with the therapeutic relationship, people (clients) will firstly consider, if they hold expectations, that it will or could be meaningful. If people (clients) begin with an expectation of little or no meaningfulness, this has severe consequences for the building of the therapeutic relationship. The expectation of meaningfulness often occurs prior to or within a short time of meeting. For example, a young woman in her third foster placement was referred to counselling by her social worker. Throughout the session she politely responded to my inquiries while indicating boredom and covert clock watching. I asked her if she had talked with other people about her life. She confirmed that she had talked with numerous counsellors and social workers. I asked her to disregard any consideration for my feelings and tell me truthfully if there was anything interesting about our conversation or if it was more of the same. She laughed and said it was more of the same. I said that I disliked boring people and asked what could we talk about that wouldn't bore her. She responded and we began a conversation with an agreement that she'd indicate if I was moving into boring territory.

This example demonstrates negotiating a beginning point, a point where a person considers there is a possibility of meaningfulness.

Expectations of meaningfulness have considerable implications when therapists and clients belong to different cultural groups, sexualities, genders or classes. Whenever such a difference exists we can support the therapeutic relationship by respectfully acknowledging this difference. This acknowledgement allows for a conversation about the potential lack of meaningfulness when differences exist in the therapeutic relationship.

For example, Paul (therapist) was meeting Len (client) for the first time. Paul felt that he was working very hard to engage Len in a conversation that went beyond terse responses to his questions. Paul expressed his wondering about this. He asked if Len was finding the conversation difficult. He asked what Len's thinking had been about coming today. He asked what were Len's thoughts/feelings about talking with another man about his concerns and feelings. At this point Len said that he would have preferred a woman counsellor. Paul then asked Len's permission to talk a little more about his preference. Len agreed and after the conversation, Len indicated that he felt more at ease with

Paul and that this had been a different experience for him. He still indicated, however, that he would prefer to see a woman counsellor. Len's preference was respected and supported by referring him to a woman.

Having a conversation that makes visible and prioritises an expectation of meaningfulness, signals a therapy that is founded on collaboration. Collaboration is achieved when we actively negotiate the conditions required for meaningfulness; the negotiation signals a belief that people's (clients') perception of our cultural, sexuality, gender or class belonging has implications for the expectation that this therapeutic relationship will be meaningful. Collaboration is represented as a practice that extends further than an assumption of our goodwill. I believe this negotiation provides the foundation on which a respectful practice sits.

When our initial therapeutic enquiry takes into consideration the expectancy of meaningfulness, we can readily discover who has identified the family/couple/individual concerns and who strongly believes in these family/couple/individual concerns. Without this knowledge we can unwittingly find our selves positioned against families rather than with them. For example, a family identified their concerns about Andrew's temper. Family members were very involved in arguing for Andrew and interrupted my conversation with Andrew numerous times, regaling stories of Andrew strengths. As I re-searched the context that surrounded the concern, the tone of the conversations became increasingly urgent. I felt my enquiry was being experienced as an accusation. I stopped the conversational direction and asked the family members if they felt my questions were in any way accusing of Andrew. Did they feel that I was standing with them on this concern? This enquiry direction clarified that the family members didn't believe Andrew had the temper problem. They were in a longstanding dispute with the school where they felt Andrew was treated unfairly. They had come to see me at the school's insistence. The family experienced any exploration of Andrew's relationship with the temper as an indication that I was siding with the school. Their response to this was to close ranks and argue with me.

I believe that the process of negotiating the expectation of meaningfulness sets the scene for a collaborative and negotiated therapy.

FINDING THE BALANCE
Therapeutic relationships involve a dynamic balance between connectedness and detachment within the bounds of the therapeutic

relationship understanding. Finding the balance between connect-edness and detachment within the therapeutic relationship was, for me, a process of trial and error. During the period, I worked predominately with people (clients) who had been subjected to sexual, physical and emotional abuse, often I was teaching in the morning followed by an afternoon where I saw four or five people (clients). In order to survive, I had to invent strategies for putting the emotional, intellectual and spirit-filled knowings away between sessions and at the end of the day. During this period there was a time where the work seemed to demand all my life's energy. It was as a consequence of this exhaustion that I re-viewed the expectations I carried of myself. I did this while reflecting on the discoveries I had made in the clinical work. I believe emphati-cally that we can work well with people (clients) who have been subjected to sexual, physical and emotional abuse while also providing care for our selves. Indeed, I think that it is only within an environment of self care that we can adequately engage with life/hope.

We can support the development and maintenance of an environ-ment of care by ongoingly reflecting on the balance of connection and detachment in the therapeutic relationship. The connection I describe is founded on a belief that we are willing and able to meet (emotionally, physically, intellectually, spirit-filledly) people's (clients') uncensored descriptions of their experiences. At the same time people (clients) also believe that we are willing and able to meet them.

Here is an example where a colleague was not willing to connect with the person's (client's) experiences. It arose when I was consulting with a colleague who felt her work with a man who 'flashed' at women was 'not going anywhere'. She discussed her lack of ease in talking with this man because she felt that this behaviour was totally outside of her experience. She also indicated that she was worried about the way he would be looking at or considering her in the therapeutic relationship. At this point there was a lack of willingness to connect with this man's (client's) experience.

The consultation process involved discussing a number of enquiry directions which prepared the therapist for a conversation about the therapeutic relationship given her lack of ease.

Terri: I just don't understand this behaviour.

Johnella: When you haven't understood behaviour in the past, how have you started?

Terri: I've just begun by re-searching the behaviour — the context and the thinking — but this is different.

Johnella: What's different?

Terri: I don't want to know his behaviour, the context and his thinking. I know I should but I just don't want to know.

Johnella: I'd like to talk a little about what it is that you don't want to know.

Terri: It's not what he does. I've heard that before, it's not that, I don't know what it is, it's something creepy.

Johnella: Okay. Think now in this moment about asking the questions that help you to get to know the thinking, the behaviour, the context. What's the thinking and feeling as you reflect on these questions?

Terri: I'm feeling angry, irritated, I think he's getting off on the details and he's sitting there and looking at me while he talks about other women.

Johnella: How would it be if we experimented with a conversation you could initiate that might set the scene for a respectful therapeutic relationship?

Terri: I'd like that, if it's possible.

Johnella: Let's begin where I interview you as Stefan (the client). Is that okay?

Terri: I'll try.

Johnella: Stefan, I'd like to spend some time today getting to know the thinking that supports flashing.

Terri: Yeah.

Johnella: Before we begin I'm wondering how my being a woman will affect the telling. Do you think it would be easier or hardier to tell if you were telling a man?

Terri: It's easier with you. I mean a woman.

Johnella: What makes it easier?

This interview represents a consultation process where the unwillingness was named and that naming provided us with an enquiry direction. The enquiry involved beginning to negotiate a climate of respect. This then has the potential to expose taken-for-granted gender relations assumptions and practices. After articulating a possible negotiation of an environment of respect the consultee felt able to facilitate an enquiry where an environment of respect was negotiated.

In the following example which I am repeating from Chapter Three, I have indicated my willingness to speak what is often unspoken. I have positioned myself as a potential challenger to objectification. Jack is 23 years old and is involved in counselling as a result of being caught intruding on people's property while looking through windows at women. After 15 minutes of conversation, Jack's eyes have not left my chest.

Johnella: Jack, I've noticed that since we've been talking together your gaze hasn't shifted from my chest. I'm wondering if you have any other ways of gazing at women or at men?

Jack: You've got to be joking, I don't look at blokes like that.

Johnella: What sort of look would you be using if I was a bloke?

Jack: (shifts in his chair looking down and to the side, runs his hand through his hair) I dunno.

Johnella: I noticed when I talked about your talking with a bloke, you looked down and to the side. Is that the look you use with blokes do you think?

Jack: I dunno, it could be.

Johnella: There are possibly two looks we've discovered. One for women and one for men. I'm wondering if you know any other ways of looking?

Jack: I dunno.

Johnella: If the look you use is down and to the side, how does that effect listening?

Jack: What do you mean?

Johnella:	Okay. If you are using the look you find your self using with women, I don't want you to use that look right now. Just think about it. If you used that look, how would that effect listening?
Jack:	I dunno.
Johnella:	Would you find your self listening to my words or would you be listening to the words in your mind?
Jack:	Like what words?
Johnella:	I don't know. As you're imagining the look used on women, do you find your self thinking things?
Jack:	Yeah, I do.
Johnella:	What do you find your self thinking?
Jack:	I don't want to say.

When I negotiate an environment of respect, the relational externalising conversation enables me to engage as a subject within the therapeutic relationship. Re-searching 'looking' and 'listening' requires Jack to reflect on his intentions and thinking habits.

In the process of negotiating an environment of respect I am indicating my willingness to name the process of objectification. The naming represented in the example with Jack indicates that I am willing to explore Jack's willingness to expose and challenge these processes. The first challenge is within the therapeutic relationship. We cannot guarantee that people (clients) will respect the therapeutic relationship understanding. However, we can provide people (clients) with an opportunity to re-view their engagement within the therapeutic relationship.

We might believe that we are willing and able to meet with people's (clients') experience. The people (clients) we are working with also need to believe in this possibility. For example,

Les:	Do you know what it's like to be made redundant and then be out of work for three years?
Johnella:	Other people have told me about this sort of experience Les. I haven't however been out of work for a significant period.

How will this knowledge about me effect the confidence you have in the counselling?

Les: To tell you the truth, it gives me no confidence, no confidence at all. I don't believe anyone who hasn't been through this will come within a brass razoo of understanding.

Johnella: Would you be interested in our beginning to talk together, and if by the end of the session there's still no confidence we could talk about what to do next?

Les: Now I'm here I might as well give it a go but I think I'll be wasting your time.

In this example, Les and I are negotiating his willingness to experiment with the possibility that I might be able to meet his description of his experience. If there was no willingness to experiment with this or if a feeling of no confidence remained at the end of the session, the therapeutic relationship is untenable.

People (clients) who believe that we are willing and able to understand their experience also carry the belief and the experience of us as being able and willing to detach enough from their experience to survive. For example,

Chris: I don't think I should tell you this. It's just too awful.

Johnella: What are your thoughts or experiences about how the telling will impact on you and on me?

Chris: It's upsetting enough for me to think about what happened. Why should you have to know this, carry this around?

Johnella: Has your belief in the protection of others from what happened stopped telling before?

Chris: Yes, really that's the main reason I've kept it to myself.

Johnella: If you felt free to tell, what difference would it make to your life?

Chris: I feel like it would be a relief, a weight lifted off me.

Johnella: Okay. What do you need to know about me, to know
             that I can cope with the telling?

Chris: Hmm, I'd like to know what you do, how you cope, with
             the terrible things that you hear.

In order to engage in the style of conversation that is represented in this
example, we must also believe we have the strategies to detach enough
to survive. Maintaining the balance between connection and detachment can be particularly demanding on the therapeutic relationship
when people (clients) have been affected by considerable abuse —
physical, mental and/or emotional. Whenever there is a shift in the
connection/detachment balance, an opportunity is provided for exploration in supervision/ consultation and within the therapy.

Identifying a shift in the connection/detachment balance within the
therapeutic relationship requires alertness to the signs of over-
connection and over detachment. Alertness requires the following:

▼ A sensitivity to ourselves (thinking, emotions, body).

▼ A sensitivity to people's (clients') experiences within the therapeutic relationship.

▼ A sensitivity to the therapeutic process, for example, knowing if
   the therapy is stuck in some way.

OVER-DETACHMENT

A nun who had recently retired from work in prisons was interviewed
on a BBC radio programme. She was asked, 'How did you cope with
working with people who had often done horrific things?' She replied,
'Oh, they were all nice lads. I never had any difficulty with them. I made
it a point to never ask them what they had done.'

As therapists we need courage to truly understand what has been
done to some people or what some people have done to others. Courage
to reflect on our participation in practices and with ideas that have
denied, humiliated and punished others. Courage to reflect daily on the
congruency between the stated principles we live by and our ability to
live within and practice those principles. Courage to know the
limitations of our understandings. Courage to speak the words that
describe brutal, judgmental, torturing and abusive behaviour. Courage
to do all this and retain hope and compassion. Without courage we are
tempted to concur with people's (clients') pathological self descriptions.[1]

When we lose courage we over-detach. This will happen to all of us at some times. We can protect the therapeutic relationship by attending to the signs of over-detachment using self and other reflection (other reflection refers to utilising a consultant or supervisor or colleagues).

The following practices indicate that we have moved into over-detachment:

▼ Disembodied words and metaphors, disinterest, reinterpretation, conversational pace and 'Yes, but . . .'

Disembodied words and metaphors

We can hear people's (clients') experience as though through a medium or third person. When we do this words are heard in a disconnected manner, interesting but irrelevant to the self of the therapist. When therapeutic metaphors that hold immense emotional significance are used as disembodied stories, then we are over-detached. Using a metaphor such as prisons or concentration camps, without knowing or being willing to know what it means to be robbed of self determination, to be treated as less than human and threatened with death of the spirit or body, is disrespectful and non-therapeutic. In this instance we are using words in a technical sense, believing the words themselves will act as the salve to emotional wounds. In contrast, embodied words resonate with emotion as we speak what we know or have discovered.

Disinterest

Over-detachment can be preceded by disinterest. Disinterest occurs when our attention is focused away from the other (client), for example, thinking about tonight's dinner, last night's movie or looking out the window at someone or something. Whenever we notice disinterest it can be useful to ask the following questions:

▼ What was the conversational theme before disinterest took over?

▼ Has that theme got any relevance to my life, past or present?

▼ What question would I ask or what question would I have thought of if I hadn't been taken over by disinterest?

Reinterpretation

Over-detachment is indicated when we reinterpret people's (clients') experience in order to protect us from people's (clients') experience.

For example,

Johnella: You are incredibly courageous, you've withstood the abuse and carried on with your life successfully.

Carol: I wasn't courageous because I felt broken. If I hadn't gone to school, hadn't acted normally, I would have been beaten.

Johnella: Well I think you were courageous.

We can find our selves reinterpreting people's (clients') descriptions of events out of a sense of fear or a sense of arrogance. The fear can be prompted by a belief that to explore what it means for a person to feel, e.g. broken, would propel the person into distress. Arrogance is connected to a belief that our version of the world is the right and correct one.

Conversational pace
Conversational pace can contribute to over-detachment. It is important for us to respect people's (clients') conversational pace. When we impose our pace on the therapeutic process we risk silencing people (clients). We can avoid this by checking with people (clients). For example; Do you feel comfortable? Have you had enough time to think? Do you think I am moving too fast or too slowly? When we act insensitively to people's (clients') search for words or coherence in telling their story by interrupting with questions and statements, we can supersede people's (clients') conversational direction. Whenever I catch myself imposing my conversational pace I know that I have become too involved in self or singular thinking.

'Yes, but . . .'
'Yes, but . . .' by either the therapist or client is information that an understanding has not been reached. If we continue to 'Yes, but . . .' we risk silencing people (clients) by imposing our understandings on to their experience. 'Yes, but . . .' may indicate that we are moving too fast and our ideas have jumped ahead of people (clients). It may indicate that we are attempting to persuade people (clients) that our ideas are correct, for example, 'I know best'. It may be a sign that we are unable and/or unwilling to attempt to understand people's (clients') experience.

Whenever we catch a 'Yes, but . . .' we need to make sense of it. We can do this by reflecting on:

▼ The relationship between ourselves and prevailing cultural ideas and practices: for example, a male therapist may need to reflect on his actions, thoughts and gender relations when his reflections are being challenged by a woman who is a client and he is responding with a 'Yes, but . . .'.

▼ The relationship between ourselves and our family of origin and intimate relationships: for example, we may avoid engaging with our relationship with pain and discomfort by persisting with ideas that distract us from the feelings of helplessness and despair we hold.

▼ Our thinking and feeling within the therapeutic relationship: for example, we may be unwilling to or we may feel fearful about connecting with people's (clients') experience as it takes us into the unknown.

The 'Yes, but . . .' reflects a desire to insist on an explanation that is within our (therapists') knowledge base or comfort zone. These questions will help re-search the 'Yes, but . . .' :

▼ What idea/feeling is supporting this 'Yes, but . . .'?

▼ Where does this idea/feeling belong, does it belong to my life or the therapy?

▼ If this idea/feeling belongs to my life, how do I re-search the effects, development or influence of this idea/feeling in my life?

▼ If the idea/feeling belongs to the therapy, how do I re-search this idea/feeling in the therapy?

Whenever people's (clients') lived experience takes us beyond our experience (which includes our professional experience) we are often required to engage with ethics. If people (clients) have been forced by circumstances to act in ways that challenge their sense of moral rightness, we are also challenged to engage in conversations that help people (clients) find ways to live free of the torment that they acted immorally. We may need to consider engaging with morality in inhumane circumstances. We may be required to consider what collection of circumstances would force us to act against our ideas of morality.

Failure to consider and engage with ethics may be reflected by the presence of the 'Yes, but . . .' in the therapeutic conversation.

The 'Yes, but. . .' can often precede a statement. When the 'Yes, but . . .' belongs to us, the statement reflects certainty. Once we catch this certainty we can re-position our selves with an enquiry that reflects a wondering or a partial knowing.

The presence of disembodied words and metaphors, disinterest, reinterpretation, conversational pace and the 'Yes, but . . .' indicates that we have moved into over-detachment. I believe it is essential to the therapeutic relationship that we remain moved by human tragedy and amazed by people's resourcefulness. This does not adequately describe the enormity of always being open to connection with another, being emotionally moved, amazed, overwhelmed, awed and humbled by people's (clients') experiences. If we are unable to connect in these ways then it is possible that we have moved into a relationship with over-detachment. Reflecting on the therapeutic relationship is thus a critical therapist self-reflective tool.

OVER-CONNECTION

Over-connection occurs when we lose the ability to stand beside people (clients) in their experience. Instead we become lost in the experience. Becoming lost in people's (clients') reflections on their experience can signal that we have been propelled out of the conversation into an engagement with our experiences. The loss of contextual space/vision has the potential to blur the bounds of the therapeutic relationship understanding. Over-connection can:

▼ Draw our attention towards our selves and therefore away from the therapeutic relationship.

▼ Result in our assuming that the understanding we've made in relation to our experiences reflects other people's (clients') experience.

▼ Move us into a disconnected or numb state.

▼ Result in our movement towards concurring with 'the hopelessness arguments'.

▼ Persuade us to stop the enquiry process because we now know people's (clients') experience.

▼ Draw our attention away from re-searching the contextual environment within which people (clients) live.

In order to engage with the therapeutic relationship understanding we attend to any sign that our concentration has moved away from people (clients). This includes reflecting on any experience of stuckness, strong feelings, specialness and pervasive hopelessness, both in and outside of the therapy.

We can detect the presence of over-connection by listening very closely to our thinking, feeling, and physical state and dreams. A few indicators of over-connection are:

▼ Being overwhelmed with strong feelings that seem to reflect people's (clients') feelings. This includes experiencing physical symptoms that reflect the physical experiences of others (clients).

▼ Out of the ordinary nightmares and sleeplessness.

▼ Out of the ordinary fears, e.g. fear of using the lift, social gatherings.

▼ Changes in desire for sexual intimacy.

▼ The creation of a special relationship.

Propulsion out of a conversation into engaging with our experiences includes engaging with direct and indirect experiences. Direct experience encourages us to see/know the other's (client's) experience as though it is reflective of our experiences. Indirect experience encourages us to join with the experiences described by people (clients). Direct experience tends to incline us towards telling others what to do or think, while indirect experience tends to lead us towards feeling so lost in the other's (client's) experience that we feel or think in a similar way to the people (clients) we are working with. This over-connected feeling and thinking is dangerous for people's (clients') lives. It encourages us to believe in hopelessness, helplessness, depression, anxiety, rage, suicide as the only options available for people (clients).

The advent of over-connection is not an indicator of failure. It is an indicator of the need to have supervision/consultation.

THE EFFECTS OF CONNECTION
Connection within the therapeutic relationship requires us to use our abilities to understand, sense and feel for another's experience. Whenever we use our imaginations in order to find ways of assisting people (clients) to authentically represent their experience, we too are touched by their experiences.

For example, when I was working with a number of people who had experienced horrific ongoing abuse from family members. The level of malevolence and evil-doing was beyond anything I had heard, seen or read outside of institutional torture.

The imaginative ability that allowed me to engage with people's (clients') words and feelings didn't leave me after the session, nor did my emotional response. When you've gazed upon people's capacity for atrocity, a cup of tea does little to dislodge the images and knowing. I found myself unwilling to discuss my experiences with anyone as I believed the only worthy discussion was an authentic one. What would it mean for me to authentically describe what I knew? What would it mean to the listener? Would it help ease this knowing? I decided it wouldn't ease the knowing and authentically telling the story would leave another person with this deep knowing. I needed to put the knowing somewhere inevitably accessible but not in my everyday.

The memory my imagination created is available to me although I would rarely call on it. However, the intellectual knowing that behind the doors of respectability unspeakable abuses are perpetuated, this stays with me forever.

We are touched and changed by our engagement within the therapeutic relationship. When we hold the knowledge that the balance between connectedness and detachment is dynamic, this precludes us from ever taking the therapeutic relationship for granted. Our commitment to the therapeutic relationship understanding is maintained by ongoing self and other reflection.

We will be affected by our experiences within the therapeutic relationship even when there is a balance between connection and detachment. Over time the effects can accumulate. These effects are often identified by us (therapists) as exhaustion.

Many institutions have failed to recognise the implications for workers of engaging in therapeutic relationships where people (clients) have been sexually, physically and emotionally abused. This lack of recognition has encouraged over-detachment and over-connection as we struggle, often in isolation, to survive. It is essential that we are assisted in this work with intellectual explanations and technical skills. It is also essential that we reflect on how we can balance connection and detachment. Adherence to the idea that the balance between connectedness and detachment is dynamic prepares us to be continuously watchful of this balance. From a state of watchfulness we are also able re-search the strategies and environments that assist this balance. I have found the following strategies useful in my practice:

Breath consciousness

When hearing and discussing shocking events we may prepare our selves by physically tensing. This tension can impact on breathing. We can find our selves holding our breath or breathing shallowly. The result over time can be hyperventilation. Exercise, yoga or relaxation between sessions can maintain a consciousness around our breathing. This consciousness can then assist us during sessions.

Body consciousness

Physical tension can be expressed in numerous ways, e.g. moving forwards in the chair, holding the body in a particular posture for long periods of time, lifting the shoulders, clenching hands, tension in the face and neck. During therapy sessions we can check this by moving our attention to our bodies and releasing tension.

Activities to move knowings into memory

This involves experimenting with ways to put the knowing to one side rather than staying in the knowing. Centering rituals can assist us in this, as the rituals symbolically move us from one place to another. These rituals can be as everyday as completing written reflections, putting these away in a filing cabinet and putting the thinking away with the notes. Moving around the room, opening windows or participation in prayer, meditation or visualisation can be helpful. Centering is necessary because most of us move from one therapeutic session to another and we need to find ways to be available to our selves in order to be available to others (clients).

Activities to connect or reconnect with feelings

The therapeutic relationship understanding requires us to be aware of our feelings and to use feelings for the benefit of other people (clients). At times what we hear will result in feelings that belong entirely with and for our selves. Putting these feelings to one side for the duration of the interview may result in an inability to access them later; they may instead remain submerged, appearing as exhaustion or tiredness.

Activities such as relaxation, exercise or massage can help us reconnect with feelings. We can also use a consultative or supervisory process to reconnect with these experiences.

OVER-DETACHMENT AS NORMAL CLINICAL PRACTICE

Very little has been written in therapeutic literature about over-detachment, whereas over-connection has had considerable exposure. The consequences of over-connection have been labelled in various ways as burnout or compassion fatigue. It is not uncommon to hear a worker being criticised for being over-involved, while it's rare to hear a criticism of under-involvement. This bias relates to the value placed on the objective, the scientific and the idea that professional detachment goes with expert knowing. When this relating style is dominant in a therapeutic process it results in an under-estimation of people's (clients') experience and an over-estimation of professional certainty. Inevitably the therapeutic conversation is directed towards evaluation, diagnosis and intervention.

It is my experience that men who are therapists are more vulnerable to over-detachment whereas women who are therapists are more vulnerable to over-connection. Therapies that link poststructuralist ideas to the therapeutic work continue to focus primarily on providing new theoretical explanations. There is a lack of engagement with both the therapeutic relationship as a vehicle for meaning-making (and thus a focus for change) and the therapeutic relationship as an arena for emotional experiences for both therapist and client. Pre-occupation with a poststructuralist explanation contributes to an invisibility of the emotional climate that exists in the therapeutic relationship. This invis-ibility put therapists at risk of engaging with over-connection or over-detachment practices. In contrast, when we both (client and therapist) use the emotional climate to explore and engage with making sense of people's (clients') thoughts and experiences, we are also open to be affected by our experiences within the therapeutic relationship. We are part of the emotional climate. When we are not affected this may indicate that we are using a therapeutic practice that relies on over-detachment. However when we don't acknowledge the effects of our participation in this emotional climate we risk becoming over-connected.

A therapeutic environment that supports us to balance detachment and connection also enables us to remain connected with our own physical, emotional, spirit-filled selves. This type of therapeutic environment sits outside of many of the established conventions for therapeutic practice. A therapeutic environment that supports connection/detachment balance may precipitate reconsideration of our relationship to the environment, time, change, movement, humour, touch and community. So begins the process of reinvention.

REFLECTING ON CONNECTION AND DETACHMENT STRATEGIES

Over-connection and over-detachment are inevitable when the effects of connection are not acknowledged. Over-detachment is inevitable when over-detachment practices disappear from scrutiny under the auspices of preferred or normal psychological practices. We can provide our selves with the strategies that protect and respect our emotional and physical selves while engaging with the effects of connection. Using these strategies prevents the movement into over-connection or over-detachment. Over-detachment can deaden our selves to our selves. We can use this strategy of over-detachment to distance our selves from that which we see or hear. This, however, can move into our lives, isolating us from our own experience. In order to experience re-enlivement, we may resort to using substances such as alcohol and drugs.

The strategies I have suggested in this chapter for maintaining the connection/detachment balance act to remind us of simple pleasure. We can actively orientate our selves towards taking opportunities to enjoy our life. From this place of replenishment, we are able to engage more coherently with life/hope. Looking for or developing strategies for replenishment is a different experience from using stress management techniques.

In some institutions, strategies have been developed informally to help workers detach from the repeated experience of listening and being emotionally available as people (clients) move out of silence to articulate their experiences of abuse. These strategies have often detached workers from their own experiences. A common practice is for workers to use black humour. This practice may have advantages. However, it is important that its function is re-searched and explored. It is possible that the use of black humour detaches the worker from her/his experience of horror. This horror may represent the worker's exposure to the actions of one human being who has systematically tortured and tormented another. This knowledge may raise deep philosophical concerns, for example:

▼ What constitutes human nature?

▼ Does evil exist?

▼ Is there anything about this abuser that is recognisable in me?

▼ How is hope sustained and supported after such experiences?

▼ How can hope for life and grief for what has been suffered exist side by side?

Whatever our response to people's (clients') life experiences we must name it, speak it, re-search it, in order to stay connected in our lives. All the strategies we and institutions use, including black humour, need to be personally and collectively re-searched so we can understand the implications these strategies have for our lives and for the therapeutic relationship.

There is no line that can be drawn to provide us with a point of balance between detachment and connection. It is a dynamic process that requires us to willingly engage in daily reflection on thoughts, actions and language both in and out of the therapeutic relationship. This reflective process is founded on curiosity and wondering, it is not a search for definitive answers. Experiences provoke a search for questions that, in turn, provide answers that develop a process of relating with the therapeutic relationship.

Transparency with our selves is the cornerstone of any therapy that recognises that every psychological theory and practice is vulnerable to conscription into ideas and practices that invisibilize others. This can be illustrated with a simple rule of practice. Whenever the therapy feels stuck, I wonder to myself:

▼ Is there something that I don't understand?

▼ Where did I begin to lose understanding?

▼ What is the understanding that I'm working within?

▼ Is that the other person's (client's) understanding?

▼ What are the presuppositions that support the understanding I'm working with?

This reflective process protects the therapeutic relationship from stuckness becoming evidence of people's (clients') lack of willingness to comply with helpful ideas and strategies. Instead it assumes a lack in my (the therapist's) knowing.

Discovery through the therapeutic conversation is situated in the present moment. We ensure that people (clients) are recalling or looking back to the past while firmly situated in the present. Situating people (clients) in the present moment enables a connection with the past while retaining enough detachment to protect people from experiencing the experiences of the past. In positioning our selves to stand beside people (clients) as their discoveries unfold, we also ensure our separateness or detachment from people's (clients') experiences. The therapeutic relationship is vibrant, therefore the movement and the balance between connectedness and detachment must always be available for reflection. I find it useful to continually reflect on the signs of over-detachment and over-connection in order to monitor their balance within the therapeutic relationship.

Maintaining the balance between detachment and connection in the work with people who have been sexually, physically and emotionally abused requires courage. It is the courage to know what it is to be human.

THE ETHICS INVOLVED IN BUILDING THE THERAPEUTIC RELATIONSHIP

What are the ethical implications of the balance between detachment and connection in the therapeutic relationship?
Achievement of the balance between detachment and connection is necessary in order for us (therapists) to intimately get to know people's (clients') experiences without being overwhelmed by this knowledge. When we achieve this we are effectively standing beside people (clients), as they engage in the process of reflecting deeply on their lives. The balancing of connection and detachment protects people (clients) from our assumptions. These assumptions include the idea that we know or feel people's (clients') unique experience or that our specialist knowledge provides us with a way of coding behaviour so that people's (clients') experiences fit our comprehensive theoretical explanations.

Over-detachment has a long history as a valued positioning of the professional self towards the other. It is a strategy used in medicine to move the body from a subject into an object which is assessed, intruded upon, and operated on. It is a strategy of modernism, where it is considered possible for an observer to collect the 'objective' data that supports truth claims. It is a strategy of those psychological and psychiatric practitioners who adhere to the belief that it is possible to assess people without reference to historical and cultural constructs. It is a strategy of all therapists who hold to a definitive theory of psychological development that is given preference to and presides over the intimate and domestic details of people's (clients') lives.

Over-detachment draws a distinction between us and them. In the world of problem evaluation, over-detachment secures an enquiry that searches out the etiology of the problem and presents an intervention. There is no room in the world of problem evaluation to re-search the strategies for making sense of experiences or to search out competence, abilities and strengths.

In over-detachment we don't wonder about how reported experiences would feel, how a child, woman, or man at this point in time, within this particular cultural context, carrying the burden of that marginal-ization, would make sense of experiences. In over-detachment we don't take those wonderings and develop an enquiry process that further researches people's (clients') experience. In over-detachment we don't consider how the knowledges we carry (including lived experience knowledges) both support and hinder our enquiry. Over-detachment situates us (therapists) as colonisers of people's (clients') lives.

In the professional climate where over-detachment is valued, any movement towards connecting with another's experience is considered an over-connection. Any challenge to the prescriptions or interventions of over-detachment is negated as being evidence of the person's over-involvement.

For example, a general practitioner refers a man (Ben) to the local psychiatric out-patients unit. Ben has been deeply depressed since the death of his father six months ago. He was interviewed by a social worker who discovered that Ben was seriously considering suicide. She also learnt that Ben had been sexually abused by his father. Ben reported that this was the first time he'd talked about the events from the past. By the end of the session the social worker assessed that the suicide risk factor had reduced sufficiently to allow Ben to return home. He was given another appointment for the following day.

At the case conference meeting that day the social worker was reprimanded for failing to admit Ben. She was told to visit him at home that day to arrange admission. When she met with Ben, he told her that although he was still feeling shaky, he could 'see a light at the end of the tunnel'. His response to the idea of admission was to say the following; 'To put me in the looney bin would truly tip me over the edge.

It would make me feel hopeless. It's been my greatest fear for years that someone would find out that I really was mad. Even that I made it all up, the abuse I mean. I'll keep my word to you. I know it would get you in to trouble if I didn't.'

The social worker went back to the consultant and informed him of the conversation. His response was, 'You've got too emotional about Ben, you're over-involved.' The social worker, Ben and the consultant met the next day. The consultant agreed that the suicide risk factors were low. However, he wanted to admit Ben to be on the 'safe side'.

Questions:

▼ Who's side is the 'safe side' on? Did the consultant's fears belong to Ben or did they belong to the recent public exposure of the suicide levels among psychiatric patients?

▼ What constitutes a safe side for Ben?

▼ How could a safe side be negotiated to include Ben's, the consultant's, and the social worker's concerns?

▼ What role did over-detachment play in the lack of exploring and making sense of, and giving credence to, Ben's experiences, thoughts, and feelings?

▼ What role did gender relations play in the dismissing of the social worker's assessment as over-involved and emotional?

In a milieu where over-detachment becomes invisible under the guise of normal professional practice, it remains unavailable for re-view and reflection. Its invisibility inevitably visibilizes connection within the therapeutic relationship. This in turn creates the conditions where connection is available for scrutiny and problematising. The appearance of over-connection and over-detachment in the therapeutic relationship has severe consequences for people (clients). Ethically we must consider becoming alert to both of these states. In doing this we will be challenging taken-for-granted professional detachment practice.

If the connection/detachment balance replaces detachment as a professional practice, what are the consequences for us (therapists)?
Therapists/counsellors and administrators have established a relationship with time that has a strong association with the production of

therapy as an economic activity. Institutions frequently require workers to note down all activities in order to assess productivity. These activities rarely include any strategies to maintain the connection/detachment balance. The work is thus defined as having no implication for the wellbeing of the workers. In this environment, conversations that explore, name and contextualise tortuous and traumatic events are equated to an accountant's work on a balance sheet.

In order to survive many workers gravitate towards over-detachment. There are however personal and professional consequences to both over-connection and over-detachment. These consequences can be avoided by linking productivity with workers' wellbeing. In other words, strategies for maintaining the connection/detachment balance need to be legitimised and incorporated into the expectation and practices of therapy/counselling.

WORKING WITH THE TEXT

How do I (Client) participate in building the therapeutic relationship?

In order to participate in the therapeutic relationship first consider your willingness to engage with this relationship. If you are entering this relationship because someone else (GP, partner, friend) thought it was a good idea, ask your self:

▼ Even though this is not my idea, am I willing to consider that this could be useful or meaningful?

▼ How would I know if it was?

▼ How long would I give the therapy in order to decide if I want to engage in it?

When you meet the therapist, consider your first impressions and ask your self:

▼ How will this impression impact on this relationship? If the therapist appears to belong to a different cultural group, gender, class or sexuality from you, ask your self:

• How will this difference affect my attitude to the therapy?

For example:

- Will I present myself in a particular way?
- Are there some things that I won't say?
- Can I express myself fully in this environment?
- Will I protect the therapist from my thoughts and feelings?

You are entitled to check out with them your impressions of the therapist's ethnicity, class, professional experience and qualifications, attitudes, sexuality and religious affiliations.

If you identify a difference and you believe the difference will affect your ability to engage in the therapeutic relationship then take this information seriously. Either continue to have a conversation with the therapist that explores and negotiates the differences or end the therapeutic relationship. If the therapist conducts this conversation defensively or unwillingly, then this is not an environment that can respect differences.

Therapeutic relationships involve a dynamic balance between connectedness and detachment. It is the therapist's responsibility to be alert to this balance. If you find, however, that you are holding back thoughts, feelings and/or memories in order to protect the therapist, consider the following:

▼ What do I think will happen to the therapist if I confide these thoughts and memories?
▼ Is there any evidence for this worry?
▼ What will I need to know about her or him in order to check out this worry?

Holding back thoughts, feelings and/or memories often encourages screening. (Refer to Chapter Five.)

A therapist's over-connection can be signalled by the following:

▼ When the therapist discloses information about herself/himself that adds to your knowledge of the therapist's life but doesn't benefit the work.
▼ Whenever the therapist's emotional response results in your thinking or feeling that you need to care for the therapist.

▼ Gestures, touch or disclosure that leaves you feeling uncomfortable.

A therapist's over-detachment can be signalled by the following:

▼ You leave a therapy session in which you have attempted to speak
your concerns with a sense that the therapist doesn't understand
your thoughts, feelings and experience.

▼ You feel that something of life significance to you is treated glibly.

▼ The conversation feels superficial rather than substantial. You
can signal this experience of over-detachment by saying, 'I don't
feel that you truly understood what I was saying last week,' or, 'I'd
like to negotiate uninterrupted time during our sessions.'

▼ If the therapist allows ongoing interruptions to occur during the
therapy session.

If the therapist's response to your queries is genuine consideration of
the experience you hold while wondering about what needs to change
in order for you to experience understanding, then the therapeutic
relationship understanding is maintained. If the therapist's response is
to consider the experience you hold in a way that diminishes it rather
than extends it, then the therapeutic relationship understanding is
contravened. In this instance the therapist is unwilling to consider her
or his participation in the lack of understanding. Remaining in this
situation puts you at risk of ongoing detachment experiences, which in
turn separates you from your own knowing and wisdom.

How do I (therapist) participate in building the Therapeutic Relationship?

When you experience your self as working hard in a therapeutic
relationship one explanation is that people (clients) do not expect that
the therapeutic relationship can or will be meaningful. Instead of working harder to facilitate engagement, stop and consider the following:

▼ Is there a significant difference between myself and the other
people (clients)? This difference can be reflected in ethnicity,
gender, class, sexuality, age.

▼ What are people's (clients') expectations of therapy/counselling?

▼ What have been people's (clients') previous experiences of
therapy/counselling?

▼ Who is most concerned about this concern inside and outside of the family?

These questions can both help you in a self-enquiry and become part of your enquiry with people (clients).

Building the therapeutic relationship involves a dynamic balance between detachment and connectedness.

In order to truly understand what has been done to some people or what some people have done to others you need courage. Reflect on:

▼ What are the beliefs, technical abilities and experiences in my life that allow me to consider people's capacity to injure others without succumbing to thoughts and feelings of despair?

▼ What are the beliefs, technical abilities and experiences in my life that encourage me to look for and support people (clients) to rediscover life/hope even when they are gripped by hopelessness?

▼ How do I catch the judgments I hold in order to protect people (clients) from the imposition of this judgment into the conversation? An example of a judgment is, 'No one could possibly love someone who did that.'

▼ What are my ideas about how I can use a knowledge of these judgments to inform the therapy? For example, 'When Mary (client) carries that judgment, how is it turned against her or turned for her?' Does Mary censor her thoughts and feelings out of fear that this judgment will be carried by me or others? How has this judgment impacted on Mary's life?

▼ What strategies do I use to know people's (clients') experiences without getting lost in the experience?

▼ What alerts me to over-detachment or over-connection?

▼ What strategies does the institution I work in use to encourage detachment or connection? Within the therapeutic relationship, re-search the implications to your self and the therapy of this strategy.

▼ What strategies have enabled me to stay connected while acknowledging the effect of connections?

▼ What strategies assist me to re-search my thinking and experiences within the therapeutic relationship?

Another way to reflect on over-connection and over-detachment is to ask your self the following:

▼ When I come home from work, what strategies do I use to fully re-enter my life?

▼ How do I protect myself from replicating my engagement with the obligations and roles of the therapeutic relationship understanding in other relationships in my life?

Re-searching stuckness
Whenever the therapy becomes stuck in some way it is useful to reflect on the possibility of over-connectedness or over-detachment.

Reflect on a time when you identify that the therapy was stuck in some way

▼ Was the person's (client's) experience outside of my experience?

▼ How did I negotiate an understanding of this difference?

▼ Was the person's (client's) experience similar to mine?

▼ How did I protect the relationship from the assumption that I knew the other's experience?

▼ Where did I begin to lose the understanding?

▼ What was the understanding that I was working within?

▼ Was this the other person's (client's) understanding?

▼ What questions could I have asked people (clients) in order to have further explored the understandings they held?

Externalising stuckness within a self and other reflective process allows us to re-search the conditions that surround stuckness both in and outside of the therapeutic relationship. This protects the therapeutic relationship from either therapist self-blame as in 'I'm not a good enough therapist' or client blame as in 'she/he isn't working hard enough'. Re-searching the stuckness emphasises that the therapy is always a negotiated collaborative process. Given that the balance between connection and detachment within the therapeutic relationship is dynamic, evidence of stuckness may signal either over-connection or over-detachment.

CHAPTER FIVE

. . . .

Working with Contradictions

A FICTIONAL STORY

Once upon many times there lived, in a land like yours and mine, a young woman. This young woman, whose name was Anne, lived with her family.

It was a rather ordinary family whose members lived rather ordinary lives. They were so ordinary, no one really noticed them. In fact, to a certain degree, they had achieved the impossible — they were 'invisible'.

Anne had the ability to bring them all into visibility. She didn't want to, by any means. She preferred invisibility. She knew it caused her family members various degrees of pain to stand exposed.

Her father, in particular, feared the visibility light and said to her many, many times, 'If you expose me, I will have to leave. And when I leave my love goes with me, leaving you and everyone else bereft. Your mother will feel this pain deeply and she will know that you are the cause of her loss.'

Anne's father, whose name was Simon, said this without a hint of malice or anger. Instead he looked at her with sad, watery blue eyes.

The look struck her deeply. Anne wanted invisibility. In fact every night she prayed to her God to help her keep the family safe.

Visibility came against her will. It took the form of shaking. Every now and again Anne would shake from her head to her toes. Even the tips of her ears vibrated. The shaking drew stares from everyone, and eventually Anne was sent to a doctor who gave her anti-shake medicine which didn't stop the shake at all but did stop her eating.

Out of desperation the doctor decided to shake up her mind with ECT treatment. That didn't stop the shaking either but it did help her forget.

Many diagnoses later she was sent to a therapist who wondered out loud, 'Sometimes people shake from fright. Is there anything that has, or is frightening you?'

'I don't think so,' said Anne. 'The thing that frightens me most is that my dad gets very upset with this shaking, so upset that he might leave. He doesn't like people staring at us.'

'What does he worry that people will see, when they stare at him?'

'It's silly,' said Anne, 'but a long time ago he abused me. It was just once or twice. I've confronted him, you know, and he's admitted it. It's all over now. No one else needs to know. My mum, she'd get upset if she knew, so it's better this way.'

▼ Is it all over now, bar the shaking?
▼ What can be done in the face of this contradiction where in an apparently close family, this closeness is maintained by secrets?
▼ What can be done when words of love are spoken by the same body that has abused?
▼ What can be done when a loved one requires the sacrifice of the other?

In Anne's situation the sacrifice is life itself. Love is conditional on the loss of the self. In order to secure the love that many children take for granted, Anne is required to deny what she knows, what she has experienced and what is happening now. She is obliged to reconstruct and enact a child's relationship with parents where she is the protector and guardian of safety, while in fact living in an environment of parental abuse. She is expected to trust and respect the person who is untrustworthy and disrespectful. When Anne inevitably falls short of these expectations she reprimands her self and is reprimanded by others (family members, friends, professionals) as a failure, as guilty, as stupid, as a trouble maker, as difficult, as untrustworthy, as a liar, as precocious, as nervy, as mentally ill. Finding ways to live with these contradictory conditions provokes profound dilemmas that are often carried by children into their adult lives. In this work we (therapists) are required to know the conditions that support love and the conditions that support the death of the spirit.

When people (clients) are abused (physically, emotionally and sexually) by members of their family, contradictory experiences and emotions abound. In this story it's clear that Simon is responsible for sexually abusing Anne (his daughter). In order to protect himself and his place in the family and society, he intimidates Ann with the threat, 'If you tell I will be forced to leave and you will be blamed.' This statement is possibly true. It is likely that Simon would have to leave the family if sexual abuse was disclosed and it is possible that Anne would carry the burden of blame for this. Simon, however, requires Anne to take responsibility for this possibility, thereby removing any responsibility from himself. Anne, in order to protect the family, agrees to hold this secret. Holding the secret begins the separation between her self and her experiences and thus her self and others. The cost to her of holding this secret is high, however the cost of telling is also experienced as high.

What kind of love requires a person to sacrifice their emotional, spirit-filled self? What kind of loving person says that he is loving you, not abusing you and then threatens to blame you if you tell? These contradictory conditions pervade the intimate, daily moments of family life. It is these everyday moments that young people such as Anne are required to negotiate their way through.

If we are not prepared for these contradictions we risk undertaking a simplistic enquiry that continues to alienate people (clients) from their experiences. Our preparation usually includes studying academic texts. However, professional journals and psychologically orientated texts provide a limited resource in illuminating the complexity of this 'narrative in action' and our relationship to it.

In moving past the simplistic ideas of 'solution' we prepare to engage with the complexity of both living in and re-searching human relationships. This complexity has acted as inspiration for musicians, writers and artists throughout the centuries. In the arts the emotional coherence of a piece of work is judged by its ability to resonate with the viewer, listener, reader. In the coherent therapeutic relationship resonance is achieved when there is mutual understanding, joint vision and emotional exchange. To achieve resonation we must extend our sense of morality so we can sit with the contradictory experiences and feelings that pervade people's (clients') sense of their lives. Within this place we, together with people (clients), work towards knowing and exploring ways of living well in the presence of these contradictions.

Membership of the elite professional classes often requires us to practice a conversational style that is self referential and objectifying of 'the others' (members of the client class). The literature often reflects this style, as academic writers rise from clinician to university professor; reflections on the therapeutic practice consequently conform to an academic style, where thoughts or ideas are validated through textual referencing.

Whenever we believe this self referential literature and impose these understandings on people's (clients') experience we fail to extend our sense of morality. When we apply abstract detached explanations we classify experience rather than engaging directly with an intimate exploration of people's (clients') experience. This intimate exploration transports us to both the edge of and inside of the parameters within which love and hatred, good and evil, helplessness and resilience, all reside. If we apply abstract detached explanations by using binaries such as good/bad, well/sick, then we risk both simplifying experience while at the same time contributing to people's (clients') continued experience of soul persecution.

People (clients) can find themselves struggling to find a way to live with contradictory feelings. These contradictory feelings may include anger/rage together with feelings of love and connection. All of these feelings can be directed towards the abusive person/s. When we (therapists) are faced with contradictions, we must resist siding with one position over another. Instead, we explore the context that surrounds and supports the contradictions, in order to understand the contradiction's development and its impact on people (clients). In this exploration we inevitably expose issues of responsibility and the impact of secrets on people's (clients') relationship to the self and their relationship with significant others.

When people (clients) explore the effects of defying the secret's requirement of silence, with the self and with non-familial significant others and with family members, they often reconnect with the abuser's terror strategies that have maintained the secret over many years. Consequently people (clients) often experience strong, emotional responses and this calls for a re-view of safety strategies both in and outside of therapy. Exploration of the situation that requires secrecy can expose how the contradictions have imprisoned the person (client) in a particular meaning paradigm. This understanding then enables us (therapist and client) to find ways to challenge the contradiction or to live with the contradiction liberated from the effects of blame, shame, guilt, fear and secrecy.

Living with the contradictions can mean that people (clients) experience two selves: the self who holds the secret knowledge and experience; and the self who takes part in the world. The self who takes part in the world is often regarded as the false self. All accomplishments and friendships are diminished by the secret knowledge; 'If they knew who I really was or if they knew what I'd really done, they'd think differently about me.' People (clients) who exist within the contradic- tions highlighted in Anne's story, often occupy the borderland. The borderland is a place haunted by the past. People (clients) rest uneasily here as they are neither in the world nor outside of it. The stresses of living here can result in what is considered mental illness and/or drug and alcohol use. Living on the border so disconnects people (clients) from life that death can become an attractive option. People (clients) living within contradictions are frequently labelled with the psychiatric diagnoses of 'Borderline Personality Disorder'. They are labelled this way because we have failed to engage with the complexity of their experience. Our intellectual, technical and imaginative failure subjects those people (clients) who have already suffered immensely to even more suffering.

When the contradictions and secrets are exposed and explored, it is possible for people (clients) to reclaim the accomplishments and friendships they had previously considered as belonging to the false self.

A relational externalising conversation is essential to exploring these contradictions. Within this style of conversation we can name and explore actions that humiliate, threaten, bully, abuse and diminish others physically and emotionally while holding people's (clients') positive memories of that same person. In this exploration we may be required to reconsider our ideas about the concept and lived experience of love and attachment.

In the following example consultant number one will approach

Trevor and Rose's situation using an internalising discourse. Consultant number two will use a relational externalising enquiry process. In the example, what is externalised is italicised to emphasize the fluidity of relational externalising in a conversation.

Trevor is eight years old. Rose, his mother, was referred for family counselling by social workers employed by a statutory organisation. They were concerned that Trevor was being physically neglected by Rose. Trevor's school had alerted the authorities because Trevor had begun to steal and frequently attended school inadequately dressed and unwashed. He had subsequently been mercilessly teased by other children. Trevor's father, Steve, had been physically abusive to Rose and had left the relationship within a week of Rose discovering that she was pregnant. In the initial interview, the therapist discovered that Rose had suffered enormous shame as a child because of a club foot. This physical difference, together with the effects of poverty, e.g. different clothing, no school lunches, the school paying for the costs of stationary and school trips, culminated in Rose feeling and being isolated within her community.

Rose found Trevor a nuisance and an irritation. She expected him to live independently of her by making his own meals and determining when he came home, got up, and went to bed. Whenever he approached her looking for connection, support, sympathy or love, she responded with irritation, e.g. 'Why does everyone want something of me, I just can't give him what he wants, he annoys me.' Trevor presented in the interview as quiet and detached from the conversation. When he was engaged in the conversation he responded eagerly. However, he would often look anxiously towards Rose. Trevor appeared animated when he talked about 'Nana', a 50-year-old woman who had been a neighbour eight years ago and had been very supportive of both Trevor and Rose. The therapist was concerned with the direction of therapy and approached two consultants.

Consultant number one began the consultative process by making the following comments:

> Consultant: I am really worried about this situation. Rose appears to have been unable to attach to Trevor. It's likely that Rose was unable to form an attachment with Trevor as a baby. What was her emotional engagement with Trevor in the room with you?

Therapist: Well, throughout the whole interview she barely looked at him.

Consultant: Did she touch him at all?

Therapist: No, he touched her once after he had completed a drawing. He was trying to draw her attention to the drawing.

Consultant: How did she respond?

Therapist: Well, she sort of sighed and gave it a cursory look and waved him away.

Consultant: Um, that's really worrying. How does she respond to meeting his basic physical needs?

Therapist: Not very well, it's almost as if he's not really there. When he is loud and rowdy, she responds to him, however it's often an angry response. The situation can then escalate where he throws a temper tantrum. She either throws him in his room or smacks him.

Consultant: When she hits him, is she in control or out of control?

Therapist: I checked that. She says she doesn't really lose it, she generally hits him once or twice on the bottom. She says if she's about to lose it, she gets out of the house. I've checked with the social worker and the school and there isn't evidence of physical abuse.

Consultant: I think that Rose has been unable to attach adequately to Trevor. I suspect that there was no attachment at birth. That places him at serious emotional risk. I am really worried about him. Is there anyone else that he could live with?

Therapist: There is the person they both call Nana, but from what I can gather she can only be involved occasionally, maybe once a week or fortnight.

Consultant: Well, that's a real problem. What about a foster placement?

Consultant number two began:

Consultant: What question does *this situation* leave with you?

Therapist: Well basically I don't know what I can do. It was hard work engaging with Trevor and I'm worried that this together with a lack of engagement between the two of them in the session indicates an attachment problem. What can I do when the mother hasn't attached to her child?

Consultant: Okay. Would it be okay if we talked for a moment about *this attachment idea* and perhaps *the climates that support attachment*?

Therapist: That would be great.

Consultant: These are some of the questions that come to my mind. They may be questions that you've asked.

Consultant: I'm wondering how Rose related to being placed on *the outside* as child, because of *these differences*?

Therapist: She was incredibly ashamed. She says that she tore up all the photos of her self as child. She looks back at that time and feels she was pathetic and revolting. It's a time that she'd prefer to forget.

Consultant: When she looks at Trevor, what does she see? Is there anything in the way Trevor looks or the way he acts that reminds her of her memory of her young self? If there is, what is she reminded of *in the looking*? Does *the looking* include any feelings of revulsion that emerge when she remembers *the memory of her young self*? What impact would *the feelings of revulsion* or any of *the other feelings* have on the *relationship* between Rose and Trevor? What do you think of these questions — can you see that I'm wondering if *the turning away from the past* is a strategy for surviving and then Rose finds the past is reflected in a child. I'm wondering what effect that might have on *the relationship*?

Therapist: Yes, that could be interesting.

Consultant: Okay, I'd like to talk about an enquiry around attachment. I'm wondering if we move away from *the idea of
attachment or not,* could we consider *the possibility of
forms of attachment.* I'm wondering about an exploration of *the early mother/baby activities* of attachment. I'm
wondering about the *changes* to and with attachment as
the baby becomes a toddler and the toddler becomes an
active boy.

I'm wondering about *the environment* and *the ideas
and practices* that support *attachment-thinking and
attachment-practices.*

I'm wondering about Rose's relationship with *the
experiences of attachment* with her self and with another
person in *the present* and in *the past* and *the hopes* she
carries for possibilities for *the future.*

I'm wondering about what would constitute *good
enough attachment* or *beginning attachment.*

I'm wondering if the relationship between Nana and
Rose provides Rose with *the experience of attachment.*

I'm wondering if *the relationship* between Nana and
Trevor provides Trevor with *the experience of attachment.* I'm wondering if Rose notices differences or
similarities in *the experience of attachment* or connection between her self and her parents, and her self
and Trevor.

I'm using *the language of attachment* in this enquiry, but
that may need to be negotiated and changed in conversation with Rose.

Therapist: That helps me to explore *the experience of attachment.*
However I'm worried that even if we could establish *the
climate for building a relationship of connection or
attachment* that this would take time and would effect
Trevor's wellbeing.

Consultant: Over this time is it possible to negotiate a regular
connection between Nana and Trevor and Rose? Could
Nana become a supporter of Rose by helping her
develop or explore *the relationship of attachment/
connection* with Trevor?

Therapist: The social worker said that Nana was as involved as she could be.

Consultant: Would you consider inviting Nana to a session to negotiate her involvement? I'm imagining negotiating *the beginning of a supportive relationship* rather than *a taking over relationship*. I'm also wondering about exploring *the strategies for holding on to the experiences of connections* with, for example, Nana and then between themselves. This may mean exploring ways to consider *the memory of experiences of connection or attachment* that can act to support people in the everyday.

Therapist: That sounds an interesting idea to explore, I hadn't considered involving Nana. What about the level of physical neglect?

Consultant: This may be connected with the other issues we've discussed, including the possibility that this neglect is somehow connected to Rose's removal of feeling or acknowledgment from the relationship with Trevor because of what he represents. *The possible removal of feeling* could then support a vicious cycle in that *the neglect* strengthens the association between Trevor and Rose's *memory of her young self*. Maybe you could develop an enquiry around the connection between *the self* and *the experiences of self and other care*. What do you think?

Therapist: I think I have a lot of ideas to follow up in order to understand what's effecting the relationship between Trevor and Rose. This conversation has highlighted that there's a lot I don't yet understand.

The first consultant brings certainty and her theory of attachment to the consultation process. The second consultant is interested in a further exploration of the conditions that surround attachment/connection and levels of possible attachment/connections in the relationship. She is also interested in looking for possible attachment/connection relationships beyond the biological relationships. This consultation highlights what remains unknown to the therapist. The consultant's wonderings reawakens the therapist's curiousity and sense of not knowing.

Engaging with certainty precludes an exploration of life possibilities within the contradictory nature of people's (clients') experience. This experience is often totally outside of professional people's experience and people (clients) consequently are vulnerable to a pathologising interpretation of life events.

When I consider the limitations of my experience, I prepare and support my ability to engage empathetically by using literature, music, art and film. This preparation extends my imaginative abilities. Willingness to extend and engage with our imaginative abilities prepares us to explore the dilemmas presented, not as detached representations of other's experience, but as though it could be our experience. This practice helps us to engage with a living morality that challenges simplistic ideas of right and wrong.

WORKING WITH LIFE/HOPE
In the therapeutic work with people (clients) who have experienced the effects of physical, emotional and sexual abuse on their lives, the therapeutic relationship can act to support them by providing experiences of hope and trust. When we are unprepared for the work in these areas we can find our selves succumbing to a sense of hopelessness followed by the blaming and further labelling of people (clients). We can avoid this by finding ways to explore the experience of hope and trust in our lives as well as in the lives of others. Exploration of hope and trust within the therapeutic relationship prepares us to engage in conversations that will challenge fears within a climate of safety. This work requires that we act at times to hold, within the therapeutic relationship, the knowledge of the potentially complex and contradictory relationship people (clients) have with hope.

Hope is a simple word with a simple/complex meaning. Hope in the therapeutic context does not mean being cheerful or looking towards the positives in people's (clients') lives. Hope means knowing that while experiencing great despair, there is somewhere a belief in the possibility of life: life-hope. When people (clients) experience great despair, we hold and maintain the possibility people (clients) will rediscover the hope for life. The therapeutic relationship can sometimes be the only site for hope in people's (clients') lives. This can be frightening for both therapist and client.

Working with people (clients) to build or rebuild a sense of life/hope, must be undertaken with caution and awareness of the supports that are necessary in order to maintain life/hope. We can only support life/hope effectively when we closely know people's (clients') life circumstances. This knowing includes the life events that have impacted on people's (clients') lives together with the emotional consequences of those events. In order to work with life/hope we are required to know its presence and its absence.

These questions may help us reflect on our work with hope:

▼ What are the ideas and experiences that act as the foundation stones for your engagement with hope in your life/in your work?

▼ How close have you been to experiencing life-taking hopelessness?

▼ How did the hope for life re-emerge in your life?

▼ What ideas or people stood on the side of hope in your life?

▼ How have you used this knowledge and experience to retain life-hope in the face of hopelessness?

We can position our selves for the work with life/hope by holding to the idea that life circumstances can be unpredictable; for example, a chance encounter on a bus may alter someone's perception of hopelessness. This knowledge encourages us to continue to be alert for life/hope experiences both within the therapeutic relationship and outside of it. For example, Tony felt a surge of hope while sitting on his surfboard. Prior to this experience he had been going through the motions of surfing. Then, 'The sun broke through the clouds and diffused rays of light danced on the water, the board and on my skin. At that moment I felt a sense of joy I had previously thought was lost.'

When these moments of life/hope are discovered through the conversation we attempt to capture this life/hope moment and move the experience into a knowing. With this new knowledge of life/hope people (clients) can then be equipped with a resource to challenge the despair knowledge.

WHEN WE (THERAPISTS) LOSE HOPE
When we fail to hold the possibility that life/hope will be rediscovered within the therapeutic relationship it is often as a result of being either over-connected or over-detached. If this happens it is important, in fact critical, to seek supervision/consultation. The task of supervision/

consultation is to discover what is impeding our holding on to the possibility of life/hope. If we are unable to rediscover life/hope possibilities, then we know we are no longer able to be vigilant for opportunities to discover, negotiate, explore and experiment with life/hope within the therapeutic relationship. People (clients) are then at risk of slipping further into despair.

For example, I heard a therapist tell the following story. 'I was working with a young woman, she was 23 years of age and had had a longstanding involvement with psychiatric services. She had experienced sexual abuse by several members of her family, consequently she had withdrawn from any involvement with her family. Episodes of depression had interfered with her ability to complete university, maintain relationships and hold on to employment. She was presently on the sickness benefit. She had a comprehensive argument for ending her life. Over time I came to believe her argument, and she subsequently killed her self.'

The first indication that we are beginning to believe in the argument to end life, signals that the therapy is stuck. Once we join that thinking, it permeates the therapeutic conversation. People (clients) often see only one option and that is suicide. When the therapy is stuck, we urgently need to engage in a supervisory/consultation process.

Reflecting on our experience of hope in the therapeutic relationship is a useful self-reflective tool. Limited hope, no hope, and disengaged hope may indicate that the therapeutic relationship is stuck. Disagreement between therapist and client in respect to life/hope may indicate that we are siding with life/hope in overbearing way. We may be pushing for life/hope without comprehensively understanding people's emotional experience of despair.

HOLDING LIFE/HOPE

When **we** (therapists) solely hold the possibility that life/hope will be rediscovered by people (clients), this position can only be a short term emergency strategy. This holding of the possibility that life/hope will be rediscovered provides us with both a valuable resource and time to work with people (clients) towards rediscovery or reconnection with **their** relationship with experiences of hope.

This resource can be described as the 'belief in possibilities' even when those possibilities are yet to be discovered. When we hold this resource we are subsequently orientated towards listening for life/hope possibilities within both people's (clients') reflections on life events and the conversational or experiential moments that occur in the therapeutic relationship. When we move away from a binary relationship with hope, i.e. hope and hopelessness, the potential for life/hope possibilities are expanded. The binary position, i.e. hope and hopelessness, provides us with an extremely limited field for exploration. Within this limited field people (clients) can experience pervasive hopelessness which acts to obscure other avenues of thinking and experiencing that supports life/hope.

In moving past a binary relationship with hope, we are provided with linguistic strategies that are only limited by our imagination.

For example:

▼ Limited hope.

▼ Protective hope.

▼ Hope with safety.

▼ Pretend hope.

▼ Wait and see hope.

A conversation that moves beyond the binaries while utilising a relational externalising process is represented in the following example, where I have reflected on protective hope.

Rachel: I have lost my belief in everything. It's just too hard. I don't see the point in carrying on.

Johnella: When did the loss of belief start to get this big?

Rachel: It started to build up after that visit from Mum and Dad. I had just thought that this time it would be different, and it wasn't, it was just the same, in fact it was worse.

Johnella: What made it worse?

Rachel: Before the visit, I'd had a couple of phone calls with Mum that had been really relaxed. She seemed pleased that I'd got the lecturer's job at university and had even suggested that she makes some curtains for my new flat.

Johnella: How did those different phone calls impact on your expectations for the visit?

Rachel: I just created this huge picture of the two of us, Mum and me, doing all the things we've never done. Talking, going shopping, just ordinary things.

Johnella: Have those ordinary things ever been present in the relationship?

Rachel: No, never. Just an ongoing battering of criticism, and that's how it was from the moment I met them at the airport. She criticised my clothes, the hug I gave her was too tight, the car was too hot, too noisy, smelt of petrol and on it went.

Johnella: When you met your mum and dad at the airport, how open was your heart to the possibility that this visit would be different?

Rachel: It was totally open, totally open. After the first few hours in her company I felt exhausted, battered. It was as though I was punch drunk. I went through the motions and sighed with relief when they left.

Johnella: As you went through the motions, did your mum notice this happening?

Rachel: Oh no, she just carried on, the egg was too soft, the stove was too dirty, when was I going to get a decent boyfriend!

Johnella: What happened to you as you were in the motions?

Rachel: I sort of disappeared. I just held on until they left.

Johnella: Was going through the motions and disappearing part of your survival strategies when you were younger?

Rachel: Totally, I feel like it's only the last two years that I have been in my life.

Johnella: What have you done to keep in your life over the last two years?

Rachel: Well for a start I've limited my contact with Mum and Dad, and the contact I've had has been on my terms.

Johnella: Were your terms part of this visit?

Rachel: No, I let down my guard. I thought it would be different but it wasn't. I just feel so empty.

Johnella: In the letting down of the guard, did hope for a different style of relationship with your mother come in?

Rachel: Yes, totally.

Johnella: When hope for a different relationship with your mother diminished, what was left?

Rachel: Total hopelessness.

Johnella: Hopelessness for the relationship or hopelessness for your self?

Rachel: Both I think.

Johnella: It seems a failure of hope for a relationship has turned on you. Failure of hope for the relationship has as a result of this visit become a failure of hope in you.

Rachel: Yes, that's true.

Johnella: If you had found a way to hold on to this sense of guard during this visit, what would have happened to this sense of hope in life?

Rachel: I think I wouldn't be feeling so awful, so hopeless.

Johnella: If you thought that there was a way to have hope with guard or hope with protection in your relationship with your mum and dad, what would you think or feel about this?

Rachel: That would be good if I could do that. I think though I'd have to face the possibility that I probably won't ever have my dream relationship with my Mum.

This example is not a complete conversation, it illustrates an exploration that moves past the binary of hope and hopelessness in order to consider a variety of engagements with life/hope.

We can only sustain the holding of life/hope within the therapeutic relationship for short periods. We can judge the extent of our life/hope holding by reflecting on our experiences in the therapeutic relationship. We can reflect on our:

Exhaustion	'I don't think I can face another client'.
Irritation	'I wish Mary would act on my suggestions.'
A sense of Hopelessness	'I don't know what else to do. This is just hopeless.'
Self-doubt	'I'm just not good enough. If Mary was seeing another therapist, she/he would be able to help.'

Sustained solo holding of life/hope can inevitably result in our over-connection with people's (clients') lives. In order to prevent this, we work with people (clients) to identify what is limiting the holding of life/hope. This requires us (therapist and client) to reflect on our mutual experiences of hope building and hope loss in the therapeutic relationship. We can experience considerable fear when doing this, fear an enquiry into life/hope will be experienced as a threat to remove life/hope from the therapeutic relationship thus leaving people (clients) bereft of hope, with death as the result. The reflective process requires preparation including using supervision/ consultation to discuss our thoughts, feelings and the therapeutic relationship. It also includes an enquiry direction that helps to explore people's (clients') experience of life/hope within the therapeutic relationship. We need to be supported through this process, supported by supervisors/consultants and colleagues who carefully monitor the process of achieving therapeutic distance while maintaining therapeutic connectedness. For example,

Sue: I feel so exhausted about this. Every time I see Lisa (client) she begins by presenting me with the week's disasters and concludes the litany with a declaration of despair. In exploring what's happened during the week, we find lots of possibilities for hope, indications of strength and examples of her taking a stand for her life. By the time the session is winding up there's a sense of optimism. Lisa leaves feeling strong and enthusiastic. Then next week's it's the same thing. Maybe I'm just not skilled enough.

Sue and Lisa agree to an interview with Johnella (consultant). Johnella interviews Lisa while Sue listens.

Johnella: Lisa, Sue has noticed that when you come to these sessions you are often gripped by strong feelings of despair. By the end of the session these feelings are replaced by optimism. What happens in the session to support the movement from despair to optimism?

Lisa: I'm not sure. I feel really black when I arrive. Sue helps me to see other possibilities or reasons for things. It really helps.

Johnella: When you arrive for the session, how much belief do you have in the truth of the blackness?

Lisa: What do you mean?

Johnella: Blackness usually comes with thoughts and feelings. Is that how blackness comes to you?

Sue: Yes.

Johnella: Do you believe in these thoughts and feelings when you arrive for a session?

Lisa: Oh yes, totally.

Johnella: How does that 100 per cent belief get shaken?

Lisa: Sue asks questions that help me see differently.

Johnella: Does the seeing differently help you feel stronger/ weaker, more confident/less confident?

Lisa: Stronger. More confident.

Johnella: What happens to the belief in the blackness?

Lisa: Oh it drops away, it never totally goes but by the end of the session it's in the background.

Johnella: After you leave the session and walk down the stairs where is the blackness?

Lisa: It's still in the background.

Johnella: After an hour, where is the blackness?

Lisa:	It's moving forward.
Johnella:	How long does the blackness take to overwhelm feeling differently — feeling strong and more confident?
Lisa	Oh, about six hours.
Johnella:	You feel this strength and confidence in the room with Sue. What changes when you leave here?
Lisa:	When I'm not here in this room the feelings fade.
Johnella	Does this relationship support your discoveries of strength and confidence?
Lisa:	Yes, I think it does. When I'm not here I can't hold on to it.
Johnella:	When you leave here, do you leave the memory of the relationship behind you?
Lisa:	Yes, I think I do. This is like a special place and when I leave I think I leave it behind.
Johnella:	If you could take your memory of the relationship with you, do you think it would strengthen your discoveries?
Lisa:	I think it might be possible.

In this interview I (as the consultant) supported Sue (therapist) by exploring the movement from blackness to experiences of strength and confidence. We also explored how the experiences of strength and confidence could be maintained outside of the immediate experience of the therapeutic relationship. The therapeutic relationship is for many people (clients) the site for experimentation with experiences of hope for life and trust in relationship to another person. This experience can be named and then explored to provide people (clients) with a relationship knowledge that can be used in aspects of their everyday life. When this occurs, people's (clients') experience of the therapeutic relationship can be re-searched as a unique experience.

RE-SEARCHING THE THINKING AND ACTIONS THAT LIMIT LIFE POSSIBILITIES

Whenever we identify that the therapeutic relationship is the only locality where hope for life is held, this often indicates that people (clients) are for some reason unable to act on, and for, their lives. We can work with people (clients) to identify and explore the thinking and actions that limit life possibilities. The following experiences are common:

1. Lack of practice — This occurs when people (clients) have limited experience with acting for or on their lives.

IAN (THERAPIST)

Geoff is 35 years old, married with two children. He had had substantial involvement with psychiatric services, and has been diagnosed as chronically depressed. Geoff always attends therapy and seems really interested in the ideas we develop together. When we discuss how these ideas could be put into practice, he's enthusiastic. However the next time I see him, he hasn't moved from TV watching.

GEOFF (CLIENT)

Life sweeps over me, like waves. Sometimes this is soothing and other times I'm buffeted about like a piece of driftwood. I feel very much like that — adrift. Life feels pointless, aimless and frankly disappointing. Sport is my refuge. If they had sport on TV, seven days a week that's where you'd find me. I don't know why this therapy isn't working. I expect something will change sooner or later.

In this example the conversational focus is redirected towards exploring Geoff's relationship with acting for and on life. This includes re-searching the history of his relationship with acting for and on life.

When Ian (therapist) pursued this he discovered that Geoff had very limited experience in acting in and for his life. The focus of therapy moved towards Geoff finding and experimenting with an 'acting on and for life practice'.

2. Lack of success — Whenever people (clients) have acted for and on their lives they have experienced punishment and/or failure.

CHRISTINE (CLIENT)

When I was little I discovered that I could make myself very small, so small that people would scarcely notice my presence in a room. It worked a lot of the time at school though sometimes I was trapped into reading from my workbook in front of the class. I was terrified, the words would run around the page, so I consequently made the most ridiculous mistakes. The other kids would laugh, even if the teacher told them to keep quiet. When we talk about doing things here I really want to, then I just get terrified and I can't. I just can't.

Christine's past experiences increased her sense of vulnerably and sense of visibility whenever she felt an expectation from another person. The therapeutic focus was directed towards Christine catching her belief that the therapist carried an expectation of her. Whenever this occurred the belief was caught and checked with the therapist. The conversation moved towards drawing a distinction between a self expectation and an expectation that was thought to emanate from another person. Christine could then decide what she needed to do or say in order to maintain a sense of safety.

3. Ideas about the therapeutic relationship — People (clients) can expect that we (therapists) are experts who act on their lives.

PETER (CLIENT)

I have been coming to therapy for a while now. It doesn't seem to be helping much. I suppose my therapist knows what he's doing. I wish he'd just tell me what to do. I mean he's the expert. My last therapist told me that I shouldn't get involved in another relationship for two years because I needed that time to grieve. I've waited two years but I don't feel any better. I'll wait and see what this therapist suggests.

After a time, both therapist and client can experience frustration at the lack of progress in the therapy. At this point it's useful to re-view the expectations of the therapy and the therapeutic relationship.

These questions may begin an enquiry:

▼ Peter, what did you expect from the therapy at the beginning?

▼ Have those expectations changed since we've been meeting?

▼ Which expectations have been met and which haven't?

▼ What are your ideas about how this therapy could be more helpful to you?

The idea that we (therapists) are experts who act on people's (clients')
lives may be situated in understandings of the therapeutic relationship
based on other expert client relationships, i.e. doctor, patient, lawyer,
client. It may also be situated in past experiences of therapy.

4. Lack of belief in the self — People (clients) may not believe that
their lives are worth fighting for.

RITA

> She (therapist) gets so concerned about whether I live or die. I
> suppose it's part of her job. Why would I want to live? I feel like shit.
> I have a shithouse life. Look at me, what have I achieved? Nothing.

When this belief is exposed, a conversation occurs that explores the
conditions that would support Rita to engage in a process of life/hope
discovery. Without this commitment Rita's life is seriously at risk. This
commitment isn't just a verbal or a written agreement, it is embodied
in the conversation. People (clients) can give a verbal agreement not
to act on suicidal thinking in order to comply with us. However, if
commitment isn't embodied in the conversation, then people (clients)
continue to be at risk.

5. Overwhelming fear — People can be terrorised by the belief that if
they claim life then it will be taken away.

NINA (CLIENT)

> When I was little I learnt to hide any pleasure I had over a toy or a
> pet or even food. I remember the day I decided never to want any-
> thing. A stray puppy had followed me home. I tried to shoo it away
> and lose it by running across streets and hiding in people's backyards.
> I even had to scare it by throwing stones and yelling. It just kept
> coming back. It was as though it had made up its mind that it
> belonged to me.
>
> I decided she was a girl and called her Sam. I made her a kennel
> out of a wooden box and saved her scraps from dinner. It was
> imperative that no one knew about her. I couldn't trust them not to
> take her away. A month passed and I thought I was so clever.
>
> I don't know what it was that alerted them, was it my happiness,
> or did someone see me sneaking over to my secret place? One day

I came home from school and she was gone, the kennel was smashed. I lost it. I ran home screaming. I kicked at the doors, smashed windows until Dad knocked me out, smashing two of my front teeth. The next day no one spoke about what had happened. I rang the SPCA on the way to school and walked for miles calling her name and asking if anyone had seen her. No one had.

A month later I knew for sure she was gone and it was then I decided.

Given people's (clients') life experiences these fears are often realistic. The task of the therapy is to get to know intimately the requirements for safety within the therapeutic relationship, in order to catch fears early and then to continually negotiate strategies for safety that directly challenge these fears.

6. Loyalty choice — This can occur when more than one therapist is working with people (clients). People (clients) can experience power-lessness when faced with different therapeutic options that seem to require a loyalty choice. In this instance we need to work hard to liberate people from the obligation of loyalty. We can use a relational externalising enquiry to re-view people's (clients') relationship to 'the therapy'. This re-view supports people (clients) to consider the benefits of both relationships while identifying ways to keep safe from confusion over issues of loyalty. Using this enquiry process allows people (clients) to explore the options available to them outside of the binds of loyalty to either therapist.

7. Disconnection and pervasiveness of 'In The corner' ideas — Disconnection acts to isolate people (clients) from their experiences, thoughts and feelings, preventing them from acting for, and on, their lives. This is discussed in detail in Chapter Nine. Whenever people (clients) strongly believe in the 'truth' of persecutory ideas, hopelessness abounds.

DISCUSSION
The seven areas described above hinder people's (client's) ability to hold life/hope. To effectively challenge hopelessness, alternative beliefs and practices must be sought out and practised. These alternative beliefs and practices often reside within the person's (client's) experience. In

the enquiry we attempt to capture and re-search these experiences thereby providing people (clients) with a resource that's available for their use in the present.

These alternative life/hope experiences are often brought forwards when we move away from the binary of positions, hope and hopelessness in order to explore the subtleties of people's (clients') relationship with and to life/hope. Whenever we (therapists) experience sustained hope holding, we can assume that there is a restraint acting on life/hope which needs to be identified and explored with people (clients). Identifying and finding ways to challenge the ideas, practices and experiences that restrain life/hope, within a safe context, provides people (clients) with the opportunity to experiment and take control of life/hope. This is often a turning point in the therapeutic relationship.

When we use a relational externalising enquiry to explore people's (clients') relationship with life/hope, people (clients) are protected from professional interpretations of ongoing hopelessness. The most common interpretation is one that suggests that people (clients) are resistant to change. This idea of 'resistance' can quickly become the platform for professional withdrawal and blaming of people (clients). The relational externalising enquiry allows for no-change to be named while exploring and building a context of understanding with people (clients). This understanding often provides the platform for people's (clients') active relationship with life/hope.

KNOWING HOPELESSNESS

In order to work with life/hope we need to be knowledgeable about the environments that perpetuate and support hopelessness and the ideas of hopelessness. The pervasive or strong logic of hopelessness frequently offers people (clients) only one option and that is death. The internal dialogue of hopelessness can completely dominate people's (clients') thinking, thus reducing the possibility of rediscovering life/hope. We can intrude on this thinking by challenging the logic of hopelessness. Alternative ideas and experiences are then brought out through an enquiry centered on a pursuit of life/hope.

In such a conversation we (therapists) are not neutral. The therapeutic relationship understanding places us on the side of life. Being on the side of life requires us to be available to a deep knowing (intellectually and emotionally) of the conditions that have nurtured and supported hopelessness, while we continue to hold the possibility of life/

hope. The holding of the possibility of life/hope is reflected in a compassionate enquiry that explores people's (clients') experiences of hopelessness. When exploring and exposing hopelessness we (therapists) also deserve and require support from colleagues and supervisors. We do not need to do this alone. This support may include a colleague or supervisor sitting in on sessions.

When hopelessness takes hold, it often has a pervasive and strong logic. We can explore and challenge this logic through the enquiry process. For example:

Lisa: Human beings stink. They destroy the planet. They destroy animals. They cause pain wherever they go. I don't want to be part of that. There is nowhere to go.

Johnella: Have you ever thought about being an exceptional human being? One who shows by her actions and beliefs that she cares and respects the planet and those who live on it?

Lisa   I suppose I could but . . .

The question provides Lisa with an opportunity to enquire into the possibility of living life by extending the options available to her. This extension challenges a choice between dichotomising ideas where a logic is constructed that leads inevitably to death.

In order to assess the degree of life risk we need to know the logic of hopelessness and be available to engage in an exploratory conversation that reflects our belief in the possibility of life/hope. To immediately implement institutional strategies for safety, when people (clients) acknowledge hopelessness, puts people (clients) at risk of experiencing increasing alienation within the therapeutic relationship. Safety is incredibly important. However, our fear for people's lives can direct us to detach from the therapeutic relationship, thereby removing a vehicle for life/hope exploration and experience. Rather, safety is achieved when we work with people towards an agreement that is respectful of the therapeutic relationship understanding and people's experience of hopelessness. A contract for safety is only effective when it is a contract of trust within a meaningful relationship.

If hopelessness cannot be challenged then people need to be held physically in a safe place. Sometimes a safe place can be a hospital and at other times a safe place can be created in the community by using general practitioners, friends and relatives. We can work with the friends and relatives to develop an environment that supports safety, which will include a commitment to physically and emotionally holding people (clients). For this to happen it is essential that people (clients) provide caregivers with concrete evidence that hopelessness will not be acted on. A contract can be negotiated with people (clients) around action steps that will be taken if hopelessness takes over. It is important to engage both the friends and family, and the people (clients) at risk, in watchfulness around the signs of growing hopelessness. In order to prepare for growing hopelessness or re-emerging hopelessness, strategies that will challenge hopelessness are discussed and agreed upon. People (clients) must be a part of, and aware of, all discussions with the supporters of life/hope.

INSTITUTIONAL HOPELESSNESS

I believe it is important to consider the impact of institutions on our experience of life/hope. A therapist's hopelessness can sometimes mirror institutional hopelessness. The formal and informal talk in ward rounds, corridors and tea rooms often provides indicators of institutional hopelessness. For example, in one institution, formal and informal talk was unequivocally hopeless when it came to therapeutic work with those diagnosed as 'borderline'. Hopelessness pervaded the institution, with people being referred to counselling with remarks like, 'It will take at least two to three years for any change if you're lucky.' In this environment of hopelessness, it is often extremely difficult for us to hold life/hope for and with people (clients).

TRUST AND THE THERAPEUTIC RELATIONSHIP

Trust is defined in the *Oxford Dictionary* as 'the firm belief in the reliability, truth or strength of a person or thing'.[1]

The therapeutic relationship provides people (clients) with opportunities to experiment with trust; trust in a worthwhile self, trust in another person and trust in a relationship.

The development of a trusting therapeutic relationship takes time. Trust cannot be demanded, it is freely given. Many people (clients) have reflected that it took six months to really trust the therapeutic relationship. They add, however, that if they had been asked in the first month whether they trusted the relationship, they would have said yes. The experience of trust in the first month can be intellectual trust. People (clients) judge us according to a number of criteria, for example, openness, willingness to connect, warmth, understanding, honesty, reliability and reputation.

The trust experienced here at six months occurs as people (clients) explore experiences, memories and feelings that challenge the perceived family and/or societal descriptions of the self. Disclosing the experiences, memories and feelings requires people (clients) to risk that the experiences, memories and feelings will not be greeted with scorn and derision.

Conventional usage of English positions us only to consider the binaries trust/lack of trust. When we engage with this binary our enquiry process becomes severely limited. In moving away from the binary, a repertoire of possibilities becomes available to us. Some of the possibilities are:

intellectual trust,
head trust,
embryonic trust,
partial trust,
heart trust,
core trust,
wide-open trust,
moving-towards trust.

In the following example, I was exploring with Leslie her changing relationship with trust within the therapeutic relationship. There are a number of opportunities here for me to use language outside of binaries, e.g. 'taking the risk to bring out trust'.

Johnella: It's interesting that, when I talk with people who have been sexually abused in their past, they have highlighted the issue of trust; trusting the self, trusting the therapist, trusting others. You talked about trust in your self and the trusting of feelings. It was then you said that you actually started to feel not crazy. You used feelings as a resource, as a way to keep your self safe, to give your self information. You placed trust in your self.

Leslie: Yeah, and I could move on once I could start to do that. I couldn't move on until I could do that, I guess. That's been a really big one with me, trust. And also trusting other people.

Johnella: What do you think made the difference around that? What helped in the discovery of self and other trust? I'm really interested in that. If we use the example of the therapeutic relationship, do you think it took a while before you felt you could trust in me or the therapeutic relationship or did that happen quite early on?

Leslie: Yeah, I was quite wide open, I felt like I'd been split open. But I still think it took, it has taken me, a long time too. I guess there are levels of trust and I could trust you on one level probably quite quickly, and maybe on the next level quite quickly. But to really trust you with kind of truthful things inside, that's been really hard because I haven't trusted that myself, because when I was growing up I learnt that those deep feelings weren't valid or something. They weren't to be trusted because I didn't get it validated anywhere. So I think, it's like the core or something. The core of me. And I think that took a long time, to get to that. I think, in some ways maybe I'm still getting there.

Johnella: Did you sometime in the process become aware that you were going there and you didn't want to?

Leslie: Sometimes . . . I sort of remember that something would be triggered when we were talking and I'd have a thought that I would kind of think, Ah, that's a true thought or feeling about something that happened. But ah, God, I'm not going to say that. Still trying to manipulate the situation whereby sieving out what I'm honest about or what I'm truthful about. And in some cases I wouldn't say anything, and so you wouldn't even know it had happened. And then in other cases I would risk it and bring it out. And they were really powerful times and I think after a few times of taking that risk, it got easier to bring it out because it was so powerful when I did, really powerful because it would kind've clear it out. It would be dealt with. Whether it was a big

thing that needed working on, or whether it was
something that I'd carried around and it was not
important or something that could be dealt with really
quickly. But to bring it out in the open, I started to learn
the value of that. The value of trusting enough to be
open and honest, and it was just so scary before.

We can under-estimate the enormity of experimenting with the relationship with trust in the therapeutic relationship. Once we know the
courage it takes to speak about thoughts, feelings and life-events, we
can provide platforms for trust-building throughout therapy sessions.

The therapeutic relationship provides people (clients) with an
environment to experiment with different relationships with trust. This
requires us to be alert to moments where people (clients) have taken the
risk to disclose feelings, thoughts and actions. These moments are
potentially unique experiences that can be re-searched in order to
become available to people (clients) as a future resource.

For example, in the conversation with Leslie, I could research in
detail the process by which she engaged with 'bringing it out'. Here are
some questions that would assist such an enquiry.

▼ What would alert you to the possibility that there was a
   movement towards a 'bringing it out' time?

▼ Was it a thought, feeling, body sensation or something else?

▼ As you remember standing on the edge of deciding to go with
   'bringing it out', what tipped you towards 'bringing it out'?

▼ Once the 'bringing it out' had happened, what happened next?

▼ How did this (above) experience impact on future 'bringing it out'
   times?

▼ What sort of conditions and/or relationships would encourage a
   turning away from 'bringing it out'?

This work inevitably requires us to focus on experiences within the
therapeutic relationship, thereby exploring the present as the primary
focus for unique experiences. For example:

Monica: I've just tuned out.

Johnella: When did you notice that happening?

Monica:	I'm not sure.
Johnella:	Okay, I'm just going to go back a little, let me know if *the tuning* out is happening again — is that okay?
Monica:	Yes, yes it is.
Johnella:	Okay, we were talking about you and Libby, your daughter. You were saying that you sometimes get scared, scared that something will happen to her and that these feelings push you to check on her in ways that leave you feeling exhausted but also vulnerable that other people will think you're silly or over-protective. Is this what you understand we were talking about?
Monica:	Yes.
Johnella:	Has *the tuning out* happened while I was talking?
Monica:	No, not like before, but I've got a panicky feeling, my heart's racing.
Johnella:	When did *the panicky feeling* begin?
Monica:	As soon as you talked about me being scared that something would happen to Libby. I'm so scared. (Monica begins to cry.) Just terrified that if I let her out of my sight I won't be able to protect her and she'll be hurt like I was. It's stupid, I know it is, I try to tell myself not to be silly but it doesn't work. I feel really stupid just talking about it and now I'm crying.
Johnella:	Monica, how does *the feeling* that its stupid to talk about being scared for Libby's safety . . . how does *this feeling* affect our talking about this?
Monica:	Well, as soon as we started talking and I felt sort of panicky, I thought, Here we go. I'll be crying soon and then that's pretty pathetic.
Johnella:	Do you think *the tuning* out was a way to stop the crying?
Monica:	Well it certainly worked.

Johnella:	Monica, what do you think I would have thought or did think when you began crying as you talked about *those scared feelings* for Libby?
Monica:	I'd think you'd think I was ridiculous, stupid, because that's what I think.
Johnella:	Is there any way that we could hold *off the idea that these feelings are stupid* so that we can get to know *these scared feelings* better? Is there anything you might want to know from me that would help?
Monica:	Do you think it's stupid?
Johnella:	No, I think *this stupid idea* is stopping you from discovering what *this scared feeling is about* or where *it belongs*. I think *the scared feeling* is telling us something, we just don't know what that is.
Monica:	So you think it would be okay to talk about it?
Johnella:	I'd like to get to know it a little better because it seems to be very present in your life.
Monica:	It sure is, it's around all the time.
Johnella:	If we talk a little more about *the scared feeling*, could you tell me if the idea that 'this is stupid' or 'she thinks I'm stupid' comes up, because if it arrives it will effect the conversation?
Monica:	I think I can do that.
Johnella:	Is there anything I can do or say that would help with that?
Monica:	No, I don't think so, it really helps to know that you don't think I'm stupid.
Johnella:	Do you think if you keep *the thought or memory in your mind*, 'that I don't think you're stupid', do you think that could help you speak up, if that thought comes forward?
Monica:	Yes, I think that will help.

In this example Johnella and Monica are negotiating a safety platform to continue to experiment with trust.

TRUST AND SAFETY

Disconnection from the therapeutic conversation is often an indicator that people's (clients') safety boundaries have been transgressed. Negotiating alternative safety strategies is an essential prerequisite for a future conversation where people (clients) experiment with moving past what feels comfortable or safe. Another safety strategy that has implications for the development of trust within the therapeutic relationship is screening out thoughts and feelings from the therapeutic conversation. Often we won't know this is happening unless we ask. I find it useful to ask questions about screening if the therapy appears to be stuck in some way.

These questions could facilitate an enquiry around screening:

▼ Do you (client) ever find your self engaging with a private dialogue through this conversation?

▼ Can we talk about it as screening practice, is that okay?[2] Is there anything you need or want to know from me in order to begin this conversation?

▼ When do you notice the screening?

▼ Does it appear when we're talking about certain things?

▼ What do you think I might think of you if you were to speak without the screening?

▼ Do you think you could tell me when the screening is happening?

▼ Does screening take you away from our conversation in that you begin to consider or argue with certain ideas?

▼ Is there anything you would want to know about me or from me that would support you to challenge the screening practice?

▼ How do you notice the screening practice effects the conversation?

▼ Does the screening happen all the time or occasionally?

▼ Does the screening have different strengths?

▼ How do you think the screening will affect the therapy?

If we negotiate a process by which people (clients) feel safe enough to signal in the conversation when they are engaged with holding back screening or censoring certain ideas, then initially it is this practice that we re-search and understand. Knowledge of this practice allows us to negotiate with people the conditions that support an environment of safety within the therapy. With safety it is possible for people (clients) to experiment with disclosure or to negotiate a decision to not disclose. (In this instance, I'm referring to disclosure of thoughts.) A decision not to disclose can be connected to the person's (client's) expectations of meaningfulness (refer to Chapter Four). In this context it is possible for us to negotiate accessing the alternative resources that people (clients) need, e.g. a priest or minister, trusted figures in the person's (clients) cultural and social group, alternative and conventional medicine. Opportunities to experiment with trust become apparent as we identify needs and negotiate meeting those needs with people (clients).

THE ETHICS THAT SUPPORT WORKING WITH CONTRADICTIONS

(De-centering our experience)

I have written earlier about the necessity of preparing for the limitations of our experience by using literature, music, art, dance and film as mediums to extend our imaginative abilities. Engagement with the arts however, doesn't guarantee imaginative extension. We can use the arts to confirm that our viewpoint or experience of the world is the true and correct one, thus strengthening our sense of certainty. Extending our imaginative abilities in order to engage with the contradictory conditions that shape people's (clients') lives, requires an ongoing search for decentering opportunities. Decentering involves exposing our selves to difference. Literature, music, art, dance and film can ask of us that we reconsider our relationship with ethics, values, traditions, knowledge, language, relationships, family, children, movement, space, time, the physical body, sensuality and sexuality. By engaging with the difference we can call on our imaginative abilities while we draw on all our senses. We stand with and in the difference while looking back to where we had previously stood. We then have an opportunity to look over at the self and make apparent the assumptions, ideas and cultural practices that invisibly or unknowingly shape our lives. In this experience of movement we can experience change, as what is invisible or unknown becomes visible and known. *In our therapeutic practice we can also de-center our selves by assuming that people's (clients') experiences are unknown to us.* We continually negotiate a climate of respect by maintaining an assumption that we do not know this person's unique experience.[3] We combine this stance of not assuming with a desire to know as much as another person outside of the direct experience can know. In the therapeutic environment, we acknowledge that differences exist within a hierarchy that privileges one difference over another. When the hierarchy and privileging of differences is recognised, its existence forms part of an ongoing exploration and negotiation in the therapeutic conversation. If the existence of the hierarchy and privileging of one difference over another is unacknowledged, the *experience* of the therapeutic conversation can reflect another abusive environment. For example, Lois, a heterosexual counsellor, is working with Sarah, a lesbian.

Lois: I understand what you've been saying about the effects of invisibilization. It must have been very hard for you. I think all of us women suffer in one way or another from being made invisible in our culture.

Sarah: (Thinks to her self,) She hasn't been listening to me, she doesn't understand what I'm saying. Since I was twelve years old, I've had to lie to my family, pretend I was somebody else. I just about went crazy from loneliness and shame. Even now I can't walk down the street with my arm around Jessie and feel safe. I'm so angry with Lois, I'm not here to educate her. This is just more of the same.

In the above example Lois is unaware of the hierarchy and privileging of heterosexuality over lesbianism.

In this further example, Jackie (counsellor) is working with Sue who is in a lesbian relationship.

Jackie: This 'marriage' seems to have been struggling for some time. What do you think happened that changed your vision for this 'marriage'?

Sue: I don't consider that I'm in a 'marriage'. That's not how I would describe my relationship. The relationship changed substantially when I went back to university to study for my PHD.

Jackie: What were you studying?

Sue: Philosophy.

Jackie: That's interesting. In my experience many marriages
               come under stress when one partner goes back to study.
               How did you experience the changes?

Sue: I am not in a marriage.

This is an example of a member of the privileged group (Jackie) inviting
the other person to join with her in her descriptions and understandings. The invitation to join with the privileged 'marriage'
description expresses the desire 'you and I are the same'. Apart from the
fact that legal and social discrimination prevent lesbians and homo-
sexuals from marrying in New Zealand, Sue may object to the institution of marriage or she may have a preference for other relationship
descriptions. Jackie's construction of sameness denies Sue's experience
of a difference which is institutionally maintained and supported.
Jackie's commitment to the 'good intention' of affording Sue's relationship the status of marriage acts to close down conversational possibility, most obviously the impact on relationships and individuals of being
excluded from institutional legitimization processes and institutional
supports.

When we (therapists) actively seek out environments that provide
a decentering experience we are acknowledging the power relation
within the therapeutic relationship. We know we can be implicated
in the ongoing pathologising and marginalising of people (clients).
This knowledge accords us the responsibility of continually tipping
our selves out of our intellectual, emotional and practice comfort
zones.

THE ETHICS OF HOPE

We cannot prescribe or necessarily imagine for people (clients) how
their life would change if it was free from despair. The life/hope
we hold in the therapeutic relationship rests on the possibility that
the therapeutic enquiry will support people (clients) to discover such
a life. While people (clients) engage with us in a therapeutic relationship we can assume that the hope for life still has a presence in
their lives. This life/hope may not be presented by people (clients)
either verbally or non-verbally. Its existence may be indicated by

people's (clients') physical presence in therapy/counselling.

We cannot afford to glibly decide to, and then begin, a conversation that explores life/ hope with people (clients) who are struggling to know hope for life. In these conversations we may be required to decenter our selves in order to understand the circumstances that produce and support despair. In the decentering we may also find our selves lost in hopelessness for people's (clients') lives. Supervision/consultation that facilitates a rediscovery of life/hope can precipitate a meaningful conversation of discovery between therapist and client. A relational externalising conversation can expose the initiators, supporters and circumstances that perpetuate hopelessness. In this process we are working with people (clients) to discover, see, experience, know what has been, and is, acting on their ability to engage with hope. In these moments, people (clients) often begin to re-negotiate a relationship with life/hope.

The therapeutic relationship understanding requires that partici-pants in the therapeutic conversation contribute to the exploration of hope, hopelessness and the activity of holding on to hope. When we are solely engaged with the activity of holding hope for people's (clients') lives, we risk encouraging dependency. Depending on the therapeutic relationship is inevitable if we remain the principle vehicle for life/hope. Dependency on the therapeutic relationship leaves people (clients) bereft of the experience of actively engaging with maintaining and creating their own life direction. It is, however, our responsibility to explore the activity of holding hope in order to resource people (clients) with the knowledge of their engagement with hope. This exploration locates life/hope in relationship to the therapeutic relationship, which protects people (clients) from thinking life/hope belongs to the thera-pist's person.

When we are willing and able to move beyond predominant cultural prescriptions for a successful life we increase the resources available for negotiating possible life supporting conditions. This may include exploring alternative relationships with work, family, friends and lovers/ partners as well as concepts of home and community. The exploration may also include re-viewing what constitutes meaningful connection and contribution. In these circumstances our explorations may deeply challenge our own definitions, experiences and ideas of what consti-tutes a meaningful life.

Creating the ethical conditions that identify and illuminate contradictions

Anne's story (refer to the beginning of this chapter) illustrates the contradictions within which many people (clients) struggle daily. The conditions that support the ongoing existence of contradictions in people's (clients') lives include a requirement for silence and secrecy. Living with this contradiction is extremely wearisome. Its existence in the everyday perpetuates circumstances that equate to the movement of the sea slowly and imperceptibly wearing away the stone. Contradictions in people's (clients') lives have a 'wearing away' effect on their emotional and physical wellbeing. In its unnamed state, the contradiction remains disguised as a condition of despair that belongs to people (clients). In other words the disguise creates a situation where people (clients) are solely culpable and responsible for the presence and effects of distress.

The movement of what is unnamed to that which is named occurs in a therapeutic relationship where there is an ongoing reflection on what provides safety. Talking about past events in people's (clients') lives can provoke terror and evoke abusive incantations of harm.

The movement involved in naming the unnamed is akin to a weaving motion. We weave among the events, feeling, thoughts, and experiences, exploring and unwrapping the extraordinary from the shorthand language of the everyday. We weave among that which is fleeting, hidden, discounted and overwhelmed by the dictates of events and people who claimed irrefutability and truth. We weave among the truths that are strengthened and supported by the everyday circulation of ideas and beliefs. In this weaving motion an environment is created that generates tentative naming. People's (clients') experience of safety in this environment is heralded by our willingness to negotiate and act on people's (clients') needs, for example, 'I can't talk about this in a small space. I need to walk.' People's (clients') experience of safety is only confirmed when we are able to engage compassionately with life contradictions, e.g. 'I know he abused me and sometimes I hate him but he's the only father I have. Sometimes I look over at him sitting in his favourite chair and my heart goes out to him.'

People's (clients') movement to naming highlights the experiences people (clients) have carried outside of everyday consciousness, while moving from silence and secrecy in itself changes people's (clients') relationship with the contradictions. When the contradictions are exposed, people (clients) can experiment and explore a different relationship with the contradictions. In this climate of experimentation we are continually invited to engage with the complexities of people (clients), relationships and lives. Failure to create the climate for experimentation by imposing simplistic notions of right and wrong subjects people (clients) to a practice that silences and separates them (clients) from their experiences. This failure is often an act of compliance to institutional ideas and practices that continue to privilege one experience over another in order to maintain the coherence of institutional ideas and practices. For example, institutional requirements of mothering suggest that a mother outside of this ideal (i.e. a mother who is unable to protect her child from physical abuse by a partner) could not provide experiences of a loving relationship for a child. This child's loving memories and love for her/his parents are therefore institutionally invalidated.

WORKING WITH THE TEXT

What Do These Contradictions Mean for Me (Client)?
I hope when you read this chapter that the explanations you have carried for the experiences of despair, desperation and hopelessness in your life may move away from self-blame towards an appreciation of the struggle inherent in living with contradictions.

Therapy that respects the complexity of living in contradictions requires therapists to struggle with you to find new ways to understand events from the past. When you know and experience the consequences to you of living with contradictions that were shaped and determined by another (often a caretaking adult), you may have a range of strong emotions, i.e. elation, rage, sadness, fear, hope. The appearance of these strong emotions can signal a reconnection with your sense of a self free from the binds of contradictions.

Therapists can explore and hold life/hope in the therapeutic relationship for a short period of time. If you experience no relief or only short term relief from experiences of hopelessness, it's important that you alert the therapist to this. If you're struggling to hold on to hope this may indicate the following:

▼ Exhaustion.
▼ Limited practice in holding on to and maintaining life/hope.

▼ Limited past successes.

▼ Ideas about the therapeutic relationship.

▼ Limited belief in the abilities you hold.

▼ Overwhelming fear and confusion.

▼ Disconnection from thoughts and feelings.

▼ Physical illness (including depression).

The therapist can work with you to identify what is interfering with your ability to hold and support life/hope. Sometimes people are so exhausted and worn out in their daily encounters with the ideas and practices of hopelessness that additional life supporters are necessary. These life supporters can include medication, establishing supports that may involve twenty-four hour companionship and care, and negotiating emergency therapy sessions.

Screening

The survival practice of screening out thoughts and feelings and presenting what you think other people want to hear, limits the therapeutic conversation. However it has developed for real safety reasons. You can catch the screen-out practice by remaining alert to two conversations. One between the therapist and you, and one between your self and certain ideas. This second conversation is had in silence. If you notice the screening out practice ask your self the following:

▼ What do I think will happen if I speak these thoughts and feelings rather than screening them or keeping them to myself?

▼ What could I do or say in the therapy to check out these fears or worries?

▼ Has there been any evidence in the therapy that these fears and worries are safeguarding me?

▼ If there has been evidence, how can I safely leave this therapy?

▼ If there has not been any evidence that these fears and worries are safeguarding me, what can I do or say to negotiate a beginning conversation about the fears and worries?

Safety

Your safety within the therapeutic relationship is often an ongoing negotiation throughout the therapy. You may respect and trust the therapist but still experience fear and lack of safety in the therapy sessions. Whenever this happens it is important that you take these experiences seriously. Consider what you will need to do or say to create an environment of safety that supports you to express your experiences of fear and danger. It is not a slur on the therapist's integrity to experience fear and danger within the therapeutic context. The appearance of fear and a sense of danger often creates an important context for new discoveries, including your entitlement to keep your self safe.

Whenever you experience fear and a lack of safety in therapy take it seriously and reflect with your self and others on your experiences in the therapeutic relationship. These feelings may also be telling/highlighting to you that something is happening in the therapy that contravenes the therapeutic relationship understanding.

What Do These Contradictions Mean for Me? (Therapist)

We all live within contradictions. For the people (clients) we work with, these contradictions can be life threatening. Reflect on the contradictions you live with. For example:

▼ A good mother is available to and for her children at all times.
▼ Women on the Domestic Purposes Benefit should be required to go back to work as soon as possible.

Doing this will involve you reflecting on gendered prescriptions, cultural prescriptions, class prescriptions, sexuality prescriptions, family of origin prescriptions, relationship prescriptions, parenting prescriptions, etc. If you are in a group, once you have named these contradictions in twos, interview each other in order to develop an intimate knowledge of how these operate in your lives (remember to use a relational externalising enquiry).

You can reflect on your understanding of contradictory moments in the therapeutic relationship by catching your preference for the outcome of a particular direction of enquiry. When your preference is challenged by people's response, for example, 'But I still love him,' this is an opportunity for further exploration. This exploration contrasts to arguing for a particular position (which is often represented by a 'Yes but . . .'). This exploration may encompass re-searching the meaning and experiences of love, re-searching the meaning and experience of love being lost, re-searching the meaning and experience of belonging, re-searching the meaning and experience of secrets and lies, re-searching the meaning and experience of responsibility, re-searching the meaning and experiences of adult/child relationship, etc. etc. This exploration represents an attempt to work with people (clients) to find new and liberating ways of living with contradictions. This enquiry process requires a willingness to grapple with the complexities of human lives. Engaging with these complexities can shift our relationship with current psychological theory and extend our appreciation of human resourcefulness.

Hope

The relationship that you have to and with 'hope for life' will either support you or hinder you in this work. Although you cannot know someone else's experiences, you can attempt to get close to those experiences through using the imagination. While using your imagination consider the ideas, values, knowledges and/or experiences that would assist you to continue to believe in life/hope.

Reflect on the hope exercise in this chapter. Ask your self, 'Are there any areas of work that I find myself losing life/hope in?' Re-search this with another person.

If you believe that you have been engaged in a sustained holding of life/hope with a person (client), reflect on the thinking and actions that may have limited life possibilities, and, possibly with someone else, develop questions that would support an exploration of these possibilities with people (clients).

Trust

The development of a trusting therapeutic relationship is often taken for granted. The achievement of this is therefore unavailable for re-search and re-view, and is therefore lost to people (clients) as a life resource. In order to encourage you to appreciate people's (clients') engagement with trust in the therapeutic relationship, consider these questions:

Remembering a time that you experienced a betrayal of trust.

▼ How did this betrayal impact on your sense of your self?

▼ How did this betrayal impact on your ability to trust others in relationships?

▼ What helped you to regain a sense of trust in the relationship within which you experience a betrayal of trust?

Screening

Screening thoughts and feelings out of the therapeutic conversation is a common experience. We often use screening to protect the relationship, i.e. 'I don't think he (client) can take this feedback,' or to protect the self, i.e. 'If I say this, he'll (client) take me apart.'

Reflecting on your engagement with screening practices is a useful self-reflective tool.

Attempt to catch your self screening, then note the context and the information that was screened, held back or kept to your self.

Interview someone else, and have them interview you, about instances of screening using a relational externalising enquiry. The questions on page 198 could act as a guide for the interview. (Remember to negotiate safety in the interview process and to reflect on screening as a possible safety technique.)

CHAPTER SIX

· · · · · · · · ·

Working with Time

TIME

People's (clients') relationship with time is a principal focus for exploration in therapeutic work. We call on memory in order to extract from the past the genesis of present day thoughts and feelings. We ask people (clients) to bring the present moments into focus in order to intentionally feel, think and experience the relationship between the self over time, the self and other/s, and the self and the environment. We enlist the imagination in order to anticipate the experiences that may be provoked by adherence to certain ideas, behaviours and beliefs. This accords dynamism to the concept of future. In this chapter I focus on the strategies I use within my clinical work to engage with an exploration of time.

REFLECTING ON THE PAST

People's (clients') narratives of the past exist within a social, moral and value-laden cocoon. When people (clients) tell me about experiences I am interested in each persons (clients') particular representation of experience. In the therapeutic conversation I attend to an exploration of what and who has influenced this representation of experience. As the representation of experience is located contextually, meanings that have been subordinated come forward. These subordinated 'new' meanings can also be located contextually (refer Chapter Two: Contextual Enquiry,).

For example, Bonnie reports that she feels detached from her life. She finds it difficult to understand why this is as she is 'in a relationship where she feels cared for'. Here is a fragment of our conversation:

Bonnie:	I have never been very good with money. Phillip looks after that in the relationship.
Johnella:	What does this 'not being good with money' mean?
Bonnie:	I'm not very orderly. I don't have any sort of system.
Johnella:	How does Phillip's looking after the money in the relationship affect the conversations about money or access to money?
Bonnie:	Phillip makes all the money decisions, that's only fair because he has the responsibility. I have a $50 allowance — don't get me wrong, I can ask if I need more.
Johnella:	How was the decision made in respect to who in the relationship would look after the money?
Bonnie:	I don't know, it just seemed logical.
Johnella:	Bonnie before you met Phillip, what was your relationship with and to money?
Bonnie:	(laughing) Oh, a bit haphazard!
Johnella:	In the past, before the relationship, was money a problem for you? In other words, were you in trouble in your daily life because of this relationship with money?
Bonnie:	No, I did quite well really. I'd paid off my small home unit and I had a superannuation fund.
Johnella:	Did your relationship with money ever cause the bank or the superannuation fund to be concerned?
Bonnie:	Oh no, the money just came straight out of my wage packet.
Johnella:	Who organised that automatic payment?
Bonnie:	I did.
Johnella:	You were organised enough in your relationship to

money to put arrangements in place to support your self.

Bonnie: Yes, I did.

Johnella: Given there were regular payments going out, did your relationship with money mean that at times you couldn't pay other accounts, for example electricity or food, etc.?

Bonnie: Oh no, the main bills were always paid.

Johnella: How did you do that?

Bonnie: I knew approximately what the everyday costs were, so I took that into account.

Johnella: It sounds like in the past, you had an accounting way of managing money. Did this way work for you?

Bonnie: Yes, I suppose it did.

Johnella: Would other people that knew you in the past have thought you had an accounting way of managing money?

Bonnie: I don't know. My Mum and Dad were really impressed that I'd paid off the mortgage, I knew that.

Johnella: When we began this conversation, you said that you have never been good with money. Yet when we talk about the relationship you had with money before the relationship with Phillip, you had a system to account for money that worked. What is your understanding of this difference?

In this example, Bonnie's present description, 'I have never been good with money,' is juxtaposed with 'the accounting way of managing money'. The accounting way of managing money is situated in an exploration of the past. As this interview progressed Bonnie and I would go on to explore the context that has supported the 'forgetting' of her past relationship with money. We would also explore the impact of remembering 'the accounting way of managing money' on an understanding of the self, and on present relationships. The effect on present relationships would be explored using a contextual enquiry. This enquiry has the potential to expose the effects of gender socialisation and gender relations on people's (clients') lives and relationships.

This kind of questioning will often provoke people (clients) to reflect on the influences that shape memory while also wondering about the consequences for their present lives if alternative explanations for the past events were more dominant.

For example, Michael suffers under the weight of severe self-criticism. His achievements in life turn to dust under criticism's relentless diatribe. When he reflects on his life as a child, he is very disparaging of the child he remembers. He regards this child as weak and 'tied to his mother's apron strings'. This is a fragment of our conversation.

Johnella: When you hear the words 'he's tied to his mother's apron strings', whose voice do you hear?

Michael: Oh, that's easy. It's Dad. He was forever on at my mother, blaming her for the things I did.

Johnella: What were those things that he was upset about?

Michael: I was captain of the debating team and I was really into drama. You'd need to know my Dad to understand. He played rugby for Manawatu for years. He's a real man's man. When I arrived, I mean was born, he was over the moon. He desperately wanted a son. I was not the son he wanted. I am quite athletic really, but I wasn't that interested. He tried and I tried, but it just wasn't any good. I remember the day that I said, 'I don't want to play rugby any more.' The way he looked at me. That's all he did. He didn't hit me or shout, he simply folded his newspaper, stood up and said, 'Well that's that then,' and went out to the pub.

Johnella: What do you think you took from the words, 'well, that's that then'?

Michael: I think he cut me off from that moment. He did all that was required of him but he cut me out. He never spoke to me about it, but he raved on at Mum, blaming her for how I'd turned out.

Johnella: Do you think this disappointment about how you'd turned out went both ways? I mean if we consider that your dad experienced disappointment in the relationship, do you think you also experienced disappointment?

Michael: I don't know about disappointment. I know at times I feel very angry.

Johnella: What's the anger made up of?

Michael: Oh, so many things. What could have been, I suppose, that's the disappointment. Sorrow, that he didn't do a better job as a father.

Johnella: Do you think the anger has any sadness with it?

Michael: It could have, I don't know. I really don't like to think about this very much.

Johnella: When there's no thinking about these strong feelings, where do you think the feelings go?

Michael: Maybe underground, I don't know.

Johnella: When you began talking today, you mentioned the strong above-ground feelings that are directed at your self. Do you think that there's a relationship between those above-ground feelings and these underground feelings?

Michael: There might be, I've never thought about it.

In this example Michael and I are beginning to explore the relationship between 'the above-ground feelings', i.e. criticism, and the underground feelings. The explanations, feelings and thoughts about the self in the present are explored in relationship to past events and feelings. I am interested in what has influenced the past-sense that Michael has made and what other past-senses are available to him.

Engaging with memory is not a passive activity, it involves re-viewing events and feelings from a number of perspectives. Reflecting on the past involves a dynamic process of enquiry and response that creates conditions for the discovery of possibilities.

When we reflect on the past, the conversational process will evoke memories that have escaped people's (clients') attention. These memories may contradict the following:

▼ A prevailing description of the self held by others (family members and friends).

▼ The prevailing cultural and/or societal views.

▼ A constructed memory that excludes traumatic events.

For example, Lynda said:

> For quite a long time I made myself up. Whenever I met people I would create a story about myself. I would support the story using photos that I'd brought at secondhand stores or by using cuttings from old newspapers. I really entered the story, believing totally in the character. The character had an entirely different history from mine. After a while, I began to feel dizzy, unstable. I had created an ever-shifting reality that in the end threatened to overwhelm me. I became incredibly depressed. When I look back, I just think that making up my life was the only way I could think of to cope with the years of abuse. I couldn't find a way to live with it, so I became other people. The other people I became entered every relationship, including my friends, my partner and the counsellor I had at the time.

We search with people (clients) for those memories that sit in the shadows. When we explore the past, it is important that we have a grasp of the conditions and beliefs of that time. Past relationships and events that are reflected on in the present make a different sense if the historical context within which these relationships and events are situated is also known.

Margaret Forster in *Hidden Lives* (6) writes of the lives of three generations of women in her family. When Margaret entered high school, her mother saw a gulf opening up between them. Over time that gulf remained. Here is the conversation between Margaret and her mother Lilly, while Lilly is dying in hospital (pp. 300–303).

> My mother said, 'I feel as if I'm in a waiting-room. It's so tiring, waiting, waiting. I wish my turn would come. I wish I didn't have to wait. I want to leave. I want to go somewhere nice.'
>
> 'Where? Where would be nice?'
>
> 'Oh, Silloth, of course. I'd like to be on the Green at Silloth. Lovely.'

'Who with?'

'Jean and Nan and Peggy Farish'.

'What would you do? Have a picnic?'

'No, no, the grass is too damp.'

'So what will you do?'

'Oh, sit on a bench for a while, then have a walk along the sea wall, watch the tide come in, have an ice-cream, watch the men fish. Plenty to do.'

'What will you wear?'

'My blue dress, the one with the sailor collar.'

'And what . . .'

'Oh STOP IT!' she suddenly snapped. 'This is *silly*.' It was said so viciously, with a strength I didn't know she still had, and yet I'd thought she was enjoying what seemed a harmless game, a soothing fantasy. I could have played it for hours. I *wanted* to play it for hours. She tossed and turned on her pillow and sighed. 'Anyway,' she said, 'I've had enough.'

'What of?' I asked, nervously, knowing I mustn't anger her by starting another evasive dialogue.

'This. I've had enough. I want done with it. It hasn't amounted to much, my life.'

'Mum, *please* . . .'

'No, it hasn't. It's been all work and worry. I've done nothing with myself.'

It was the old cry, the more painful for being said, as it was said now, without any desire to arouse sympathy, without the slightest hint of wishing to be contradicted and persuaded otherwise.

'Mum, please, listen. You've led a good life, you have . . . You've done so much good in it. You've been a wonderful daughter and wife and mother. Nobody could have been better . . . You've had and brought up three children. You've always put your family first . . . Isn't that making something of your life? Isn't it?'

'No. It isn't what I mean. Look at you . . .'

'Mum! I can't bear it. You go on as though I'd climbed Everest or discovered penicillin. I haven't done any more than you have. My life is no more commendable than yours. There's no real difference in what we've achieved. A few

skittery books doesn't amount to much . . .'
   'It's how I feel. And I've had enough anyway.'

This conversation occurred in 1981. Lilly (Margaret's mother) was born in 1901. Margaret writes about Lilly's decision to marry:

> She made her bargain, trading a job she loved and good money, and a comfortable home with her mother, whose company she found more than congenial, for marriage to a man she cared for, but for whom she did not feel overwhelming attraction, in order to fulfill her destiny as a woman and have those children for whom she yearned.

There was no other possibility for Lilly's life given the institutional and cultural limitations on women at that time. Throughout Margaret's life, changes to institutional regulations, attitudes and values provided an environment that supported Margaret's ambitions. Lilly judged her self inferior and inadequate to Margaret's achievements; in other words she understood her daughter's achievements outside of context and time. Consequently Margaret's achievements reduced her achievements.

In conversation with Lilly we would direct our enquiry towards the context within which she made her life decisions. This would enable Lilly to see the conditions that determined her life direction.

Johnella: Lilly, before you were married you were in a job that you really enjoyed. How was the decision made to leave this job after you were married?

Lilly: There was no choice about that. Married women just weren't employed in the public service.

Johnella: Was this an informal understanding or was there a rule that enforced this?

Lilly: It was a regulation.

Johnella: Okay. When you were young, women's lives were regulated by rules that determined if they could work or not.

Lilly: Yes, that's right.

Johnella: It wasn't an issue of choice?

Lilly: No, no it wasn't. Don't get me wrong, I wanted to be a
              mother. Being a mother was very important to me.

Johnella: How is it Lilly that you did 'the right thing' in that time
              which involved being a wife and mother, and Margaret
              did 'the right thing' for this time where she was able to
              seek education and work without legislative restraint
              then she sought marriage and children?
              How is it that the experience of Margaret's 'right thing'
              in her time has turned your 'right thing' in your time
              into a wrong thing?

Any attempt to reassure people, as Margaret attempts to do when Lilly
is dying, is often experienced by the other as alienating. Reassurance
does not soften or challenge beliefs. An enquiry, focused on the cultural
prescriptions that determine the boundaries within which meaning is
made of individual lives, challenges people (clients) to reassess critical
self-judgment and to consider how life decisions are constrained and
shaped by societal, cultural, economic and familial circumstances. In
re-viewing the past contextually, memories of achievements, and the
striving to support oneself and others, can replace judgment and
criticism. This challenge to self-judgment liberates people (clients) to
find ways to realise, acknowledge and use their strengths to live with
life's circumstances. In such an enquiry we challenge the idea that
individuals solely determine their fate. We move the focus for
psychological wellbeing away from isolated internal experiences
towards the self in relationship to historical, cultural, familial and
economic circumstances.[1] This style of enquiry locates people's
experiences within a context, thus illuminating the forces that shape
and determine the meanings we make of our lives. When people
(clients) can explore and see these shaping forces, people (clients) have
the opportunity to consider their lives and others' lives with respect and
compassion.

WHAT AND WHO FALLS FROM MEMORY
Doris Lessing, in her autobiography *Under My Skin* (17) reflects on
memory as she calls on memory in the writing of her life. She
comments that women often get dropped from memory and then from
history. It is obvious that members of the dominant group within

society have foremost access to the resources that promote visibility and thus acknowledgement and legitimisation. This visibility, acknowledgement and legitimisation then provides the means for discerning the superiority of ideas and practices. The ownership of these ideas and practices is thus confirmed as belonging to members of the dominant group.

When people are dropped from memory and then from history, the effects are profound. Experiences and knowledge that belong to forgotten groups are then determined to exist only within the individual who 'discovers' them. This individual, more often than not, belongs to the dominant group. Those who are alienated from the dominant group will then defer to this group as the carriers of true knowledge.

For example, in an article written on the subject of gender relations in couple work, the writer acknowledged the influence of feminism on his thinking. However a check of the references revealed that the texts used to support the article were written solely by men. There are, of course, numerous texts on the psychology of gender to which women have contributed. These women could and should be referenced and therefore named. Glowingly absent from this particular text and many others is also any acknowledgement, appreciation and authorship of dozens of women in every community who have defied the majority voice and insisted that their experiences and ideas be listened to. This is the oral and moral contribution that almost always disappears under the traditional approach to authorship of psychology texts.

When people are dropped from memory and then from history, they are robbed of the knowledge and experience of being active in maintaining and creating the community in which they live. The next generation is then presented with a version of their heritage that excludes the activities and ideas that originated from part of their community. In therapy I reflect with people (clients) on the past in order to bring forward knowings and experiences which have been relegated to the inconsequential, thereby robbing them of knowledge of their resources. Reclaiming memories that have previously been regarded as inconsequential is achieved within a framework that explores and exposes how memory is shaped and claimed.

THE FIXING OF MEMORY

Doris Lessing (17) reflects, 'How do you know that what you remember is more important than what you don't?' Virginia Woolf (38), in writing on her earliest memories, wonders why some things are remembered and some are not. The thought that accessible memories are in some way exceptional is juxtaposed with the question, 'What makes one event more exceptional than another?' Virginia Woolf explores this question by giving an example of a memory that would seem to be one that as a child she would remember. 'Why remember the hum of bees in the garden going down to the beach, and forget completely being thrown naked by father into the sea? (Mrs Swanwick says she saw that happen.) Doris Lessing (17) comments that 'I spent a good part of my childhood fixing moments in my mind'.

When I work with memory, I explore what is remembered and wonder what supports the fixing of that moment in a child's or adult's mind. If we believe there are moments that are fixed in memory, then there are also moments that are not fixed.

When I use my clinical experience to consider what it is that supports forgetting, the following determinants came to mind.

Firstly, memory is more easily fixed if others concur with a description of events. For example, there are two people walking along the same beach. One person sees and feels sand, the sea, the sun. The other person sees droplets of water dancing in the space between the wave and the sky. Both people speak about these visions. The first description is supported by the other 300 people that were on the beach as reflecting their experience. No one supports the second description.

Experiment with answering these questions:

▼ How does it feel to have the memory you hold of the experience supported by others?

▼ How does it feel to not have the memory of the experience supported by others?

▼ How do you continue to believe in this experience?

▼ How do you continue to believe in this experience when it is unsupported by others?

▼ How will this lack of support influence the memory you hold of the experience?

▼ If one other person in the 300 had a similar experience to the one you hold, do you think they feel able to join you, or would they concur with the majority voice?

When traumatic events remain secret and are locked within the contradictory moments that inevitably occur in situations of family abuse, it is interesting to consider what the memories are that then become fixed, and what the memories are that fade into the background, often leaving behind those remnants of memory — shame, guilt, terror, anger and sadness. Traumatic events that remain secret while immersed in contradictory moments inevitably lack witnesses. The lack of witnesses deprives people (clients) of memory supports. In the therapeutic work, we are equally interested in the memories that people (clients) easily access and the memories that people (clients) struggle to access.

A second element in remembering and forgetting is that whatever is forgotten is often that which has been considered by people (clients) as normal and everyday. The normal and everyday does not always warrant fixing. For example, Jess was frequently horrendously beaten by her mother, Fran. The beatings involved several hospitalisations. After the beating, Fran repeatedly told Jess that the beatings were her own fault. When the beatings resulted in an investigation by the authorities Jess had been tutored into an explanation that contained fragments of what occurred. All these incidents were then recorded as accidents. Consequently as an adult Jess viewed her self as essentially bad and deserving of beatings. She acknowledged the beatings but minimalised the severity and frequency by talking about her self as a 'difficult' child. Jess did not remember the hospitalisations until the fifth session. In the remembering she again reduced the severity of the incidents. It wasn't until she viewed her hospital records that she began to reflect on the past evidence differently.

The forgetting I'm addressing reflects those memories that aren't immediately accessible. For example, if I ask someone to tell me in as much detail as possible about their relationship with their mother, the end point of the narrative consists of what is easily accessible. If at that end point I begin an enquiry of the account, new information will come forwards which extends and alters the original account. One way to extend the account is to make apparent and then explore the normal and the everyday, thus the taken-for-granted.

The third aspect of what is forgotten is often that which is saturated in contradiction.

For example, I say that I love you, which is demonstrated by my public behaviour towards you and reinforced by others' good opinion of my loving, while in private I physically hurt you and threaten to kill you. Within this contradiction what is the memory that can be held?

Each person (client) determines this uniquely according to individual circumstances.

To continue with examples of contradictions, Phillip is a minister of the church. He is regarded as a respected, ethical man that others approach for guidance and counsel. Phillip is also sexually abusing Lucy, his 6 year old daughter. Lucy has no language to adequately convey her experience while surrounded by other people's expressions of the relationship between her self and Phillip. 'You're so lucky he really loves you, Lucy.' 'I wish my husband would spend as much time with the children as you do Phillip.' 'Lucy, you're a lucky girl.'

I believe that immersion in contradictions can act against the fixing of memories that are unsupported by others. When contradictory moments occur in the domestic sphere daily, those moments frequently remain unnamed, unacknowledged and unwitnessed. In these environments what is there to remember? I believe that living with these domestic contradictory moments can cause lack of ease, unhappiness, worry, etc. This is what people remember and is often explained by a pathological view of the self. For example, 'I get the blues every now and then', 'I cry over nothing', 'I've just lost all interest in sex, maybe I've got a low sex drive'. What is remembered in these circumstances is a problem-saturated self. This problem-saturated self may attend counselling in order to make changes to the self. A contextual enquiry of the past offers people (clients) the opportunity to explore different relationships with the past.

The enquiry that I have with people (clients) around remembering and forgetting, challenges conventional beliefs that memory is fixed and individually created. My enquiry arises from a belief that a scaffolding of beliefs determines, shapes and constructs the meanings made of memory.

Re-viewing the scaffolding of beliefs can involve engaging with the presuppositions that underpin the maintenance of significant relationships including the relationship with the self. For example:

Johnella: Jess, how old were you when these beatings took place?

Jess: It happened throughout my childhood and stopped when an aunt paid for me to go to boarding school.

Johnella: Do you think your aunt knew what was happening?

Jess:	I think she knew that things were difficult between me and Mum.
Johnella:	Do you think there are any circumstances where a child deserves to be beaten to the extent that she is admitted to hospital?
Jess:	I was a difficult child. Mum had lots of pressures, she tried really hard.
Johnella:	Would you consider taking a similar position with your children?
Jess:	Oh no, I'd never do that.
Johnella:	What's the difference between you as a child and the children you're imagining?
Jess:	Nothing really. I'm just afraid, afraid that if I really look at this, everything will change. I'm afraid I'll lose my mother.
Johnella:	I'd like us to move really slowly because I'd like to understand this fear — is that okay? If you think anything I'm saying or asking is moving you in that fearful direction, could you tell me and I'll stop. Is that okay?
Jess:	Yes, yes that helps.

In this example, the scaffolding on which the meaning of the past sits is partially constructed by the fear of loss. It seems easier for Jess to shoulder the familiar construct of self-blame than it is to enter the unknown, where she fears she will lose her relationship with her mother. In our work together we would get to know this fear. We would re-search the following:

▼ How the fear has shaped the present mother/daughter relationship.

▼ Who and what the fear actually protects.

▼ What the mother/daughter relationship could become if the fear was no longer present.

▼ How the fear shapes an engagement with the past and how this engagement reflects on Jess's sense of self.

In this therapy I am interested in exploring how Jess can be liberated from self-blame and how that liberation will act to reconstruct Jess's experience of the mother/daughter relationship.

In summary, my hypothesis of what contributes to the fixing of memory is:

▼ Memory is more easily fixed if it is supported by other people's account of the events.

▼ What is often forgotten is that which is considered normal and everyday.

▼ What is forgotten is that which is saturated in contradictory ideas and circumstances.

We can assist people (clients) in the re-search of their memory by supporting an inquiry process outside of therapy by looking at photos, talking to family members and so on. I encourage people (clients) to experiment with expressing their wonderings, flashes of memory or gut feelings. This experimentation is just that, a wondering out-loud. We are not in a position to arbitrate on meaning.

Doris Lessing (17) comments further that 'memory is a careless and lazy organ, not only a self flattering one.' It is interesting to observe the conditions that support self flattering memory and the conditions that support less than flattering memory. Self-flattering memory tends to include experiences that represent success — societal, cultural and familial success. The people (clients) who don't qualify as 'successful' as a result of ethnicity, gender, economic status, physical disability, and sexuality often make sense of their lack of access to resources by seeing it as a result of personal deficit. This making sense is supported by a memory search for evidence of that deficit such as, 'I never worked hard enough at school,' 'I was really good at sport but I didn't have that winning above everything else streak,' 'I'm lazy I guess,' 'I really loved reading, I guess I was pretty selfish when I was younger.' In the therapeutic work, the enquiry places memory in a societal, cultural and familial context.

Here is the beginning of an exploration of Trish's statement. 'I really loved reading. I guess I was pretty selfish when I was younger.'

Johnella: Was it hard to give reading away and help out?

Trish: It was and it wasn't. I knew Mum really appreciated me helping out and I knew that she was really exhausted by the end of the day.

Johnella: What was it that encouraged you to give up something you loved, to help?

Trish: Seeing Mum's face, she was often really white and looked quite ill. It was hard for her looking after five children on her own.

Johnella: You gave up something you loved for the love of your mother?

Trish: Yes.

Johnella: How have you come to see the giving up of something you loved for the love of your mother?

Trish: I didn't do this straight away — these were lots of times that I'd disappear into the back shed to read when Mum needed me.

Johnella: How old were you then?

Trish: About eight or nine.

Johnella: How old were you when you decided to give up reading to help?

Trish: I was 10 years old.

Johnella: How many 10 year olds do you know that are required by circumstances to give up something they love to help?

Trish: I don't know any children now who have done that.

Johnella: When you reflect back on your self at 10, holding in your mind other 10 year olds that you know, would you judge the 10 year old that sacrifices what she loves, to help out as generous, loving and resourceful or as selfish?

RELATING TO MEMORY

I encourage the people (clients) I work with to engage as re-searchers of their lived experience. At times people (clients) cannot find collaboration for the memory of their lived experience. In these instances we focus on what supported the memory's appearance and the impact of the memory appearing in that particular way. The stand I take is to be available to an exploration that encompasses broad and numerous possible explanations. It is not our responsibility to provide definitive explanations for people's (clients') memories.

For example, Sally was alienated from her mother. Sally had experienced that relationship as emotionally and physically abusive. She had a memory of her mother acting on her body in a way that could have been interpreted as sexually abusive. When we explored this memory further and the context that surrounded the memory, it appeared more likely that the memory was that of a medical procedure. The medical procedure was experienced by the child as traumatic because it was applied in a climate of physical and emotional abuse and was administered in a particularly brutal manner.

When memories cannot be collaborated, I encourage numerous contextual possibilities that could provide an explanation to surround and support the memory. There is no hierarchy for traumatic events. Experiences of emotional abuse can have as substantial an effect on wellbeing as does physical and sexual abuse. Knowing this enables a wide contextual enquiry rather than one that is directed by the therapist's assumption of what the memory means.

THE EFFECT OF BEING STRUCK DUMB

People (clients) talk about memory in an interesting way. When people (clients) remember past events, it is as though they are known and yet not known. Physical, emotional and sexual abuse can exist in the shadowland between belief and disbelief. This shadowland can occur as the result of contradictions and silence. Within the silence, children and sometimes adults have no words to describe the myriad of emotions that sustain the knowledge that what happened is/was wrong. This knowing that what happened is/was wrong, can exist despite the threats and the context of the abuse, i.e. its secrecy. If there are no words however to describe traumatic events and no venue to experiment with expression, including verbal expression, what happens to the knowledge of the event? In many instances it moves into an everyday forgetting. Its retrieval is often precipitated by flashing images or overwhelming emotional responses or unexplainable physical pain. The retrieval can occur independent of any external stimulus.

A relational externalising enquiry process takes fragments of memory and re-searches the environment that surrounds the memory, thus bringing the memory into focus. The relational externalising enquiry positions the person (client) as a viewer, re-viewer and re-searcher of the past in order to prevent immersion in the experience of the past. This positioning attempts to maintain the person's (clients') sense of control in the exploration and retelling process. It does not preclude experiencing strong emotions. I am dedicated, however, to a process of working with people (clients) where retelling is an activity of the present. The relational externalising process is central to creating the linguistic space that supports people to *reflect on their relationship with the past* in contrast to *being immersed in the past* events and emotions. This conversational process allows people (clients) to experience in the present a sense of agency over the exploration of the past.

SURVIVING

One of the methods used to survive traumatic life events is to forget or to rationalise, with statements like, 'It was a mistake, it only happened once.' Significant life changes, such as commitment to an intimate relationship, birth of a child, or an opportunity to re-view life experiences by reading or viewing others' lives, or talking with someone else about life experiences, can provoke strong emotional responses 'out of the blue'.

The strong emotional response is often frightening for people (clients) and those close to them. The precipitating event to the emotional outpouring can seem trivial in relation to the response. People (clients) will often conclude that they are having a nervous breakdown or going mad. Tobias Wolff in his book *This Boy's Life* (37) writes about his relationship to memory when his parents separated. Although his father was physically abusive to him, as a child and adult he had thought, 'He was no monster — he'd had troubles of his own. Anyway, only crybabies groused about their parents.'

Tobias Wolff then records how his understandings of the past changed. When his first child was born he experienced extreme distress at the inadequate performance of a medical procedure on the baby. He then writes of a shift in his relationship with memory.

> When I finally got my hands on him I felt as if I had snatched
> him from a pack of wolves, and as I held him something hard
> broke in me, and I knew that I was more alive than I had been
> before. But at the same time I felt a shadow, a coldness at the
> edges. It made me uneasy, so I ignored it. I didn't understand

> what it was until it came upon me again that night, so sharply
> I wanted to cry out. It was about my father, ten years dead by
> then. It was grief and rage, mostly rage, and for days I shook
> with it when I wasn't shaking with joy for my son, and for the
> new life I had been given.' (pp. 101–102)

In this autobiographical account that strong emotional response made
no sense 'until it came upon me again that night, so sharply I wanted
to cry out. It was about my father, ten years dead by then'. This is often
an experience that precipitates therapy or occurs in therapy when
people engage in talking about past events. In the process of making
sense of strong emotional responses, people (clients) can experience
enormous relief. The past is therefore a dynamic feature of our lives,
we carry it with us, using the strategies available to us to make sense
of, and to sometimes survive the events of the past.

Through a relational externalising enquiry process, people (clients)
experience themselves as in relationship to the past. This defies conventional thinking, i.e. the past is in the past, 'what's done is done'. Past
events cannot be made to disappear, however the meaning made of past
events can be re-searched, reflected on and related to in ways that are
liberating. When people (clients) engage with the process of negotiating
the meanings that can be attributed to past events, our questions draw
people's (clients') attention to the power relationship inherent in one
meaning being privileged over another. The exposure of this power
relationship provides people (clients) with an opportunity to engage
with the relationship between ethics, morality and memory. This
engagement challenges the conventional belief that memory is self-
contained and possessed by the individual.

THE PRESENT
The therapeutic relationship provides a unique environment for
experimenting with the self in relationship with another. People
(clients) take risks to disclose thoughts, feelings, memories and events
that have often remained hidden for survival purposes. Our response
to these disclosures determines the meaning that will subsequently be
made of these events.

For example, Lyle told his therapist that he had been sexually abused
when he was seven years old. The therapist acknowledged this with a
nod and made a comment about sexual play. The difference in the ages

of Lyle and the abuser was eight years. The therapist's response completely silenced Lyle who took from this response that he was to blame
for what happened and that he was exaggerating his feelings. It took
Lyle many years to risk disclosing this experience to anyone else.

My first response is to take people's (clients') experiences seriously,
then re-search the experience using a relational externalising enquiry
that places the experiences in a societal, cultural, historical and family
context. The unique nature of each person's (client's) experience
requires us to be cautious about generalizations. We can use collective
knowings as a possibility as in 'a number of people have said'. This
possibility is presented as the beginning point of any enquiry.

When people (clients) take the risk to expose thoughts and feelings
we have an opportunity to reflect on a unique experience. Exploration
of this unique experience can present people (clients) with new self-
knowledge about the process of risk-taking.

For example:

Lilly:	There is something I haven't told you, I feel really bad about not telling you. I've tried several times but I just couldn't.
Johnella:	What was the thinking or the feeling that stopped the telling?
Lilly:	I think that you'll think I've made it up, or if you do believe me I think you'll think I'm disgusting.
Johnella:	How much is this thinking affecting the therapy?
Lilly:	Lots, every time I come I get myself geared up to tell. I think about it the whole time and then I don't. I feel so stupid.
Johnella:	If you were to take a risk with telling, what could I do or say to support you in that?
Lilly:	I don't know. I just don't know.
Johnella:	There are many forms that telling can take, there can be telling by using speech or talk, telling by writing and telling in pictures. What form of telling would most support you?
Lilly:	I think I'd prefer to write it down, give it to you to read

and then leave the room while you read it.

Johnella: When you imagine leaving the room while I read, what do you think that you'll be thinking?

Lilly: I'll be thinking the worst, I'll be terrified to come back.

Johnella: I'd like us to explore these two things. Firstly what are the ways that you can be supported in the waiting and how can we make the coming back easier? In the waiting, what can you carry with you about your experiences of this therapy that will support you?

Lilly: What do you mean?

Johnella: Have there been times that you've thought I would be critical or blaming in the therapy and I wasn't?

Lilly: Oh yes.

Johnella: Can you remember some particular times?

Lilly: Yes I can, it might be hard to hold on to them though.

Johnella: Okay, is there something I can write or give you from the room, that you could take with you to remind you of the past support?

Lilly: If I could hold something and look at it. I think that would help me remember what you've done in the past. What about that green shell on the window sill. Would that be okay?

Johnella: Yes that's fine. Do you feel that you could experiment with the waiting with the support we've discussed?

Lilly: I'm willing to give it a go.

Johnella: You talked about your concerns about the coming back . . .

Lilly: Yes but I think now that I have some ideas about the waiting it will make it easier to come back.

Johnella: Would the coming back be more or less supported if I came out to you after the reading?

Lilly: I think I'd like you to come out to me.

Johnella: Okay. In the discussion we've had about the telling, what
              helped you to bring it out in the open? It was you that
              brought my attention to the telling.

Lilly: I just knew I had to.

Johnella: Have you thought 'I have to' during other sessions?

Lilly: Many times.

Johnella: What was different about this time?

Lilly: I just told myself this is silly and reminded myself of all
              the times that I've felt supported by you.

Johnella: Were you reminding your self before you came today
              and during the session?

Lilly: Oh yes, right up to the moment that I told.

Johnella: At the moment and before the moment of telling today,
              have ideas about support in this therapy helped you
              with the telling?

Lilly: Yes, yes they did.

Johnella: It seems as though today you have experimented with
              using the method of support we were discussing.

Lilly: (Nods)

Johnella: Do you think this knowledge of your success today
              could be added to the memories that will support you
              in the waiting?

Lilly: I think that's a good idea.

The therapeutic relationship can provide people (clients) with the
opportunity to experiment with challenging fears. Whenever fears are
challenged, people (clients) can find themselves moving past a long
established and often lonely experience of silence. In this movement
people (clients) make apparent and challenge longstanding negative
descriptions held by themselves and others. Our (therapists') role is to
take the opportunity to highlight and explore those unique experiences
that occur from within the therapeutic relationship. These experiences
within the therapeutic relationship provide people (clients) with an

experimental resource. Often the experimental resource involves negotiating and experimenting with safety, exposing the secret self-defining ideas and practices. Once these ideas and practices are exposed and negotiated, relational strategies for safety can then be taken into other relationships.

The following conversation was a consultation about a therapeutic process that had become stuck. In the conversation we turned our attention towards the unique experience of 'deciding to mention it'. Once a unique experience is identified it can be further re-searched, providing people (clients) with the resources for change.

Stephen is representing his client, Wayne, in this consultation.

Johnella:	If the therapy was to be successful, what changes do you think would occur?
Wayne:	I'd be myself.
Johnella:	When you talk about 'I'd be myself', what self have you been over the years?
Wayne:	If I was myself I wouldn't tell lies, I'd be myself, be a father to my children. I've been weak, I've been phony, not able to stand up for myself.
Johnella:	Has there ever been a time when you think back over your life that you've thought, 'That's myself.'?
Wayne:	The time when I told my ex-wife Cherie to get out rather than continuing to take her nonsense. That was taking a stand.
Johnella:	Is a self for you a 'taking a stand self'?
Wayne:	Part of it, not always backing down, not always afraid of the shit hitting the fan, Cherie's yelling and screaming.
Johnella:	What other parts of your self is a 'taking a stand self'?
Wayne:	By just saying the other day that the two boys were having a sleep-out at school. Their mother told me, and asked me if I wanted to go and sleep there. I was afraid to mention it to Linda, afraid that she'd freak out. Instead I should have told Linda and said, 'I'm taking the tent, these are my lads, I'm doing this.'

Johnella:	Are you somebody who over the years has been quite sensitive to others' ideas or opinions?
Wayne:	It seems I'm more afraid than sensitive so I wouldn't have thought so.
Johnella:	It sounds like you're quite knowledgeable about what Linda might feel?
Wayne:	Every time I mention Cherie, Linda goes ballistic. I've tried over three years and its not working. I'm losing my lads.
Johnella:	You experimented by mentioning it for a couple of years, and then by not mentioning it?
Wayne:	Yes, I'd make up stories, lied and sneaked out to see the kids, however sooner or later she'd find out.
Johnella:	So this experimenting, has it resulted in you feeling less of your self?
Wayne:	Yes, that's not how I want to be. That's how I've been most of my life, sort of weak. I've recently been going to the gym. I still remember when I was a kid, stronger people used to pick on me.
Johnella:	Before this not mentioning it, did you have a stronger sense of self, or weaker sense of self, or just the same?
Wayne:	By not standing up for myself I avoided hassles. It seemed easier at times.
Johnella:	Are you saying that you've had a history of not mentioning things?
Wayne:	I've been to other counsellors before Stephen and they've said, 'That's her problem.' But that doesn't seem to work.
Johnella:	In other areas of your life, for example work, can you mention issues and other things?
Wayne:	Other areas in life are really in the shit, work's not going well. I can't mention it to Linda, she goes, 'Ah you should have done this and that.'

Johnella:	What do you find it easy to mention — with Linda, with friends?
Wayne:	Easy to mention with Linda? Nothing is easy. Just recently I got more determined to do that after three years of it not working.
Johnella:	Has Linda caught up to your determination to mention it?
Wayne:	She's off to Australia, she needs a break to think. While she's there she'll see if she if misses me, if not that's it.
Johnella:	Wayne, in a situation where for three years you experimented with 'the not mentioning it', does Linda know about this decision to mention it?
Wayne:	We hardly talk, talk is argument.
Johnella:	So there's been no talking, and within the no talking you've made a decision to start to mention it?
Wayne:	I need to be me.
Johnella:	When you look back, has this mentioning it ever been a decision? You said no — shaking your head — is that a no?
Wayne:	My dad, he never talked about stuff, kept it inside, maybe I learned to do that.
Johnella:	When you first got involved in the relationship with Linda, could you mention feelings of love?
Wayne:	Not really. I was still trying to get over Cherie, Linda was sort of pushing.
Johnella:	One of the things that strikes me right this minute, for someone who's spent a long, long time not mentioning things such as feelings of love, struggle, fear, is how have you been able to mention it in therapy?
Wayne:	Well, when I first came with Linda to see Stephen, even now when she's there I can't talk to Stephen. When there's just the two of us I can do it.
Johnella:	What supports you in doing it at that time?

Wayne:	He listens, not telling me I'm doing it all wrong, stupid. Not like other counsellors. I got angry and worked up with them.
Johnella:	Have you ever found in these talks that you've been tempted not to talk about it to Stephen?
Wayne:	Yes.
Johnella:	So when that's happened, what have you done?
Wayne:	Well, the time before last I rang him up, said I wanted to see him. I felt I needed to talk about this stuff, there's no one else to talk to, I can't talk to mates, my dad's dead, and I can't talk to Linda.

The focus of the consultation was to find an enquiry direction that moved past the stuckness. Highlighting the unique experience within the therapeutic relationship provided the therapy with a new area of exploration.

The therapeutic context, which is situated in the present, is saturated with exceptional moments where people (clients) take enormous risks to move beyond their relationship with fear. Exploration and re-search of these moments provides people (clients) with the following:

▼   Hope for a different relationship with the self and with others.

▼ The opportunity to practice identifying, naming, reflecting and acting on fears within the therapeutic relationship.

▼ A knowledge resource that can be used outside of the therapeutic relationship.

Within the therapeutic relationship, in the present moment, people (clients) experience the aliveness of the past. We are engaged in a relational externalising enquiry that re-searches the effects of the past (events, thoughts and feelings) on the present. The understanding that I bring to the therapeutic work is that the past is in relationship to the present. In the present, we have an opportunity to explore and negotiate the effects and implications of this relationship.

The experiences that occur within the present moment provide the therapy with an invaluable resource for making sense of the past in the present. People (clients) move from using a detached representation of events to engaging with an exploration of the past in the present.

Engagement with the presentness of the past challenges the suppositions that we need to go back to the past or that we must move on from the past. When the past is restored to its place in relationship to the present we are concerned with the following:

▼ How does the past represent itself in the present?

▼ What sense of the past are we carrying?

▼ Who and what contributes to this sense of past?

▼ Who and what benefits from this sense of the past?

▼ Who and what suffers from this sense of the past?

▼ In re-viewing this sense of the past, what are the implications to wellbeing of carrying this sense of the past in the present?

THE FUTURE

In a relational externalising enquiry that asks people (clients) to consider stepping outside of the bounds of their experience, it is necessary to use imagination. The enquiry process can begin with an 'If' question. For example:

▼ If you were to consider for just one moment being free of waiting, waiting for Greg's decision for this relationship or the other relationship, how would you live your life differently?

▼ What would a day look like?

▼ How would relationships change?

▼ In this freedom from waiting state what could entice you back to believing in waiting?

On agreeing to an enquiry that enlists the imagination, people (clients) join with us in a playful exploration of an imaginary self in relationship to both time and a community of values or people. For example, 'If you were to consider . . . how would that alter your view of these past experiences?' 'If you were to bring this altered view from the past into the present, how would life change?' 'From this position of change, how do you imagine the future might look?'. Using imagination provides an opportunity for creating conceptual space. People (clients) can then engage as an audience to part of their imagined future life. This allows people (clients) to see the relationship between what is thought of as real and what is thought of as imaginary. Using imagination allows people (clients) to entertain possibilities because the enquiry is not rooted in facts, certainties or limitations. For example:

Mary: If I change, everything will fall apart.

Johnella: What do you do in order to stay the same and hold
           things together?

           If someone else could take over doing what you do in
           order to hold things together, how would life change for
           you? How would life change in the family? How would
           life change in the relationship?

These questions explore the person's (client's) activity versus passivity
in staying the same. The idea that Mary is active in staying the same
then allows us to enlist a future enquiry in order to consider possibilities for her life direction.

A future-oriented enquiry calls for exploration of the consequences if
present-day concerns remain unaddressed. The fears, worries or doubts
that can paralyse people (client's) and stop them acting on their
concerns are put into a smaller perspective when a future life with the
concerns is imagined. Alternatively, imagining a future life without the
concerns can strengthen people (clients) both in their resolution to
address the concerns and in confronting the concerns.

Jan: When I consider a life free of the guilt that dominates
           my every moment, it's quite overwhelming. I think in
           order to do that, I'd need to consider claiming a new
           morality that was free of the Church and family guilt
           messages. I just see someone who's happier. Someone
           who can react to whatever and whoever is there in that
           moment rather than someone who has disappeared into
           a conversation with guilt. I think it would be fantastic,
           that's where I want to be.

When we explore a possible future life without the present concerns we
assist people (clients) to consider the steps they would need to take to
move towards this life. People (clients) can consider these steps before
committing themselves to a new life direction. This provides people
(clients) with the experience of engaging with their life rather than
being passively acted on by life. Working with the future requires the
same depth of enquiry as working in the past and present. All involve

supporting people (clients) to seriously consider the implications of a continuing relationship with certain ideas, practices and people. Throughout the therapeutic process the future can be experienced in relationship to the present and the past, which can in turn challenge the idea that the future just happens to us.

THE RELATIONSHIP BETWEEN TIME AND MOVEMENT

A relational externalising enquiry over time (past, present and future) generates a fluid relationship with time. This fluidity is represented by an enquiry that moves boundlessly through time. This enquiry over time (past, present and future) inevitably creates a sense of movement, movement towards or movement away. The experience of movement challenges people (clients) to view their lives as evolving rather than static. In this environment it is then possible to see/know the conditions that support people's (clients') lives and the conditions that undermine people's (clients') lives.

For example, Jenny was six years old. Her parents reported that she had always wet the bed. They had tried numerous methods to help her achieve bladder control. None were successful. This is a fragment of our conversation:

Johnella: Jenny, has there ever been a time that you listened to your bladder and got up at night or had a dry bed?

Jenny: I don't know.

Johnella: Staying at friends or with family?

Jenny: Last year when I stayed at Nan's place I didn't wet the bed.

Johnella: How come, what's different at Nan's place that helps you hear your bladder?

Jenny: Mum said to me Nan's too old to wash sheets.

Johnella: That's very interesting. Do you think those words helped you to listen and hear your bladder somehow?

Jenny: I don't know.

Johnella: Did Mum tell you that before you went to Nan's place?

Jenny: Yes.

Johnella:	How long before you got to Nan's place, just before or in the car, or when you arrived at Nan's place?
Jenny:	I think before we left home.
Johnella:	When do you go to bed Jenny?
Jenny:	Seven o'clock mostly.
Johnella:	From the time you arrived at Nan's place to the time you went to bed, how did you hang on to those words?
Jenny:	I don't know, in my mind I guess.
Johnella:	Those words stuck in your mind. Did you know your mind could hold the words that helped you hear your bladder?

In this example I'm highlighting my belief that people often don't know what they know as they are preoccupied with the strength of the concerns, in this case, bedwetting.

A unique experience like the one in the example often gets lost within the daily experience of problems. Its existence will only be brought forward by an enquiry that has as its focus the evolution of concerns and abilities over time.

The enquiry over time inevitably exposes movement; movement to strengthen or to weaken a concern or ability or idea or practice. This movement constitutes a change. Exposing this change inevitably challenges the totalising meaning construction made of experience. In the movement towards or the movement away from we have opportunities to explore the conditions that either support or undermine concerns, abilities, resilience, health, illness, etc. Movement generates opportunities for unique experiences. Once we locate this possibility we have a venue for exploring the context which surrounds and nurtures this unique experience.

A relational externalising conversation that uses time to re-search both concerns and abilities significantly challenges the concept of the autonomous, independent individual, while introducing the concept of relational self-determination. Engaging with the past and the future in relationship to the present enables a consideration of a relational self that can determine and negotiate life directions.

This way of engaging with time constitutes a principle source for our (therapist and client) relationship to and with hope. Whenever we actively relate to time we are constructing our present life in relationship to the past and the future. Life constructed within this relational paradigm is subject to movement whenever we take the opportunity to reflect on the self in relationship to the past, present and future; in relationship to concerns, abilities and strengths; in relationship to the therapeutic relationship; and in relationship to the contextual environment.

Time is stripped of the power which it holds under determinism where, 'What's in the past, stays in the past.' 'Our future is already determined.' 'We are pawns of time.' Instead we engage with possibilities while restoring the presentness of the past and imagining the future within the present.

ETHICS AND TIME

The ethic of possibility

The ethic of possibility contravenes the dominant ethics held by many psychological and counselling professionals. Diagnosis and categorisation require clinicians to focus on the clustering of symptom behaviour and thinking into a disease etiology which then translates to limitations and sameness. A diagnosis implies homogeneity. Within homogeneity clinicians are encouraged to conform to the limitations inherent within the disease etiology. The search for the diagnosis is further shaped by static engagement with language and a fixed relationship with time. Any therapy within this paradigm requires us to firstly diagnose and then produce the answers or cures for people's (clients') difficulties.

The ethic of possibility is reflected in the way we position our selves with people (clients). Our psychological theories are held as one possibility that may be added to, abandoned or confirmed. The ethic of possibility allows us to engage with the past and the future in the present moment. Consequently, the enquiry over time assists us (therapist and client) to expose how particular meanings have constructed, shaped, limited or expanded lived experience. We are searching out the supporters for one construction of meaning for life events over others, and we are reflecting on the ethics embedded within each construction of meaning.

When I engage with the ethic of possibility I use the relational externalising enquiry. This enquiry confirms and affirms a relational self.

When we engage with the ethic of possibility we become attentive to the exceptional, to differences, to the one-in-a-million, to the 'perhaps' and the 'maybes', to 'once I did something different'. Working with the ethics of possibility raises the prospect that when considering the limitations of therapy we need to also reflect on the limitations of our imagination.

When we engage with the ethics of possibility we enter the therapeutic relationship willing to have our therapeutic models and explanations added to and/or overturned. Every therapeutic relationship provides us with an opportunity to re-search in the present moment the limitations and strengths of the ideas we use as clinical supports. The ethic of possibility embodies the idea that therapeutic models are incomplete representations of the activity of therapy. Therapeutic models are therefore always in the process of evolution.

Within the ethic of possibility I remain continuously alert for signs of people's (clients') resilience or strength. I also actively move language from what isn't to what is. The what is, as in trust, includes all that it isn't. I explore all that constitutes trust by using a myriad of externalisation such as the development of trust, the building of trust, the movement away from trust, the betrayal of trust, the reclaiming of trust. Shifting language in this way brings forward the experience of unique experiences over time. The ethic of possibility is founded on the idea that people (clients) can be active in making changes in their lives. When people (clients) have previously held the belief that there was no possibility for change in their lives, the introduction of possibility creates a climate of hope and activity. The possibility of acting on our lives is implied whenever there is a consideration of choice. Within this consideration of choice, knowledge and experience are represented by using language that reflects activity. When ideas and practices are reflected in language as activities, we enter the process of living rather than making the best of living with the finished product.

Ethics and working with the past
There has been a furore recently challenging the plausibility of what has been termed 'recovered memory'. There are indeed examples of clinicians' inappropriate responses to information given to them by people (clients). In the late 1970s and early 1980s I was aware of numerous examples where all indications suggested that children were being sexually abused, and this evidence was blatantly disregarded by therapists, social workers and psychiatrists. In fact, in one case a

disclosure by a child of sexual abuse was ignored by authorities until many years later when the abuser admitted abusing this child.

The recent vitriolic attack on therapists is interesting because it stands outside of a call to reflect on therapeutic processes in order to prevent therapists imposing meaning within the therapeutic conversation. This imposition occurs when therapists define or diagnose the meaning of events and this definition or diagnosis then dominates people's (clients') explanation of events. Traditional psychiatric and psychological practices are saturated with methods of working with people (clients) that require an imposition of meaning. In fact, whenever a diagnosis is applied professionals are imposing meaning.

In this book I have attempted to present a way of working that reduces the possibility of therapists imposing meaning in the therapeutic conversation. I believe we overstep the therapeutic relationship understanding whenever we argue against or for the possibility of an adult (client) being abused as a child. There are ways to position our selves in relationship to people (clients) that protects the therapeutic relationship from our limitations. I believe, however, that the recent vitriol directed at therapists goes beyond a call for reflecting on therapeutic processes. Instead it is a call that supports a complete (or near complete) denial that traumatic events can be experienced as forgotten and then remembered. This idea totally contradicts my experience.

Toni Morrison (19) refers to her commitment to reflect 'the aesthetic tradition of Afro-American culture'. She describes the commitment in this way.

> If my work is to confront a reality unlike that received reality of the West, it must centralise and animate information discredited by the West — discredited not because it is not true or useful or even of some racial value, but because it is information held by discredited people, information dismissed as 'lore' or 'gossip' or 'magic' or 'sentiment'. (p. 217)

Similarly, the recent movement to discredit therapy goes beyond exposure of the poor practice of a few therapists. We are all discredited simply by belonging to the counselling profession. Discredit is directed particularly at those therapists who work with people (clients) who have been emotionally, sexually and physically abused. We are accused of being central players in creating and maintaining the sexual abuse myth. Our discredit hits at the most vulnerable group in our community, those who have experienced physical, sexual and emotional abuse within the 'sanctuary' of their families. The belief that we have introduced the idea that people (clients) have been abused and that this idea is subsequently believed, directs attention away from all members of the community. I include myself in this community. I challenge all those involved in the debate to redirect their attention to supporting those who have been emotionally, physically and sexually abused and to preparing for a future free of abuse.

It is challenging for us to consider that children continue to be physically, emotionally and/or sexually abused within our homes and communities. It is challenging to ethically re-view the policies, environments, ideas and practices that continue to support the abuse of children. It is challenging to stand aside from the vilification of abusers as monsters and consider that the abuser could be a loved member of our family, a trusted friend or valued neighbour. It is challenging to resist the accusation that therapists and counsellors are perpetuating a myth and instead turn our attention towards what is happening locally in our families, our neighbourhood and our community. It is challenging to confront the complex conditions that support those people who abuse. It is challenging to do all of this without resorting to simplistic and inane solutions that maintain status quo conditions that perpetuate abusive thinking and practices.

WORKING WITH THE TEXT

How Do I (Client) Relate to Time?
When you read this chapter you will get a sense that there can be a number of accounts of the same event. In therapy we are interested in the following:

▼ Identifying these accounts.

▼ Exploring what and who supported or supports each account.

▼ Exploring the consequences of one or more person's accounts being excluded from the 'official' account.

▼ The consequence for people's sense of wellbeing when each account is realised.

▼ Reflecting on the ethics that support maintaining one account over others.

▼ Reflecting on the ethics that support the account people believe represents their experiences.

Memory inevitably effects the account you hold of past events. It is interesting to reflect on what is remembered and what is not. Exclusion of certain events from memory can be part of a protection strategy; protection of the family unit, protection of relationships, protection of economic stability, protection from outsiders, protection of the self. A protection may exist for many reasons and may even have been supported by the understandings of the day. For example, 'It's better if she forgets it and just gets on with her life,' 'You must hold the family together at any cost,' and 'Your strength must compensate for his weakness'. Reconnecting with the memory of your experiences may liberate a raft of new ways of making sense of the past, present and future. For example, 'I now understand that peculiar statement my mother made to me on my wedding day. She said, "Don't let anyone tell you that you're not a virgin, you're a virgin in your heart".' These new ways of making sense of events may also include strong emotions such as experiences of loss.

Often when people remember what they thought they had forgotten they say something like the following:

Dorothy: It's funny, I didn't remember the abuse until after that third session. It's strange, we weren't even talking about sexual abuse, we had been talking about the way I feel detached from life, even from my kids who I love. When I went home that night, I remembered the times my brother abused me on the farm. I never really forgot it, it was always there, I just shut it away.

Whenever you work with the past, it is important that the therapist supports your discoveries. Therapists rarely position themselves definitely, for example by saying, 'This means the following.' In working with the past, you will find your self exploring a number of explanations for past events or feelings. This exploration may involve re-search that includes talking with family, friends and neighbours or reading the files of statutory organisations.

Memories of the past are sometimes very explicit and sometimes very unclear. When they are unclear therapy can assist you to find a way of living well while balancing knowing and not knowing.

In moving the past into the present you have the opportunity to decide how you will engage differently with important relationships. Many people report that moving past experiences into the present heralds the possibility of new ways of being in present relationships. These relationships have been unburdened from past silences and secrets that have previously interfered with them. Engaging in a future enquiry with the therapist or on your own has the potential to help you establish safety parameters. You can consider each step towards a future vision/possibility while re-viewing the supports that can be put in place to make the passage easier.

How Do I (Therapist) Relate to Time?

A relational externalising enquiry that explores people's (clients') relationship to and with time provides us with a principal focus for exploration. We move back and forth over time, drawing together fragments of understanding that support the ongoing enquiry.

In order to experience a contextual exploration of the past think of a past parental relationship and reflect on these questions on your own or with someone else:

▼ What is/was your experience of that relationship? (answer this question in as much detail as possible)

▼ What ideas/values/experiences shaped her/his (your parent's) expectations of the following — her/his self, the parental relationship, children? Answer this question in your parent's voice at different points in time including the present. Then in your own voice as the observer of your parent's relationships at different ages — child, adolescent, adult.

▼ How did those expectations get expressed in the relationship between parent and child, parent and adolescent, parent and adult?

▼ What sense did you make of your experience of these expectations in action?

▼ What sense did your parent make of the experience of these expectations in action?

▼ How did the different or similar experience of the expectations in action impact on the relationship?

▼ Is this impact still impacting on the relationship?

▼ If the impact could be changed, reduced or strengthened what would change in the relationship?

As you do this exercise you will find your self developing further questions in response to the answers. In answering these new questions, you will experience the movement across time as more akin to a weaving and linking motion rather than a linear progression.

Afterwards reflect on these questions:

▼ What questions bring the experience of the past into the present?

▼ What questions move the exploration into the future?

In this next exercise draw a three generational genogram or 'family tree'. Name an ability that relates to your counselling/therapy practice. Reflect on the movement or development of that ability through the generations. In this exercise people have reported that abilities have jumped generations, are not specific to gender, are specific to gender and that the ability is renamed over time. This exercise emphasises that connections over time are often not apparent unless we searched for them.

A future-orientated enquiry provides people (clients) with freedom to experiment with future possibilities in the present. This enquiry necessitates engaging enthusiastically with possibilities. The future is unknown, however the questions which connect people (clients) with their imagination liberates the potential for discovery in the present. These discoveries in the present can provide new foundation blocks for the future. A future enquiry conducted in the present thus creates conditions for change and a sense of actively shaping a self direction.

A facility to engage with the imagination provides us with another resource for developing hope in our lives and in the lives of others. You can practice engaging with this future-orientated enquiry in relation to your ideas of a future life as a therapist.

For example,

▼ If I was the therapist/counsellor that I want to be, what would change?

▼ How would I know that I had become the therapist/counsellor that I want to be?

CHAPTER SEVEN

· · · · · · · · · · ·

Where There is a Relationship, There is Gender

Over the nine years that I have been facilitating workshops on gender and the therapeutic relationship, I have become convinced that we are not adequately engaging with people (clients) in an enquiry around gender relations.[1] Fear that therapeutic conversations that enquire into gender relations will be experienced as politically centered rather than client centered contributes to this lack of attention. The fear often arises from a belief that it is possible to have a therapeutic conversation and be gender neutral. This belief is in turn maintained by the consistent lack of attention in clinical texts and training to the implications of gender relations for clinical work.

The fact that we are all inevitably immersed in the ideas and practices of gender relations contributes to gender relations blindness and creates a responsibility to ongoingly reflect on this gender blindness. The main obstacles to such a reflection are:

▼ Lack of a safe environment for re-viewing clinical practices that promotes conversations which centre on gender relations.

▼ The promotion of gender relations as a fixed knowledge rather than an ongoing relationship to ideas and practices.

▼ The styles of conversations that internalise and blame.

▼ The implications for our lives of reflecting on gender relations in our practice.

▼ The failure to acknowledge historical and institutional influences on the development and maintenance of gender relations.

▼ The reluctance to focus on power relations as enacted in everyday life.

▼ The privileging of detachment in the therapeutic relationship.

The continuing failure of texts, teaching institutions and supervisors/consultants to emphasise the importance of gender relations in therapy implicates therapy as a principal vehicle for maintaining gendered practices and ideas that oppress and silence people (clients).

GENDER AND THE THERAPEUTIC RELATIONSHIP
It is extremely rare for writers of clinical texts to wonder about the impact that the therapist's and client's gender has on the negotiation of meaning in the therapeutic conversation. This absence, together with references to feminism, seems to signify that those writing these texts have reached a gender nirvana. When gender relations is only acknowledged through theoretical ideas there is an implication that reflection on gender relations as a practice is no longer necessary. The readers of these texts are indirectly offered the reassurance that if they follow in the footsteps of the 'master therapist' they too will reach this nirvana.

I continue to be surprised by disembodied writing, where the writer's gender is not considered as a factor in the making of meaning within the therapeutic relationship. This lack of consideration of the therapist's/writer's gender, along with many references to feminism, create an impression of a universal truth. If your experience sits outside of this thinking, you are left to wonder if there is something wrong with your practice.

Therapists' everyday immersion in the prevailing cultural ideas and practices of gender relations contributes to gender relations blindness. I believe this requires us to scrutinize our work and our selves in respect to gender relations throughout our career. A number of years ago, when I was working with a heterosexual couple around the issue of sexuality, I asked the following:

Johnella: Mr Smith, what are your thoughts about your body?

Mr Smith: I don't think about it.

Johnella: If you were to think about that question now, what would you answer?

Mr Smith: I don't like my body. I ignore it.

During the interview we continued to explore Mr Smith's relationship with his body and the effect this had on the issue of sexuality.[2] When I reflected on this interview, I realised that it was unusual for me to ask men about their experience of their bodies. At subsequent workshops, I have discussed the above dialogue with women who are therapists and discovered that many felt uncomfortable about asking such questions. The discomfort arose from the women's (therapists') unfamiliarity with initiating conversations that scrutinized the ideas men hold about their bodies. Men who are therapists have looked slightly embarrassed throughout these discussions, indicating later that it hadn't occurred to them either to ask these questions.

This example reflects my belief that the therapeutic conversation and reflections on it are fertile ground for discovery about gender relations. Discoveries will only be made, however, if the context supports discovery.

In another situation I was consulting with a male colleague around his work with Harry (client) who was masturbating to the extent that his ability to engage in life was severely limited. Even though Harry felt tormented by this behaviour, every intervention and suggestion was overridden. Harry was 40 years old and this concern had been long-standing. My colleague, who had carefully re-searched events and thoughts that occurred prior, during and after masturbation, was interested in considering any ideas I might have. I asked my colleague a number of questions that I would have liked to have asked Harry. Here are some of my questions:

▼ Harry, when you touch your penis, what sort of touch is it? For example, is it a loving touch, a disengaged touch, a caring touch, a non-caring touch?

▼ Harry, when you think about the masturbation, is it an act of self-care or love, or is it an act that hurts you or shames you?

▼ Harry, if you were to think about a loving touch, what would that be like?

▼ Harry, if this is an act that hurts or shames you, what or who has
   supported the development of hurt and shame?

These questions did not provide the answer to this clinical problem.
What shifted during the consultation was that the therapist realised that
he had not explored Harry's relationship with his penis. Subsequently
in the therapy this relationship was re-searched for the first time,
allowing the therapy to take a different direction.

When I considered both these situations I was left wondering. What
does it mean to therapeutic conversations that are exploring sexuality,
if men's ideas/feelings about their bodies are unavailable? This omission
in couple counselling directs the clinical focus towards women as the
carriers of the problem, and in individual counselling supports men's
detachment from their bodies, emotions and others. I also wondered
what the conditions were that enabled me to consider enquiring in
these directions and what else is unavailable to me as a result of my
immersion in gender relations.

SPEAKING THE UNSPEAKABLE

At the 1991 New Zealand Family Therapy Conference in Nelson and the
1992 New Zealand and Australian Family Therapy Conference in
Melbourne, I presented a workshop entitled, 'Are You Interested In
Men?' The workshop was prompted by a realization that men frequently
escaped clinical attention. They either didn't attend counselling, were
labelled difficult, or contributed so little to the therapeutic conversation
that they became witnesses or passengers. When I discussed this
observation with male colleagues, a common response was, 'Women are
so much easier to work with. The worked is more rewarding.' Over the
last four years the men that I work with have challenged this idea.

I believe that men have been neglected as subjects for clinical
attention for the following reasons:

▼ Women (clients) have little hesitation in agreeing with professionals and others that they are the problem.
▼ Women (clients) often actively participate in creating and maintaining a connected therapeutic relationship.
▼ Men's (clients') behaviour that contributes to family, couple or
   individual concerns is often seen as normal and therefore
   becomes invisible.

▼ The pressure to keep men (clients) in the counselling process has resulted in therapists avoiding the issues that are central to men's, couples' or family concerns. This avoidance comes from a fear that talking about the issue will be too confronting or too difficult.

▼ Therapists' gender socialisation may inhibit the way we engage in therapeutic relationships. For example, a woman (therapist) may automatically relate to a man (client) by using 'pleasing' strategies, or a man (therapist) may automatically relate to a man with 'advice giving' strategies.

In contrast, women have frequently been subjects for clinical attention (refer to clinical texts or video presentations and reflect on how many women are represented as clients). Psychological and counselling theory is often based on or illustrated by work with women. These texts ignore both the absence of men as clinical subjects and the gendered therapeutic relationship. Immersion in gender blindness inevitably limits the potential therapeutic conversation.

For example, when I was interviewing a family which consisted of a mother, a father and two children, I became aware that the man was staring at me. He had pushed his chair back and had his arms folded, directing his whole attention to me, not to the responses of the family members. I felt uncomfortable as this man was not following the conventions of the therapeutic relationship. I felt that his positioning reflected my experiences in social settings where women are subjected to men's gazes.

A male colleague indicated that he would have responded to that behaviour by exclaiming, 'What are you staring at?' On reflection, I was aware that I had moderated my response for several reasons. Firstly, out of a sense of loyalty to the man's partner; I didn't want to embarrass her. Secondly, I was concerned that a woman saying, 'What are you staring at?' would be perceived as aggressive and responded to aggressively.

My moderated response in this interview was not satisfactory, however, as it left the subtext of the man's behaviour unavailable to the therapeutic enquiry. It isn't my responsibility to determine the meaning of this behaviour, it is however my responsibility to negotiate the meaning of this behaviour with people (clients). In this instance, I needed to take time outside of the clinical setting to reflect on what I had experienced. This reflection involved experimenting with the naming of the event/s so that meaning could be re-searched rather than implied in the therapy. Immersion in gender relations can impact on our (therapist and client) belief that this conversation will or could be meaningful. When we experience direct and indirect signals that gender relations is affecting the therapeutic relationship, the first challenge is to find a way to name the interaction. This naming allows for a nego- tiation of meaning rather than an assumption of meaning. In the negotiation of meaning, people (clients) are asked to consider their relationship to a particular behaviour or idea. Once this occurs we can explore the implications for useful and ethical therapeutic relation- ships.

THERAPEUTIC CONVERSATIONS ARE ALWAYS GENDER- INFLUENCED

A number of clinical experiences convinced me that I needed to continue to reflect on gender relations in my life and work in order to challenge my participation in the normalizing, and thus rendering invisible, of gender relations.

A principle that underpins my work is that therapy is always a gender- influenced conversation. Each person participating in the conversation (therapist and client) is gendered and this influences the expectations and assumptions of therapist and client within the relationship. The gender of therapist and client also potentially influences the inform- ation available to the conversation. When a man chooses to work with a woman who is a therapist, it is useful to re-search what or who has supported this choice. There are numerous possibilities:

▼ My best friend said that you were the person to see. I trust his judgment.

▼ I feel more comfortable talking with women. I don't know why. I just prefer talking about these things with a woman.

▼ I don't trust men, really, maybe it goes back to my boarding school days.

Whenever people (clients) choose the gender of the therapist, this is fertile ground for an exploration of the implications of gender relations on their lives. When people's (clients') gender is different from that of the therapist, it is inadequate to engage only in permission-getting where the therapist asks, 'Do you feel comfortable meeting with me as a man/woman?' The therapeutic relationship provides us with a unique opportunity for re-searching gender relations in the present moment.

This question doesn't take into consideration the power relations that inevitably exists within the therapeutic relationship.

Jane Flax (5) states that 'the single most important advance in feminist theory is that the existence of gender relations has been problematized. Gender can no longer be treated as a simple, natural fact'. (pp. 43–44.) I am interested in making gender relations apparent in therapy. Once gender relations has been liberated from universalizing and essentialising ideas, the practices of gender relations are available for enquiry.[3] Ideas and practices that constitute gender relations can then be explored and scrutinized.

Here is an example of questions that expose and explore a common-place gendered arrangement:

▼ How was it decided that Jennifer would take on the tasks of primary parenting and George would take on the tasks of primary income earner?

▼ What was your understanding of the financial arrangements when you both took up these occupations?

▼ Jennifer, how do you think George acts to show you he values your contribution?

▼ George, how do you think Jennifer acts to show you she values your contribution?

▼ If either of you wanted to renegotiate this arrangement, how would you go about this?

▼ If this arrangement was reversed what would be the consequences for each of you, for the relationship, for parenting?

▼ How would you inform each other about the total responsibilities and expectations of each occupation?

This is not a neutral enquiry as the questions imply a negotiation of roles, expectations and tasks according to gender. Not to enquire in this way is also not neutral as the silence implies a division of work on biological grounds, as in 'women mother, men earn'. The therapeutic conversation can provide people with an opportunity to examine the influence that gender relations has on their lives. Once gendered arrangements are named the implications of and meanings attributed to them can be consciously negotiated.

A gender relations enquiry is 'relational'. We are asking people (clients) to reflect on the following ideas:

▼ The relationship between the self and certain ideas and practices, for example, 'How does this "pleasing" impact on your life?'

▼ The relationship between certain ideas and practices on the relationship, for example, 'What are the relationship practices that bring forward this "pleasing"?'

A relational externalising conversation is an essential ingredient for a conversation that moves us away from the universalizing and essentialising ideas of gender relations. Such a conversational style allows us to name and re-search the gendered ideas and practices that have previously existed as a biological imperative for both men and women. A belief that gender relations is biologically determined requires people (clients) to accept and live with differences. A relational externalising enquiry, however, asks people (clients) to re-search the differences and the similarities in their gendered lives in relationship to historical and cultural constructs. When we orientate our selves towards re-searching people's (clients') gendered knowledge and experiences we also protect the therapeutic relationship from our gendered limitations and assumptions. In the following example, 'the provider' ideas and practices are situated historically and culturally in relationship to the self.

Johnella: How has the idea of being 'the provider' impacted on your life?

Craig: Tremendously. I thought that I needed to establish myself in that way, in fact I remember one day looking at my house and deciding I didn't like it. It didn't represent me.

Johnella: What did it represent?

Craig: It represented success, that I was successful.

Johnella: What is the relationship between 'the provider' ideas and success?

Craig: They go together. It's important to reflect material success.

Johnella: When did you notice that this idea first appeared in your life?

Craig: I can remember thinking consciously in my early 20s, I
            can't get involved with this person. I've got nothing to
            offer. I haven't got anything behind me.

Johnella: What does that mean — not having anything behind
            you?

Craig: My career wasn't established. I didn't know where I was
            going.

Johnella: Do you think the idea of being 'a provider' is primarily
            what's offered in the relationship, rather than your
            person?

Craig: It seems so.

Johnella: Has this idea got a history in your family?

Craig: Yes, it was really important to my father.

Johnella: How did you know that?

Craig: Just the way he lived his life. He worked really hard, was
            successful and it was important to him that we were
            successful too.

Johnella: If 'the provider' idea hadn't dictated your choice of
            house, would your house have been different?

Craig: Yes very different — it would have been mine.

Johnella: Are there any advantages to being 'the provider' in
            relationships?

Craig: I suppose so. When you're successful it feels good.

The responses to the two final questions expose a contradiction; there
are benefits to 'the provider' ideas and practices as success is affirmed
and affirmation 'feels good'. In order to claim this success, however, the
person's (client's) unique way of representing himself in the world is
suppressed, hence the contradiction.

    This 'provider' example highlights the importance of situating gender
relations within a historical and cultural context through an enquiry.
In this enquiry people (clients) experience themselves as in relationship
to ideas and practices that are institutionally and economically
sustained. This engages them in a relationship with gendered ideas and

practices that goes beyond what 'I think or feel is just'.

Failure to place a gender relations enquiry in a historical and cultural context allows the development of grievance lists. The proponents of grievance lists vigorously defend the superiority of their particular grievance over others. For example, some proponents of the men's movement have addressed men's issues, such as the number of men committing suicide, by producing men's grievance lists as a counter to their perception of women's grievance lists. This list production does little to expose the historical and cultural constructs of gender that influence men's present experiences of alienation and isolation. The list production also draws our attention away from the historical and cultural benefits of one construction of gender over others. The development of grievance lists by those who belong to a dominant group is often an attempt to escape blame and a sense of powerlessness. These lists, however, entrench differences and increase antagonism. A relational externalising conversation that explores gender relations and acknowledges the implications of historical and cultural contexts moves people (clients) away from personal blame. At the same time people (clients) are asked to consider the effects of gendered ideas and practice on their lives and on others' lives. This exploration consequently makes the unequal distribution of privilege and benefits overt.

The relational externalising conversation moves us to ongoingly consider our relationship with gender by providing us with a language strategy that challenges explanations of gender difference. If these explanations of gender difference are accepted without any exploration, gendered inequalities remain invisible to people (clients).

People (clients) attend counselling to escape, understand and change emotional pain. I believe that a major contributor to this pain is the belief and practice of gender relations which result in a person believing she/he is acting correctly, only to feel wrong or unhappy. Feeling wrong can be interpreted as an individual failing or the result of a fault in someone or something else. This is not a malicious act on the self or others; it is a desperate attempt to make sense. Another way to make sense can be to make the effect of gender relations visible using a relational externalising conversation.

ENGAGING WITH TEXTS
It is totally inadequate to relegate an analysis of gender to a 'special'

therapeutic issue. Gender relations is present and influential in every conversation, including every therapeutic conversation.

There has been more interest in philosophical discussions around gender relations than in experimenting with both the languaging and practices that explore gender relations in the domestic and personal spheres. Consequently, gender relations is most often explored in workshops and in books as an intertextual, theoretical activity rather than as a practice.

A writer belongs to the privileged group that has access to the resources required to write and publish. If the writer is male and is commenting on gender relations then his position of privilege is increased. If the writer is male, commenting on gender relations and illustrates his work with clinical examples that involve women as clients, then this further increases his position of privilege. This privilege makes it likely that his interpretation of meaning will be the dominant meaning. If he indicates that a relationship is constituted in a particular way, then who is there to argue that it is not?

Who, within the power relationship inherent in the therapeutic relationship, the teacher/student relationship, the supervisor/consultant-supervisee/consultee relationship, the author/reader relationship, will be able to hold on to the integrity of their ideas/experiences if they contradict the ideas/experiences of the author, teacher, consultant/supervisor? When this holding on occurs, however, we are positioned to challenge the conditions that maintain a hierarchy of ideas or practices. The relational externalising conversation supports us to name these contradictory ideas/experiences in order that the relationship between these ideas/experiences and the 'privileged' ideas and practices (this includes texts) is explored and exposed.

Lack of acknowledgment of the practice of gender relations in the privileged environment of texts presents them as gender neutral. Readers/clinicians/students who do not have their clinical or personal knowings reflected in these texts often struggle to replicate what the texts support. Consequently these readers/clinicians/students can dismiss their clinical or personal knowings as wrong or inadequate. When the writers of texts are men and the readers/clinicians/students are women, this lack of attention to gender relations in practice can feed women's ongoing sense of lack of competence. When I have spoken over the last 10 years about the ideas and practices I use that are not represented in clinical texts, many women have expressed relief. This relief is often voiced this way: 'You have put into words, what I think and do,' 'You've put into words the struggle that I've had with these ideas.' 'I've just thought there was something wrong with me and what I was doing.' Men have made similar comments. However, the vast majority of comments come from women. I believe this lack of attention to the practices of gender relations in texts has contributed to the reluctance of many women clinicians to write or facilitate workshops.

Feeling wrong as a result of not being represented in text contributes to silence and, sometimes, secrecy. I encourage you to be aware of the gap between text and practice and to use this gap to re-search, wonder and extend your clinical practice. Silence and secrecy are not conducive to experimentation, dialogue, mindfulness and accountability.

Awareness of my privileged status as someone who writes and teaches alerts me to the possibility that privilege may protect me or blind me to what I don't know. Privilege carries an obligation to make our selves available to that which we don't know. In entering accountability practices we avail our selves to challenges of the premises on which our clinical knowledge is founded. This availability may take the form of accountability practices where we subject our selves to critique from those people outside of our community of belonging.

MAKING SENSE IN CONVERSATION

In an article written by Michelle Fine and Susan Merle Gordon (3) they argue that, 'If psychology has generated two primary positions in response to the "Gender question" with the first arguing for Gender differences, the second represents psychology as inherently Gender (and power) neutral. The search for "truth" can be navigated through questions of Gender like all other questions. Gender presumably represents a dichotomous variable that can be examined within a laboratory, in a survey, through observations, or with an interview. Absent from the formulation is Gender as a relational concept, knitted with power, context and intimate meanings.' (p. 154)

Therapy provides a unique environment where 'Gender as a relational concept, knitted with power context and intimate meanings' is enacted.

Challenging entrenched beliefs and interactions requires us to experiment with language which resources a relational externalising conversation that exposes intimate meanings. If a man in a hetero-sexual relationship says that this is a relationship of equality and a hundred per cent believes this, using feminist texts to support his hypothesis, is it equal? It may be and it may not be. Believing in a principle (equality) is one thing. Knowing what it means to practice this principle and continuing to experiment with and negotiate this practice in life is something else. Without a commitment to the practice of equality in our everyday living, we can unwittingly continue to participate in practices that silence and oppress others. I am interested in the way that ideas, such as equality, are constituted in practice. Immersion in conventional gender relations inevitably results in a number of ideas and practices disappearing into the taken-for-granted.

The meanings and practices of gender relations can operate throughout a therapeutic conversation in silence. What is experienced as normal becomes invisible and therefore unavailable for scrutiny. When a principle such as equality is discussed without an exploration of the principle as a practice, then the principle is policed by whoever has dominance. This dominance is maintained by the invisible privilege of belonging to the dominant group.

Two restraints that limit an open gender relations enquiry are gender relations blindness and gender relations shorthand. When these restraints are in effect we are either unaware of gender relations in the therapeutic conversation or we experience impotent awareness. Impotent awareness is the consequence of experiencing a sense that something isn't quite right in the therapeutic relationship; which can include the appearance of strong feelings. Whenever we attempt to make these experiences and strong feelings disappear we lose an important opportunity for enquiry. Strong feelings may indicate that gender assumptions are operating within the conversation. Whenever I experience strong thoughts and feelings in the therapeutic relationship I take the time to name and explore these thoughts and feelings. If I decide that these feelings and thoughts belong in a therapeutic relationship, I begin to search for a way to name what might be occurring. Naming is the first step in preparing for a relational externalising conversation that explores rather than judges experience.

GENDER RELATIONS BLINDNESS

Gender relations blindness is a restraint to a gender relations enquiry. It is difficult for us to reflect on the impact of gender socialisation on our lives and work. Immersion in the dominant cultural ideas creates a gender relations blindness that is difficult to challenge with self-reflection. Reading texts on gender relations does not adequately prepare therapists for therapeutic conversations where the focus is on the practice of gender relations. It is more effective to use a supervisory or facilitated process where gender relations is the focus of attention. The practice of exploring gender relations brings to consciousness what is made invisible and undetectable by its normality. Self-discovery in respect to gender relations has implications for our lives and partnerships, and it is important to acknowledge and prepare for this. When I have facilitated workshops on gender relations a number of people (therapists) have identified their lack of readiness to subject themselves to a self-enquiry on this. I have encouraged these people to continue to explore the factors limiting the readiness to address gender relations because these factors will also have implications for their clinical work.

Gender relations blindness needs to be placed in the same category as other life issues that we may be immersed in, such as a death in the family or a recent relationship separation. It is assumed in these situations that firstly we need time to be in the experience, followed by assistance to then make sense of these experiences before we are able to find the balance of connectedness/detachment that facilitates our work with people (clients) on these issues. Gender relations blindness needs to be accorded the same attention.

When I found myself in a debate with a man who was a client, my initial response was that this was an issue of power. After the session I explored what had been happening in the therapeutic relationship and decided to name it 'the debate style of conversation'. This naming allowed me to engage in a relational externalising conversation that explored the implications of the debate style of conversation on the man's life, including the effects of this conversational style on his relationships. The therapeutic relationship is a venue for the operation of gender relations — 'gender as a relational concept, knitted with power, context and intimate meanings' (3). The relational externalising conversation requires us to use language differently. This difference generates a spirit of discovery that allows us (therapist and client) to fully explore gender relations in action. This is exciting and challenging work.

We find the language to describe those ideas, behaviour and experiences that are central to people's (clients') meaning-making processes. Once these become apparent and visible they lose their place among what is considered natural, inherent or characteristic of men and women. The search for a consensus of language and then the subsequent enquiry provides an arena for exploration and hope, as individuals, couples and family members discover the influence of gender relations on their lives and relationships while experimenting with new possibilities.

THE DEBATE STYLE OF CONVERSATION

In couple work, exploration of the effects of behaviour and/or words on the relationship and on the self and the other, requires a relational language of enquiry. This style of enquiry can be challenging for men and some women. Listening to someone's experience without thinking that it reduces one's own experience, together with the belief that listening and enquiry may in fact extend one's knowing of one's own experiences, is a radical departure from individualistic thinking such as 'I am what I am'.

One of the challenges in couple work is to explore the dominant style of talking that relies on individualistic knowing, that is, the debate style of conversation.[4] The debate style of conversation is based on the idea that knowing is located in the individual and that there is a hierarchy of knowing, i.e. one person may know more than another. (It can also be considered a friendly activity such as playful verbal sparing.)

The debate style of conversation can be very challenging if we find our selves competing to win a point. The debate style of conversation stops any listening beyond the listening required to find flaws in someone else's reasoning. It stops listening for what is partially said, listening to the emotions, listening to the body, listening to the self, listening to the other. Listening on these levels is a very connected activity.

For example, a couple attended therapy as a result of one person socialising more and more on her own. Her explanation for this was that her partner had systematically alienated all her friends and made socialising stressful. On exploration it was obvious that he enjoyed a debate style of conversation. He played the 'devil's advocate' and enjoyed dismantling arguments. This debate style of conversation did not take into account the strength of meaning attached to a particular belief. Playing the 'devil's advocate' with people's strong convictions was thus experienced as an imposition and in some cases a violation.

The following questions are an example of beginning an exploration based on the above example:

▼ What are the implications for the relationship of you playing 'the devil's advocate' while the other person experiences this play as a violation?

▼ How will you ascertain that both of the people in the conversation are willing participants in a fun debate style of conversation?

▼ How does this debate style of conversation impact on family relationships?

The debate style of conversation is neither right nor wrong. Once a particular style of conversation is identified it is explored in order to ascertain its strengths and weaknesses in the negotiation of meaning. Styles of conversations have implications for the experience of intimacy in relationships. I define intimacy as a relational experience which is achieved when people are able and willing to explore the meaning made of emotions, interactions and words, and the impact of this meaning on relationships.

Externalising the debate style of conversation implies that this is one style and that there are others. If this is so, then what are the conditions that promote the use of this style of conversation over others?

Once conversational styles are named, they are available for exploration. They are also available for practice. Extracting conversational styles from essentialising beliefs such as, 'Men are just like that,' or 'I've always been like this,' creates the possibility of change and provides people with the choice of one conversational style or another. For example:

Johnella:	Bryan, does the debate style of conversation enter your relationship with your children?
Bryan:	I like to play the devil's advocate a bit around them, I think they like it, it's just a bit of fun.
Sarah:	(softly) Bryan, Tess (14 year old daughter) doesn't like it. Remember last week we'd had a lovely family day at the beach and then the two of you had an argument?
Bryan:	Tess is too sensitive, she knows I was only kidding.
Sarah:	No she doesn't Bryan. She was in tears. You know membership of the school council is really important to her.

Bryan	(shrugs) I think she uses words like socialism too flippantly.
Johnella:	Bryan, what conversational styles other than the debate styles do you have access to?
Bryan:	What do you mean?
Johnella:	Well, if you wanted to know what Sarah was thinking or feeling, how would you go about that?
Bryan:	I'd just ask.
Johnella:	Okay, would you be prepared to show me?
Bryan:	Nods.
Johnella:	I'd like you to find out what Sarah was thinking and feeling while you were talking with Tess?
Bryan:	Okay, Sarah, what were you thinking and feeling?
Sarah:	When you started, I just had a sinking feeling in my stomach. It was like you were bantering her, leading her on. At one point I tried to intervene, stop the conversation, but it was too late. Tess was already upset.
Bryan:	You shouldn't worry so much. Tess has to learn to stand up for her self.
Sarah:	That's not right Bryan, you weren't listening to her.
Bryan:	I was listening. I could quote the whole conversation to you if you like.
Johnella:	This feels a little bit like the beginning of a debate style of conversation. Sarah puts her point, Bryan counters, etc, etc. I'd like to go back a bit Bryan. Do you think you understand what Sarah was thinking or feeling about the conversation between you and Tess?
Bryan:	I think so.
Johnella:	Sarah, do you think Bryan has an understanding of your thinking and feeling?
Sarah:	Not in the least.

Johnella:	Bryan, if Sarah doesn't believe you have an understanding and you believe you do, what is the outcome for the relationship?
Bryan:	I guess we'd argue.
Johnella:	Do you think argument strengthens the debate style?
Bryan:	Yes it does.
Johnella:	Would you be interested in exploring a different style of conversation that might help you to further understand what Sarah is thinking and feeling?

The debate style is one of many conversational styles. In order to create opportunities to explore other conversational styles, consider the following:

▼ Name the different styles of conversation that people engage in.

▼ What supports each conversational style?

▼ What is the effect on a conversation of two people having the same conversational style?

▼ What is the effect on the conversation of two people having different conversation styles?

▼ Can two different conversation styles co-exist?

▼ How do you remain alert to the presence of one or more conversational styles?

STATUS OF VOICES

If we consider Michelle Fine and Susan Merle-Gordon's (3) idea of 'gender as a relational concept, knitted with power context and intimate meanings,' (see p. 259) then in therapy it is important to consider the status of voices. If one voice assumes more status or authority than another, this voice will dominate meaning making.

For example, a heterosexual couple attend counselling. The Pakeha woman is a professional aged 34: the Maori man is a student of law, aged 28. The relationship is three years old. The woman is financially supporting her partner although he has recently won a prestigious scholarship. The last six months have been particularly volatile, with not a week going by without a significant argument. The therapy needs to take into consideration the status of voices, as it becomes clear in the therapeutic process that the woman's status as patron resulted in her belief that her voice carried more authority and this stopped her listening to her partner's experience.

The status of voices has considerable implications for the therapeutic relationship. Women's gender socialisation and life experiences may encourage them to believe that their voice carries less status than men's voices. Men's gender socialisation may encourage them to act and believe that their voice carries more status than women's voices. This can determine the way meaning is made within any therapeutic conversation.

Tena, for example, works in a real estate office. The team were meeting to discuss sale strategies. Tena proposed that lists of the last month's housing sales in the area be made available to prospective purchasers at each open day. Members of the team agreed with the idea. The team manager said it was an interesting idea, however they'd need to consider whether it was worth the extra cost and effort. Three weeks later Ted, the team manager, suggested the same idea as though the previous conversation with Tena hadn't occurred. Tena challenged him and he responded with genuine surprise. He couldn't remember the previous conversation.[5]

With this example I am suggesting that the status assumed by men's voices can result in women's comments, discoveries and ideas being conscripted into the male voice. Translation of the information into the male voice automatically eliminates the identity and gender of the originator of the idea.

There are many instances of men's and women's failure to acknowledge the contribution of others to their ideas and work. However, in this instance I suggest that gender socialisation creates a hierarchy of voice that can literally eliminate women's voices from men's memory, leaving the memory of the idea in a man's voice.

In work with heterosexual couples, I have often noticed that when I have commented on an idea or theme, the man has enthusiastically received the reflection as though it is a new possibility or thought. The woman has retorted, 'How is it that when Johnella suggests this, it's a great idea? I've been saying it for years!'

This is an interesting therapeutic moment to hold and to wonder, What are the conditions that encourage the listening to me? Does the authority given to the role of counsellor support listening to my voice? Is a comment, suggestion or idea which is given to a man, by a woman, (outside of the therapeutic power relation) experienced by this man as diminishing, as in 'I should have thought of this, she's thought of it before me therefore I feel exposed'? My guess is that the process of conscription goes something like this. Gender socialisation can impact on people's (clients') ability to relate to a new idea as simply a new and interesting idea. Instead, the idea can promote an experience of exposure which may precipitate either argument as in 'What a stupid idea' or debate as in 'I don't agree with this because . . .' or withdrawal. Withdrawal, physically, emotionally or through the debate style of conversation, prevents the creator of the idea from articulating the complexity of their idea. This withdrawal can leave the listener with the kernel of the idea, which can then be conscripted and expanded so that it emerges as newly formed. Women have often commented, 'If I want something done, it's best if he thinks that it is his idea.' How do women achieve this? I suspect by presenting an idea as partly formed, as a wondering that can be conscripted and then repeated with the certainty of ownership. I believe these thinking and conversational habits are longstanding and infiltrate every sector of society, including the therapeutic profession. If we believe in gender equity then these local, intimate moments of thinking and interaction must be exposed and explored.

GENDER RELATIONS SHORTHAND

Gender relation blindness frequently results in gender shorthand remaining invisible, unnamed, and therefore unavailable to the therapeutic conversation. Gender shorthand consists of indirect messages conveyed verbally by body language. These messages frequently communicate, 'I know that you know that what I really mean is . . .' Gender shorthand contributes to and maintains gender blindness.

When we experience strong feelings a possible explanation is that we have been subjected to gender shorthand. Naming and then exploring gender shorthand can give us information about people's (client's) understanding of the therapeutic relationship. Once the gender shorthand is named we can participate with people (clients) in exploring the impact that gender is having on the therapeutic relationship understanding. For example:

Johnella: You have said that you regard women as emotional
            rather than logical and you have also indicated that you
            value logic. Given that I am a woman, how will you give
            value to what I say?

Johnella: I have noticed your sighs. Can you help me understand
            what you are thinking or feeling?

Johnella: When I asked you about your thoughts and feelings with
            respect to the recent separation, you answered by saying
            you were all right and then told me about your visits to
            massage parlours. What are you hoping I will learn
            about you from this information?

Johnella: When I was asking Allan about his relationship with his
            father, Sue you seemed to be looking at me very intently.
            Allan was upset as we were talking. Was there some-
            thing that you wanted me to know? What did you want
            me to know from that look?

Johnella: Stephen, there has been considerable negative talk
            about women generally today. I wonder what that
            means to the therapeutic relationship given that I'm a
            woman?

Johnella: George, I've noticed that you are shaking your head
            when Margaret talks. Have you noticed this? What does
            the shake mean to you? What do you think Margaret
            makes of this?

If we challenge our gender relations blindness, then it is possible for
gender relations and gender relations shorthand to become available to
the therapeutic enquiry. Moving the operation of gender relations from
out-of-consciousness to consciousness allows people (clients) to
participate with and negotiate the influence of these ideas and practices
in their lives.

THERAPISTS AND GENDER BLINDNESS — WOMEN
Lack of practice in the privileging of one's knowledge and experience,
together with a lack of recognition of this knowledge and experience in
the literature or in workshops, has implications for women therapists'
professional development. Women (therapists) often fail to recognise,

utilise and believe in their ideas and experiences in both therapy sessions and as members of the professional community. I have noticed that when there is a discrepancy between women therapists' experiences of the therapeutic process and the dominant therapeutic knowledge, women frequently discount and invisibilize their experiences. This results in women attempting to fit their practice into what is acceptable and as a consequence they lose access to their own resources and experiences.

A self-reflective process that accesses women's resources and experiences is only possible when the influence of criticism and doubt is understood and quietened. We can support self-reflection by using an enquiry facilitated by others (colleagues, supervisors, consultants) which exposes our relationship to criticism and doubt. In the following example, I was asked to express an opinion on how much time is optimal for a therapeutic session? Instead of answering the question, I tried to encourage engaging with the question.

This conversation was between Celia Griffiths and Johnella Bird. It was held during an Advance Family Therapy Intensive at The Family Therapy Centre.

Celia: What are your ideas about the use of time? I would like to be able to use time with flexibility, sometimes 75 minutes, sometimes 90 minutes. In my agency other people work on the hour. I sometimes worry I'm doing something wrong.

Johnella: If you brought your own practice into the foreground and re-searched it, you could ask your self the following questions:

▼ What ideas do I have about the value of extending sessions?

▼ When in these sessions do I make this decision?

▼ How do I decide that it is useful to extend the session to 75 minutes or 90 minutes?

▼ Are there particular client concerns that I find myself spending more time in conversation about?

▼ What are my clients' thoughts and experiences around the issue of therapeutic time?

Would you find these questions interesting?

Celia: Yes.

Johnella: If I had answered your question, I would claim the
              status as the expert on time, whereas if you answer
              these questions you claim the status of expert. Self-
              doubt is inevitable whenever our practices challenge a
              collective practice. Doubt limits the possibility of a self
              enquiry into this practice, consequently your practice
              around time will either be conscripted into the dom-
              inant practice or it may be maintained in secret.

In this example I am supporting Celia to develop ideas and vision, in
contrast to producing my ideas or vision for her. After this conversation,
Celia could explore her ideas about time using the above questions.

To withstand being co-opted into believing in other people's ideas and
practices (including dominant counselling/therapy ideas and practices),
we can employ a practical deconstructing enquiry. Practical deconstructing involves the following:

▼ Locating these ideas and practices historically and culturally.

▼ Reflecting on the genderization of these ideas and practices.

▼ Reflecting on the utility of these ideas within a therapy practice
  based on a collaborative ethic.

▼ Noting contradictions between the representation of therapy
  practice and the actual practice.

This practical deconstruction invites a living relationship with the
ethics of therapy rather than complying with these ethics. A living relationship with the ethics of therapy prepares women to re-search
difference rather than see their difference as inadequacy.

It is no coincidence that men dominate the international teaching
arena and appear to be the originators of many new clinical directions.
Women (therapists) are inclined to focus on what they don't know,
whereas men (therapists) are inclined to focus more on what they know.
When supervision/consultation relationships employ a practical deconstructing enquiry, what is known and what is not known is more likely
to be highlighted for both men and women.

Entitlement

Asking questions about gender relations requires a sense of entitlement and a sense of personal safety. Past and present experience may have informed a woman therapist that this isn't a safe practice. Adherence to personal safety in her life may limit a woman's therapeutic practice. To question culturally-sanctioned gender behaviour requires that the therapist give her self permission to do so, because no one else will. In questioning gender blindness and gender relations shorthand she is breaking a powerful, cultural taboo by suggesting gender arrangements are a set of socially sanctioned ideas and not an inherent truth.

To expose and then invite men to participate in a gender relations enquiry requires women (therapists) to position themselves outside of socially sanctioned gendered practices. We can do this safely and respectfully by positioning our selves in relationship to gender relations. This relational perspective allows women to look in on the relationship rather than being subject to the relationship. Being subject to the relationship can bring forward out-of-consciousness gendered behaviour where we focus on anticipating and reading the reactions of the other. However, when we look in on the relationship we are positioned to wonder, 'What does this mean?' The naming of and enquiry around gender relations indicates that we are re-searching the other's ideas and experiences within the therapeutic relationship understanding. This re-search is not dominated by our thoughts about what 'he' or 'she' will think or feel about me. Re-search is presented as 'I wonder what this means' as distinct from 'I think this means this, I'd better respond this way' or 'In order to keep myself safe I'll make sure he or she feels comfortable and comes back' or 'This will stop him from feeling angry' or 'What can I say to placate or please him or her'. Any construction of behaviour or language that is based on an anticipation of men's or women's needs and desires requires us to anticipate men's or women's thinking and intentions in the therapeutic process. We need to put aside our gendered training in anticipation as this denies men and women the opportunity to reflect on their ideas and practices. Consequently we can engage more directly with the men and women we are working with. It is important we give our selves permission to enquire and negotiate the meanings that can be made of ideas and practices. We do not assume meaning. An enquiry process that reflects a negotiation of meaning is mostly experienced by people (clients) as respectful and unafraid. Lack of fear is implicit in our willingness to name what frequently goes unnamed.

Participating in conversation direction

People (clients) give us authority to facilitate an enquiry that explores experiences and ideas. This may result in people (clients) re-viewing the ideas and practices that have served as the foundations of their relations with self, others and the community.

Women therapists who are not practised in speaking with a sense of authority may find it difficult to ask questions around gender relations blindness and gender shorthand. They may not have had practice in questioning cultural practices within their family of origin, within their present relationship, or in their workplace, or they may have experienced a negative reaction to any such enquiry. Old habits of pacifying, peacemaking and distracting, combined with fear, anxiety, and the invisible influence of gender relations, can hinder women therapists' ability to challenge gender relations blindness and gender shorthand.

Here are some questions that can expose conversational habits:

▼ How often do you find your self facilitating the conversation towards men's interests?

▼ How often do you find your self facilitating the conversation towards women's interests?

▼ When you watch other women in conversation, what do you notice?

▼ When you watch men in conversation, what do you notice?

▼ Has there been a change in your conversational style over the years?

▼ What or who has supported this change?

▼ If you asked others about your conversational style, what would they notice?

Women can feel/experience a lack of authority in negotiating conversational direction. If this is a woman's dominant experience then it has implications for the therapeutic relationship.

THERAPISTS AND GENDER BLINDNESS — MEN

The following set of questions helps to facilitate a self-reflective process that asks men to consider that their experiences are not the universal experience. It also highlights the issue of the status of voices when men who are therapists work with women and couples.

▼ How do men who are therapists learn about women's experiences?

▼ How do men who are therapists learn about men's experiences?

▼ How do men who are therapists continue to challenge what they think they know about women's experience?

▼ How do men who are therapists continue to challenge what they think they know about men's experience?

▼ What do men who are therapists notice is different/or similar about conversation styles between men and men, women and women, women and men?

▼ How are those conversational styles affected by race, age, sexuality, disability?

▼ How do women who are clients experience their experiences as reflected to them by a man who is also a therapist?

▼ How do men who are clients experience their experiences as reflected to them by a women who is also a therapist?

▼ How easy is it for a woman client to challenge a man's (therapist's) assumptions and therapeutic directions, given the authority he automatically assumes from his place in society plus the authority his role as therapist has given him?

▼ How easy is it for a man who is a client to challenge a man's (therapist's) assumptions and therapeutic directions, given the authority he automatically assumes from his place in society plus the authority his role as therapist has given him?

▼ What is the outcome when men work with women, and these questions have not been articulated, let alone answered?

▼ What is the outcome when men work with men, and these questions have not been articulated, let alone answered?

Participating in the conversational direction exercise (p. 263) is also a useful self reflective tool as it moves the process of conversation to a practice rather than a taken-for-granted, everyday experience. For example, if the debate style of conversation dominates, this has serious implications for therapy. The debate style of conversation includes a particular form of listening. This involves alertness for a confirmation of your ideas and/or waiting for a weakness in a person's logic that confirms your ideas. In this situation there is a significant risk that conversational meaning will be dominated by one person. The effect of this domination on relationships can vary from a misunderstanding to a profound injury that affects intimacy.

When men (therapists) engage in a conversational style that is self-directed, this can restrict or hinder the therapeutic conversation where the therapist is required at times to give precedence to the other's direction and thinking. The listening exercise in Chapter Nine is a useful tool for challenging a self-directed conversational style.

Constructing the relational
Constructing the relational requires us to be in the conversation while at the same time distant enough to enable consideration of our partici-pation in the conversation. We inevitably ignore the influence of power relations when we are primarily preoccupied with subjecting people (clients) to our enquiry. This enquiry style ignores our influence in determining or shaping meaning. In order to challenge this style we need practice in re-searching the relational assumptions and meanings with others and with the self.

Men often have less gendered training in the consideration of the relational, consequently men who are therapists may need a focus on the relational in their work.

This section entitled 'Therapists and gender blindness — men' has less material in it than the one entitled 'Therapists and gender blindness — women'. This is a consequence of my gender. When I write about the issues facing women, these are issues I have directly experienced as a woman. In men and gender I have attempted to present my observations for men's discussion.

COMMON EXPERIENCES FOR THERAPISTS
When people (clients) enter the counselling room the following manifestations of gender relations can emerge.

Over-connection with the woman/man(client).
This may result in a sense of helplessness, a sense of being overwhelmed, disgusted or angry. In couple work the disgust or anger is generally directed towards the partner's (client's) behaviour, but it can also be directed towards the woman/man who is effected by this behaviour — 'If only you'd see!' The experience of helplessness is often precipitated by the therapist's belief that she/he won't be able to influence this person's (client's) behaviour and beliefs. It generally also indicates that

a relational externalising conversation has been lost. Over-connection is indicated when we agree with people's (clients') gendered assumptions or ideas rather than re-searching these assumptions and ideas. When this occurs consultation/supervision is warranted.

Establishment of a gendered hierarchy by direct action
For example, people (clients) starting the session for you, interrupting when you are speaking, using body size, using touch, telling you what you think and using inappropriate language and behaviour (including challenging the boundaries of the therapeutic relationship by suggesting an intimate connection). Direct action can also include the ongoing deferring to you. Deferring occurs within a power relation where people (clients) give over authority to the therapist.

Attempts to establish a gendered hierarchy by indirect action
For example, sitting back from the conversation with an attitude of 'catch me if you can', playful distractions, 'see what you can do with this', and attempts to engage you in discussing the merits of a particular therapeutic idea in the hope of facilitating an interesting discussion between the two of you while identifying that the problem belongs to the partner. This behaviour can identify people's (clients') unwillingness to engage with vulnerability in a therapeutic relationship, or it can represent a cultural or gendered habit.

Protection of women (clients)
You may be limiting the therapeutic enquiry by holding the idea that naming your observations may be experienced as challenging by the man (client), or may embarrass his female partner or put her at risk. Whenever you take a protective stance, this needs to be taken seriously by enquiring around people's (clients') safety. Whenever we take a protective stance, self reflection is necessary as protection of women may be a life-habit.

Protection of men (clients)
This may be encouraged by the following ideas: 'He won't be able to take this' or, 'He won't be able to take this and still engage in therapy'. These ideas may be derived from the therapist's experience rather than from sensitivity to the other (client). In a number of workshops women therapists have identified the following dominant family idea: 'The women are the strong members of the family while the men are actually weak. However, the women pretend that the men are strong and the men believe that they are strong.' When this idea is held by the therapist

it will influence the direction of the therapy. Protection of men (clients) may enter the therapy through the lifelong practice of a partner. This person may then attempt to warn the therapist of the male partner's vulnerability by using indirect messages such as eye contact or verbal distractions. Rather than complying with these signals, we can name the interaction in order to re-search it. Whenever we notice our selves protecting people (clients) or notice a protective stance by others, it's important to identify and re-search this rather than provide the protection.

These examples are generalizations. In the therapeutic work we are prepared to meet experiences and ideas that contradict our expectations of gender relations.

When the influence of gender relations in the therapeutic relationship remains unavailable to the therapeutic conversation, gender relations blindness flourishes. This places severe limitations on the clinical work. When thoughts, feelings and practices that reflect gender relations are identified, we can find ways to make these thoughts, feelings and practices visible/apparent so that they are available for enquiry. Gender relations blindness or shorthand, however, will frequently only be exposed by reflecting on the work using live consultation, video or audio tape. This reflection requires that gender relations blindness is recognised as a persistent and significant issue for us all.

In the novel written by Alice Walker, *Possessing The Secret of Joy* (31), Walker discusses cultural ideas about female mutilation/circumcision and implores us to retain our willingness to challenge cultural ideas. She presents people's belief in the value of female mutilation/circumcision as being so profound that women too were conscripted into practices that tortured or humiliated them. When these ideas have been discussed in training groups, trainees express horror at these cultural ideas and practices. It is clearly so much easier to identify and take a stand against another cultural practice than it is to critique our cultural practices. When we reflect on gender relations we also see/know that we too have similarly been conscripted into ideas and practices that humiliate and torment people in our communities.

The experience of the women and men that we see in therapy challenges and adds to the descriptions of their lives by theorists and philosophers. We need to make our selves available to that experience, which may be very different from our experience. To do this we need to enhance our ability to listen to alternative and/or marginalised knowledges and enquire with an openness that suggests that experiences within the therapeutic conversation may act to change us. In therapy, we have a responsibility to locate marginalised knowledge in a context that recognizes that there are ruling knowledges that have greater access to material and social resources. We can do this while remaining watchful of the insidious influence of privilege, which can dull us to the knowledge that individual change does not create a more just community. In other words, therapy does little to challenge the institutionalized gendered assumptions and practices that can torment people and limit their lives.

ETHICS AND GENDER RELATIONS

Addressing the power relations of everyday life

Poststructuralism's decentring of the subject occurs in a theoretical framework that does little to develop a living practice informed by post-structuralism. Therapists and counsellors are involved with everyday situations that demonstrate the consequences for individuals of remaining within the dictates of powerful discourses. I work to challenge the 'truth' of these discourses by exposing one structure of meaning-making among many. I also attempt to expose the advantages and disadvantages to people (clients) and others in adhering to one structure of meaning-making over another by using the relational externalising enquiry, where I raise questions that expose the taken-for-granted.

In order to engage effectively in this work, we also must expose the operation of these discourses in our lives. This is sometimes challenging, as we may have benefited from adherence to particular regimes of truth, such as women being naturally intuitive.

If we are interested in a living practice informed by poststruc-turalism, it is also probable that we are interested in ethics, justice and equality. This interest requires that we continually re-view, reinterpret and challenge our understandings. We defy the stasis that comfort generates by re-viewing the taken-for-granted and actively seeking to include those people's voices/ideas that are made invisible by processes of exclusion.

Reflect on these questions:

▼ What are the principles of justice and equality that support your vision/understanding of an ethical individual, family and community? Consider your principles in relation to each of the following:

The Individual — re-view the ethics you hold regarding:
- An individual's relationship and responsibilities to the self.
- An individual's relationship and responsibilities to the family.
- An individual's relationship and responsibilities to the wider community.

The Family — re-view the ethics you hold regarding:
- The family's and community of belonging's relationship and responsibilities to the individual.
- The family's and community of belonging's relationship and responsibilities to the family and the community of belonging.
- The family's and community of belonging's relationship and responsibilities to wider community.

The Community — re-view the ethics you hold regarding:
- The community's relationship and responsibilities to the individual.
- The community's relationship and responsibilities to the family and the community of belonging.
- The community's relationship and responsibilities to the wider community.

▼ When you read what you've written or reflected on what you've said, what are the historical, cultural and gendered assumptions inherent in the construction of these ethics? (Develop questions using a relational externalising process.)

▼ Which group/s benefit most from your initial construction of ethics?

▼ Imagine how someone of a different race, gender, sexuality than yours, would answer the first three questions.

▼ What structural changes (i.e. changes to education, law, economics) would support the principles of justice and equality that you believe in?

▼ What practices indicate a willingness to listen to people who have been excluded from the resources of the institutions that hold power? What listening practices do you, your community, institutions (such as government, law, medicine, education, church, family) use?

▼ What practices support a willingness to change in order to encourage inclusion?

Exclusion and inclusion occur in a context. In reflecting on justice and equality we re-search and negotiate personal experiences and ideas to illuminate the historical and cultural context which shapes and influences meaning. For example:

Jeff: It makes me really angry, those feminists have had it their own way for too long. They've got the changes that they've wanted but we've had to wear all the bad press. Things have swung too far the other way. I mean, if I separated from Suzy and we went to court, she'd be sure to get the children. I'd be relegated to a weekend Dad. That just isn't right, I've got as much right to be equally involved in parenting as her. It's discriminatory.

Johnella: How do you think those ideas and practices of women taking on the role of primary parents evolved?

Jeff: Yeah, but that was a long time ago now, women can go out to work too if they want to.

Johnella: Jeff in your work practice and in the work practices that you know of from male friends, how many workplaces welcome men taking time off to look after sick children or take time off for school holidays?

Jeff: No, I must admit that's pretty impossible. I would like to do it, but there's too much work pressure.

Johnella: What dictates that work pressure in your work place?

Jeff: The bottom line is profitability, if we don't produce we don't get paid.

Johnella: So economics dictate work pressure and work pressure restricts your participation as a man in care for your children.

Jeff: Yeah, I suppose.

Johnella: If you thought past, current and economic regimes have and were affecting your right to parent rather than feminist's, what would you do or think differently?

Jeff: Yeah, that's interesting but you know I read about some
               guy talking about how men had lost their place in the
               family as fathers and how feminism had affected that. I
               think he's right, we need to go back to the values of the
               '50s.

Johnella: How do you think Jeff, that the economic regimes of the
               '50s after World War II impacted on the roles of women
               and men in the workplace and in the family?

In this example, I am highlighting the importance of considering the
feelings and experiences of exclusion in context, in order to protect
marginalised groups from often vitriolic attacks by disenfranchised
members of the dominant group. It is easy to focus on those who are
different (i.e. Pakeha women, Maori men and women, Pacific peoples)
to explain our experiences of disenchantment, unfair treatment and
anguish. It is harder to reflect on being betrayed by the structures and
belief system that supported our expectations of privilege.

Our experience with the power-relations of everyday life doesn't
readily follow any prescribed direction. We are confronted by
ambiguity, contradictions and opposing representations of the self and
others. We witness moments of profound change where individuals find
the strength to oppose institutionally supported ideas and values by
setting a different life course. Moment by moment in the therapeutic
conversation we engage with the ethics of the everyday. This engagement demonstrates a willingness to continually negotiate meanings,
including identifying and negotiating the effects of the ethics that guide
our lives. There is no longer the offer of rest within certainty. It is no
longer possible to rest within the terms of reference for justice and
equality that we individually believe in. Anna Yeatman (40) refers to this
by talking about 'the multiple interests in emancipation' (p. 228) and
drawing attention to the position of insiders and outsiders.

        Each reforming achievement which transforms policy in the
        name of equality, establishes a new regime of governance. All
        governance works in terms of a bounded community, a
        community of identity and thus establishes insiders and
        outsiders. (p. 229)

Engaging with the power relations of the everyday requires us to acknowledge the comfort we receive from our insider position. Acknowledgement can then support us to make our selves ethically available to the voice of those on the outside. Being available to those who are on 'the outside' provides us with both powerful moments of realization of what we have taken-for-granted and the experience of responsibility for others' pain and exclusion.

WORKING WITH THE TEXT

What Has Gender Got to Do with Me (Client)?
The therapeutic conversation is never neutral. A simple way to reflect on the impact that the gender of the therapist might have on your participation in the conversation is to consider the following questions:

▼ If I was talking with a man who was my therapist, what would I be tempted to focus on in the conversation? What would I be tempted to leave out?

▼ If I was talking with a woman who was my therapist, what would I be tempted to focus on in the conversation? What would I be tempted to leave out?

▼ Would my expectations of the therapy change according to the gender of the therapist?

▼ If I disagreed with or wanted to correct or challenge the therapist's assumptions, ideas and or behaviour, how would I go about this if the therapist was a woman? a man?

▼ What would I expect of the therapist in response to my questioning challenge or correction if the therapist was either a man or woman? How would these expectations shape what I say or do?

▼ Do I have a preference in respect to the gender of the therapist? If I do, what supports that preference?

▼ Could I stop the conversational direction if I was finding it unhelpful? Would the gender of the therapist have an impact on my ability to do this?

▼ Could I acknowledge if I felt discomfort rather than push on through the discomfort? Would the gender of the therapist have an impact on my ability to do this?

▼ If I discovered a gender preference while in the therapy, what would support me to act on that new knowing?

You can expect a therapeutic conversation that explores the impact on your life of gender socialisation and gender relations will be both respectful and useful. If this is not your experience, then the therapist is contravening the therapeutic relationship understanding. You can ask the therapist to stop the conversational direction or you can end the therapy.

Therapy that ignores the impact of gender relations and gender socialisation on your life is not neutral therapy. This therapy in its lack of acknowledgement is enabling the invisibility of gender relations, thereby keeping it as an invisible fact of life. You may suffer within this invisibility as you may be left believing that life events are your fault, or the result of your inadequacy.

For example, Daphne attended therapy, identifying depression as the problem. She said that her ongoing moping around the house was driving her partner mad and their relationship was under threat. We discovered that Daphne was physically beaten regularly over a 10-year period and strongly believed that it was her responsibility not to provoke her partner. No matter what strategies she used to please, there was always something, such as dinner being five minutes late, that provoked violence.

In this example, 'pleasing' is a strategy that Daphne used in order to ward off violence. When Daphne was beaten she blamed her inability 'to please' effectively and went on the search for more effective 'pleasing' strategies. 'Pleasing' can be re-searched as:

▼ A gendered strategy to avoid violence.

▼ A consequence of immersion in the abuser's accusations of incompetence, fault and provocation. These accusations are excuses for the ongoing perpetuation of violence.

▼ A consequence of immersion in dominant western cultural ideas about gendered roles and obligations.

▼ The most available strategy when people are emotionally and physically worn down by strategies of humiliation, fear and violence.

▼ The most available strategy when people are economically dis-advantaged.

▼ The result of living within the contradictory moments of the relationship where love is spoken of after beatings.

▼ The result of living within the contradictory moments generated by the public and private displays of the relationships. For example, in public there are never any displays of violence towards Daphne, although there are secret signs of control such as him twisting her wrist while he holds her hand.

To help you reflect on any therapeutic conversation that focuses on gender relations and gender socialisation ask your self:

▼ Was this conversation useful and respectful?

▼ Was I able to speak about ideas and experiences or did I move into silence?

▼ If I moved into silence what would help me to speak?

What Has Gender Got to Do with Me (Therapist)?

There are two dominant restraints to exploring gender relations. Firstly, there is the belief that it is possible to have a therapeutic conversation and be gender neutral. Secondly, there is the idea that gender relations is constituted by textual/theoretical knowledge. This textual knowledge colonises our minds and distracts our attention away from the daily experience of 'Gender as a relational concept, knitted with power, context and intimate meanings'. (3) Believing that gender relations is constituted by textual knowledge is demonstrated by the comment, 'Oh, I did gender in my training' or 'I've done gender, I did a two-day work-shop on it three years ago.'

If, after reading this chapter you are interested in exploring the meanings and practices of gender relations, then inevitably there are implications for your life. Creating a safe context for doing this work may make it necessary for you to alert people around you, you can then negotiate the following:

▼ The conversational styles that explore experiences and challenges blame and judgment.

▼ The timing of conversations.

▼ The safety requirements of the individuals who engage in the conversation.

You can't know what you don't know. You can't know what it is that you take for granted. The only way to make gender relations apparent and visible is to establish an ongoing dedication to self and other scrutiny. This means asking colleagues/supervisors/consultants to re-view your work and colleagual relationships with a focus on gender relations blindness and shorthand, thus providing opportunities for a gender relations enquiry. This request requires a negotiation of safety for all participants in the conversation. Any safety negotiation needs to consider the relationship between ethnicity and gender relations before proceeding with any exercises.

These following ideas could be useful in determining safety.

Suggestions for negotiating safely with colleagues/supervisors/ consultants

▼ Discuss the impact of the following — tone and loudness/softness of voice, the effect of strong emotions on listening, physical proximity between participants.

▼ Agree to alert each other to any restraints operating on listening. These restraints may include arguing back in your mind, the presence of certain ideas and the presence of certain emotions.

A gender relations enquiry
This includes the following:

▼ Someone identifies something they have noticed and all participants negotiate what could be externalised in order to begin an exploration, for example, talking time taken by one person in the group.

▼ The observer explores this theme with the other person for 15–20 minutes (more or less can be negotiated) using a relational externalising enquiry.[6]

▼ Participants agree to the conversation stopping if one person wants to.

▼ On stopping, discuss what needs to be put in place in order to continue the conversation. This may include negotiating a time to discuss issues of safety.

▼ Discuss the outcome of the conversation in respect of therapeutic practice, colleagual relationships and personal relationships.

▼ If either participant doesn't feel safe to begin a conversation or doesn't feel safe during any part of the conversation, stop. When there is a lack of safety participants have agreed to respect the request to stop. Each person has previously agreed to involve a negotiated third party when a lack of safety is identified.

▼ If you recognise that you are holding back a thought or feeling while engaged in the conversation, firstly name this thought and feeling to your self. Secondly explore the thought and feeling by both reflecting on when it emerged and by finding a description that can be externalised. This reflection can either come back to the conversation or if a lack of safety is recognised, refer back to the previous item.

Creating a context for exploration of each person's safety conditions assists us to have conversations that move us beyond what we know. In this instance a lack of safety provides us with an opportunity to re-search conditions that construct experiences of safety. When we use a relational externalising conversation, safety, and the lack of safety, moves away from being an internalised experience. This movement acts to eliminates experiences of blame and helplessness. A belief that gender relations is constructed in a social environment assists us to overcome the idea that we will be found wanting or wrong. If we believe that gender relations is constructed within a social environment, we are encouraged to explore the strategies of domination and silencing. A conversation that liberates gender relations from universalizing and essentialising ideas such as 'women are like this,' and 'men are like that' creates a platform for exploration. This exploration exists within a plethora of determinants that shape meaning making.

Socially determined gendered arrangements support the holding of certain benefits. It is challenging for us to acknowledge that we hold benefits that silence and oppress others. In acknowledging this we are confronted by the options of knowingly continuing to hold such benefits or actively making changes that redistribute the benefits.

CHAPTER EIGHT

. . . .

Trust and Fear

There is often a recurring relationship between the development of trust in a therapeutic relationship and the appearance of fears. Often, as trust grows in both the therapeutic and other relationships, fear also grows. This shows itself when people (clients) take steps forward in trusting the self and others, only to lapse into doubt and fear by the following session. I became interested in trust and fear when I realised that I had over-estimated my knowledge of people's (clients') relationship with both. My ignorance and assumptions became apparent when people (clients) continued over time to struggle with the experiences of fear and distrust in the therapy. I was prompted to study their relationship with trust and fear in minute detail. I discovered the most commonly identified fears were the fear of physical and emotional abandonment, of being overwhelmed by emotions and going mad, of losing what has already been achieved in life and of being disbelieved. These fears are often strengthened by continuing life experiences that confirm the 'truth' of the ideas that are generative of fears. The challenge is to find a way to identify and act on the fears in safety, thus providing people (clients) with an experience of creating safety.

Fear can be increasingly debilitating as it interferes with important and sustaining connections with family, friends, activities and the therapeutic relationship. The subsequent isolation can feed and maintain self-doubt and self-criticism and this can culminate in hopelessness.

I found the ideas of fear and distrust difficult to challenge because while people (clients) know that fear and distrust place unnecessary limitations on their lives, they also know these ideas have at times helped them to survive. No one should be expected to throw away a life-saver. Therefore it is important for us (client and therapist) to draw distinctions between the fear and trust ideas and practices that are life-saving, and the fear and trust ideas and practices that are life-taking. In order to do this I assist people (clients) to identify and re-search the fear in order to determine if it is life-saving or life-taking. Life-saving fears can then be retained while life-taking fears are challenged.

In order to re-search the ideas and practices of fear, we (therapist and client) need to know the signs of fear. The first signs may be physical such as a racing heart, nausea and perspiring hands, together with thoughts like 'I don't want to get on this bus', or no thoughts, namely 'the numbing out' that affects the mind and body. Once fear is acknowledged, it can then be reflected on further. For example: When did I start feeling uncomfortable? What have I been thinking? What precipitated these feelings and thoughts? This process of making sense of fear ideas and practices assists us (therapist and client) to determine whether it is life-saving or life-taking.

An example of a **life-saving** fear is, 'I started to feel uncomfortable when that man kept staring at me while he was reading a pornographic magazine. This fear is life-saving for me. What can I do now to keep myself safe?'

An example of a **life-taking** fear is, 'I started to feel uncomfortable when I remembered my last bus trip. I was so nervous I was sure I was blushing. Other people must have noticed. This fear is life-taking because it is stopping me from doing what I want. What steps can I take to reduce the effects of fears?'

By reflecting on the ideas and practices of fear, people (clients) can establish their parameters for safety. People (clients) who have been sexually, physically and emotionally abused have the right to determine their own parameters of safety without being judged by us (therapists).

People (clients) can minimise the impact of fear in the therapeutic room in response to feelings of shame (shame you will know and see them in a distressed state, shame they have let you down). At other times people (clients) are unable to name what is happening to them and we can assist in identifying the feeling state. When the physical effects of fear are extremely disturbing it is helpful for people (clients) to be coached in relaxation skills, breathing and mind control. If fear is people's (clients') dominant experience, we can practice controlling the physical effect of fear in therapy sessions in order to expand people's (clients') experience of safety. This practice is then available to people (clients) outside of therapy.

Once fear is identified we can work with people (clients) to achieve an experience of control. This is made possible by naming and making sense of the experience and negotiating action steps in safety. People (clients) who are totally in the grip of fear can be supported to obtain a sense of physical control before being asked to reflect on, understand, name and rename the experience. The physical experience of excessive fear can be terrifying. People (clients) have reported the following:

I felt as though there was an enormous pressure building up in my head. I thought I would disappear out of my head. I was overwhelmed with fear. I felt desperate and I wanted to hide, crawl into a small place, any sort of space.

People (clients) can protect themselves from the effects of fear by disconnecting. This disconnection can be indicated by looking out of the window, asking for a question to be ongoingly repeated, not remembering what had been discussed previously in the session. There are numerous explanations for people's (clients') disconnection from the therapeutic conversation. One possibility is to use disconnection to escape from the feared consequences of engaging with memories or certain ideas. If we (therapists) are overwhelmed or fearful of physical manifestations of fear we need to ask for immediate assistance from colleagues, supervisors or consultants. In these circumstances our relationship with fears can endanger people's (clients') lives.

COMMONLY EXPERIENCED FEARS

As previously noted, the most commonly expressed fears are of being overwhelmed by madness, of physical and emotional abandonment and of being overwhelmed by emotions. These fears are represented uniquely in each person's (client's) life. Fear of being overwhelmed by emotions can be connected to fear of madness in that a person (client) may equate a loss of emotional control with behaviour that could be construed by witnesses as 'crazy' or 'mad'. Past experiences may reinforce this belief. Fear of being overwhelmed by emotions can be connected with fears of visibility and vulnerability. When people (clients) guess that connecting with the experiences from the past may provoke strong emotions, for example grief that represents itself in substantial distress such as crying for a week, they may fear other people's reactions or response to this vulnerability.

We need to explore, negotiate and make sense of the ideas and practices of fear in the context of each person's (client's) life. This exploration supports people (clients) to acknowledge the fear while staying connected with their experiences and feelings.

The fear of being overwhelmed by 'madness'

Fear of being overwhelmed by 'madness' frequently precedes disconnecting. Whenever a feeling, for example, sadness, shows itself, fear can intervene by introducing thoughts such as, 'If I let go I'll never stop, I'll go mad.' Disconnecting is a strategy that frees the person from the fear of madness. Disconnecting involves shutting down cognitive processes, which may mean people (clients) then move into a trance-like state.

While disconnecting protects people (clients) from feelings it also robs them of the opportunity to make sense of experiences and feelings in ways that allows them to then act on their lives. Disconnecting can result in self harm. For example, people (clients) have talked about cutting themselves as a way to re-engage with themselves. It can also put people (clients) at risk of harm by others; a person who disconnects in response to insults or abuse is unable to protect her/his physical self by taking action and leaving. This may result in the person being subjected to ongoing abuse.

Disconnection can promise liberation or relief from the fear of madness while actually creating conditions for ideas and behaviour that can attract the attention of mental health professionals. The seduction of the liberation promise thus creates and maintains conditions that subject people (clients) to their worst fear. It is a crucial task of therapy to assist people (clients) to recognise and resist disconnection in order to experience and make sense of feelings and thoughts. This takes enormous courage, and people (clients) need to be supported through this process by information from others who have successfully emerged from fear, by friends and loved ones, by books and ideas and by our knowledge, experience and willingness to continually negotiate the safety conditions in therapy.

The following extract is from a conversation between Leslie (client) and Johnella (therapist). It centers on Leslie's experiences of fear, in particular the fear of 'being crazy'.

Johnella: You were talking about the prospect of being committed to a psychiatric hospital. Were you worried about that?

Leslie: A lot. And yeah and along with . . . and that became very intense, too. Along with feeling suicidal and feeling violent towards other people because when I had fits, afterwards I would think, if someone in authority saw me, then I would be locked up. And also part of me believing that maybe I should be locked up because any 'normal' human being shouldn't act like that, shouldn't lose it like that.

Johnella: So you were engaged with labelling your self in that sense? This is crazy behaviour?

Leslie: Yes, I've always done that all my life I think. Because I was abused very young and I think that I've just carried it with me, that really I'm sort of quite crazy. I have a lot of insanity. It's just that I fooled a lot of people. I fooled everyone. And, then when I turned 30, I sort of thought I can't hide it any longer. I can't hide this. I can't keep it down. Someone is going to see and I'm going to end up in prison, or I'm going to end up dead. And then that made me have to look at why? Why I was like that? Why did I feel like that? Why did I do those things? Was I crazy? Was I really crazy? I found out I'm not.

Johnella: Do you remember when you first engaged with the thought, I'm not crazy, I'm okay?

Leslie: I can remember early in therapy, I would often rush home and write. And I remember early on sort of writing things like, maybe I am okay. But it was kind of a big question mark — sort of hah, hah, hah! Who's she kidding? Because okay, that had huge implications for my whole life up to now. For my family. For my reality that I'd been living. If I wasn't crazy, then nothing else in my life really made sense. It didn't fit in with my reality.

Johnella: That's an interesting idea, there was a small bit of you that was saying, 'maybe I'm okay?' and that was a huge

challenge because you're saying it challenged everything.

Leslie: Yes, and it was very scary and I resisted that for quite a
bit, for quite a while. But it kept coming up because I
would come here and get validated that I was an okay
person. And so . . . and belonging to an incest survivors'
group and talking with friends, I would . . . I was getting
some feedback from people, kind of out in the open,
that I wasn't crazy. Like before it wasn't talked about in
the open because I didn't go around saying 'I think I'm
crazy'. I just thought it. I was just in the belief. But I was
actually starting to say to people, well you know I've
probably got problems. And I was being challenged.
That's what it was. I was challenged. Well, what are you
doing that makes you think you're crazy? Ah well I'm
doing this and I'm doing that. Yeah, and then it would
be pointed out that yeah, I'm not very happy. I'm
actually just really unhappy and that I'm reacting to
things that I've carried around for years. And situations
that I'm in now, with my family, I'm reacting to that and
it makes me feel crazy, but I'm not actually crazy. And
that idea just snowballed too, that maybe I'm not.

Johnella: Was it like there was an alternative? The explanation
was that maybe there were some things that were
happening and had happened that made you feel crazy,
but that you're not crazy . . .

Leslie: Yes, and then I started to recognise when I felt crazy. It
was when I started to think that maybe, even though I
was a victim of all that abuse, in my family, that maybe
I wasn't an incest survivor, or maybe it doesn't matter
anyway. Those were the times I would feel craziness. I
would go right off. And also if I was around my family
and things came up, then I would think that there was
really something wrong with me. When I could recognise those times and things, it put the craziness into
context or something. I could see that it was something
to do with the situation or my frame of mind, something

I was putting on myself. As soon as I started challenging the thought that what happened to me as a child, and a teen, is gone, lost, and it hadn't affected me, that there's nothing wrong with me I'm just being stupid. As soon as I started challenging that I would start to feel powerful. I would start to feel power. I would think yeah, I am okay.

Johnella: When you didn't discount that experience, when you saw that experience for what it was . . .?

Leslie: Yeah, that's when I could feel powerful and in control which to me meant sanity.

Fear of physical and emotional abandonment

Fear of physical and emotional abandonment is often sustained with evidence that has been accumulated by people (clients) over their lifetime. This evidence includes the following:

The words of the abuser,

Abuser: If you tell, no one will believe you, they'll think you're a bad girl and send you away to a home.

Past events

Phil: I told my mum. She said she believed me but for the sake of the family it was better if I were to live with my Aunt and Uncle up North. I hardly ever saw my mum again. He wouldn't have anything to do with me and said he'd leave Mum if she tried to see me. I can't believe she went along with him.'

Present events

Jackie: When I told Simon that I was coming to counselling he wanted to know why. I wouldn't tell him, but he just didn't let up. In the end I was so worn down by him that it just came out and I told him what had happened to me as a child. He was quite supportive at first, then I just felt him get more and more distant. He avoids touching me and when I touch him he tenses up. He won't admit it, but telling him has changed everything.

Future Predictions

Riley: I couldn't tell anyone about this. I can hardly bear to

come here knowing that you know. Look, I know what
people think, I've been with groups of guys laughing and
joking about this, I've even joined in. It's a great laugh
to them, they think you're lucky to have your leg over
some older sheila. Maybe they're right, I wish I felt that
way about it.

Fear of emotional and physical abandonment can be identified and
explored so that each person (client) can negotiate their relationship to
this fear. Once the fear is exposed, people (clients) can decide how to
position themselves in relationship to this fear in order to achieve an
ongoing, safe experience of connection to their lives.

The following extract is, again, from a conversation between Leslie
(client) and Johnella (therapist). It centers on Leslie's experiences of
fear, in particular the fear of physical and emotional abandonment.

Johnella: When you talked about getting some distance from the
            family in order to make your own discoveries, did that
            leave a gap in your life?

Leslie: A very large one. A very large, scary, sad gap. It was
            incredibly painful. It kind have felt like my family had
            died. I knew they hadn't, not physically anyway, but the
            picture that I had had of my family had died and also I
            wasn't having contact with them, so initially the contact
            with them wasn't there. But that probably gave me
            space to let the old story of my family die, because I did
            a lot of grieving. Even though I could ring my mother
            up or she would ring me, it was very emotional. I had
            to keep lots of physical space between us, but it was very
            much an emotional letting go. Because I grieved for my
            mother and for my family, the one that I actually never
            had. I thought I had but I didn't have . . .

Johnella: I can remember something we talked about. I don't
            know whether you remember this or not, but one of the
            ideas that you had was that somehow it was your job to
            bring the family with you on the journey. I can
            remember talking with you and you were saying that
            you had this place where you wanted to be and that you
            wanted to carry them with you to this place.

Leslie: Yeah, I wanted to carry them with me and that was an old pattern, too. And that was a part of my role. I've always been kind of the emotional leader or something. I led my family through different things and I did think . . . I'd do that again. Yeah, that's a while ago now, but I remember thinking that it would be necessary for me to drag them along with me and that actually made it seem impossible.

Johnella: Ah, it would be pretty hard work if they didn't want to go.

Leslie: Yeah, I know, and I thought of my mother and my sister and trying to get them to come along with me on this huge emotional journey. That was really off-putting because that would be impossible. And I think it got easier once I realised that I didn't have to do that. That I couldn't do that. That was a big release, you know, I was relieved that I didn't have to do that. That I could actually change without them changing. I think I thought that the whole lot of us would have to change and that's just an impossible task. Just impossible.

Johnella: So during that time, when you were feeling that sadness, that grief for the family and the gap, what did you do to look after your self?

Leslie: I had my group by then, which was really supportive because they all identified with what I was going through. I was coming here intensely so that really helped. It was the support. And I was reading a bit of *Courage to Heal* then. I think I was just generally doing all sorts of things to validate what I was doing. I made sure that I wrote in my diary every day and challenged any thoughts I had that weren't validating to myself. I was pretty committed to supporting myself through it because I knew that I would actually lose it. Yeah, because it was quite a big deal.

Johnella: Was it quite a turning point for you?

Leslie: Yeah, it was.

Johnella: That you actually had to fight for your own life in a way?

Leslie: Yeah.

Johnella: That's hard work, to write every day and challenge the thoughts and . . .

Leslie: Yeah, and I think at some stage I came here and told you that it felt really hard, what I was going through. And you actually said, 'Well, you're fighting for your life.' And I held on to that sentence and I held on to that throughout the whole thing of, well, if I don't go through with this I'm not going to survive. And that really helped, thinking okay, this is the way I can survive — yes that was really helpful.

The distance from her family that Leslie talks about was put in place for a short period of time. It gave her the opportunity to connect with and experience her relationship with grief. Connecting and making sense of her emotional knowings allowed her to negotiate a way to reconnect safely with her family. Family members who know that physical, sexual and emotional abuse has occurred can attempt to obliterate this knowing by forgetting or refusing to acknowledge the existence of the abuse. When one or several family members then acknowledges the past, they can be ignored or blamed by other family members. Consequently silence or blame raises the possibility that speaking out about experiences and feelings may endanger the speaker's belonging in the family. In order to protect belonging, the person (client) may disconnect from feelings and thoughts, therefore abandoning any connection with self-knowledge.

We work with people (clients) to find ways to safely stay connected with emotions, thoughts and experiences. This may mean experimenting with strategies to articulate and honour experiences that are relegated to invisibility by family members. People (clients) often confront an unbearable dilemma: in order to connect with their emotional, physical, spirit-filled self, they acknowledge past abuse/s and the emotional consequences of the abuse/s while emotionally holding the possibility that exposure of past abuse may threaten their belonging in the family. We can negotiate strategies with people (clients) that will assist them to navigate through this uncharted territory. It is not necessary for people (clients) to choose between belonging in the family and self-survival, although some people (clients) have found that choice needs to be made. We can stand beside people (clients) as they negotiate their way through. We can experiment with strategies that protect the self and protect the belonging. This is never an easy journey. From within the therapeutic relationship understanding we articulate possibilities, discoveries and strategies.

For example, Viv found that whenever she went to a family gathering, by the end of the evening she was often left feeling suicidal and depressed. We discovered that she would space out or disconnect whenever her father raised his voice to articulate his displeasure at something. Her silence would be noticed by others who would 'get on her case' about her life, often supported by her father, who would lecture her on toughening up. Viv experimented with noticing when she was about to space-out and instead of entering this state she would leave the situation. On leaving she would access the physical supports she brought with her that would remind her of her strength, resilience and determination.

The physical supports mentioned in this example can include letters, photos, symbolic objects and words. These supports must be meaningful to the person (client). They can be used to interrupt cycles of disconnection that rob people of the opportunity to negotiate a new relationship with the past.

We do not attempt to resolve this belonging dilemma for people (clients) by suggesting a particular course of action. We can however talk about the limitations of therapy. For example, Lucy is 19 years old. She is a university student and lives with her mother and her stepfather. Lucy's stepfather sexually abused her between the ages of nine and 11 years. Lucy left home when she first went to university and at that stage entered counselling and disclosed the abuse for the first time. She returned home because of financial difficulties. Lucy's mum doesn't know about the abuse. Lucy has taken up the strategy of shutting down her emotions in order to survive being at home. She identifies that she often feels worse after counselling because in counselling she 'allows her self to feel'. The counsellor and Lucy negotiate the following:

▼ What sort of therapy will support Lucy in her decision to live at home?

▼ What are the consequences of 'the shutting down' on Lucy's life?

▼ Is there a way to have 'the shutting down' at home while switching on elsewhere, for example with friends, etc.?

▼ Can Lucy consciously choose ' the shut down' or 'switch on' rather than it just happening to her?

▼ Can Lucy tell the therapist if she's feeling 'the therapy' is acting to switch on too many thoughts or feelings for the present circumstances?

In this example I am presenting therapy as always a negotiation between therapist and client within the bounds of the therapeutic relationship understanding. The questions acknowledge Lucy's present living circumstances and provide her with an opportunity to reflect on and negotiate a way to survive these circumstances.

The fear of being overwhelmed by emotions

This letter was written by a person I was working with. The letter highlights the fear of being overwhelmed by emotions:

MY DEAR FRIEND,

One Saturday morning just a few weeks ago I had a phone call from my son-in-law. He was very upset, tears, shame and fear all intermingled. Mum, I don't understand what's wrong with me, I feel so bad. He told me in tears over the phone. All I was able to do was to explain to him what I had just gone through.

When my husband and I made love, because of my past I disconnected from my body and it bled through my neglect. It was the sight of this that tipped me into sadness. At first I fought it with all my being. The fear of the sadness was overpowering.

Johnella and my husband and myself had discussed my grief at therapy a week before. I had told them at the time how terrified I was that it was going to destroy me.

One day while feeling emotional, it came to me that this was how I felt when I was a child. Those who had hurt me could not allow others to see my hurt. They named my grief as feeling sorry for myself, and that was a sin. They did this because they wouldn't have been able to explain the depth of my pain to anyone, would they? This thought made me come to the conclusion that I was not feeling sorry for myself, I was just plain sad. Sad just as I was as a child. The sadness took over. I cried when I made my bed, cried over the dishes. The sadness was so intense, but throughout that week it had its way. If tears wanted to spill, they spilled. You see this person for the first time was given permission to cry, and she did.

Johnella had warned my husband about this and it was a great help as, in the past whenever my grief would sneak through my guard, this would of course worry him sick. When I saw his worry this would then make me fight for control.

So my advice to my dear son-in-law was, Don't be afraid, you will come to no harm, you didn't in the past, you won't now. If you want to cry, cry, it does subside sooner than you think. Let all that pain just come and flow out with your tears.

Today I feel a peace and a tranquility that once eluded me. There is just one more thing I want to say, the fear of the grief was a hundred times worse than the grief itself. Trust your self.

When people (clients) identify a fear of being overwhelmed by emotions, we need to take the fear seriously by getting to know the way it operates in their lives. Fears thrive when people (clients) believe the release of tears or sadness will precipitate a collapse or that accessing feelings of anger will provoke uncontrollable rage. The therapeutic conversation centres on taking fear seriously. Exploring the fear is complemented by exploring the effects on people's (clients') lives of complying with it. For example, Jess never allowed feelings of sadness about the past into the present. She came to therapy because she wanted to be sexual with her partner. Sexual relations were difficult because Jess habitually disconnected from her body.

We take Jess's fear seriously by exploring and negotiating the conditions of safety necessary to entertain the possibility of connecting with both experiences and emotions. The conditions of safety include the following:

▼ The length of time for the session or sessions.
▼ The space between sessions.
▼ The physical locality.
▼ Space between people in the therapy room.
▼ Touch.
▼ The people present in the session.

▼ Opportunities and signs that indicate stopping the session or pausing.

▼ After session care.

▼ After session support people.

▼ Clothing that maximizes comfort.

▼ Identifying any movement away from a sense of safety.

The preparation demonstrates a critical value, which is that people (clients) are entitled to maximize the conditions they require to feel safe.

It is extremely courageous for people (clients) to experiment and strengthen their engagement with the self/voice by describing to another person the experiences and thoughts they hold. It represents a turning point in the work as people (clients) trust us and others with life-vulnerability. The experience of the therapeutic relationship thus becomes an important location for the discovery and exploration of unique experiences.

I use life-vulnerability to distinguish from the common everyday usage of the word vulnerable. Life-vulnerability involves deeply exposing the self to another person and risking mortal injury. Whenever this occurs in therapy it is common for past experiences, memories and words to reappear in overwhelming ways. The experience is best described as terror. Naming this experience as fear underestimates it. Consequently we (therapist and client) place unrealistic expectations on people (clients) to deal with this terror. In the midst of terror, the only reasonable expectation is that we work with people (clients) to create a sense of safety both in the therapeutic context and outside of it.

Over time people recognise the early signs of terror and can act for their own safety before being overwhelmed. A person who has visual memories can practice reducing the physical size of the memory of the past abuser, or people (clients) can put words to the terror, such as, 'When you spoke I felt overwhelmed with this idea, I thought you would hurt me. I know you won't but that's what I feel.' Or people (clients) can take the risk to ask for support from the people in their lives for example, 'I need you to sit on the floor with me and just hold me.' It is very common for us to underestimate the experience of living with fear/terror that permeates every life interaction, fear/terror that lives in each inhalation and exhalation of breath. To work with these fears/terror we (therapists) must know them without being overwhelmed by them.

WORKING WITH LIFE-TAKING IDEAS AND PRACTICES

I work to expose past and present life-taking ideas which dominate people's (clients') thinking within a therapeutic enquiry. These life-taking ideas often centre around the themes of criticism, doubt, guilt, fear and shame. While exploring these themes I also work to discover and strengthen people's (clients') abilities. Reflecting only on the influence of criticism, doubt, guilt, fear and shame maintains ideas of powerlessness as these ideas have frequently been strengthened and sometimes nurtured by significant people and cultural practices. The following exercise reflects the process of identifying the ideas/voices of criticism, doubt, guilt, fear and shame while practising using a self-voice that can challenge life-threatening ideas. People (clients) have found this exercise useful in identifying, catching and practicing a challenge to specific life concerns. The knowledge collected outside of therapy thus becomes a resource to and for the therapy. This exercise is unsuitable if people (clients) have a tenuous hold on life, for example when re-searching guilt one person discovered that it came into her life three hundred times a day. In this example criticism is being external-ised. However, the exercise could also be used with other significant experiences such as doubt, guilt, fear and shame.

PRACTICE EXERCISE

▼ Practice becoming alert to the thoughts, feelings, pictures of criticism. This may mean being vigilant to certain ideas, thoughts and/or actions.

▼ Whenever you notice the thoughts, pictures and feelings of criticism, take a note of what is thought, said, seen and/or felt. You may need to have access to paper and pen at all times. If you are not comfortable writing and/or drawing, you could use a small dictaphone.

▼ Attempt to identify a source for the thoughts, pictures, feelings. Where do they come from? Who has said this before? Who is holding the camera or taking the picture? The sources can be specific people's beliefs and practices and/or institutional and cultural beliefs and practices.

▼ Write, feel, draw a challenge to criticism. Look at the criticism and attempt to find a challenge to it. This challenge may involve thinking about the times you've done or said something that defies the 'truth' of the criticism statement. Or it may be a challenge to the absolute nature of criticism words like 'you never do . . .'. If this is difficult, imagine that you are your own best friend. What would she/he say, do, feel in order to challenge the criticism of you?

▼ Think about ways you could support that challenge to criticism. Decide who or what you believe. Do you believe the criticism or do you believe your self or your own best friend? Reflect on who is more supportive in your life, your own best friend or criticism?

▼ If you believe your self or your own best friend, write down/ decide on the steps you can take to strengthen these ideas and beliefs.

▼ If you believe criticism, write down and/or decide on steps that could weaken the impact of criticism. For example, some people have found it helpful to do the following: read strengthening books and/or words; talk to friends; remember strength-giving occasions and/or words; hold on to objects that symbolise strength, listen to certain music.

In therapy I re-search the source of ideas such as criticism. This encourages people (clients) to challenge the 'truth' of these ideas by exposing the totalising impact of language, as in, for example, 'I am very critical.' The linguistic space created by relational externalising provides people (clients) with the opportunity to see/experience the conditions that amplify or reduce the effects of certain ideas on their sense of self. People (clients) also have the opportunity to expose the societal structures and systems that benefit from people's (clients') adherence to these totalising ways.

A therapeutic process which uses relational externalising introduces people (clients) to ideas and practices that engender hope. For example, 'It is possible that I am not bad.' This introductory challenge to pervasive ideas often lacks the strength, however, to counter the relentless nature of the life-taking ideas and experiences. Finding ways to continually make life-taking ideas and experiences apparent requires persistence and a willingness to experiment.

People (clients) can use writing, drawing, talking, music, in fact any medium that enables the creation of linguistic space. From the position of being in relationship to the ideas (guilt, criticism, doubt, fear and shame) people (clients) can reflect on the possible relationship between two or multiple sets of ideas and experiences. People (clients) can then view or reflect on the two or multiple sets of ideas and experiences, and determine which ideas/experiences they believe in or feel more attracted to and what/who supports that decision (this includes institutional supports).[1]

This work is not done once, twice or even three times. It is a process that needs to be engaged in many times. Distancing the self from life-taking ideas and practices provides people (clients) with the experience of life-hope. Distancing enables them to see/experience themselves in relationship to these ideas rather than having these ideas as an intrinsic part of their nature. The work of fighting for a life that is free from life-taking ideas and practices is thrilling, exciting, difficult and exhausting. The therapeutic hour does not provide enough of an alternative experience to sustain life-enhancing ideas and practices. Consequently within the therapy people (clients)will need to reflect on their willing-ness and readiness to ongoingly engage with the vigilance required to catch the emergence of life-taking ideas and practices outside of the therapy.

WORKING WITH LIFE-TAKING IDEAS/PRACTICES
The conversation between Leslie and Johnella continues:

Johnella: It's as though you stood outside of it by saying, 'I don't deserve this.'

Leslie: Yeah, that's what I did. I would act like a fly on the wall really and just look at exactly what was going on. And I never would do that before, I was in it. I was part of it but because I'd started to remove myself a bit, it was easier to look at my role in it all and see what was going on. It gave me a clearer view of what was happening and I guess that just gave me a wider view instead of being right in it.

Johnella: What do you think promoted that idea, that skill in a way, to be a fly on the wall? What gave you that idea?

Leslie: For me that happened just spontaneously after I started pulling away and because of the anger. And because I'd decided I was not going to be angry with myself any more. As soon as I'd challenged that, I thought, Okay, who will I get angry with? Okay I'll be angry with my family now. It's like these stages of anger and right . . . it's everyone else's fault in my family except me, and so that enabled me to stand back physically, just keep away, but also emotionally . . . 'No you're not going to pull me in. I'm not going to fall for that.' And that led to being able to stand back.

Johnella: The way you're describing it. It's like you saw that the family could pull you in. You saw what could happen to you?

Leslie: They would try to and I would even know my usual responses and I wouldn't do it. And I'd just think, yes normally I'd go . . . for a period of months, just about every week, I'd have an example of it, . . . God in that situation I normally would have done 'da da da etc' or I would have gone rushing over there, and I didn't. This happened just time and time again. And I built up this kind of evidence that it really was my role. I could see it really clearly, but also evidence that I was able to keep out of it. I just had all these stories of how usually, or in the past, I would have done this, but I wasn't doing it, and that gave me strength to go on because I started building up this picture and thought, I don't want to be part of it.

Johnella: Building up a picture of how the family were and how you were in it?

Leslie: Yes, and how I was in it.

Johnella: And how that left you feeling . . . being in that place.

Leslie: Yes, and this was happening all along with challenging the idea that I was crazy. And it started to fit in together and I thought 'yeah, of course', now if I'd said such 'n such and that would have happened, then I'd be left feeling like I was a bit crazy. Where as it almost feels like

I've just developed some kind of self protection now and they can actually say what they want. But it's not going to get me, because I'm validating myself instead of validating them.

Johnella: You're not going to be pulled into the old ways of interacting? It's almost like, the way you describe it, it's like you're re-searching the family, the self and the relationship. For example, 'I used to respond this way, then I would say this and they would do that and I would do that,' — you're sort of standing back by saying, 'Now I'm going to do this.'

Leslie: Yes, and I think it is like re-searching and it's an ongoing thing. Like it's not short, it's not even the ideal place right now, I'm not where I'd like to be, but I'm in the process of it, or sorting out what I want and how I want it. But the first part of it was validating myself instead of accommodating the family and then I felt like I started to have a grip on things, to have a hold on life.

When people (clients) have learnt to distrust experiences and feelings, they are at risk of further emotional and/or physical abuse from others and the self. Alienation from self-experiences is also a threat to a person's (client's) mental and physical health. We can experiment with activities that assist people (clients) to move from self-alienation to self-determination. It is important that we work with people (clients) to create resources that can be used outside the therapy room. The following exercise provides an example of the building blocks that have been found useful in creating activities that support people outside of the therapy room.

EXERCISE

▼ Looking in. Practise listening for and to the experience and to the feelings. This practice can begin in the therapy room.

▼ Experiment with naming the experience and the feeling.

▼ Looking out. Place this experience in a context by asking a number of questions. When did I start to have this feeling or thinking? What was said or done? Who said or did this? How did

I engage with what was said or done? Did it set some thinking off? What did I do? What did I think? Did I feel stronger or weaker? What were the strengthening actions or thoughts? What were the weakening actions or thoughts?

▼ Concretise the experience in some way, e.g. with words and/or pictures. It is critical that the experience moves from the internal (i.e. in the self) to the external (i.e. out of the self) and then in relationship to the self. This makes visible influences that may have remained invisible and secret.

▼ Re-view what you have said and/or written. Ask your self, — What do I experience as I read, hear or see what's said, written or drawn?

▼ Collect opinions. Ask trustworthy people what they think of these reflections.

Beginning to trust thoughts and feelings

The conversation between Leslie and Johnella continues:

Johnella: It's a lot to fight against, the strength of the old relation-ships and that story of who you were and how you were, in relation to the past. It was a longstanding story and you stepped aside and started creating your own sense/ story, which included its own history and experiences. You talked about the groups you've been involved with and how it helped to hear other people's stories and to be challenged by other people.

Leslie: It helped a lot because every time someone told a story I would be able to relate to a part of it. I hadn't really ever verbalised the idea that when I spent time with my family I felt crazy. But I sat in a group and someone said, 'Whenever I'm around my family I just go crazy and when I leave my family I have to do things to comfort myself.' And I just sat there and thought, God that's me. That's what happens to me. And I started to check out the theory that that's what happens to me and sure enough I would come away from my family thinking, 'I've just been kind of screwed around in my head.' And then I could look at changing it. And just hearing other people with their experiences, and I identified with it so much and I could see that they were doing it with me to. You just . . . I think it's really, really valuable because you think you're the only one. You think you're unique. Like I thought I was unique. I thought no one else on this earth is like me. Even though there's people who say they're incest survivors, it didn't matter. I was unique and no one actually knew me and knew my problems and my screwy head. Well I found out that a lot of people feel like me and yeah. And that thing of no one was as clever as me at hiding my stupidity of my . . . I just thought that I was the ultimate actor, but there are a lot of us out there. There's heaps and we've got, it's . . . I don't know.

It's just, I guess I was able to shed a lot of that from hearing other people talk, I thought, Ah, maybe we're all just sort of real people underneath but thinking that we're fooling everyone or something.

Johnella: It certainly would make you feel less alone, hearing those things. I don't know whether this happened or not but if you thought that other people were doing and experiencing the same thing it would then become like a phenomena in a way. Like it wouldn't be just you, something particular to you, or peculiar about you, it would be something that people do in order to survive. Rather than . . .

Leslie: Yeah, and that's what I started to look at it as, survival. They were survival techniques rather than my personality and I had thought that all that rubbish I carried with me was my personality. That's it. Yeah, and from sitting and talking with other people I was able to see patterns and things that were common with my behaviour and the group would start recognising them as survival techniques.

Johnella: Which is a whole different way of describing what's happening. This is a survival technique . . .

Leslie: Yes, because it's not actually part of my soul, it's just something that I've had to learn . . .

Johnella: Something you can either choose to continue or choose . . .

Leslie: Yes, you've got control over it. I don't think I really thought that I had any, that I would ever have any control over it. But to look at it like a way of survival then you do have hope. There's hope in that.

Re-searching life-taking ideas requires an ongoing vigilance which will only occur when people (clients) are able to take their experiences seriously. People (clients) struggle with this, as they consistently under-estimate experiences and feelings because other significant people, past or present, have minimised them. The therapy will suffer immensely if we also act and think in ways that minimise experiences and feelings. Consequently we need to remain alert to our own possible over-detachment and over-connection in the therapeutic relationship.

THE ETHICS THAT STRENGTHEN THE WORK WITH TRUST AND FEAR

What's in a name?
Throughout this chapter I make distinctions between different experi-ences of fear, for example, life-taking and life-saving fears, the physical effects of fear, fear of being overwhelmed by emotions, fear of being overwhelmed by madness, fear of physical and emotional abandon-ment. These descriptions of people's (clients') experiences of fear became apparent through my work. This by no means a comprehensive or complete list. Within each category we will, in conversation with people (clients), possibly discover other fears operating in their lives.

Negotiating and experimenting with the language used to describe people's (clients') relationship with fear provides us (therapist and client) with an opportunity to draw distinctions. The physical manifes-tation of fear may be predictable. However, people's (clients') emotional and cognitive relationship with fear may vary significantly. When we do not negotiate and experiment with the language used to describe people's (clients') relationship with fear we reduce their experiences to generalisations. Generalisations often lead us to suggest strategies that we believe will help people (clients) to challenge these fears. When people (clients) are unable to use these strategies we are tempted to make sense of this by drawing on pathological explanations such as diagnosing 'resistance' or wondering if the problem benefits the person (client) in some way. At these moments we can use the power that is culturally given to professionals and diagnose and evaluate people (clients). The problem is thus seen/known to exist in people (clients) rather than being seen/known to be in the therapeutic relationship. Drawing distinctions by experimenting with the language I use to talk about people's (clients') relationship with fear provides me with a language resource to begin a relational externalising enquiry. This enquiry then generates a climate of discovery in respect to the intimate workings of the particular fears that are operating in people's (clients') lives.

Whenever the therapy is stuck in some way (what stuck means to me is that the therapy is not moving and within this stasis the problem grows and/or stays the same), this indicates to me that there is something that I don't yet understand or know. Taking this position provides us (therapist and client) with an opportunity to re-view 'the therapy' (refer Chapter nine).

When the therapy is stuck it is possible that the language used to explore and understand people's (clients') lives is inadequate. We may have heard the description of people's (clients) experience without attending to the minutiae of potential meanings. At these moments we are operating within gross assumptions. For example,

Sharon (client):
>   At some point in the therapy I just get scared. I sort of wanted you to stop, but I also know that it's important to keep going. I then get panicky and start to have trouble with breathing.

Johnella: Is there anything I can do or say to reduce the scared feelings?

Sharon: No. I feel good about this relationship.

Johnella: What are the scared feelings?

Sharon: I just feel scared. I want to leave.

Johnella: Where do you feel scared?

Sharon: My stomach gets knotted and I feel sick.

This conversation could get stuck here as the enquiry is both too generalised and is locating the scared feelings within the person. Another example:

Sharon: My stomach gets knotted and I feel sick and scared.

Johnella: What's the point in the therapy where the scared feelings happen?

Sharon: It's hard to pinpoint, I think it was when we were talking about sexual feelings.

Johnella: If we think back to that, where do you think the conversation was going when we began that talk about the sexual feelings?

Sharon: I thought hell, she's going to ask me to start experimenting with acting on sexual feelings.

Johnella: The thought 'she's going to ask me to experiment with acting on sexual feelings', did this thought begin the scared feelings?

Sharon: Yes, I just wanted to leave, run away. I began to feel cornered.

Johnella: What would have happened if I had asked about the sexual feelings and discussed acting on the sexual feelings, could you have said, 'Johnella, I don't want to do that'?

Sharon: No, I don't know what I'd have done, I could have left the room.

Johnella: What feelings or thoughts would have been around before you left the room?

Sharon: Shame, embarrassment, feelings of exposure.

Johnella: So the scared feelings and the idea 'I want to leave the room' have within them shame, embarrassment and feelings of exposure. So do you mind if we explore this some more? Before we do I want to reassure you that I won't be asking you to experiment with acting on sexual feelings. That would be a negotiation between the two of us. At the moment I am interested in our getting to

understand the shame, embarrassment and feelings of
exposure, and how the scared feelings operate in your
life. Do you think that is an 'okay' beginning point?

The generalising nature of the way we talk about everyday experience
such as 'I am a really fearful person' requires us to remain alert to
re-searching the context that surrounds and supports people's (clients')
definitions. Re-searching can then generate the development of
descriptions that more adequately represent the complexity of people's
(clients') experiences, as in 'the fear of failure as a man drove my early
ambition to dance underground'. Development of these very specific
descriptions directly contravenes the generalised descriptions that limit,
categorise and pathologise. Diagnostic categories can also become
generalised descriptions of lived experience. Once experience is
categorised the carriers of institutional power assume that we know
all we need to know about people's experience. Adherence to this
belief robs people (clients) of opportunities for self-discovery and self-
determination. Adherence to these generalised descriptions has the
power to drive people (clients) beyond despair.

When we experiment with the naming of experience in order to
mirror the integrity of people's (clients') relationship to the experience,
this can directly contravene professional naming. In doing this we can
put our selves at risk. The risk we carry is that we may find our selves
on the margins with the people (clients) we work with. In contrast to
the people (clients) we work with, we are more resourced to operate bi-
lingually. We can protect our selves and the therapeutic relationship by
finding ways to negotiate our way through the static and totalising
paradigms inherent in generalised and diagnostic descriptions of life
events. We inevitably need allies in this enterprise.

The ongoing process of negotiating the naming of experience,
together with negotiation of the meaning of lived experience (including
the meaning of stuckness in the therapy), assumes a therapy founded
on collaboration.

The battle for meaning

Past and present life-taking ideas that dominate people's (clients') lives
are parasitic. Their settling on, and eventual attachment to people
(clients) occurs with such subtlety that people (clients) believe that they
have generated the ideas themselves. Weedon (32) writes:

Although the subject in post-structuralism is socially constructed in discursive practices she nonetheless exists as a thinking, feeling subject and social agent, capable of resistance and innovations produced out of the clash between contradictory subject positions and practices. She is also a subject able to reflect upon the discursive relations which constitute her and the society in which she lives and able to choose the options available. (page 125)

The two self-directed exercises in this chapter attempt to expose the development, maintenance and repetitive nature of certain ideas. Once exposed the ideas can be reflected on and other ideas can be named and considered. People (clients) are therefore able to consider acting on their lives by choosing a direction, idea or practice that supports their beliefs and values. The act of choosing or experimenting will significantly alters people's (clients') relationship with what has previously been considered 'true'.

The therapeutic process can expose the existence of life-taking ideas. However, I want to reinforce my earlier assertion that an hour a fortnight often does little to shift their strong hold. The work to counter past and present life-taking ideas is predominately done outside of the therapeutic context. I believe that the conversations that draw attention to both the strengths and limitations of therapy are useful in setting a climate for discovery and experimentation outside of therapy. It is in these conversations that therapy is experienced as a collaborative enterprise where trust and fear are related to rather than produced or eliminated by the therapist's expertise.

WORKING WITH THE TEXT

Trust and Fear — How Do I (Client) Identify and Challenge Fears ?
Although living with fear is debilitating, fear can also be life-saving. It is important for you to get to know the fears that are part of your life. The first signs of fear's presence may be physical or may be thoughts. Once you've identified that fear is around, move your self (physically or psychologically) to a place of safety and ask your self:

▼ When did I first notice the fear?
▼ What was happening at that moment?
▼ What thoughts were around?
▼ Does this fear belong to the past or to the present?

▼ If it belongs to the past, how can I comfort and support myself
without believing this fear belongs to my present?

▼ If it belongs to the present, what can I do to keep myself and
others safe?

Fears that belong to the past are sometimes more aptly described as
terror. Whenever you experience this have compassion and care
towards your self. Partners and friends may need to be informed of the
effects of terror and what specifically you want and need from them.
You can be supported in initiating this conversation with partners and
friends by asking your therapist to be present and to speak on these
issues.

Other fears such as the fear of being overwhelmed by madness,
of physical and emotional abandonment, of being overwhelmed by
emotions, often show themselves in therapy. Their appearance can
sometimes be signalled by your disconnection from the conversation.
When you alert the therapist to these fears, she/he will attempt to get
to know and understand them. If you feel pushed in the therapy to
confront the fears before you are ready, it is very likely that you will
either disconnect from the conversation or experience strong feelings.
Both are protection strategies. Disconnection or strong feelings can
inform you both (therapist and client) that there is something that you
both don't understand or that the therapy is moving too fast.

It is important that the fears are taken seriously. It may be necessary
to negotiate detailed conditions of safety in order for you to feel ready
to name and confront them. A context of safety may involve having
support people, taking time off work, a longer than normal session and
arranging after session care.

If you are suffering from the influences of criticism, doubt, fear and
shame, then the two exercises in this chapter may help you develop
ways of challenging these influences. If you feel overwhelmed or upset
in any way, don't consider doing the exercises until a sense of strength
has returned. If you feel overwhelmed or upset in any way while
engaging in the exercises, stop, note the upset and discuss it in therapy.

How Do I (Therapist) Identify and Challenge Fears?
The word fear describes a myriad of body, visual and auditory experiences that are triggered by innumerable stimulants. The most common

response in work with fears is to underestimate its effect and pervasiveness. We need to experiment with language that accurately represents the experience in order to find ways to distinguish between the fears while developing contexts of understandings in respect to the fears.

In the text you will notice that a distinction has been drawn between life-saving and life-taking fear, between fear and terror, between the fear of being overwhelmed by madness, the fear of physical and emotional abandonment and the fear of being overwhelmed by emotions. Drawing these distinctions allows for a conversation that focuses on discovering a more accurate representation of experience in language.

Simplistic notions like 'feel the fear and do it anyway' invalidate past, present and future consequences of challenging fears. This also deprives people (clients) of a possible resource. For example, sensitivity to the subtle nuances of an emerging danger can provoke a fear response before any intellectual recognition that this is a dangerous situation.

Developing a knowledge of the way fears operate allows people (clients) to actively negotiate safety both in and outside of therapy. This negotiation has the potential to provide people (clients) with a unique experience of acting to develop safety in their lives. The conversation that negotiates safety will also protect you from taking people's (clients') ability to challenge fears for granted. Whenever you find your self repeating previous strategies developed to challenge fears, it's an indication that you have over-estimated your understandings of the way this fear operates in the person's (client's) life. When I reflect on this description, 'Fear that permeates through every life interaction. Fear that lives in each inhalation and exhalation of breath,' it helps me to continually take people's (clients') relationship with fears seriously.

To work with these fears we must know them while not being overwhelmed by them. When we are overwhelmed it is possible that we have developed an over-connection with people's (clients') experience of terror while forgetting to remain connected with opportunities in our lives for love, laughter and safety. If fear enters your life in the form of nightmares, out of the ordinary vigilance, fear of taking risks, going to social occasions and so on, remember, this is telling you something. It is not a personal deficit. Take time with someone you trust to make discoveries about the appearance of these fears in your life. You may find you can counter fears by activities such as watching comedy, or you may find that you are on the edge of reinventing your relationship with ideas about humanity by thinking about issues like, 'What ideas, environments, relationships, support me to recognise injustices while still believing in people's capacity for love, tenderness, generosity?'

The life-taking ideas which manifest as criticism, doubt, guilt, fear and shame can be present for people (clients) in an overwhelming and tortuous way. These ideas, however, are present in all of our lives and they may both support and limit us. Their appearance can herald an attempt by the prevailing cultural ideas to pull us back into line. Whether these ideas support us or limit us it's useful to neither disregard or comply with them. With the exercise on pages 298 and 299, you can engage actively with these ideas. The presence of criticism, doubt, guilt, fear and shame could also be alerting you to your negative actions in respect to a relationship as in, 'I feel guilty because when Suzanne asked to borrow my book I said I'd lost it because I didn't want her to use it and write a better essay than me.' In this instance you may agree with the criticism which says you could be more supportive and share what resources you have. Instead of suffering under the criticism, however, you could engage in further exploration of criticism. For example:

▼ What ideas or experiences support my sense of needing to do better?
▼ Is doing better internally or externally measured?
▼ If it's external, is there a limit to how many people can 'do better'?
▼ Who or what benefits from this evaluation procedure?

These questions illustrate a way that you can engage in a self-reflective process that isn't shaped by the socially constrained ideas about what is right and wrong.

These exercises are not answers. Predominantly, they create space between the person and certain ideas and practices. This space/relationship then creates the opportunity for exploration.

On your own, or with someone else:

▼ Throughout the week catch experiences of criticism, doubt, guilt, fear and shame and go through the first exercise and then extend the conversation as demonstrated.
▼ Remember to focus on an externalising conversation, i.e. ask your self and your partner, 'What am I externalising?' It is also useful to be alert to assumptions about gender, ethnicity, race, sexuality and disability.

For example:

- How would guilt operate if the other person in the relationship was a man/woman?
- Is this guilt gendered in any way? Would a man/woman hear the voice of guilt differently?
- What assumptions support the appearances of guilt?

It was while working with people (clients) who were often gripped by terror that I recognised the importance of experimenting with the naming of experience. The everyday language used to represent experience was a poor reflection of people's (clients') actual experience. Together (client and therapist) we would search for a coherent expression of experience and in this process we would often negotiate and renegotiate the language used.

It is a huge challenge for us (therapists) to ongoingly consider how little we know about people's (clients') unique lives. However, when we hold this knowledge we prepare our selves to always wonder and enquire about the meaning of the language used to represent experience.

CHAPTER NINE

· · · · · · · · · ·

Disconnection and Desperation

DISCONNECTION

In this book I refer often to 'connection' and 'disconnection'. Whenever I use these words I am describing people's ability to relate with consciousness. I prefer these terms to 'disassociation' for the following reasons:

1. I am interested in re-searching in therapy the movement between a connected relationship to consciousness and a disconnected relationship from consciousness. This re-search requires attention to the following:

    ▼ A connected relationship between the self and consciousness.

    ▼ A disconnected relationship between the self and consciousness.

    ▼ Signs of movement away from a connected relationship with consciousness towards disconnection.

    ▼ Signs of the movement away from a disconnected relationship with consciousness towards connection.

    ▼ The sense made of any movement away from or towards connection.

2. Disassociation has a strong association with psychiatric classifications and pathology.

3. Generating language that reflects the movement between a connected relationship to consciousness or a disconnected relationship to consciousness challenges conventional language strategies that position us on either side of the binary of 'normal' or 'dissociative' states. (refer Chapter One.)

Disconnection describes people's (clients') ability to move their relationship with consciousness away from immediate experience. This immediate experience can include conversation, connection to the body or parts of the body and connection to the immediate environment (including people and things). Connection describes people's (clients') ability to relate with consciousness to immediate experience (including thought). Disconnection prevents people (clients) from connecting with consciousness to their direct experience or their memory of experience. This subsequently restricts their ability to reflect on either the past or the present. The strategy of disconnection will have, at times, been life-saving. Many children who are physically, sexually and emotionally abused quickly learn that their survival depends on their ability to disconnect from the abusive experience. The practice of disconnection frequently generalises to other parts of the child's life, affecting emotions, relationships and learning. Over time, disconnection can become an automatic response to any threatening situation, for example meeting a new teacher or starting a new unit of school work.

The life-saving strategy of disconnection can also be life-taking. Disconnection robs people (clients) of their relationship with their experiences. Disconnection robs people (clients) of the opportunity to challenge the strongly held ideas that frequently belong to their abuser/s. Disconnection also excludes people (clients) from an intimate connection with the self and with others.

A disconnected world offers isolation, numbness, familiarity and safety. This can be both terrifying and appealing. Total disconnection provides the peace of self-elimination, a self lost to madness and death. People (clients) who negotiate a balance between connection and disconnection live with the extreme emotional pain of this balancing act. Whenever disconnection operates automatically in people's (clients') lives, they are left seeking explanations for their behaviour because it seems outside of what is 'normal'. Frequently people (clients) conclude that their actions are the result of a personal deficit. These self-explanations can confirm and maintain the truth of societal or the abuser/s opinions, such as, 'You're weird. Why don't you act like normal people and join in?' This balance between connection and disconnection may have been established and practised over many years with a strong belief that this is the only way to achieve safety. The practice becomes so familiar it disappears into the everyday and is experienced as 'that's the way I am'.

DISCONNECTION IN THERAPY
The practice of disconnection is often automatic. When we are alert to the signs of disconnection we can use the therapeutic conversation to explore and understand the process of disconnection with people (clients). People (clients) then have the opportunity to take back control of their lives by increasing their awareness and appreciation of this practice. Awareness thus creates a basis for self discovery.

A millisecond is all the time needed for someone to move from connection to disconnection. Once we are alerted to the practice of disconnection we can discuss with people (clients) strategies for re-establishing connectedness in the therapy room. These strategies may include: verbally alerting people (clients) as in 'I think you've left — have you?'; movement for example, encouraging people to move around the room, get a drink and so on; changing eye focus. As an example of the last strategy, a number of people I have worked with have used the connection strategy of looking at my colourful socks whenever they caught themselves moving from connection to disconnection.

Disconnection provides the ideal environment for maintaining life-draining ideas. While these ideas remain invisible and thus unchallenged people (clients) experience periodic desperation.

What is Connection? — A conversation between Leslie and Johnella

Leslie: It's the difference between living a real life and being in a movie, I guess. You begin to feel things and that's very scary too, but it's also incredibly powerful as you know you're alive. The last year or so I've felt more alive than in my whole life.

Johnella: Interesting isn't it? It's like a living death in a way. Being in a movie is not living.

Leslie: And sometimes now I have these sort of flashes of 'Oh
             God, I wish that I didn't have to feel this quite so much',
             because the feelings are really intense. They're real
             feelings. They're quite overpowering. But there are also
             the good things with that and I know that once I go
             through the feelings I'm going to pop out and be real.
             You know. The fog's not going to be there. The numb-
             ness isn't going to be there. The feeling is okay. It's okay.

When people (clients) move into a life of connection with consciousness
(connection with self, including body, emotions, ideas, connection with
others, connection to the environment) the intensity of feeling can be
exhilarating, exhausting and frightening. For example, Louise was
gardening and accidentally cut her finger with the secateurs. The pain
she felt was sharper than any pain she had felt in previous accidents.

It is interesting to reflect on the actual prevalence in everyday
Western cultural life of people's connected relationship with consciousness. I suspect a disconnected relationship with consciousness is
more 'normal' than a connected relationship with consciousness.

DISCONNECTION AND 'IN THE CORNER' IDEAS
Disconnection sentences people (clients) to ongoing persecution by
strong, life-taking ideas, and locates these ideas within the person
(client), where they never see the light of day and thus can never be
argued against and discounted. These ideas can be described as 'in the
corner' ideas because they provide no escape or way out.[1] When people
suffer these ideas they can experience extreme hopelessness.

These are some examples of 'in the corner' ideas:

▼ You are so screwed up you will never be able to be in a
   relationship.
▼ You will go mad. It's only a matter of time.
▼ If people really knew you they would be repelled and disgusted.
▼ You are damaged goods.
▼ Nothing will ever change.

The first step in challenging these ideas is to expose them. This requires
people (clients) to risk exposure by challenging the rationale for secrecy
that has maintained and sustained the ideas over many years. This takes
immense courage.

Here is a beginning conversation that exposes an 'in the corner' idea.

Johnella: How often do you find your self listening to the idea, 'You will never amount to anything'?

Lucy: It's there all the time, sometimes it's like a low hum and other times it's so loud I can hardly hear anything else.

Johnella: When you hear the words in a low hum, how does that affect you?

Lucy: It's an irritation, I'm sort of distracted . . . not totally there.

Johnella: When it's loud, what's that like?

Lucy: Umm, it's like the words take up all the space, nothing else seems to get through, it's incessant pounding. Sometimes I hit my head to try and stop it, I hurt myself.

Once the truth of the 'in the corner' ideas is exposed, the ideas can be challenged. When 'in the corner' ideas are dominant in people's (clients') lives they often go unrecognised unless they are accompanied by a strong feeling state such as despair. Inexplicable feeling states may signal the appearance of 'in the corner ideas'. Whenever strong feelings like despair are identified, people (clients) can ask themselves the following questions:

▼ When did I first notice the appearance of despair feelings?

▼ What ideas were circulating that may have thrown me into this despair?

These questions indicate the beginning of an enquiry that can alert people to the influence of these ideas.

When people (clients) are in the grip of despair, they often cannot isolate the ideas that are producing the despair because the ideas are experienced as truths. We can assist in identifying these ideas by re-searching the events that surrounded the appearance of the first sign of despair in people's (clients') lives. These events are often commonplace and don't stand out. When the event is re-searched it often becomes obvious that it has triggered the 'in the corner' ideas.

For example, Billie was asked to facilitate her group in a university tutorial. She was given a week's notice. She suffered enormous anxiety and subsequently called in sick. When she attended her next counselling session she was feeling desperate and suicidal. The enquiry identified a trigger for the anxiety. This trigger was the fear of saying the wrong thing and belonged to childhood experiences of physical abuse. The anxiety provoked a number of 'in the corner' ideas including, 'You might as well give up university now, if you can't do such a simple thing.'

The relational externalising enquiry helps to create space between the self, these 'in the corner' ideas and the subsequent emotional response. This space makes a detailed enquiry of everyday experience possible. We situate the initial appearance of the 'in the corner' idea in time, in order to begin to re-search its 'truth'. Once we establish its origins, we often find that it belongs to a significant person in the person's (client's) life. 'In the corner' ideas often provide a lynch pin for the safety of the abuser, while people (clients) are continuously tormented by their belief in these ideas. The enquiry process can create an experience of control, hope and joy as it challenges the secrecy and irrefutable nature of the 'in the corner' ideas. We can also discover, however, that people (clients) carry a strong loyalty to the arguments and practice of 'in the corner' ideas. This can prevent them from even beginning to imagine a counter argument or practice. In the example below I have created conceptual space by guessing a counter argument or practice.[2]

Therapist in dialogue with the fear of madness:

Therapist: Okay, tell me why I should believe in you?

Madness: Oh, you know very well why. Madness runs in the family and there is heaps of evidence that says madness is inherited.

Therapist: Well, I can provide heaps of information that would challenge that idea.

Madness: There is nothing conclusive though, it would be your opinion against mine.

Therapist: When I look at my life you have always threatened me. You have always threatened to be there, but you never have been. You are a liar!

Madness: Well maybe I am a liar but maybe I'm not.

Therapist: Well, I'm just not going to believe you. There is no substance to you.

Madness: Oh, I wouldn't do that if I was you. I'm always just over your shoulder. Just as you're relaxing, I will appear.

Therapist: You're always threatening that you might be there. Well, I'm tired of your blackmail. It robs me of my life. So what if you appear in one year or 10 years. While I believe in you, I don't have a life. If I believe in myself at least I'll have a life for as long as I can.

In order for us to attempt to represent 'in the corner' ideas we need to have an intimate acquaintance with them. After using this process, it's important to check the authenticity of the representation with people (clients). The above dialogue personifies madness so that we can reflect intentions and emotions. This assists people (clients) to reflect on 'it' rather than being immersed in 'it'.

THE NOISY CHORUS

'In the corner' ideas frequently do not come alone. In fact there is often a chorus. This chorus is deafening, overwhelming and encourages disconnection. Consequently these ideas are extremely dangerous and need to be taken seriously. When we notice disconnection it provides us with an opportunity to reflect on the presence and strength of 'in the corner' ideas. For example, here is a conversation between Johnella (therapist) and Bridget (client).

Johnella: I noticed that as we were talking about the depression you were staring out of the window. Is that a sign of disconnection?

Bridget: Yes.

Johnella: When did you notice that happening? What were we talking about?

Bridget: I think we were talking about work.

Johnella: Okay. Do you mind if we talk about work a bit more so that you and I can understand what's happening?

Bridget: Yes, that's okay.

Johnella:	You noticed the depression taking hold when you were at work on Thursday. Is that right?
Bridget:	Yes.
Johnella:	Were there any ideas hanging around with or before depression?
Bridget:	Yeah, either with or before, I'm not sure. It's pretty noisy now.
Johnella:	What are the ideas you are aware of now?
Bridget:	I keep hearing and thinking, 'You're hopeless, you'll never hold down a job.'

We can explore the context that maintains and provokes the 'in the corner' idea along with exploring alternative explanations.

Johnella:	What happened that day at work? Can you remember what happened before you noticed the depression and the appearance of the 'in the corner ideas'?
Bridget:	Oh, um. . . the boss had asked me to retype part of page two of an important report. He had marked some changes that he wanted done. I suppose I thought that he was looking a bit cross and I thought that he probably didn't think I did a very good job.
Johnella:	What were the changes he was asking for?
Bridget:	Oh, he was just adding some things and changing paragraphs and that sort of thing.
Johnella:	So when you think of it now do you think you did a good job with the information that you had initially been given?
Bridget:	Well I suppose, but you know, maybe I should have changed the paragraphs myself and taken the initiative.
Johnella:	Do you think your boss expects that of you?
Bridget:	Well, no, I don't really think so.
Johnella:	Do you think these ideas come from a pretty unrealistic expectation that you should guess what your boss needs

and wants? Do you think it is possible that these ideas look for problems and trouble rather than looking for success and ease?

Bridget: Well . . . I suppose it's possible.

We can directly challenge the truth of the 'in the corner' ideas by presenting alternative possibilities.

Johnella: There are several ways of interpreting what happened at work. One way brings forward a sense of competence and success and the other way, which is fed by the idea 'You're hopeless, you'll never hold down a job' brings forward feelings of depression and hopelessness. When you think of the ideas that maintain a sense of achievement and success, what happens to the feelings of depression? Right here and now as you are thinking about the ideas of success and achievement, do you feel the depression lifting or strengthening?

Bridget: I feel . . . I feel lighter . . . yeah it feels better, more possible somehow.

Once the truth of 'in the corner' ideas is challenged, the ideas of badness and madness are also challenged. This can consequently dramatically reduce feelings of depression and despair. People (clients) can discover that they have been subjected to a lifetime of persecution by 'in the corner' ideas. This discovery is generated in a relational externalising enquiry. The linguistic space relationship introduces both movement and the possibility of escape from these ideas, thereby generating hope. Hope provides the impetus for the struggle ahead. This struggle is often the struggle for life.

Challenging 'in the corner' ideas is often terrifying for people (clients). We can alert people (clients) to the possibility of the presence of 'in the corner' ideas while continuing to explore issues of safety. For example, 'A lot of people tell me in counselling that they engage in two conversations; one between the therapist and themselves, and one between themselves and certain strong ideas. Is that true for you?' We can provide opportunities for people (clients) to re-search safety by a process of enquiry. For example:

Johnella:	What do you think I will think or do when you say these thoughts out loud?
Ellen:	You will think that I'm crazy.
Johnella:	What can I do or say to reassure you that I won't think that?
Ellen:	There is nothing you can do.
Johnella:	Has there been another time that you have thought, 'She'll think I'm crazy if I tell her that,' and you did tell me?
Ellen:	Yes, there was a time when I said that I sometimes imagine my father as dead.
Johnella:	What happened? What did you think I thought, or what did I do?
Ellen:	It was okay. We talked about it and it was okay.
Johnella:	What helped you to take that step to tell me what you were thinking?
Ellen:	I don't know, I suppose I thought, Why not give it a try.
Johnella:	When you remember this success, would this support you to give it a try?
Ellen:	Yes, I think it would.

People (clients) commonly experience the following constraints to continuing conversations that expose, explore and challenge 'in the corner' ideas:

▼ Fear of exposing the secret, as previous life experiences confirm that exposing secrets is extremely dangerous.

▼ Total belief in the truth of the idea. For example, 'I can't argue against this. It's true isn't it?'

▼ Limited practice at arguing for the self. For example, 'The loudest voice is always right.'

▼ Arguing back against the 'in the corner ideas' and thoughts is too exposing. People (clients) are paralyzed by the possibility of making a mistake, of looking foolish and/or getting it wrong.

Awareness of possible constraints to engaging in conversations that expose, explore and challenge 'in the corner' ideas enables us to move slowly with people (clients). Intellectual awareness of these ideas is the first step to recognising and countering them both in and outside of the therapy room. People (clients) can experiment with catching these 'in the corner' ideas, followed by experimenting with ways to reduce the strength of these ideas. Acting on these ideas is a direct challenge to being acted on by these ideas. One of the strategies to 'action' is to strengthen self-determined ideas. Other strategies include physical activities (including self-care), talking with others, reading therapeutic or self-written letters, and reading literature.

FOREIGN TERRITORY
It can be difficult to navigate our way through the often complex and comprehensive logic of 'in the corner' ideas. The logic of these pervasive, negative ideas can overwhelm any information or experience that challenges its truth. Alternative ideas do not survive. We can find our selves arguing strongly against these ideas, which people (clients) then experience as us arguing against them. This can send the 'in the corner ideas' underground.

For example:

Johnella: When you said . . . that is a real victory, too.

Marie: (thinking) She doesn't really know how pathetic you are. Anyone can do that.

When confronted with seemingly intractable persecutory ideas we can behave like English speaking people, who when faced with a different language and culture, speak loudly, slowly and repetitively. If this occurs in therapy we know we have entered foreign territory!

When we (therapists) find our selves in foreign territory, we can guess it is possible that there are several conversations going on in the therapeutic process. One powerful silent conversation could be between people (clients) and the pervasive 'in the corner' ideas. This conversation needs to become part of the therapeutic conversation, in order that it may become understood and to provide an opportunity for people (clients) to re-view the ideas. To do this we first need to know that we have entered foreign territory. When we are in foreign territory we can use the following guidelines:

▼ Don't assume we know the territory.

▼ Be available to learning, and ready to challenge our assumptions.

▼ Negotiate a safety net.

▼ Negotiate the meaning of the words that carry emotional significance.

▼ Move slowly.

▼ Listen for certainty in our internal conversation. Once certainty is caught, turn it into a question.

▼ Be available to have our thinking challenged by the answer to the question.

Being in foreign territory has taught me a number of things. The first is humility, knowing that I have limited knowledge of the many aspects of people's (clients') experience. The second is appreciation of the need to gain a consensus of understanding when using common expressions and words. The third is knowing that even in foreign territory I won't get lost. I will find a way through with people (clients) because although I don't know this particular path, I have substantial experience in navigating in foreign territory. The fourth is that being in foreign territory may fundamentally change what I know or believe.

Therapists, counsellors, psychologists, social workers and psychiatrists who operate with certainty when working with people who are persecuted by 'in the corner' ideas, tend to become unwitting supporters of these ideas. The certainty exhibited by members of the privileged professional classes is thus persecutory and condemning of people (clients) in our society who have suffered significantly.

HOLDING ON TO HOPE IN FOREIGN TERRITORY
People (clients) who are persecuted by 'in the corner' ideas frequently have a tenuous grip on life because hopelessness and despair are so pervasive. We can hold the life/hope in the therapeutic relationship for a short period of time as mentioned in Chapter Five. Sustained holding of life/hope for people, however, results in our over-connection with people's (clients) lives. At this point the therapy can become stuck. Whenever this happens I find it useful to re-view the therapeutic direction and process with people (clients).

An enquiry that re-views 'the therapy' may be something like this:

Johnella: I would like you to know that I'm feeling worried about
              the therapy. When you leave my office you are feeling
              hopeful and optimistic and then within a short time
              suicidal ideas appear. These ideas gather strength until
              you act on them, ending up in A&E. Over the time we
              have spent together we have talked about strategies to
              fight the ideas and feelings that lead to suicidal action.
              We have talked about a lot of strategies. At the time you
              seem to think these will be helpful. You indicate a sense
              of hope that if these are put into place you will be able
              to successfully challenge the suicidal thoughts. In fact,
              at times you have been successful. However at other
              times it seems these strategies are lost to you. Does this
              seem familiar to you?

Ingrid: Yes. I am feeling depressed, really depressed.

Johnella: Yes, I can see that. I am really wondering about the
              therapy. I would like to ask you about your ideas about
              the therapy. I've noticed that you often rediscover
              having hope in the room and then you are taken over by
              despair and hopelessness when you leave. I wonder if I
              am missing something really important?

Ingrid: I know that I'm really hopeless and that you try really
              hard . . . I'm just useless.

Johnella: No. That's not what I'm saying. I don't think that you are
              hopeless or useless. I think I'm missing something. I
              think it's really important that you and I talk about
              what's working, and what's not working for you in this
              therapy. What do you think I'm missing? Do you think
              I'm missing something? I think I am. What do you
              think?

Ingrid: Oh. . . . I don't know. I just feel good here and then
              terrible out there.

Johnella: Yes, that's interesting. When you're here, we sometimes
              talk about strategies, ideas and action to fight off the
              despair. What happens to those ideas and strategies?

Ingrid: I don't know. I just get overtaken with hopelessness.

Johnella:	Do you think it's possible that you may think to your self that the ideas and strategies we work out here belong to me? That these ideas and strategies are not really yours and that you can only use them when I say them?
Ingrid:	Well, maybe that's true.
Johnella:	Do you hear those ideas and strategies in your voice? Could you say them to your self, out loud, in your voice?
Ingrid:	No. . . I don't think I can. . . I don't. I suppose when I leave here your voice gets weaker and weaker till it disappears.
Johnella:	And what about the voice of despair? Does that get stronger or weaker as your memory of my voice gets weaker and weaker?
Ingrid:	That's right, it gets stronger.
Johnella:	Do you think it would be useful to find some way for you to own these ideas and strategies, so that you can hear them in your voice and keep your voice strong?
Ingrid:	That's possible.
Johnella:	You're not looking too confident about that idea. What are you thinking to your self?
Ingrid:	I don't know whether I can do it.
Johnella:	Do you think your voice needs some help along the way? Do you think it could be strengthened by my voice? Do you think if we had our voices together then that would help fight the despair?
Ingrid:	Yes, if we could do that I think it could work.
Johnella:	Do you think it would be good for us to work together on this?
Ingrid:	Yes I do.
Johnella:	When you said, 'Yes. I do,' what degree of hope did you feel? None? Some? More than when you came into the room?

Ingrid: Yeah, I did feel some. It felt more than when I came into
             the room.

Johnella: How did that feel, the feeling the hope? Where did you
             feel it? Did it feel like an idea or did you feel it in your
             body or . . . ? What was it like?

Ingrid: I felt it as an idea and as a feeling. It felt warm. I felt
             warmth in my body.

Re-viewing the therapy provides us with an opportunity to reflect with
people (clients) on the direction of therapy. Ongoing hopelessness and
desperation indicate that knowledge of a vital element of people's
(clients') experience is unavailable to the therapeutic relationship. We
can succumb to helplessness or blaming people (clients) when faced
with despair that appears unmovable. An enquiry that re-views the
therapy creates enough distance to reflect on a pattern of interaction
that may not helpful. The distance generated by the relational externalising enquiry of the therapy allows for the discovery of new information
as demonstrated in the above example.

Re-viewing the therapy demonstrates to both the therapist and the
client that the therapy is a collaboration. Concerns in respect to the
therapy become joint concerns even though each person in the therapeutic relationship has particular responsibilities within the therapeutic
relationship understanding.

TAKING THE THERAPY HOME

We can totally underestimate the pervasive nature of 'in the corner'
ideas. People (clients) experience these ideas as essential truths and
they are often buoyed up by secrecy, fear and indoctrination. The therapeutic conversation sometimes offers puny resistance to the unrelenting
evidence-collecting that reinforces the truth of these ideas. Outside the
therapy room people (clients) can strengthen themselves by collecting
concrete resources such as friends' opinions and letters, therapeutic
letters and tapes, books, films, videos, photographs and poetry. For
example, Karen placed all her self-strengthening resources in a box. She
decided that whenever she noticed the appearance of 'in the corner'
ideas she would immerse her self in the things that gave her strength.
This lack of engagement with the 'in the corner' ideas protected her
from being overtaken by them. Phoebe carried a therapeutic letter with

her, so that she could read it and gather strength when faced with an 'in the corner' idea.

Whenever 'in the corner' ideas overtake people (clients) this provides information about the supporters of these ideas and the strength or veracity of the ideas. It is not a failure to be overtaken by such strong ideas. People (clients) can slip, however, into a sense of failure, which in turn supports despair. Whenever I notice this I turn our enquiry towards understanding the event/s together with an emphasis on people's (clients) self-care. For example, Toni came to the session gripped with despair. Ideas such as, You're hopeless, you'll never get out of this, you can't live in this world, were consuming her. She had been unable to access the strengthening strategies we had discussed and consequently felt that she had let me down. Toni didn't know what could have precipitated the despair. When we explored the events that had occurred in her life over the last two weeks, we discovered an event that Toni had dismissed as unrelated to her experience of despair. She had attended a team building day with the organisation she worked for. Within the first hour each participant was asked to stand and address the group. This 'joining' exercise was set to encourage participants to speak about their strengths. Toni literally froze. She knew most of the members of the team apart from four new recruits. The closer it came to her turn to speak the more anxious, sick and frozen she felt, until unable to bear it any longer she raced from the room. Although she returned, she felt incredibly exposed, vulnerable and stupid.

Toni clearly experienced the effects of enormous anxiety. In exploring what may have precipitated the anxiety we discovered a link with visibility. When Toni was a child, finding ways to be invisible had been life-saving. When she was suddenly required to be visible during the exercise she experienced the terror associated with her early experiences. This was identified as a vulnerability that she could psychologically and physically prepare for future situations where visibility was called for.

In this therapy we take people's (clients') experiences seriously. In order to take the therapy home, people (clients) are encouraged to take their experiences seriously. Whenever people (clients) are gripped by strong emotions, this is a moment to re-search the experience. To engage in this re-search implies willingness to believe in the possibility of a worthwhile self. This can be very challenging for people (clients) who are oppressed by 'in the corner' ideas. It also requires prioritising the self by giving time to self-discoveries. This may be very challenging to past ideas and to gender socialisation.

Experimenting with 'taking the therapy home' can provide the therapy with information about the ideas and practices that continue to persecute people (clients).

THE IMPACT OF DESPERATION ON THE THERAPEUTIC RELATIONSHIP

In a supervision session, a supervisee reported that she had been asked to act in a support role with a person (client) while the person's (client's) primary therapist was on holiday. The consequence of the primary therapist's departure was that the person (client) called the support therapist daily and was talking frequently about suicide. The supervisee felt under immense pressure and was using descriptions and words like 'acting out', 'attention seeking' and had begun to set 'firm limits', such as not speaking on the phone. The situation had deteriorated to the extent that the supervisee was considering admitting the person (client) to hospital.

The process of supervision involved asking a number of questions about the person's (clients) desperation such as,

▼ Was the ongoing therapeutic relationship an important relationship for the person (client)?

▼ Had this relationship acted at times as a life-line for this person (client)?

▼ Do you think it's possible that the person (client) is feeling at a loss and panicking since this relationship has gone on hold?

We quickly determined that the person (client) could be feeling increasingly desperate as a result of the loss of the therapeutic relationship. I suggested externalising the desperation in order to explore the person's particular relationship with desperation, including their knowledge of what helps to limit or reduce desperation. If desperation was growing as a result of the absence of the therapist/counsellor, I suggested beginning to negotiate a way that the person (client) could use the memory of the therapeutic relationship to keep desperation at bay.

The supervisee reported that the conversation she and the person (client) had was a great relief to them both and they successfully negotiated strategies to reduce desperation. The threat of suicide and hospital admission disappeared with that session.

The most misdiagnosed people in the community are people suffering from desperation. In psychiatric services they are commonly described as manipulative, splitting, attention seeking, dependent and finally may receive the formal diagnosis of Borderline Personality Disorder. This group of people is also the most punished by therapists and psychiatric systems. When we (therapists) get desperate, we withdraw, depersonalise and label people (clients)!

WHY IS WORKING WITH DESPERATION SO DIFFICULT?
This is because it requires a deep understanding of another's experience, an understanding that often asks us to go the core of what it is to be human.

There are very few experiences and relationships in life where one person trusts another person with their emotional life. The therapeutic relationship potentially provides therapist and client with this experience. Therapist and client, however, inevitably experience the therapeutic relationship differently.

People (clients) who have significant life relationships can practise and experiment with the ideas and experiences generated in the therapeutic relationship in other settings. People (clients) who have limited relationship resources may find themselves wanting to continue to have the experience of the therapeutic relationship when they are not in it. This need, combined with the knowledge of the limitation of the therapeutic relationship, will often culminate in people (clients) experiencing, and acting on, desperation.

Desperation can be defined as fear of not receiving what is needed, coupled with frantic efforts to have the need fulfilled. We may experience people's (clients') feelings and actions of desperation as pressure and respond with reason, fear, irritation and/or anger. People (clients) who act on feelings of desperation are consequently often labelled and punished. The actions and thoughts of desperation are understandable, however, when people's (clients') experience is truly appreciated. Our failure to understand people's (clients') relationship with desperation is often expressed when we feel desperate, as in, 'What else can I do?'

People (clients) practice and establish a sense of self-determination with the support of another (the therapist). People (clients) who have limited relationship resources can experience themselves differently in the therapeutic relationship, only to have a profound sense of loss and panic when the therapeutic relationship is unavailable.

One hour a week/fortnight is often not enough to sustain new self knowledge that facilitates movement towards other life-sustaining relationships. The therapeutic relationship becomes a lifeline. No one who is struggling for life lets go of a lifeline. The lifeline connects people (clients) to us and this can result in desperate thoughts and behaviour that are uncomfortable and unsatisfactory. We can appreciate people's (clients') experience of desperation by empathising deeply while holding on to a sense of life/hope. This is not easy as we may find it difficult to balance connection and detachment. Connection allows for empathy and detachment allows for enough distance to retain hope in the possibility of finding a life-enhancing direction.

We can protect the therapeutic relationship from desperation by monitoring the ratio of our (therapists) talk to client talk. If we find our selves dominating talk time, then it is likely that people (clients) will locate all knowledge, wisdom and support in us (therapists). It therefore becomes inevitable that they will seek the therapeutic resource whenever they confront difficulties.

Desperation can be identified by reflecting on the therapeutic relationship. The actions and thoughts of desperation tend to generate strong responses/emotions, of either hopelessness/despair or anger/frustration in us. These responses/emotions are thus a good indicator of the presence of desperation. If we are unable to challenge these responses or emotions, then we risk contravening the therapeutic relationship understanding.

It is also possible to identify desperation by taking people's (clients') words and actions seriously. If people (clients) say that they are feeling desperate, believe them. If a person (client) acts desperately, take it seriously. Desperation can show itself in demands for more time, visiting outside of negotiated times and excessive contact through gifts, cards and letters.

Once desperation has been identified, we need to name it and explore it with people (clients). The actions and thoughts of desperation are understandable, in fact inevitable in certain situations. We need to also be mindful that exploring the actions and ideas of desperation can bring forward shame, anger and fear.

The therapeutic relationship can be a resource to challenge desperation both inside and outside of the therapy room. People (clients) can use the memory of the therapeutic relationship whenever desperation is around. The memory of the therapeutic relationship is then experienced as a relationship resource. People (clients) engage this imagined relational presence to strengthen or support them in challenging situations. These strategies allow people (clients) to experience acting on their life with support. It is important to create a climate of experimentation as people (clients) discover the type of support that suits them.

The following strategies have been identified as useful:

▼ I imagine us having a conversation about this in therapy. It makes me feel less alone and that strengthens me. Sometimes I even get some new ideas.

▼ I ask myself what would you say about this decision. It just helps to think about someone else's opinion.

The process of identifying, naming and challenging desperation is strengthened when people (clients) can use the memory of the therapeutic relationship whenever it is needed. The acts and thoughts of desperation are often understandable when put in the context of people's (clients') experience. Once the desperation is understood, it is challenging for us (therapist and client) to think of strategies to reduce the effects of desperation within the bounds of the therapeutic relationship understanding.

Workers in psychiatric services need an appreciation of the effects of desperation and an ability to work with people (clients) suffering from the experience of desperation. The absence of these abilities maintains abusive and depersonalising practices.

DESPERATION AND LIFE SUPPORTS
Desperation is less likely to be experienced by people (clients) if they receive adequate support. The therapy process is one component of that support. It can't be the only support. People (clients) who have limited relationship resources need more than the therapeutic relationship to sustain their movement towards life changes.

Participation in groups provides people (clients) with enormous resources that can support the therapy. Without group work, therapy will often suffer under the effects of desperation. Consider this statement, again by Leslie, in connection with ideas about desperation.

Leslie: It helped a lot because every time someone told a story I would be able to relate to a part of it. I hadn't really ever verbalised the idea that when I spent time with my family I felt crazy. But I sat in a group and someone said, 'Whenever I'm around my family I just go crazy and when I leave my family I have to do things to comfort myself.' And I just sat there and thought, God that's me. That's what happens to me. And I started to check out the theory that that's what happens to me and sure enough I would come away from my family thinking, I've just been kind of screwed around in my head. And then I could look at changing it. And just hearing other people with their experiences, and I identified with it so much and I could see that they were doing it with me too, you just . . . I think it's really, really valuable because you think that you're the only one. You think you're unique. Like I thought I was unique. I thought no one else on this earth is like me. Even though there's people who say they're incest survivors, it didn't matter. I was unique and no one actually knew me and knew my problems and my screwy head. Well I found out that a lot of people feel like me and yeah . . . And that thing of no one was as clever as me at hiding my stupidity of my . . . I just thought I was the ultimate actor, but there are a lot of us out there. There's heaps and we've got, it's . . . I don't know. It's just, I guess I was able to shed a lot of that from hearing other people talk, I thought, Ah maybe we're all just sort of real people underneath but thinking that we're fooling everyone or something.

THE ETHICS OF CONNECTION

Connection

Working with connection and disconnection in relationship to consciousness, 'in the corner' ideas and desperation requires an ability to connect with consciousness to others, the self and the relationship beyond the requirements for connected consciousness in other life relationships.

The consciousness I am referring to involves an ability to focus attention both on and in the therapeutic relationship. This attention directs all the senses towards the conversation. In order to attend at this level we self-consciously monitor our thinking. If our thinking moves away from the therapy we can deliberately move our attention back to the therapy. If our thinking moves into a hypothesis or theoretical explanation for people's (clients') concerns, we can reorientate this thinking towards a way to construct a relational externalising enquiry that re-searches this thinking as a possibility. If our thinking is solely focused on the other, we can reflect on the experience of the experience of the therapeutic relationship.

Another method of encouraging attending is to imagine the therapy is being viewed by a respected colleague. Such visibility can encourage attending, whereas a closed door approach to therapy with no one looking often supports a lack of attending to the depth of connected consciousness we extend towards the therapy.

In the work discussed in this chapter, a lack of attending puts people's (clients') lives at risk. Practising deeply connected consciousness in our everyday lives may bring out longstanding habits of disconnection that are sanctioned by predominant cultural practices, such as gender socialisation or disconnection as a life-long strategy for survival. If we wish to engage ethically in our therapeutic practice, we must draw our attention to our connection/ disconnection practices.

For example, the influence of gender socialisation on connection/ disconnection practices can be re-searched outside of the therapeutic context. Men and men, women and women, men and women in work, friendship and intimate relationships can negotiate a context of safety (refer Chapter Seven) and reflect on the following after each con-versation:

▼ The amount of talk time taken by each person.
▼ The quality of listening/attending/understanding. This is not explored by a verbatim report of what was said by each speaker. It is explored by these questions:

As the listener,

▼ Did you find your self attending with interest to the speaker?
▼ Did you find your self attending partially to the speaker and partially to your internal thinking (this internal thinking being stimulated by the speaker, or internal thinking existing entirely separately from the speaker)?
▼ Did you find your self attending to the internal thinking while still hearing the speaker or not hearing the speaker?

▼ As the listener, on a scale of 0–10, place a mark according to how you judge the listening/attending/understanding abilities you demonstrated.

▼ When and if the listening stopped or altered, what was your understanding of this?

▼ What are the implications of this understanding for the relationship?

▼ What questions extended the understanding of the other person's experience?

As the speaker:

▼ How did the listener act,what did she/he do that resulted in you feeling attended/listened to?

▼ What questions did the listener ask that extended or affirmed your sense of being listened to?

▼ On a scale of 0–10 place a mark according to feeling listened to/ attended to/understood.

▼ What would the listener have needed to do for you to feel more attended and listened to?

▼ Was there any point in the conversation when you believe the listening stopped?

▼ What was that point?

▼ What was your understanding of this?

▼ What are the implications of this understanding for the relationship?

▼ What was the impact on speaking when you believed that the listening had stopped/changed?

▼ What was the impact on speaking of feeling listened to?

The speaker and listener individually reflect on the answers to these questions and then guess how the other will answer the questions. When the answers are reflected back to each other differences are understood as differences, not as criticism. The differences and their implications can then be explored and re-searched. If worry or fear appear while you are having this conversation it is useful to introduce another trusted person to conduct the enquiry. It is also possible in these circumstances to take time out from the conversation to reflect on the thinking or feeling that has become apparent. A time can be made to return in safety to the conversation.

In this example we are re-searching the impact of gender socialisation on connection/disconnection practices. We can also re-search where our consciousness is directed or what our consciousness is connected to.

Subjectivity

Disconnection in the therapeutic relationship is maintained when we are certain about the truth of psychological theories. This certainty directs our listening towards a search for evidence to confirm these psychological theories. In certainty we can then prescribe the solutions to people's (clients') difficulties. If this doesn't change people's (clients') circumstances, we can hold on to our certainty by either blaming people (clients) or re-viewing our diagnosis.

The practice of connection within the therapeutic relationship supports us to hold our psychological theories as one possibility among many. While we re-search people's (clients') experience we position our selves for discovery.

A connected enquiry process involves:

▼ Listening for the theories that direct and maintain our thinking.
▼ Developing questions that pre-empt our belief in this thinking or theory.
▼ Listening to what is being said or partially said.
▼ Developing questions that enable negotiation of the meaning of the language used to describe experience.
▼ Listening for evidence of people's (clients') resourcefulness, resilience, abilities and strengths.
▼ Developing questions that seek out and contextualise the evidence for people's (clients') resourcefulness and resilience abilities and strengths.
▼ Listening openheartedly to people's (clients') descriptions of experiences that are horrific and terror filled.

The practice of connection within the therapeutic relationship rests on the ethic of subjectivity. When we enter the therapeutic relationship this ethic requires us to bring our willingness to engage with our humanity while openheartedly extending our sense of humanity towards others. The ethic of subjectivity requires us to always relate as one subject to another in the therapeutic relationship. It requires us to consider that all psychological theory is socially and culturally produced and is situated at a particular point in time. It requires us to consider that psychological theory may legitimise exclusion of one particular group from the benefits of such things as education, health, legal and economic resources.

WORKING WITH THE TEXT

How Do I (Client) Deal with Disconnection and Desperation?
Disconnection describes people's ability to move their consciousness away from immediate experience. When people are practised in disconnection, it can occur automatically whenever they are threatened. The threat may include a change of conversational direction in the therapy, the use of a particular word, sudden physical movement and the appearance of worries and fears. The therapist is alert to signs of disconnection. However, it is helpful to the therapy if you are also alert to the signs that disconnection is about to, or has, occurred. Some of the signs may include physical sensation, fearful or worried thinking and spacing out. After a time of disconnection you may find that you haven't heard the last question, or you can't remember what's been talked about, or you may experience strong physical reactions.

It is important to the therapy that you get to know when and how this disconnection operates in your life. This isn't something to feel embarrassed about because when disconnection occurs it occurs for good reasons. It is important to remember both that disconnection doesn't reflect badly on you and that you haven't let the therapist down in any way.

When you become more practised at staying connected to thoughts, feelings and to your body, you may initially be surprised by the strength of the feelings and sensations. One person described the differences as moving from living in black and white to living in colour: there is an elevation of the experiences of joy, love and happiness together with an elevation of feelings of loss and pain. It can feel like being on a roller-coaster for a while, then it eases.

Feeling more connected with your life provides you with an opportunity to re-view the past not only in a factual way but also in a feeling way.

I have often used this analogy: Imagine that you have been caught in a snow storm. You are bravely heading towards shelter, telling your self to put one foot before the other. In the unrelenting cold, your body begins to move into survival mode, moving the life-giving blood to the essential organs, the heart, the brain,etc. As the life-giving blood moves away from your extremities, your legs and arms feel numb but miraculously they support you towards shelter. You stumble inside and find a roaring fire, you sit in front of the fire, rubbing your arms and legs. As blood returns to each body part you experience excruciating pain. What helps you bear this pain is the knowledge that the numbing protects you while the pain signals the return of life. Re-viewing the past in a connected way can provoke feelings of grief. When these feelings of grief are around, consider giving your self the gift of time to feel them fully in a supportive environment.

If you notice in therapy that there are two conversations present, one between you and the therapist and the other between you and certain strong ideas, this has a big influence on the therapy. While the conversation between you and certain strong ideas remains private and invisible to the therapy, it will continue to dominate your thoughts and feelings about your self. Generally these thoughts and feelings are negative and often damaging of your relationship to strengths and abilities. This private conversation needs to see the light of day so that the source and logic of these ideas become available for scrutiny. It is often found that these ideas go back to the words of those who have abused you and the context within which the abuse occurred, i.e. secrecy , contradictions and betrayals. Exposure of these ideas gives you the opportunity to act against being co-opted into believing them because they have always been there.

Although you can experience therapy as a lifeline its availability is limited. You can protect your self from the limitations of therapy by asking the therapist for guidance and information about concrete supports, groups and networks.

You could at times be surprised and overwhelmed by loneliness and desperation. At these times people will often hold on to these feelings until desperation overwhelms them, resulting in behaviour and requests that can also threaten to overwhelm the therapy. This can establish a negative cycle of need and withdrawal. When desperation is around, take it seriously and talk about it with the therapist. The therapist will also be alert to the signs of desperation. Together you can develop an understanding of desperation and work out strategies that will reduce desperation while maintaining the therapeutic relationship understanding. When desperation is around you are entitled to respect

from the therapist. Desperation is not your fault. It just is. When you
are in a state of desperation, you and the therapist need to understand
it and act on it in order to reduce the effects of desperation on your life.

How Do I (Therapist) Deal with Disconnection and Desperation?

When people (clients) become disconnected it provides us (therapist
and client) with an opportunity to re-search the ideas, words, visions
and physical sensations that precipitated disconnection in a negotiated
situation of safety. To make the most of this opportunity for discovery
it is important to be alert to any sign of disconnection. This alertness is
determined by your ability to remain connected in the therapeutic
relationship. Connection involves dedicating one hundred per cent of
your attention to the other (client). This requirement is not present in
everyday relationships and many of us have learnt the skills of
appearing connected while pursuing our own thinking. Given that
people (clients) will rarely alert you to your disconnection in the therapeutic conversation, you are required to alert your self.

These questions will help with self-reflection:

▼ Have I moved my thinking outside of the therapy?

▼ If so, when did the wandering begin?

▼ What's the wandering telling me about myself or this particular
therapeutic conversation?

Alertness to the practice of connection or disconnection in relation-ship to consciousness

The therapeutic conversation can be strengthened by reflecting on
everyday conversations. While in conversation or after conversations,
ask your self the following:

▼ Have I been attending/listening in this conversation or has my
mind been drifting elsewhere?

▼ How much attending/listening have I been engaged in on a scale
of 1–100%?

▼ What is the drifting telling me about the feelings or thoughts I
hold about this conversation?

▼ If I was to increase the attending/listening, what would change
in the conversation?

▼ How does the gender of the other person/s in the conversation
effect this attending/listening?

▼ Is my mind more likely to drift when I'm engaged with speaking or when I'm engaged with listening?

▼ Do I find I'm engaged with listening for confirmation of the thinking that I value?

▼ If I don't find confirmation in the listening, what happens to the attending/listening in the conversation?

▼ Do I construct an argument to challenge the other person/s thinking before they have finished speaking?

▼ Does the enthusiasm I hold for this argument encourage me to interrupt the other's speaking?

▼ When the other person finishes speaking, do I extend my understanding of their thinking or do I move to express the thinking that I hold?

Relational externalising of ' in the corner' ideas helps us (therapist and client) to re-search and challenge these ideas rather than directly challenging or arguing against them. 'In the corner' ideas are present in all of our lives. They may have protected or supported us in an earlier time. They may now limit us. In order to develop sensitivity to the 'in the corner' ideas begin by re-searching your ideas. To support this enquiry reflect on these scenarios. Pursue the enquiry further than these questions but only if it feels safe.

▼ Think of an experience where you felt disappointment in a relationship. What idea supported the emotional response? Has this idea made other appearances in your life? What might be the origin/s of this idea?

▼ Think of a time where you did something new (a course of study or a recreational pursuit). What ideas did you notice were predominately around? What feeling states did you notice were predominately around? Has this idea or feeling made an appearance at other times when you were learning something new? What might be the origin/s of this idea or feeling?

▼ Think of a time that you met a new supervisor or consultant or therapist. What ideas did you notice were predominately around? What feeling states did you notice were predominately around? Has this idea or feeling made an appearance at other times when you were more vulnerable than the other person in the relationship? What might be the origin/s of this idea or feeling?

When the 'in the corner' ideas persist there is something about these ideas and the way that they operate in people's (client's) lives that we don't yet understand. It may be opportune to re-view the therapy with people (clients) and/or re-view the therapy with a supervisor/consultant/ peers. In the re-view, it's useful to explore the minutiae of experiences that precipitate, surround and nurture the ideas.

Whenever desperation takes hold of people's lives, either through persistent 'in the corner' ideas or external life events, take it seriously and re-search its appearance with people. When you get desperate about people's (clients') desperation you are likely to withdraw, blame and label people (clients). Listen to your desperation, don't ignore it or talk your self out of it. When you feel the effects of desperation, you and the therapeutic relationship deserve and need support. Your experience of desperation often indicates that you have become bereft of any new ideas or that you are working beyond your experience. In order to practice a conversation that explores desperation, remember a time when you felt a sense of desperation about a person's (clients) behaviour.

On your own, or with someone else, externalise desperation and reflect on the following:

▼ The effects of desperation on the therapist, the client, the therapeutic relationship.

▼ What precipitated the experience of desperation?

▼ What questions would have helped the person (therapist) explore desperation, including what action and/or thoughts could have acted to reduce the effects of desperation?

When we understand how desperation has developed and what has supported it in people's (clients') lives, we also get to know the limitations of therapy. With this knowledge we can have a conversation that explores possibilities with humility. The possibilities are not given as solutions but as part of the ongoing enquiry. For example:

▼ If I saw you for half an hour on Monday, Wednesday and Friday next week, how would that affect your feelings or thoughts of desperation?

▼ Do you have any ideas about how the therapy could support you to hold out against the effects of desperation between sessions?

▼ Are there other people or resources that could support you?

▼ What have you used successfully in the past?

These examples of questions keep us alert to a commitment to collaborate even when we are faced with the effects of desperate thoughts, feelings and actions. These questions demonstrate a beginning point for a potential enquiry. They are ineffectual without a response that makes sense of the questions.

. . . .

CHAPTER TEN

Endings

This chapter focuses on endings. Endings of therapy sessions, negotiating the progress of therapy, ending the therapeutic relationship, and the ending of this book.

People (clients) often consider that we (therapists) arbitrate endings. This belief gives us the responsibility of both determining the therapeutic direction and establishing when the therapy is completed. If silence surrounds this belief then we are both (therapist and client) robbed of an opportunity to negotiate endings, including the ending of each therapy session. Lack of negotiation leaves us (therapists) holding the authority over endings. This in turn undermines our commitment to the ongoing negotiation of the therapeutic relationship understanding.

ENDING THE THERAPY SESSION

The therapeutic conversation provides an arena for people (clients) to re-view significant life events and beliefs. In this re-view, people (clients) determine the influences that shape the meanings they have made of these events while experimenting with the implications of possible future meanings in the present.

The conversation's complexity is partially determined by people's (clients') negotiation and articulation of experiences together with the exploration of emotions that arise during the conversation. These emotions become part of the negotiation of meaning. We establish comprehensible sense when we pull together the threads of the conversation into a coherent form. This coherent form is presented to people throughout each session in order to negotiate its relevance. If it is relevant then this understanding provides the platform for further exploration. At the end of the session, we again provide a reflection of the understandings reached. In order for these reflections to be built on between sessions we can audiotape them, note them or write them as a letter.

People (clients) have indicated that concreting the reflections has been a significant part of the therapeutic process for them. It has often acted as the lynchpin that has re-connected them to their experiences of self outside of the therapeutic relationship. People (clients) have used the reflections as a strength-building resource whenever they are confronted by persistent and often overbearing life-taking ideas.

When the reflections are fixed by using audiotape or the written word, they are weighted with our authority. Once our reflections are in a concrete format it is difficult for people to refute, question or add to them. This can contribute to people's (clients') voices being drowned out by our voice.

In order to reduce this possibility while maintaining the benefits of something that pulls together the threads of a therapeutic conversation, I encourage people to have a dialogue or interaction with the reflections. Pulling together the threads by writing or recording them thus becomes a joint endeavour.

When people (clients) engage with the reflections we reduce the risk of imposing meaning. These questions may assist people (clients) to engage with the reflections:

▼ Before you read, listen to or write down the ideas or events that stood out to you in the session, ask your self, What parts of the conversation do I want to keep hold of?

▼ As you listen to or read the therapist's ideas/reflections, consider changing the speaker or author to your self. Ask your self, What parts do I want to remain in the therapist's voice? What happens or what does it feel like to re-read these ideas/reflections using my own voice?

▼ When you read or listen to the ideas/reflections, what stands out to you? What do you want to keep? Take this, together with the ideas you hold about what parts of the conversation you want to keep hold of, and construct a letter or audio tape to your self.

When we (therapists) write or speak about discoveries made in therapy, we often give these discoveries coherence. We are both important witnesses to people's (clients') private experiences, thoughts and feelings and active participants in the development of the sense made of experiences, thoughts and feelings. Our reflections thus become an important resource of other/knowledge and other experiences of the self (client) in relationship to another. We need to balance our contribution, however, by supporting the development of people's (clients') experience of their own voices and visions. In order to do this, we can encourage people (clients) to undertake self reflection that re-views the sense they make of the therapy.

The completion of each therapy session is a small ending. This ending can be negotiated in the therapy. Consider these questions:

▼ From the conversation we've had, what stands out to you, what do you want to remember?

▼ Do you have any ideas about how these ideas can be strengthened or practised in your life?

▼ Has this meeting provided you with enough ideas or strategies for us to finish here or do you think it would be helpful to meet again? If we meet again, how often would you like to meet before we re-view how helpful this has been?

Whenever we (therapists) are negotiating endings and the direction of therapy, we need to consider the impact of thoughts of self-denigration and worthlessness. Broaching the topic of endings or negotiating the therapeutic direction can catalyse people (clients) into thinking that they are wasting our time and that they are not worthy of our attention. When we engage in conversations about endings or therapeutic direction we can take the ideas people (clients) may be carrying into consideration by reflecting on these questions:

▼ In thinking about and answering these questions, can you tell me if any thinking such as 'I'm wasting Johnella's time' or 'I don't deserve to be here' comes to mind?

▼ The questions that I'm asking can provoke thinking such as 'Johnella wants to finish the therapy'. I need to know if this thinking is around so that I can respond directly and honestly to it.

▼ It is important to me that thoughts such as 'I'm wasting Johnella's time' don't determine the conversation's direction. Do you think you can tell me whenever this thinking is around? I would like to consider the possibility that you and I will determine the therapeutic direction.

▼ Is there anything I can do or say to support you to tell me if worry-thinking about my intentions for the therapy comes forward as we talk about the direction we are taking in the therapy?

NEGOTIATING THE DIRECTION OF THE THERAPY

I believe that the direction we take throughout the therapy requires a process of ongoing negotiation. When we engage in therapy over a period of time, this direction requires frequent re-view and reflection.

I refer to this re-view and reflection as 're-viewing the therapy'. In order to 're-view the therapy' we (therapist and client) come to this session after reflecting on these questions:

▼ When you reflect on the therapy to date, what stands out for you about the process?

▼ Do you think the therapy is moving in the right direction?

▼ What have you taken from the therapy that has been helpful?

▼ Have your expectations of the therapy altered over time? What are your expectations now?

▼ What direction do you hope the therapy will move in over the next month?

▼ Is there anything you want to know about the therapy that will help you to continue to engage with the therapy?

▼ Are there any factors outside of the therapy that you know are affecting the therapy?

▼ How will you know that the therapy is coming to an end? What will have changed so that ending can be considered?

ENDING THE THERAPEUTIC RELATIONSHIP

Some endings resound with pleasure while others sit poised delicately between excitement and pain. Each therapeutic relationship is different and therefore each ending is unique. When we work with people (clients) who have been tormented by their experience, we make our selves available intellectually and emotionally to hearing this experience. We do this knowing that what we fundamentally believe of our selves and others may change. We approach this believing and hoping that we will win the struggle to retain compassion and hope.

The therapeutic relationship has the potential to change both participants. The ending is meaningful for both. However, for people (clients) who have taken a life risk to engage with trust and hope inside and outside of the therapeutic relationship, the ending is of greater significance. For some people (clients) the ending feels like the loss of the only emotional home they have experienced.

I believe endings need to be negotiated rather than prescribed. We can prepare for the possibility of ending with these questions:

▼ How do you think we would know that we were coming close to the end of the therapy?

▼ What changes would you expect before we consider the ending?

▼ How can we talk about the ending as an indication of success?

▼ How can I support you to hold on to the successes, given that the ending may bring forward mixed feelings?

▼ When you think about the ending, what do you think and feel?

▼ Do you think the ending could provoke the memory of other endings?

▼ Is there anything you need to know from me in order to make this conversation easier?

The therapeutic relationship is a relationship that we (therapist and client) know we will leave. Being available for ending conversations throughout the therapy process encourages an experience of negotiation and participation. Even when people (clients) are intellectually prepared for the possibility of ending, they can be surprised by the advent of strong emotions as the therapy moves towards leave-taking.

During the last month of therapy I have often asked people to prepare for the ending by considering these questions:

▼ What can you take from your experience of the therapy and this relationship to support you in the future?

▼ Is there anything we or I can do to strengthen that experience?

▼ Is there anything that you want to know from me about my experience of the therapy and the therapeutic relationship?

▼ What are your thoughts and feelings about how we can best use the next month?

▼ How would you like our last session acknowledged?

It's important to consider that each person (client) may want to end differently. We can support people (clients) through this process. It is not our responsibility however to prescribe the process. During the leave-taking, people (clients) can be confronted with earlier memories of loss and abandonment. It is challenging to acknowledge the other memories of loss while also acknowledging the unique nature of the experience of the therapeutic relationship. It is challenging to grieve for the loss of the therapeutic relationship while celebrating and acknowledging its existence.

When I talk about ending the therapeutic relationship I mean ending the negotiated therapeutic relationship with people (clients). It may be that in the future another therapeutic relationship is negotiated. I have also agreed to people's (clients') requests to occasionally visit me at work or write the occasional letter or postcard. This is founded on a belief that an occasional reconnection helps people (clients) stay connected with the reality of their experience within the therapeutic relationship. When people (clients) take up this opportunity for reconnection I also enjoy catching up with their lives.

When the therapy is not re-viewed people (clients) are left with a belief and an experience that we arbitrate on the ending of the therapy. This belief renders people (clients) powerless in the negotiation of the therapeutic direction, the therapy progress and the ending of the therapeutic relationship.

PREMATURE ENDINGS OF THE THERAPEUTIC RELATIONSHIP

Ending a therapeutic relationship as a result of our inability to support the relationship is traumatic for everybody. I would expect both of the participants (therapist and client) to be supported by a supervisor/consultant who would facilitate the ending process. This support would involve finding an explanation that removes responsibility for the ending from people (clients) while placing it with the therapist. The explanation for the ending would also remain within the bounds of the therapeutic relationship understanding. Explanations that disclose our feelings and thoughts about the other (the client) outside of the therapeutic relationship understanding inevitably move the relationship outside of the therapeutic. For example, I (therapist) am sexually attracted to you (client). When this occurs people (clients) are left to review the past therapeutic relationship in the light of this new relationship information, which may provoke both a sense of possibility for a future relationship, for example, a friendship or lover relationship, or a sense of betrayal, such as, I feel fooled or lied to. This, in my view, contravenes the therapeutic relationship understanding and professional ethics. In order to ensure that the explanation for endings sits within the therapeutic relationship understanding, we negotiate the process (including the language used), outside of the therapy. We do this with a supervisor/consultant in order to practise languaging an explanation that leaves no room for the possibility of a future relationship.

ENDING THE WRITING

It is difficult to find a way to end what I consider will always be work in progress. The covers binding this book portray a completeness that doesn't reflect my experience of the therapeutic work. I do need to finish somewhere, however, and the place I choose reflects a recent experience.

In the introduction I write of how my engagement with ethics supports the evolution of my ideas into a practice. Although the entire book represents this engagement with ethics, ideas and practices, my most recent work in progress is a teaching and consultation process. An integral part of this teaching and consulting practice is the consultant (myself) interviewing the consultee (therapist) as the client. This interview is audiotaped and then taken back to the therapy. The person (client) is then given an opportunity to comment, reflect on and change the therapist's understanding of the person's (client's) life.[1]

While engaging with this work, several people (clients) who had received the audiotaped interviews between the consultant and consultee requested a meeting with the trainee consultation group. Meetings were subsequently arranged. In the process of introducing ourselves, I found myself stating that I had been waiting and preparing over the last 20 years for this meeting. Twenty years ago I had been repelled by the then common practice in psychiatric institutions of involving people (clients) in Grand Round meetings. In these meetings people (clients) were exhibited and talked about in an objectifying manner. I have been preparing for over 20 years for the time that I was ready and able to construct an environment where there could be an open-hearted meeting with people bound by the therapeutic relationship understanding.

In that moment when I spoke of the last 20 years I realised the significance to me of this meeting. I realised I had been following a dream. In the pursuit of this dream I have often been guided only by my adverse emotional response to ideas and practices that were regarded by the professional community as acceptable. Over the years I re-searched this emotional response rather than making sense of it as a deficit in me. This ongoing process of re-search included articulating my ideas, reading a wide range of literature and experimenting with practices that reflected ethical principles.

It was also in that moment, when I spoke of the last 20 years, that I saw/experienced/knew where I had been travelling to for those 20 years. From where I stand now, the journey reflected on is very different from the process of travelling. Writing has required a reflecting back. On the completion of writing I know that I will begin to travel again.

I hope that reading this book will encourage you to appreciate how you will uniquely relate to the ideas and practices presented here. I believe that while it is important that we acknowledge the sources of our ideas and practices, we are also obliged to reinvent theses ideas and practices in our work. Positioning our selves to reinvent ideas and practices protects us from dogmatically applying current and established ideas and practices. This book does not present or reflect a therapeutic model. This book is an accumulation of 20 years of engaging with therapeutic ideas and practices and 40 years of engagement in life. It may be challenging, exciting and perhaps daunting to now consider how you will represent your engagement with the therapeutic ideas and practices that support your work!

While I have decided how and when to finish, I hope the ending does not mean an end to our engagement with the ideas and practices presented and not presented in this book.

Notes

Introduction

1 Pakeha denotes the predominately Anglo-Saxon immigrants of the nine-teenth century. Maori are the indigenous people of Aotearoa/New Zealand.

2 I had these realisations within a professional environment that encouraged experimentation; in this regard, I am particularly grateful to June Scott, my first clinical supervisor. Although June used a psychodynamic explanation, her practice of therapy was a departure from the rigid dictates usually associated with that style of therapy. June's engagement with the work encouraged my clinical experimentation, which in turn directed me towards the burgeoning Family Therapy field.

3 Throughout the text I have written: 'people (clients)'. Although this may appear clumsy, I am attempting to ask you to always consider yourself in this description. Client is an awkward word that reflects a particular engage-ment within the therapeutic relationship. Its use can encourage the reader to objectify the other. I am attempting to encourage a subjective reading.

4 Donald E. Polkinghorne (24) has described the psychology of practice as 'the second psychology — emerged under the shadow of academic psychology.' (Page 146)

5 This quote comes from an interview with Denis Welsh, *New Zealand Listener*, June 12-18, 1999 (pp 42-43).

6 Olga Silverstein's plenary presentation at the 1995 New Zealand and Australian Family Therapy Conference stimulated these thoughts.

Chapter One

1   I write the word 're-search' and its variations in this way, in order to distinguish my usage from the 'scientific' meaning attributed to 'research'.
2   Pakeha denotes a person of Anglo-Saxon ethnicity.
3   The contextual environment is discussed in detail in Chapter Two.

Chapter Two

1   This diagram was initially presented at a workshop entitled, 'Working with Individuals' (1990 New Zealand Family Therapy Conference).
2   This book involves writing about the work and therefore it is two dimensional. The activity of the therapeutic process is greater than its textual reflections. This results in therapeutic literature having literary coherence while reflecting the actual therapeutic practice partially.
3   Johnella Bird, 'Working with Couples', unpublished.

Chapter Three

1   I published the paper, 'Coming Out Of The Closet: Illuminating the Therapeutic Relationship' in 1993. This paper was an attempt to describe the unique nature of the therapeutic relationship. It also included a description of a self reflective process which aimed at reducing the possibility that we could unwittingly impose the theories we held about life events onto the therapeutic conversation. I have subsequently expanded those ideas. The original article is in the *Journal of Feminist Therapy*, Vol. 2, 1993.
2   I prefer the therapeutic relationship understanding to be made available by providing people (clients) with a written explanation. This recognises the anxiety people (clients) often carry when they enter the therapeutic relationship for the first time.
3   I discuss endings in more detail in Chapter Ten.
4   Whenever I refer to 'other reflective process or practice', I'm proposing a conversation with supervisors, consultants and/or colleagues.
5   Parker, I. et al (22) reflect on Derrida's work: 'Derrida provides a systematic reading of philosophical texts which focus on the ways in which an argument is policed to guarantee a fixed reference point. An essential point of "truth" which the reader then takes for granted and sees as the foundation for other less important things.' This is an important consideration when reading all psychological texts including this one. Counselling texts are written by people on one side of the therapeutic relationship. The text constitutes one person's ideas about the therapy, it is not the therapy.
6   Ideas on self and other reflections is totally predicated on the ideas and practices outlined in the Chapter Two.
7   Obtaining permission to use therapeutic conversations for teaching or articles does not diminish the possibility that this relationship has or will be experienced as special.

Chapter Four

1   When I read Lawrence L. Langer book *Holocaust Testimonies, The Ruins Of Memory*, 1991, by Yale University Press, the dilemmas he presented reflected many of my experiences in the work with people (clients) who have suffered emotional, physical and/or sexual abuse.

Chapter Five

1   *The Concise Oxford Dictionary*, 6th edition, 1976, Oxford University Press.
2   The word 'screening' is introduced by me. People's (clients') response may result in a change of language. Often when I am wondering about the possible existence of a screening practice, I begin an enquiry with the question, 'I've noticed or I'm wondering if it is possible that two conversations are present, one between you and I and one between you and certain ideas.'
3   While we do not know this person's unique experience, we do bring knowledge or knowing to the therapy. This knowing or knowledge may or may not be helpful to the therapy. It is therefore held as a possibility. This possibility may be explored by using a question to determine its relevance. When we stand on the knowing/not knowing boundary we bring a commitment to add to, or put to one side, the knowing we have previously collected.

Chapter Six

1   When I consider the influences that directed my attention towards the self in relationship to historical, cultural, familial and economic circumstance, it is not the authors of poststructuralist texts that I acknowledge. Recognition of the historical and cultural determinants that dominate the privileging of one discursive paradigm over another was made powerfully apparent to me through my relationship with the writing of the following authors: Betty Friedan, Germaine Greer, Ann Oakley, Suzi Orbach, Adrienne Rich, Virginia Woolf and Nancy Chodorow. These early feminist writers shook me out of a preoccupation with my experience, towards an imagining of a collective experience which then fostered a political analysis.

   Authors of fictional texts have thrown my imagination outside of bounds of my lived experience. From this place I have had the opportunity to see, experience, sense and know difference. This difference highlights the institutional legitimisation process where one version of history is elevated over others, where one culture's, values, morality ideas and practices are elevated over another.

Chapter Seven

1   I have drawn on S. Kessler's (16) definition of Gender. 'The term "Gender" has traditionally been used to designate psychological, social and cultural aspects of maleness and femaleness,' (page 7).

2   It is important to consider that this conversation was held in the context of
    a negotiated therapeutic relationship. Issues of safety had been negotiated
    directly and indirectly.
3   Universalizing and essentialising ideas locate specific characteristics,
    qualities and attributes as inherently belonging to all people of a certain sex,
    such as men are hunters, women are nurturers.
4   The debate style of conversation is the way I have named a particular style
    of conversation. You may find that this way of naming does not fit in your
    clinical work. If it doesn't, change the way of naming what you see, feel and
    experience. It is essential that the naming is a negotiation with people
    (clients) as it needs to accurately reflect their experience.
5   This example represents an actual experience and was recalled in
    conversation with a colleague, Carol Lynch.
6   Parts of this exercise reflect an exercise devised by Michael White (36).

Chapter Eight
1   This process draws on Michael White's relative-influence enquiry process.

Chapter Nine
1   When 'in the corner' ideas are identified and named, we engage in a
    relational externalising enquiry using the language people (clients) use.
    In other words we don't engage in a relational externalising enquiry using
    the term 'in the corner' ideas. This is a metaphor I am using for this text.
    M. White has used 'in the corner lifestyle' as a metaphorical description in
    a 1987 article (35).
2   This practice was developed after listening in 1993 to a client of David
    Epston's talk with him about her relationship with asthma.

Chapter Ten
1   This work is in the process of being written up for publication.

Bibliography

1. Chodorow, Nancy, *The Reproduction of Mothering*, Berkeley, University of California Press, 1978.
2. Chermin, Kim, *In My Mothers House*, Harper Perennial, 1983.
3. Fine, Michelle and Susan Merle-Gordon, 'Feminist Transformations of/ Despite Psychology' in *Gender and Thought — Psychological Perspectives*, Crawford, M. and M. Gentry eds. New York, Springer-Verlog, 1989, pp. 146–174.
4. Flanagan, Richard, *Death of a River Guide*, Australia, Penguin Books, 1994.
5. Flax, Jane, 'Postmodernism and Gender Relations in Feminist Theory' in *Feminism/Postmodernism*, Nicolson, L.J. (ed) New York, Routhledge, 1990, pp. 39–61.
6. Forster, Margaret, *Hidden Lives — A Family Memoir*, Viking, 1995.
7. Foucault, Michael, *The History of Sexuality*, Vintage Books Edition.
8. Franklin, Margery, B., 'Interviewing and Narrative Representation' in *Toward A New Psychology Of Gender: a reader*, edited by Mary M. Gergen and Sara N. Davis, New York and London, Routledge, 1997.
9. Friedan, Betty, *The Feminine Mystique*, New York, W.W. Norton, New York, 1965. Harmondsworth, Penguin Harmondsworth, 1963.
10. Grace, Patricia, *Potiki*, New Zealand, Penguin Books (NZ) Ltd, 1986.
11. Grace, Patricia, *Baby No-Eyes*, New Zealand, Penguin Books (NZ) Ltd, 1998.
12. Greer, Germaine, *The Female Eunuch*, London, McGibbon and Kee, 1970.
13. Hoeg, Peter, *Miss Smilla's Feeling for Snow*, London, Harvell, 1983.
14. Hoffman, Lyn, *Foundations of Family Therapy: A Conceptual Framework For Systems Change*, New York, Basic Books, 1981.

15. Hume, Keri, *the bone people*, New Zealand, Spiral in association with Hodder and Stoughton, 1985.

16. Kessler, S., *Gender: an ethnomethodological approach*, New York, John Wiley & Sons, 1978.

17. Lessing, Doris, *Under My Skin*, London, Flamingo, 1995.

18. Marshall, Owen, *Coming Home In The Dark*, Auckland, Vintage (New Zealand) Ltd, 1995.

19. Morrison, Toni, in *The Anatomy of Memory, An Anthology*, James McCorkey, Oxford University Press, Inc., 1996. 'Memory, Creation and Writing' by Toni Morrison first appeared in *Thought: A Journal of Culture and Ideas*, December 1984, Vol. 59, p. 235.

20. Oakley, Ann, *Sex, Gender and Society*, London,Temple Smith, 1972.

21. Orbach, Suzi, *Fat Is A Feminist Issue*, New York and London, Paddington Press, 1978.

22. Parker, Ian, Eugenie Georgaca, David Harper, Terence McLaughlin and Mark Stowell-Smith, *Deconstructing Psychopathology*, London, Sage Publications Ltd, 1995.

23. Piercy, Marge, *Woman on the Edge of Time*, London, The Women's Press, 1979.

24. Polkinghorne, Donald E, 'Postmodern Epistemology of Practice', in *Postmodernism and Psychology*, Kvale, S. (ed) London, Sage, 1993, pp.146–165.

25. Rich, Adrienne, *On Lies, Secrets and Silence*, London,Virago, 1980.

26. Selvini-Palazzoli, M., L. Boscolo, G. Ceednin and G. Prata 'Hypothesizing — Circularity — Neutrality, three guidelines for the conductor of the session', Family Process, 19:3, 1980, pp. 3–12.

27. Shotter, J, 'Social Individuality Versus Possessive Individualism: The sounds of silence', in *Deconstructing Social Psychology*, Nicolson, L.J. (ed.) London, Routledge, 1990, pp.155–169.

28. Thorton, Lawrence, *Imagining Argentina*, New York, Bantam Books, 1987.

29. Thorton, Lawrence, *Under The Gypsy Moon*, Doubleday, 1990.

30. Walker, Alice, *You Can't Keep a Good Woman Down*, Harcourt Brace and Co, 1971.

31. Walker, Alice, *Possessing the Secret of Joy*, London, Vintage, 1993.

32. Weedon, Chris, *Feminist Practice and Poststructuralist Theory*, Oxford, Blackwell Publishers, 1987.

33. White, Michael, *Externalizing the Problem*, Dulwich Centre Newsletter, Summer, 1988/89.

34. White, Michael, *The Process Of Questioning: A therapy of literary merit?*, Dulwich Centre Newsletter, Winter, 1988.

35. White, Michael, *Family Therapy and Schizophrenia: Addressing the 'in the corner' lifestyle*, Dulwich Centre Newsletter, Spring, 1987.

36. White, Michael, Couple Therapy: *'Urgency for Sameness' or Appreciation of Difference*, Dulwich Centre Newsletter Summer, 1986/87, pp.11–18.

37. Wolff, Tobias, *This Boy's Life*, Bloomsbury Publishing Ltd, 1989.

38. Woolf, Virginia, 'A Sketch of the Past' from *Moments of Being*, London, University Press, 1976.
39. Woolf, Virginia, *A Room of One's Own*, London, Hogarth Press, 1928. Reprinted Harmondsworth, Penguin, 1974.
40. Yeatman, Anna, 'Voice And Representation', in *The Politics Of Difference*, edited by Sneja Gunew and Anna Yeatman, Allen and Unwin Pty.Ltd, 1993, pp. 228–245.